Up Your OWN Organization!
A Handbook for Today's Entrepreneur

By Donald M. Dible

Edited by Jeannine Marschner

Introduction by Robert Townsend
Former Chairman and CEO of Avis Rent a Car Corporation

Reston Publishing Company, Inc.
A Prentice-Hall Company
Reston, Virginia

Library of Congress Cataloging in Publication Data

Dible, Donald M.
    Up your own organization!

    Bibliography: p.
    Includes index.
    1. Small business—Management. 2. Small business—
Finance. I. Title.
HD62.7.D53   1986   658'.022   85-8293
ISBN 0-8359-8086-3

10 9 8 7 6 5 4 3 2 1

Printed in the United States of America

Books by Donald M. Dible

Up Your OWN Organization!
A Handbook for Today's Entrepreneur

Winning the Money Game—
How to Plan and Finance a Growing Business

The Pure Joy of Making More Money

Contents

Introduction xvii

Prologue xix

I The Entrepreneur, the Idea, the Company Image 1
1 Contemporary Entrepreneurship—Profiles and Case Histories 3
Recipe for Success, 5
There Is Security in Numbers, 11
Pert-O-Graph Is Pertinent!, 21
Elephants, Lasers and Moon Rocks: Talk about a Mixed
      Bag!, 31

2 What Motivates the Entrepreneur? 41
Factors External to the Corporation, 46
    The Desire for Personal Autonomy, 46
    The Desire for Fame, 46
    The Desire for a Personal Fortune, 47
    The Pure Joy of Winning, 48
Factors Internal to the Corporation, 49
    Inadequate Corporate Communications, 49
    Inequity Between Major Contributions and Financial
        Rewards, 49
    Promotion and Salary Policies, 50
    Employee Security?, 51
    Corporate Politics and Nepotism, 52

Red Tape, 52
Orphan Products, 53
Questionably Relevant Educational Requirements, 54

3   Personal Resources Checklist 57
Competence, 58
Motivation and the Three D's: Desire, Determination, and
        Dedication, 58
First-hand Knowledge of the Product or Service to be
        Offered, 59
Ability to Manage People and Resources, 61
Broad, Well-rounded Experience, 61
Stamina and Physical Well-Being, 63
Financial Resources, 64

4   Increased Responsibility—The Price of Success 67
The Extramarital Affair, 68
Sesame Street May Be Fine, But Kids Need Parents, Too, 69
The Myth of Working for Yourself, 70

5   Recruiting Partners 73
Former Business Associates, 73
Friends, 74
Business Consultants, 74
Competitor's Staff, 74
Referrals, 75
Classified Advertising, 75
An Owl, a Goose, and the Little Red Hen, 75

6   A Training Program for Success 79
Physical Conditioning, 79
Acquiring the Proper Mental Attitude, 80
Make Your Spouse the Head Cheerleader in Your Rooting
        Section, 80
Investigate Seminars, 80
    The U.S. Department of Commerce, 80
    The Small Business Administration, 81
    Trade Associations, 81
    The American Management Association, 82
    Colleges and Universities, 82
    Other Seminars, 83
Rediscover Books, 85
    Community Libraries, 86
    College and University Libraries, 86
    Professional and Trade Association Libraries, 86
    Bookstores, 87
    Book Clubs, 87

Periodicals, Too, 88
    Trade Journals, 89
    Bank Publications, 89
    Financial Papers, 90
    Business Magazines, 90
    Newsletters, 90
    Community Newspapers, 91
Computerized Information Services, 91
Uncle Sam Wants (To Help) You!, 92
    The U.S. Department of Commerce, 92
    The Small Business Administration, 93
Public Speaking, 94
    Toastmasters Clubs, 94
    National Speakers Association, 95
    International Platform Association, 95
    Community Colleges and University Extension Courses, 96
    Commercial Institutions, 96

7   Many People Are Glad to Help You—Just Ask Them! 97
Entrepreneurs Who Have Already Gotten Started, 98
Others in Your Trade, 99
    Suppliers, 99
    Customers, 99
    Manufacturers' Representatives, 99
    Distributors, 100
Bankers, 100
Stockbrokers, 101
College Faculty Members, 101

8   The Conception and Protection of a Product Idea 105
Mommy, Where Do Product Ideas Come From?, 105
    Former Employers, 105
    New Partners, 107
    New Product Periodicals, 107
    Doctoral Dissertations, 108
    Idea Books, 109
    Trade Shows, 111
    State Invention Expositions, 111
    Patent Brokers, 112
    National Information Referral and Exchange Centers, 113
Protection, 114
    Patents, 115
    Unpatentable Ideas, 117
Warning to Inventors, 120

9   Projecting a Good Image 121
The Importance of Image to the Entrepreneur, 122
Selection of a Company Name, 123
Pointers on Business Stationery, 123
Commentary by Robert Townsend, 124

II   The Business Plan **127**
10   The Importance of a Business Plan 129
The Business Plan Is a Sales Document, 129
    Credibility, 130
    Authority, 130
    Ingenuity, 131
The Business Plan and the Responsibility of the Founder, 131
Sources of Assistance in Preparing Your Business Plan, 132
    Public-Offering Prospectuses, 132
    The Business Plan of Another Company, 133
    Business Consultants, 133
    Lawyers and Certified Public Accountants, 133
    Public Relations Firms, 133
    Books on Writing Effective Sales Letters, 133
    Trial Runs, 134
Packaging the Business Plan, 134
    Shopping in the Financial Marketplace, 134
    Busy Investors May Unintentionally Waste Your Time, 135
Forget Everything I've Said!, 135
    Back-of-the-Envelope Advocates, 135
    The Unbelievers, 136
    "We Want to Help, Too!", 136
Super-Serendipity, 136

11   The Mini-Proposal 139
Investor Preferences, 139
    Initial Capitalization Required, 140
    Maturity of the Enterprise, 140
    Preferred Industrial Sectors, 141
    Emphasize the Highlights, 141
        Niche in the Market, 142
        Superior Qualifications of the Founders, 142
        Market Characteristics, 142
Keep It Short and Sweet, 143

12   The Formal Business Plan 145
Introduction, 145
Table of Contents, 146
The Management Team, 146
    Capsule Resumes of the Founders, 146
    References, 146

Organization Chart, 147
Who Does What, with Which, and to Whom, 147
Synergy of the Founding Team, 147
Management Assistance Required, 148
Watch the Birdie, 148
The Board of Directors, 148
How Many?, 150
Composition—Who?, 150
Compensation, 151
Supporting Professional Service Agencies, 152
How to Select a Law Firm, 152
How to Select an Accounting Firm, 154
How to Select a Commercial Bank, 155
How to Select an Insurance Agency, 157
The Market to Be Served, 159
Document Your Assertions, 159
List Major Potential Customers, 160
Analyze Major Competitors, 161
Estimate Market Share, 161
Polish Your Crystal Ball, 161
Discuss Product Timing, 161
The Products and/or Services, 162
Competitive Features, 162
Pictures, 166
Manufacturing Process, 166
Cost Breakdowns, 166
State of the Art, 167
Marketing Strategy, 167
Promotional Methods, 167
Advertising Efforts, 168
Distribution, 168
Terms of Sale, 170
Delivery/Performance Timing, 171
A New Twist, 172
Research and Development Program, 172
Product Improvement, 172
Process Improvement, 173
Development of New Products, 173
Who Pays?, 173
Plant Location and Related Considerations, 174
Founders' Back Yard, 175
Customer Proximity, 175
Supplier Proximity, 175
Personnel Availability, 176
Transportation Service, 176

Educational Facilities, 176
Investor Preferences, 177
Tax Climate, 177
Concept in a Capsule, 177

13   Appendix to the Formal Business Plan   179
Sales Forecast, 179
Pro Forma Financial Statements, 180
Cash Flow Statement, 181
Profit and Loss Statement, 182
Balance Sheet, 183
Projected Staff and Plant Requirements, 183
Head Count, 183
Floor Space, 183
Leasehold Improvements, 183
Major Capital Equipment, 183
Legal Structure of the Company, 184
Sole Proprietorship, 184
Partnership, 184
Corporation, 185
Founders' Resumes, 186
"To Whom It May Concern," 186
Key Articles by Members of the Founding Staff, 187
Founders' Personal Financial Statements, 187
Founders' Compensation, 187
Tax Aspects, 188
Salaries, 188
Equity Formula, 188
Supporting Documentation, 190
Market Surveys and Reports, 190
Newspaper and Magazine Articles, 190
Credit Reports and/or Annual Reports on Competitors, 190

III   Ali Baba and the Forty Money Sources 193
14   Introduction to Money Sources   195
Money Concepts, 195
Salt, Beads, and Grain, 195
Supply and Demand, 196
Debt Versus Equity Financing, 198
Comparison Shopping, 199
Are Venture Capitalists *Really* Thieves?, 200
What to Look for in a Venture Capital Partner, 200
Money, 200
More Money, 201
Availability of Managerial Assistance, 201
Compatibility of Objectives, 202

Investors Who Can Keep Their Cool, 203
Confidence in Team and Concept, 203
Reasonable Expectations Regarding Capital Appreciation, 204
Knowledge of the Market to Be Served, 204
Terms of the Deal, 204
Reward-Risk Ratios, 205
Return on Investment, 206
Earned Equity, 207
"Getting Out," 208

15   Forty Money Sources 211
Closed-End Investment Companies, 212
Colleges, Universities, and Other Endowed Institutions, 213
Commercial Banks, 215
Short-Term Loans, 215
Intermediate-Term Loans, 216
Long-Term Loans, 216
Equity Financing, 217
Commercial Finance Companies, 218
Consumer Finance Companies, 219
Corporate Venture Capital Departments or Subsidiaries, 219
Credit Unions, 221
Customers, 223
Economic Development Administration, 224
EDA Loan Terms, 225
Loan Eligibility Requirements and Conditions, 225
EDA Regional Offices, 226
Employees, 226
Equipment Manufacturers, 228
Factoring Companies, 229
Financial Consultants, Finders, and Other Intermediaries, 231
Founders, 233
Franchising, 235
Industrial Banks, 236
Insurance Companies, 237
Investment Bankers, 238
Investment Clubs, 241
Leasing Companies, 242
Mutual Funds, 244
Mutual Savings Banks, 245
National Consumer Cooperative Bank, 246
Parent Companies, 247
Pension Funds, 248
Private Individual Investors, 249
Private Investment Partnerships, 251

Privately Owned Venture Capital Corporations, 253
  Substantial Reserves of Risk Capital, 253
  Business Development Assistance, 254
  Long-Term Objectives, 254
Relatives and Friends, 255
Research Grants and Partnerships, 257
Sales Finance Companies, 259
Savings and Loan Associations, 260
Securities Dealers, 261
Self Underwriting, 263
Small Business Administration, 266
  Bank Participation Loans, 266
  Direct Loans, 267
  State Investment Development Corporations, 267
  Local Development Companies, 268
  Certified Development Companies, 268
Small Business Investment Companies, 269
State and Local Industrial Development Commissions, 270
Tax-Exempt Foundations and Charitable Trusts, 271
Trade Suppliers, 273
  Develop Customer Loyalty, 273
  Expand Customer Base, 273
  Create Markets for New Products, 273
  Extended Credit Terms, 273
  Direct Loans, 274
  Purchase of Stock in New Company, 274
  Lend or Lease Equipment, 274
Trust Companies and Bank Trust Departments, 274

Notes **277**

Recommended Readings **285**

Appendixes **301**
1 Annotated List of Information Sources Including
   Directories and Guides to Venture Capital Companies . . . 301
2 Directory of Membership of the National Venture
   Capital Association 323
3 Directory of the Membership of the National Associa-
   tion of Small Business Investment Companies 347
4 Six Business Start-Up Checklists 387
   Information Required from Applicant for Financing, 387
   A Twenty-Four-Point Checklist for Preparing a Business
     Plan, 391
   Development of a Marketing Program, 393
   Marketing Functions Checklist, 395

Information Needed from Prospective Portfolio
Companies Making Application for Investment
by the SBIC of New York, 398
Checklist for Organizing and Operating a Small Business, 399

Applause 411
Index 415

Introduction

Great civilizations have a natural life span.

Assyria rose and fell within 250 years; Persia, 200; the Arab Empire, about 240; Spain, 250; and Britain, roughly 230 years.

America has had 210 and many people assume we're on the way out.

Growth is the enemy. Time merely measures the rate of decay.

The same process governs organizations. Unless the leader is working full time for simplification, clear goals, and rewards which match contributions, human resources will fall into disuse, the leveling process of bureaucracy will take over, the champions will depart, and the handwriting will be on the wall.

As I see it, America has two chances to avoid the timetable of its predecessor civilizations.

One, we somehow replace all the corporate politicians who now occupy the chief executives' offices with leaders who will involve their people, draw out their commitments, and focus their energies on the goals of the enterprise. This seems unlikely.

Two, we rely on the great confidence we Americans have in ourselves *as individuals*, plus the freedom to try anything, which is a unique property of our society. Put that together with our seeming acceptance of hierarchy as the inevitable penalty of growth and we have a mechanism for driving hordes of our best people each year into the outrageous risks of entrepreneurship.

Don Dible's book *Up Your OWN Organization!* can increase the success rate of these champions, who may be America's ticket to another hundred years as a dominant civilization. Let's hope they all read it.

—Robert Townsend

Prologue

This book is written for today's pioneers: the men and women who have the desire *and* the ability to transform their dream of owning a business into the reality of a vital new enterprise. To these modern pioneers belong the financial gains and the personal satisfaction that are the just and proper rewards for creative effort.

Three basic steps are involved in the creation of a new enterprise: (1) recognition and objective evaluation of your personal needs and abilities, including the identification of your marketable product and/or service; (2) preparation of a plan for the attainment of your goal; and (3) acquisition of the financial resources necessary to make the plan a reality. *Up Your OWN Organization!* takes you through this process step by step, and answers the questions asked by everyone who thinks seriously about opening a business of his or her own.

A great many things have happened in the American economy since publication of the earlier edition of this book. Extensive deregulation has taken place in domestic financial markets. New government programs have been created to aid small businesses. We're witnessing the arrival of post–World War II "baby-boomers" on the entrepreneurial scene. Quantum leaps in technological progress continue to be made. Seminars and courses on entrepreneurship are now being taught in hundreds of universities. And a wealth of books, magazines, newsletters, and monographs on the subject has suddenly appeared. These trends all suggest that the '80s will indeed be prime time for emerging new enterprises.

This new edition not only takes into account economic changes, but it also reflects the growing incidence of new businesses started by women. I hope that *everyone* who reads this edition will find the information helpful as well as encouraging, as they move forward to realize the dream of owning their own business.

Since this book was first published, we have received many wonderful letters. Readers have told us about their success in raising money and starting their own businesses, making use of the principles described here. One man raised more than a million dollars for his business following our guidelines. Many others have raised thousands of dollars for their ventures.

We sincerely hope that you will find *Up Your OWN Organization!* a valuable and helpful addition to your business library. We delight in hearing from our readers. If the information presented in these pages helps you or someone you know to start a business and make it grow, please write and tell us about it! Mail your comments to Dible Management Development Systems, Inc., 1125 Missouri Street, Fairfield, California 94533.

I

The Entrepreneur, the Idea, the Company Image

1

Contemporary Entrepreneurship— Profiles and Case Histories

In his timely book, *The Age of Discontinuity,* internationally acclaimed business consultant Peter F. Drucker observes:

> Now we are entering again an era in which emphasis will be on entrepreneurship. However, it will not be the entrepreneurship of a century ago, that is, the ability of a single man to organize a business he himself could run, control, embrace. It will rather be the ability to create and direct an organization for the new. We need men who can build a new structure of entrepreneurship on the managerial foundations laid these last fifty years. History, it has often been observed, moves in a spiral; one returns to the preceding position, or to the preceding problem, but on a higher level, and by a corkscrew-like path. In this fashion we are going to return to entrepreneurship on a path that led out from a lower level, that of a single entrepreneur, to the manager, and now back, though upward, to entrepreneurship again.[1]

The following profiles and case histories represent a few of the structural beams, short ones and long ones, in this new edifice of entrepreneurship.

Recipe for Success[2]

Mrs. Fields Cookies
Mailing: P.O. Box 680370 • Park City, Utah 84068
Park Meadows Plaza • 1500 Kearns Boulevard • Park City, Utah 84060 • (801) 649-1304

Park City, Utah—1985

Take one large craving for fresh, soft cookies. Add lots of chocolate. Stir in generous portions of hard work and innovative marketing. Blend with an unwavering belief in your product and your people. Fold in high quality standards; simmer with personalized customer service. Serve warm . . . and watch the dough expand!

It all began in 1977 in Palo Alto, California near the Stanford University campus. Debbi Fields, then twenty years old, was eliciting rave reviews for her fabulous chocolate chip cookies. Friends suggested she share her treats with the rest of the world. Debbi began to dream of opening her own cookie store, where she would do the baking herself and meet and greet all of her customers.

Armed with a $50,000 loan from her husband, Debbi fashioned her dream into a reality. In 1977 the first Mrs. Fields Cookies store opened its doors for business.

Success did not come overnight. Mrs. Fields recalls those early days when she stood behind her counter, taking in the heady aroma of freshly baked cookies, bursting with chocolaty goodness—*unsold*. Determined not to go down without a fight, Debbi decided that the simplest way to convince people to buy her cookies was to wage a marketing campaign of the most *direct* kind. Tray in hand, she marched up and down the street, passing out free samples.

The rest is history. The Palo Alto store thrived, and a year later Debbi Fields was approached by Pier 39, a major San Francisco tourist complex of shops and restaurants, about opening a store there. *That* store thrived. Today more than 200 outlets in the United States and abroad peddle bags of fresh, warm cookies bearing the name of that starry-eyed dreamer from Palo Alto, California.

Opening a second store was a major hurdle for Mrs. Fields, who feared she would lose control over the strict quality and customer service standards that she "so desperately wanted to maintain." Fortunately, she was able to locate "incredible people," who shared her visions and dreams, to operate the Pier 39 store. She also purchased special equipment that automatically portioned ingredients, thus alleviating some of her quality control worries while still allowing for cookies to be mixed and baked on site. The remaining hurdle was a psychological one all entrepreneurs face at some point: She had to learn to delegate authority—and she did. Debbi feels it is critical to believe that the person to whom you are delegating a function will come through for you. She is convinced that with proper training and support, people *will* come through, and attributes the huge success the company enjoys today to that guiding philosophy.

Forget all those textbook cases on starting and marketing a business—Mrs. Fields prefers to do things her own way, which is often unconventional and perplexing to the traditional business mind.

While she is well trained in business basics, having devoured everything she could get her hands on before opening the Palo Alto store, Debbi sets her own rules, and more often than not, intuition and feeling are the basis of key decisions.

Her rules have served her well. Debbi loved soft, chewy cookies and believed that other cookie-lovers would warm to them also. Mrs. Fields was among the first to bring soft and chewy cookies to the market, and at a time when every survey available on the subject insisted that American cookie connoisseurs preferred the crunchy variety. Her hunch was right, and she points out that the battle at the supermarket these days is between the soft and chewy cookies. Milk chocolate chips are also faring well as an alternative to the traditional semi-sweet variety; Mrs. Fields led the way in bringing this innovation to market. "The key for me is to always be ahead, not to follow but to try things that no one has tried before."

Mrs. Fields takes her cookies seriously. Each ingredient used in her stores is natural, and suppliers are carefully selected to ensure a product of consistently high quality. Even seemingly minor details, such as the decision to use walnuts rather than pecans in Mrs. Fields Cookies, are the result of painstaking research, often carried out in the boss's kitchen. (Walnuts *taste* better in her cookies than pecans do, Debbi tells me. Furthermore, pecans absorb too much moisture from the cookies, causing the pecans to get soggy and lose their all-important crunch.)

Mrs. Fields Cookies does no external advertising; instead, the company relies on word of mouth and store location to attract customers—the *real* marketing and advertising focus is internal. As Debbi explains: "Our most important advertisement is to our people. Let's market to the people in our organization, because if they feel good about what they are doing, if they feel great about the cookies, they're going to make our customers feel great. That is the key."

Debbi tackles problems in a way that is consistent with her positive outlook on life. In fact, she doesn't even like the word "problems," she says, preferring to think in terms of *challenges,* and to learn as much as possible from each one. Probably her biggest challenge came when the company had grown to a thirty-store operation. Debbi was informed of a federal law that prohibits sixteen-year-olds from operating or being in the vicinity of the Hobart mixers used in all of the stores. The company had to release sixty percent of its work force, literally overnight, and scramble to maintain operations while looking for new employees. "It was a challenge, but we pulled it off," Debbi recalls.

Mrs. Fields Cookies is definitely a people company, and Debbi Fields is the heart and soul of the firm. She views her employees as her family, and she backs them all the way: "I believe that my people will give me 100 percent provided they are supported and cared for and nurtured." Debbi never asks her employees to do anything she couldn't do herself. She regularly travels around the country to her stores, pitching in to help *wherever* help is needed. All employees (including corporate executives) must work in a store at some point also, so they'll learn to understand the customer's point of view and will be better able to respond to problems at individual stores. With a family of 25 at corporate headquarters and another 1800 in the field, it is truly remarkable that she maintains such close ties with so many relatives!

Debbi Fields's philosophy seems to be paying off. The company is growing rapidly; 1984 revenues topped $40 million. How does the company manage this explosive growth? "We think small, even as we get bigger and bigger," Debbi explains. "Each store has its own special characteristics, its own special customers, needs, and desires. Because of this, Mrs. Fields Cookies will always be a small business."

Debbi has taken some steps to ensure that growth will proceed smoothly and that the company will continue to feel small. She has cut back on the memo flow to the stores and has installed an electronic voice mail system in every outlet, so she can deliver a message each day to every store regarding plans at corporate headquarters. She is also cutting back on her traveling, holding regional seminars and having her managers come to *her* instead of visiting each store individually. She feels "simplicity is the key" to handling rapid growth with a minimum of disruption.

Not content to satisfy American palates alone, Debbi Fields is spreading her sweet message around the globe. She has opened outlets in Hong Kong and Singapore, and is now targeting the Australian market. Despite somber warnings from the "experts" who predicted her cookies would fall flat in Tokyo ("Too sweet!" "Too big!"), sales are brisk. If you had been strolling along the famous Ginza strip in Japan's capital on a recent weekday afternoon, you would have seen the unsinkable Debbi Fields parading up and down the street, passing out those irresistible and now famous samples. As for the Australian market, the experts are back with their somber warnings about trying to sell soft cookies to people raised on hard biscuits—but something tells me they'll be indulging Down Under in no time!

With all the demands of running a thriving, multimillion dollar company, you would suspect that Mrs. Fields has neglected her personal life. You would be wrong. The cookie president is the mother of three small children, and according to her, the company is an outgrowth of her happy family life. "You see," she explained to me, "Mrs. Fields is an extension of my family. My kids and my husband come first. I feel that if I'm a good mom and a good wife, I can be much more successful in business because I won't be worried."

If you march into *this* executive suite, expect to trip over crayons and diapers, she warns. Her children have the choice of staying at home with the sitter or coming to work with Mom. Debbi thinks it is important for mothers to have their children nearby, believing moms are more effective when they know their babies are "right down the hall." She plans to create a daycare center at the company headquarters, and hopes more businesses will follow her lead.

On a typical day, Debbi Fields heads home for dinner and spends the evening with her children until their bedtime. As for dinner meetings, when they are absolutely necessary, they take place in the Fields kitchen, amid high chairs and spilled milk. Once the children are in bed, she works until late at night, preparing for the next business day. But Debbi is quick to point out that this is not *work* to her: "This is not a job, this is not a business—this is my *life,* it's my *love,* it's my *passion.*"

Looking back, Debbi told me she never dreamed that her business idea would evolve into a multimillion dollar operation. "I don't believe you can ever start a business with the primary objective of making money; I don't believe that's the way things work. You have to create a great product, you have to believe in what you're doing. If you're successful, the dollars are just a reflection of the fact that people like what you're doing."

Because of this philosophy, Debbi has never considered franchising; all stores are company-owned, even overseas, which is quite uncommon. "We're probably the only American-owned company on the Ginza strip in Tokyo," she said. "I really believe that when you franchise, you're selling something for money, and I don't think you can maintain quality."

Mrs. Fields has become quite a role model for other women looking to start their own businesses. Women often write to her for advice. She tells them not to be afraid of failure. "After all," she remembers, "everyone told me I was going to fail."

Some critics have claimed that Debbi Fields's husband Randy, a successful investment advisor, is the real force behind the Mrs. Fields success story. A few minutes with Debbi dispelled that notion. However, as she points out, she does rely on her husband's expertise in making key financial decisions, declaring she would be a "true fool" not to make use of his expertise, just as she would rely on her operations director for advice in key operating decisions.

I asked what was in the works for Mrs. Fields over the next five to ten years. "Being the biggest is not as important to me as being the best at what I do," she explained. "I'm most interested in creating an organization where people feel they count, they're important, they're treated with integrity and fairness."

What about going public? Mrs. Fields's thoughts on that are ' clear: "We've had the option. But how can I sell the company? My name is on the bag."

There Is Security in NUMBER$

Mountain View, California—1974

"If you aren't really tough when it comes to collecting your accounts receivable, you'll be out of business in no time." You'll have to agree, that's pretty sage advice. The remarkable thing is that it comes from twenty-nine year old Richard Bauer, Jr., vice president of DTI Security. Two years ago, Dick teamed up with David Schuldt, now the thirty-year-old president of DTI, to start a company in the burgeoning residential security industry. Since that time, both young men have undergone a forced transformation from salaried, big company employees to seasoned executives in their own successful enterprise.

The idea for the venture sprang from a working relationship David and Dick developed when they were both employed by Ampex Corporation. When that giant company fell upon hard times, they started thinking seriously about whether they should seek other employment or set out to start a business of their own. Since both of them had relatives who were in business for themselves, the notion of collaborating to start a new company didn't seem like an unreasonable alternative.

Interestingly, their decision to go into their own business followed the publication of the first edition of the book you are now reading by only a few months. On the recommendation of some friends, they bought a copy, even though the original price was $24.95 plus tax. David, Dick, and their wives each took turns reading the book. Since they regarded the decision to go into business as a serious one, they wanted to give themselves every possible chance for success. In particular, the wives found the discussions regarding personal sacrifice and the "extramarital affair" point of view especially sobering. Clearly, they were not contemplating a get rich scheme. (David Schuldt now describes the DTI attitude toward business as simply "Spartan.")

The next several months were spent trying to identify a suitable product with which to launch the company. Since their work at Ampex involved selling tape recording equipment to a variety of government agencies in the security and surveillance area, it isn't surprising that the security market received their close attention.

They studied a number of market surveys covering the residential and industrial security business and learned that very substantial market growth was projected. Further study of trade journals and industry association information confirmed these projections.

Having done their marketing homework, DTI's founders then had to decide whether to go after the residential or industrial markets. They learned that it would be least costly to direct their initial efforts in the area of residential security since product development and acceptance costs—as well as selling costs—would be much lower than in the industrial market.

DTI's initial base of operations—"World Headquarters," they called it—was located in David Schuldt's two-car garage. The floor was scrubbed, the windows were covered with curtains, a desk and telephone were installed, and a workbench was built.

Working evenings and weekends over a nine-month period, David and Dick produced their first product, an intrusion and fire detection network called the DSS-10 Security System. It was designed for installation by any of the 6000 home security system dealers across the country.

Once its solid state system has been activated, the DSS-10 sounds a loud alarm if any window or door in a home is opened or broken. The alarm also sounds if a special sensor detects smoke or fire. In order to compete in a market served by almost 200 other manufacturers, the product was designed with low cost, reliability, and ease of installation in mind. From a consumer appeal standpoint, however, a primary competitive advantage is the physical design of the DSS-10. In an industry where most products are covered by unattractive gray metal boxes, the DSS-10 is housed in a handsomely styled wall unit no more obtrusive than a thermostat.

Having completed the design and testing of the first product, a pilot run of twenty units was assembled to demonstrate reproducibility. All went well; a major milestone had been reached.

Now the time had come to formulate and implement a business plan. Making use of Section II of this book, a formal plan was prepared. It was determined that $75,000 would be needed to reach the next milestone.

Once again, our information services came along at just the right time. A "Donald M. Dible Seminar" on "How to Start and Finance a New Business" was presented in a nearby city, attended by more than 225 entrepreneurs. Included in the audience were David and Dick.

Armed with their business plan and the information received at the seminar, David and Dick succeeded in selling a thirty percent interest in DTI Security for $75,000 within a very short period of time. Roughly half of this money was invested by friends, relatives, and acquaintances while the balance was obtained from referrals. Shortly afterward, "World Headquarters" was moved to its present location, a modest 1000 square foot rented facility.

Since starting DTI, David and Dick have learned the vital lesson that cash is the lifeblood of any business. "The sale isn't made until you get paid," says David. Success requires not only that you produce a large sales volume, but you've also got to be tightfisted when it comes to your expenses. DTI has used a great many techniques to control its costs. To start with, David and Dick both took a thirty-three percent cut in pay when they started their own company; after all, equity capital is too scarce a commodity to be used for anything as unproductive as officers' salaries!

Whenever a major purchase is to be made, competitive bids are always obtained. Recently, when an injection mold was required to make a critical part, the Yellow Pages of telephone books for all communities within a 100 mile radius were consulted to locate prospective bidders. The lowest bidder's price was less than sixty percent of the next highest bid. The savings were well over $1500.

Another way in which DTI saves money is by subcontracting with homemakers for assembly work to be done in their own residences. These private contractors pick up parts from the company on Mondays and deliver the finished goods on Fridays. The assembled hardware is inspected, tested, and subjected to a forty-eight hour "burn-in" period at DTI before being placed into inventory or shipped directly to a customer.

The use of such a labor force enables DTI to avoid many of the problems and expenses associated with a large labor force: vacation pay, sick pay, paid holidays, dental and medical insurance, employer-matched Social Security payments, income tax collection, workmen's compensation, and unemployment compensation, to say nothing of the cost of larger facilities, workbenches, chairs, and other amenities. There is much to be said in favor of a subcontract work force for a small company that wants to handle rapid growth or variations in sales volume with minimum increase in overhead.

When I asked David and Dick what they felt was the most important personal element leading to their success, they both agreed that the moral support and active involvement of their wives in the business was essential. Since starting the company, David's and Dick's working time has averaged sixteen hours a day, five days a week plus nine hours on Saturday. Sundays are reserved for their families. With a work schedule like that, you can appreciate the strain on their wives. One of the keys to promoting harmony on the home front has been to actively involve the wives in the business. David's wife spends twenty hours a week as the company bookkeeper, and Dick's wife spends a comparable amount of time handling the correspondence of the marketing department and acting as watchdog over the accounts receivable. Not only does the involvement of their wives make for a more harmonious home life, it is also another very effective way of minimizing the company's expenses. (Remember, not only do the wives share the burden of their husbands' heavy work schedules, they also share the joys and triumphs of seeing the big sales closed and watching the business grow. It is truly a family team effort.)

A little over one year has elapsed since DTI moved its "World Headquarters" out of David's garage. In its first fiscal year, the company has come within fifteen percent of meeting its original sales and profit forecasts. On the sales front, DTI is moving ahead into several major markets.

While exhibiting at an important industry trade show in Chicago, David and Dick met the manufacturer of a noncompeting line of security hardware. This led to their subsequent introduction to a key export broker. DTI now indicates that export sales will account for thirty percent of their total sales volume next year.

Another area that has opened up for DTI is private label manufacturing. Many major merchandise outlets such as catalog and department stores have outside companies specially make products bearing their own labels. For instance, some gas station chains sell tires carrying the name of the chain, when, in fact, the tires were manufactured by a major tire producer that also markets tires under its own brand name.

At the present time, DTI is negotiating with one of the largest retail operations in the country for a substantial purchase order for security systems to be produced on a private label basis. This retail operation has its own nationwide service organization capable of installing the systems right in the customer's home in much the same way as a washing machine or custom draperies might be installed. Another advantage that marketing through this outlet offers is the ability of the retail chain to offer its customers easy financing—a sure-fire way to increase consumer sales.

Penetration of these markets was by no means automatic. Dick described the preparations for exhibiting at their first major trade show, the International Security Conference, last February. For four days and nights, Dick and David labored over the construction of their display. When it was arranged to their satisfaction, they loaded it into Dick's little Pinto station wagon along with their samples, brochures, personal luggage, and themselves. The load was so heavy that the frame of the station wagon nearly rested on the axles. It was Saturday afternoon, the day before the exhibits were to be erected when they set off on their 350 mile trek to Los Angeles, site of the trade show.

When they arrived at the hotel where the show was being held, they offered up a small "Prayer of Thanks" that the springs on the car had not broken. They then offered up the $550 rental fee on their eight-by-ten foot booth *plus* an additional $180 for rented chairs, side tables, and drapes for the three-day show. Hurriedly, amid the bedlam of hundreds of other exhibitors readying their booths, they set up their display.

Weary but proud, David and Dick admired their completed exhibit. Next on the agenda: the formal Exhibitors' Reception. Here is where much of the real trade show "action" occurs. Contacts are made, referrals are noted, and sell, sell, sell is the order of business. It was three in the morning on Monday—official opening day—when David and Dick finally got to bed. In the next three days, they each got a *total* of less than ten hours sleep. That's the way it is at trade shows.

Slightly over one year old, DTI has been through a lot. The sales backlog is close to $100,000 and should double in the next month when some "ready to hatch" orders materialize. Membership in two important trade associations is being arranged. Most important, a second round of financing is being negotiated. A major investor is considering the purchase of a one-third interest in the company for around $250,000. This should place DTI in a much more viable position in the marketplace, enabling it to respond quickly to customer demands and serve the needs of even their largest dealers.

Legislation presently under consideration promises substantial industry growth in the next few years. Many communities already require that fire detection equipment be installed in apartment buildings and multiple story dwellings. Much of the rest of the nation is expected to follow suit in the near future. Insurance companies are also beginning to offer significant premium reductions to policy holders who have security and/or fire detection systems installed. As far as David Schuldt and Richard Bauer, Jr. are concerned, there's nowhere to go but up!

Sunnyvale, California—1984
After ten years, DTI Security has grown to become one of the recognized leaders in the security equipment industry. In 1979, the shareholders of the company were bought out by an East Coast mini-conglomerate. At that time the company name was changed to Datura International, Inc. to better reflect the company's goal of expanding outside of the security industry as well as within. (The firm still markets its security products under the Datura/DTI Security logo.) After the merger, Datura/DTI made an acquisition of its own—a company that manufactures life safety equipment for firemen.

Now the company is negotiating to purchase a major interest in one of its competitors. This would put Datura/DTI at the $8 to $9 million annual sales mark, with a staff of nearly 150. Even without the merger, the company boasts a sales backlog of nearly $3 million. It's no wonder that David Schuldt, still president of the firm, was eager to tell us all the good news of the past decade.

Those optimistic market projections panned out even better than expected. According to David, the residential security market has witnessed a thirty percent compound growth rate in recent years, and the entire industry (including industrial markets) has witnessed a twenty-five percent annual growth rate.

Private label manufacturing is a big part of Datura/DTI's business. Customers include Sears, which was negotiating with the company at the time our original story was published and has now become one of their most loyal, long-term customers.

The structure of the company has changed significantly over the years. Work is no longer subcontracted. As David explains, Datura/DTI is now a "full-fledged, fast-paced, mainstream electronics firm."

Two years ago, to accommodate the tremendous growth of the firm, Datura/DTI moved its manufacturing operations from Sunnyvale to Stockton, California where it purchased nine acres of land and built a new 40,000 square foot facility with the aid of an industrial development bond. (Datura/DTI was only the eighteenth company in California to float such a bond to expand a manufacturing facility—testimony to the spirit of innovation that has led to their success.)

Datura/DTI now has a fully staffed in-house sales organization, supplemented by manufacturer's representatives. While direct mail and space advertising are used, the company still relies primarily on tracking down leads for new business. As David explains: "This industry is still technology-driven rather than market-driven."

Export sales account for roughly six percent of revenues, mostly to the United Kingdom and Europe, with some sales to Australia and New Zealand. David doesn't expect to see an explosion in the export market since the standards for security equipment vary widely among countries, making it difficult to serve different markets. On the other hand, foreign competition has been minimal, partly because Datura/DTI focuses on the high end of the market. Foreign competitors are more interested in the low end, which lends itself to low-cost mass production.

Datura/DTI has managed to finance its growth over the years with the help of a substantial line of credit at a regional bank where the company has developed a strong relationship. In addition, after the merger a few years back, the parent company provided a healthy $2 million infusion of capital.

While the picture looks bright for Datura/DTI, the going hasn't always been easy, as David Schuldt is the first to acknowledge. The company has had its share of problems. A critical shortage of electronic parts has been a "major burden" for the company over the past two years, at times forcing David personally to go parts-shopping in Hong Kong, Taiwan, and Japan. Another problem arose a couple of years ago when Datura/DTI signed a multimillion dollar contract to develop a special line of equipment for a customer. When the customer ran into financial difficulties, Datura/DTI was left holding the bag. While they managed to recoup part of the monetary loss, the lost engineering opportunity will never be recaptured. But David feels he came away from the experience having learned a valuable lesson: "Don't put all your eggs in one basket."

The most difficult experience for the company was the loss of Dick Bauer, David's partner and close friend, to leukemia in 1979. The loss was a major setback for the company and was deeply felt within the industry where Dick was well known and well liked.

David has managed to instill within the company a philosophy of strict cost control. "It would be easy to do a lot more with a lot more money. The challenge is to do a lot more with what you already have." Fortunately, he has groomed a talented financial and engineering staff to give added elasticity to his dollars.

What lies ahead for Datura/DTI? The company looks forward to sustaining a thirty percent compounded annual growth rate for the next five years. Right now, they are considering development of hotel/motel guest security systems. Plans also call for utilizing Datura/DTI's existing technology to expand outside the security industry with a low-cost modem that will enable personal computers to communicate with each other.

Incredibly, David manages to find extra time to keep active in his industry and in his community as well. He sits on the boards of electronics and security industry trade associations and on the board of a software company. He also serves on the advisory board for his district assemblyman and lectures at seminars on financing company growth.

On the home front, David tells me that while he's still very married to the business, he's also very happily married to the same woman. He feels that is somewhat remarkable and attributes it to "perseverance and flexibility on my part and on the part of my wife"—pausing to add, "probably much more so on her part."

While David doesn't take time for an annual vacation, he and his wife continue to take "mini-vacations" to places like the Silverado Country Club in the Napa Valley wine country or Hawaii. But he chuckles as he laments the fact that he still hasn't found time to play golf on Wednesdays "with all the dentists and lawyers" as he'd envisioned years ago.

Would the president of Datura/DTI do anything differently if he could turn the clock back? "Yes," he candidly admits, "I'd spend more on research and development early in the game. We weren't nearly 'high-tech' enough during the first years of operation, and it made our success that much more difficult to come by." Datura/DTI has made up for lost time, though. The company now pays top dollar for engineering talent, and employee loyalty is strong. Not a single person has left the engineering department in more than two years. In Silicon Valley, that must be some kind of record!

David Schuldt's only son will be leaving for college soon. I asked if he planned to follow in his father's footsteps. Apparently Dad won't have to worry about potential charges of nepotism; his son wants to be a pro golfer.

**HALCOMB
ASSOCIATES**

Pert-O-Graph Is Pertinent!

510 East Maude Avenue   Sunnyvale, California 94086   Telephone (408) 245-3131

Sunnyvale, California—1971

Cold steel rings as it drives nails into structural studs, and saw blades whine as they slice through two-by-fours: Workmen are constructing a classroom of the future under the roof of Halcomb Associates, an industrial consulting firm on the San Francisco peninsula. Amidst the cacophony of progress, the man who got the outfit moving reluctantly parted with a three hour chunk of irretrievable, evanescent time to reminisce for this story. "Let's see," he muses, "How *did* it all start?"

Actually, it was Mr. Bowers who did it . . . planted the seed, that is, of Jim Halcomb's entrepreneurship. Bowers was the high school teacher who gave Jim his first glimpse of the inner workings of business. Hardly a "General Business" class meeting would go by without the students hearing the exhortation, "Differentiate the product! Differentiate the product! Differentiate the product!" Jim got the message. He contends that today there are hundreds of look-alike small businesses in the highly specialized industrial consulting field of Program Evaluation and Review Technique/Critical Path Method (PERT/CPM), a unique approach to project planning that was first employed in a major program in 1958 by Admiral William F. (Red) Raborn when he scheduled the hugely successful Navy Polaris Missile Project. The unusual and atypical success of this government-sponsored effort resulted in enormous worldwide interest in the new planning process, and in the space of just a few years, more than 3000 trade journal articles appeared on the subject of PERT/CPM.

In commenting on the need for "differentiating the product," Jim points out that as many as 99 out of every 100 companies in the industrial consulting field project the same image; he attributes his own remarkable success to his never-ending efforts to be unique and different. This effort is reflected in the extensive selection of products and services offered by Halcomb Associates, including:

> The Pert-O-Graph Kit (a do-it-yourself management tool for project planning). Built around the Pert-O-Graph II Computer, this kit is so highly thought of as a time and money saver by the president of a major Florida electronics firm that he supplies one to every engineer and scientist on his staff.[3]
>
> The Pert-O-Graph Computer Watch (a Longines-Wittnauer precision timepiece equipped with the Pert-O-Graph Computer) for convenient rapid-fire project forecasting.
>
> Management Consulting to assist in PERT/CPM planning of any project, from a sales campaign to a major real estate development (clients include hundreds of corporations in North America, Europe, and Asia).

Project Management Seminars offered periodically in major cities in the United States and Canada, featuring instruction in the use of advanced project planning techniques.

Most recently, Jim has added in-house education to his service offerings—thus the noisy construction of a uniquely equipped classroom designed to make Halcomb-style education a "total experience." In fact, when ready for use, the facility will be reminiscent of a set from the movie *2001: A Space Odyssey,* replete with the most modern of visual and audio aids. There will even be a servomechanism-actuated moving whiteboard (not *blackboard,* mind you!) that will slide into the wall when the rear-image projection screen is in use. Additionally, two room-filling, horseshoe-shaped desks have been built to accommodate a class of roughly twenty students. Of course, air conditioning rounds out the amenities.

This facility was initiated because Halcomb won a $58,932 contract for the purpose of retraining a select group of jobless aerospace engineers who have highly specialized but out-of-demand skills. The curriculum is intended to qualify them for management posts in Operation Breakthrough, a federal program set up under the auspices of the U.S. Department of Housing and Urban Development. Operation Breakthrough is a national program designed to provide, in this decade alone, twenty-six million new homes for low- and moderate-income families; the project will make use of the most progressive production techniques devised thus far.

Jim is particularly well qualified to conduct such a training program. He is a former aerospace engineer himself; accordingly, he should relate extremely well to his students. In addition, his ten-year-old firm has handled more than 200 projects in the housing and construction field. In fact, as a building trades consultant, Jim has participated in such diverse projects as planning the development and building of Foster City (a major real estate complex on the shores of San Francisco Bay) and the construction of Harrah's Casino at South Lake Tahoe, Nevada.

However, unlike the students he will soon be teaching, Jim left the aerospace community because he had a carefully conceived plan (long since drastically revised!). Recognizing the enormous difficulty that most engineering managers have in getting a shot at a corporate management position, Jim decided that he would resign, go into the "management consulting" business for two years, and then return to the aerospace industry as a "qualified" top echelon manager. (Obviously, that's not the way things have worked out, but I don't think Jim has any regrets!)

For three years prior to starting his company, Jim had been a project manager in the PERT/CPM field at Varian Associates, a leading high technology electronics firm. While at Varian, Jim developed the Pert-O-Graph Computer, a circular slide rule for scientifically estimating program schedules. However, unlike its big, expensive, and complicated electronic counterparts, the Pert-O-Graph Computer is so simple to operate that most laymen wouldn't call it a computer at all! Therefore, because of the enormous and still-growing resentment against computers and the increasing public desire to "fight it," evidenced by a national flood of cartoons and jokes that point an accusing finger at The Dumb Computer, Jim's brainchild has earned him a lot of friends who rejected the electronic colossus and its priests, the programmers.

Articles describing Halcomb's new device appeared in numerous trade magazines. Varian literally gave away thousands of cardboard models of the Pert-O-Graph at trade shows as a goodwill gesture. Finally, someone on the staff of *Business Week* heard about the Pert-O-Graph. Recognizing widespread interest in PERT, the magazine sent a staff reporter over to Varian to get a news story. The response to the subsequent article was staggering. Requests for additional information came in by the tens of thousands, and even IBM wanted to know how to get a sample!

Mail volume was so tremendous that Varian transferred Halcomb to its public relations department to assist with responding to the inquiries. As a result, he decided that there were an awful lot of people—inside and outside of the electronics industry—who wanted to hear more about PERT, and he suggested a market expansion program to the Varian management. Properly, the company pointed out that its not unlimited resources should be confined to the electronics field. The customers for Jim's proposed products simply did not represent a large enough market to interest a New York Stock Exchange member corporation.

Not long afterward, Jim expressed the desire to go into business for himself and offered to buy the trademark for his creation. The enlightened Varian management (entrepreneurs themselves) authorized the necessary transfer of title free of charge and, although dubious about his prospects for success, gave Jim their blessing. In fact, to this day, Varian remains one of Jim's industrial clients.

With a chuckle, Jim recalls that his "first office, equipped with a loudly clanking radiator, would have served nicely as an anteroom for a broom closet." Its size, however, was simply in keeping with the magnitude of his "venture" capital, a mere $500 that he obtained by taking out a loan against his life insurance policy. (Today, he is a strong advocate of a regular program of personal savings. He contends that "good luck is where preparedness meets opportunity," and "financial preparedness can only be achieved by consciously planning for it.")

In reviewing the progress of his company over the last decade, Jim sums up his feelings regarding the essence of what makes for success—persistence and audacity, coupled with a very healthy measure of publicity. After listening to him for several hours, I am satisfied that Jim is persistence personified. He voices resounding agreement with the philosopher who said "Men don't fail; they just stop trying" and asserts that "If you try *enough* different things, sooner or later something has *got* to break. Pick a direction and stick with it." In pursuing such a program, *time* becomes one of your precious resources, and Jim maintains that you must "learn to be a steward of your own time. You must learn how to say 'No' firmly but politely to the unending stream of requests for 'just a few minutes of your time'."

To insure that he is never wanting for something new to try, Jim has maintained an idea file since his teenage years. Whenever he encounters *anything* of interest in his reading or conversations that he thinks *may* be of value at some future date, the concept is catalogued for easy accessibility and stored in his idea file. In discussing the value of such a file, Jim can provide a veritable verbal parade of examples of unusual successful ideas that have resulted from the amalgamation of two or more quite different disciplines. For example, consider the bringing together of ink and the roughly surfaced steel ball to make up the ballpoint pen; the packaging together of a timepiece and a receiver to make a clock-radio; and, going further back in time, the then-absurd idea of designing a radio for use in an automobile—one of countless ideas originally laughed at and now accepted as routine and commonplace. Persistence in his quest for creativity and persistence in his efforts to develop and exploit the products and services he offers are of primary significance in Jim's remarkable achievements in his highly competitive field.

Jim recalls with pleasure a time when he learned of a construction firm that had just been awarded a $2 million contract. The company general manager had never heard of PERT and was not particularly receptive to Jim's overtures. However, in the face of Jim's unrelenting onslaught, the contractor finally consented to give him a try. Following the ahead-of-schedule and under-budget completion of the program, Jim's very pleased client indicated, "I sure am glad you kept dinging me." Jim observes that in many instances people appreciate a persistent seller. Frequently, they want what you have to sell—in fact, they may desperately need what you have to sell—but they don't know how to make the time available to listen to what you have to say and to acquire an understanding of your product.

Because Halcomb recognizes that he has a large number of satisfied customers, many of whom had to be persuaded to buy his service in the first place, he is a strong believer in the importance of audacity in bringing your products and services to the attention of potential clients. With a twinkle in his eye, he says, "I could write a book on how to get past the receptionist in the lobby. One trick is to ride the elevator to the fourth floor and take the staircase to the third if that's where your quarry hides." On a more serious note, however, Halcomb acknowledges that there is a very fine balance between being persistent and being discourteous—a balance to which he is keenly attuned.

In discussing the fact that he is primarily engaged in the marketing of a professional service, Jim points out that you can't *sell* a professional service. You reach your market through *exposure*. This is where publicity gets into the act. Jim has written numerous articles on the subject of PERT/CPM for leading trade magazines and journals. Whenever anything new or unusual happens around the Halcomb headquarters, a news release is prepared and distributed to the communications media. Although such news items do not always come to the attention of individuals in top management slots, substantial numbers of middle-level managers regularly and methodically review professional and trade journals.

To illustrate the value of reaching large numbers of middle managers, consider this event in Halcomb's history. Several years ago, Jim received a call from the Comptroller of the Columbia Broadcasting System Television Division. At the time, CBS had been renting movies from Metro-Goldwyn-Mayer, Paramount, and other major movie producers for use on CBS-TV. Since the CBS management was unhappy in their role as a movie broker, they decided to build a studio of their own. At the time this decision was formalized, it was recognized that an all-out effort would have to be made in order to ready the proposed facility. Very little time remained in which to film programs for the upcoming fall season. Several of the CBS top staffers had a passing acquaintance with the PERT concept and recognized its potential value in the resolution of this timing problem. However, they needed an expert—fast! And there was no time for canvassing the industry to find one. When the problem was brought up at a CBS staff meeting, one of the middle-management attendees, having read many of Jim's articles, indicated that, insofar as he knew, Halcomb was one of the best consultants in the industry. Subsequently, Jim got the contract; and the new Hollywood filmmaking facility, known as "Studio Center," was built and staffed (Jim even helped in programming a schedule for satisfying the staffing requirements) in record time. Thus, one can fully appreciate the importance of publicity in the marketing of a professional service. Other professionals such as lawyers and accountants, who recognize the importance and value of publicity in building a clientele, regularly accept speaking invitations whenever they are afforded the opportunity.

When asked how his family has weathered the events of the last ten years, Jim beams, grinning from ear to ear. Peering into the wings of his mind, he invites his wife, Eleanor, on stage. Eleanor has borne primary responsibility for the rearing of five bright, rambunctious young men (now ages six through sixteen). Furthermore, she has been the company controller since its inception.

One of the Halcomb family pastimes is weekend boating on the delta of the Sacramento River, sometimes called the Everglades of the West. The family got started on the boating kick by renting teacup-sized sailboats at $1 per hour when the boys and the budget were thimble-sized. Today they own a thirty-seven-foot cabin cruiser. Another regular family event is the annual trout fishing trip Jim shares with his sturdy sons, angling on chill Sierra streams on the opening day of trout season—a pleasure he has enjoyed every season for the last twelve years.

Although Jim concedes that he does not have as much time for his family as he would like to have, it is obvious that his waking hours are filled with truly satisfying work *and* play. We may assume that in his nightly slumbers, he is persistently PERTing the next day's exciting events!

Sunnyvale, California—1984
Authoring destiny. That is how Jim Halcomb sums up the business he has been in for more than twenty successful years. Employing the innovative management planning techniques that Jim has pioneered, companies learn to chart a course for their future.

The PERT/CPM project management concept, an efficient step-by-step process, has caught on like wildfire among managers looking for ways to increase productivity, expand operations, or launch new products through better planning. Halcomb attributes this phenomenon to increasing foreign competition, which has focused America's attention on the need to work more efficiently in order to compete. As this awareness has grown, Halcomb Associates, Inc. has prospered.

Jim Halcomb has come to be recognized as the expert in his field—he has even been dubbed "Mr. Planner" by *InfoWorld* magazine. He's so well known, in fact, that he hasn't carried a business card in ten years; clients come to *him*. The clients are an impressive lot indeed, including such heavy hitters as ARCO, NASA, Avon, Control Data, American Express, and a host of other prominent corporations.

The *Pert-O-Graph* Kit continues to sell well. Companies use this time and money saver in all aspects of their operations. Digital Equipment Corporation, for example, recently purchased 200 kits to be used in training employees throughout the company.

Jim continues to conduct management seminars nationwide, but his major focus these days is on in-house training programs for managers. Not only does he train project managers in the process of planning and executing their projects; he often serves as a group leader in the actual development of the project plans. Jim regularly flies his own corporate aircraft in order to quickly and efficiently relocate his staff and special equipment for key assignments, sometimes in remote plant locations.

A good example of the magnitude and importance of projects that Halcomb Associates has taken on includes one for RCA Astro Electronics. RCA came to Jim with a project of tremendous proportions. The company was beginning to design and build a weather satellite system, an incredibly complicated program with more than $100 million at stake. Needless to say, careful planning of the product was critical, so RCA turned to "Mr. Planner." Jim took a team with him to the project site and over a seventeen-week period set up over ninety project management plans for the complex systems and subsystems that make up several satellites.

One feature of Jim's planning process, which helps to make it so effective, is that it provides warning signals so that problems can be detected (and corrected) early on. When a project strays from a smooth-running, "green light" condition into a cautionary, "yellow light" mode, the client can correct the problem before it reaches the critical "red light" condition of failure, delay, or cost overrun. This represents an important advantage over the "management-by-crisis" approach that is far too prevalent in American business. Jim teaches how to *plan* rather than *react*.

Apparently, Jim practices what he preaches. I asked if Halcomb Associates had run into any "red light" conditions over the years. "Never!" was the emphatic response. "We have always planned for and achieved a super-green condition."

Through careful planning, Jim has consistently managed to finance the company's growth internally. Halcomb Associates, Inc., he points out proudly, has no long-term debt and no short-term debt whatsoever.

Jim has also succeeded in maintaining a healthy balance between his business life and his personal life. When I asked him what was the most gratifying thing that has happened to him over the years, there was not a moment's hesitation when he replied, "My sons!" Jim's five sons are all grown now.

Jim feels that he and his wife have achieved an ideal lifestyle, the kind that most people only dream about. He reflects, "I spend time with my family and get involved with fascinating nonprofit projects in addition to my work. My wife and I never wanted to become workaholics and sacrifice everything for the sake of business. I believe we have achieved the perfect lifestyle." That lifestyle, incidentally, still includes weekend trips in the family yacht on the Sacramento Delta.

Another clue to Jim Halcomb's success lies in his driving determination to remain constantly in the forefront of innovation, always looking toward the future. This trait shows up clearly when Jim speaks about a recent assignment with Masonite Corporation. He recounts the project excitedly: "I spent three weeks with a team of ninety key managers from three plant sites, teaching them powerful new (1985–1990) planning techniques because, as you know, we always are expected to lead the state-of-the-art."

An example of how Jim is pushing the state-of-the-art can be seen in his incorporation of the most advanced computer technology and procedures into the planning process. Noting that a widespread aversion to computers still exists, Jim reports that ninety-five percent of all executives and managers still do not directly use computers in their jobs. Once again demonstrating his ability to "differentiate the product," Jim has helped managers embrace the technological revolution by developing a computerized planning tool that is powerful yet simple to use.

To do this, Jim took a hard look at what managers really need and want, then carefully matched a computer system, procedures, hardware, and software to those needs. Most hardware and software on the market today, he explains, produces canned information that appeals to the passive or reporting functions of managers, such as accounting or inventory control. Jim, on the other hand, responded to the manager's need for a computerized tool that would help in the "active" functions of planning and controlling group-directed projects.

Using his own proven project management procedures, along with the right combination of modern, low-cost microcomputers, software, and large-screen computer projection equipment, Jim has successfully put together a package that will allow managers to plan the future interactively, right in the conference room where projects traditionally evolve.

Jim's dream is to set up his Conference Command Centers around the country where managers, with their teams, will be able to interactively plan expansion programs, launch new products, even whole new ventures—in short, plan *any* important project—cutting costs and salvaging precious weeks of effort that such tasks would require using traditional methods.

A Vision of the Future. This is the essence of what Jim Halcomb has to offer. Considering his success up to this point, you can bet that the bright light that will signal the future of Halcomb Associates, Inc., will be "super green."

LASER TECHNOLOGY, INC.
10624 Ventura Blvd.
No. Hollywood, CA 91604
(213) 763-7091 (213) 877-8270

Elephants, Lasers, and Moon Rocks: Talk about a Mixed Bag!

North Hollywood, California—1971

The Asiatic elephant has a gestation period that lasts from twenty-one to twenty-two months—the longest in a living species of animal. However, the performance of the pachyderm and, for that matter, the rest of the animal kingdom pales in comparison with the gestation period for some of Man's ideas. Consider the case of Laser Technology, Incorporated of North Hollywood, California, which took more than thirty-five years to reach maturity as the brainchild of founder H. B. McLaughlin; and, even at that, the labor was forced!

After thirty-five years of faithful service with a major aircraft manufacturer, McLaughlin found himself the loser in a post-merger management shuffle. At the age of sixty-three, he landed smack in the middle of a recession labor market; and, since almost all companies in his industry operate under a forced-retirement-at-age-sixty-five policy, he found it virtually impossible to locate employment related to his extensive professional background. In his own words, "Thomas Alva Edison couldn't get a job in California today if he applied over the age of fifty."

Eight months elapsed before this former aerospace executive finally accepted a position as a laboratory technician. In the interim, he had sustained a vigorous campaign, characterized by remarkable persistence and ingenuity, in search of work. Because of his long and varied experience, he felt qualified for positions from purchasing agent to president. In total, he responded to hundreds of classified advertisements.

In his responses, he put his highly developed organizational talents to use and prepared a master form letter. With his wife's secretarial support, he responded to various openings with combinations of nearly seventy-five different number-coded paragraphs, each a description of one facet of his prior experience and each suitably tailored to the requirements of a particular job. Composition instructions to his spouse might read: "Honey, send this one a 12, 19, 37, 63 letter." In response, he received fourteen different offers of employment. However, in his application letters he intentionally omitted any reference to his age; and, when he appeared for his interviews, he was typically greeted with an embarrassing, and all-too-brief, period of hospitality.

After his ordeal with unemployment, McLaughlin realized that he had developed some very clear ideas regarding his future plans. For more than thirty-five years, his daydreams had been occupied with thoughts of going into business for himself. In fact, he had contemplated the prospect of turning his hobby of gemstone growing, cutting, and polishing (known as lapidary work) into a source of income to supplement his expected retirement pension.

Now his major objective was to lay the groundwork for his own company during the evenings and weekends while he sustained himself with a regular five-day-a-week job. He says "I wanted to guarantee myself a place to work for as long as I was physically and mentally able to do so."

Fortunately, while McLaughlin was filling his garage with equipment and developing his hobby of growing and processing single crystal gemstones, the space age was making new demands on industry for exotic materials and processes. The groundwork for McLaughlin's new business was closely tied to the emergence of the semiconductor industry (transistors and integrated circuits) and the superconductor industry (study of newly discovered magnetic phenomena and research in computer memories), along with advances in the field of insulator manufacturing. However, the single most significant development was the emergence of the laser market, with its demands for ultra-high-purity crystals and optically ground surfaces. Here was a field in which all of the equipment that McLaughlin had spent more than fourteen years perfecting and accumulating could be utilized. Assessing his position, he determined that he had some basis for a company (equipment), the means for economic survival (a steady job), a market to serve (the laser industry), and guts. He next set out to implement what he refers to as his eight-point program:

1. Selection of Associates. In choosing his associates, McLaughlin tried to select those individuals who had backgrounds that were suitable to the new business but that were unlike his own background. He has a very great appreciation for the valuable insights a heterogeneous team may provide a business that serves markets as diverse as jewelry to high technology.

2. Raising Venture Capital. McLaughlin and his new associates held a meeting and invited all of the individuals who had expressed interest in the new business and who were in a position to contribute either money, equipment, time, or knowledge in exchange for stock. Enthusiasm controlled the meeting; at one point a man stood up and announced "I'll take $1600 worth," without even indicating how many shares of stock he expected to receive in return for this investment. By the end of the meeting, which lasted an hour and a half, the decision to proceed with incorporation of the business was finalized in spite of the fact that the initial capitalization was only $20,200.

On several occasions shortly after this momentous meeting, McLaughlin was told by astute businessmen, "You won't last out your first year;" "Within six months you'll have to locate additional financing;" and, when McLaughlin's planned sales organization was described, "It's *impossible* to sell a thousand-dollar item by mail!" With justifiable pride, McLaughlin points out that he has indeed lasted more than a year. In fact, the company recently celebrated its seventh anniversary. Growth has been sustained through earnings without any additional financing, and several hundreds of thousands of dollars worth of products have been sold exclusively through the use of direct mail, display advertising, and publicity releases in trade journals, all of which goes to prove that the experts can be wrong. One of the most difficult factors to evaluate in weighing the potential for success of a new enterprise is the determination of the founders.

Not very long after the initial meeting, permission was obtained from the Commissioner of Corporations of the State of California to issue stock in the new enterprise and collect the money pledged. When he called on one man for his money, he was told "Mac, I know I pledged $1000, and I don't know why I did it. I guess the eunthusiasm ran so high at the meeting that I got carried away. I'm forty-eight years old and I've never had $1000 at one time in my whole life." Fortunately, this was the only instance of inability to honor a pledge, and the financing was satisfactorily completed.

3. Setting Up Shop. Next, a building was leased and the business was effectively launched. Everyone but the stenographer (McLaughlin's wife) had another full-time job outside. All of the original employees agreed to accept a $2-per-hour salary, to be paid annually in stock.

4. Building a Prototype. Part of the assets McLaughlin contributed to the new enterprise in exchange for founders' equity were models of several different pieces of equipment. However, the first product that produced an order was a prototype of a new piece of equipment called a wire saw. In McLaughlin's words, "This unit was a winner!" Interestingly enough, McLaughlin was still employed at this point by the University of Southern California, and this same institution was Laser Technology's first customer.

As McLaughlin emphasizes, not only is a prototype necessary for the procurement of new orders, but it can also be of inestimable value in garnering free publicity for the enterprise and generating interest in the product. The wire saw, the product that launched Laser Technology, functions in much the same way as a common hacksaw. However, instead of using an ordinary metal blade, the cutting blade of the wire saw is a specially formulated metal alloy imbedded with industrial diamond dust; this combination proved to be a technical breakthrough for slicing crystals and very high-density metals. Borrowing from the words of Neil Armstrong, our first astronaut to set foot on the moon, the accomplishment proved to be not only one small step for mankind but also one giant leap for Laser Technology for, subsequent to the return of this lunar vehicle, the Laser Technology wire saw proved to be one of the most satisfactory means available for cutting the moon rocks that the astronauts brought back with them.

5. Solicit Publicity. Typically, a small new company is long on enthusiasm and short on cash. That's where free publicity comes in. Laser Technology periodically supplies news releases to more than 300 trade publications that serve industries representing potential clients for their products. The key to obtaining free publicity in a publication is to persuade the editor that your message is of sufficient general interest to their readership to warrant the use of the space allocated for news. In McLaughlin's opinion, a properly handled news release may garner more free publicity than a far more expensive, paid advertisement.

6. Respond to Inquiries. As a result of the news releases issued to trade publications, Laser Technology received a substantial number of mail inquiries from potential customers. By promptly responding to each inquiry with brochures and additional information describing the entire line of product offerings of Laser Technology, a substantial amount of new business resulted; and the customer list for the new company was significantly enlarged.

7. Secure Sales. Profitable sales represent the life blood of any business, large or small. In the first year of operation, sales for Laser Technology amounted to only $3000, certainly not much by aerospace standards. However, due to the fact that the business had no employees on the payroll who were working for more than stock in the company, the drain on assets normally represented by a corporate payroll was nil. Since the first year, annual sales have doubled each year, representing a growth rate with which any company should be pleased.

One of the primary factors to which McLaughlin attributes the success of his company is its unconditional money-back guarantee on all of its products. Such a customer service program is virtually unheard of in industry circles dominated by large corporations.

The Laser Technology sales organization is run by McLaughlin's sixty-nine-year-old wife (he is now seventy years of age). She also serves as Secretary-Treasurer for the corporation. As McLaughlin puts it, "My wife didn't know that you couldn't sell a $1000 item by direct mail; and, therefore, she has been quite successful in doing it for six years." He asserts that he is confident of her ability to sell the latest product, the Environmental Diamond Wheel Chemical Polishing Machine, which carries a price tag in the $7000 range.

8. Don't Neglect Research and Development. In McLaughlin's words, "All my life I wanted to have a company where sales would bring in sufficient money to enable us to do intensive research and development work. The success of work you do today is what keeps you in business two, three, four, or even ten years from now." Presently, Laser Technology has no less than fifteen different products in various stages of development. One of their newer products is a unique, composite synthetic gemstone made of strontium titanate and cut into a diamond shape. This unique stone is characterized by multiple interior reflections exceeding those of real diamonds. However, because the basic material is slightly less hard than a real diamond, McLaughlin crowns each synthetic gem with a very thin slice of sapphire. Since diamond is the only material that will scratch sapphire, the brilliance of the underlying synthetic stone is preserved.

Another significant factor in a well-coordinated research and development program is the investigation of new applications for existing products. For example, recently the diamond-impregnated wire saw was found uniquely well suited to the fabrication of honeycomb cavities for use in air-frame structures; and the aircraft industry was provided with an entirely new manufacturing technique. As a result of this new application, the wire saw was entered in the recent Industrial Research "100" competition. Every year, thousands of inventions and ideas are evaluated by a select industry committee for the purpose of choosing the 100 best entries for an award. The McLaughlins were notified that their entry in the competition had been selected as one of the top 100 submitted. Included in the letter of notification was an invitation to attend the awards banquet in New York to accept the honor. Feeling that a trip to New York merely to accept an award represented an unjustifiable expenditure of time and money, the McLaughlins requested that Industrial Research mail the award. With unconcealed pride, McLaughlin produces a copy of the letter he received in reply and, pointing to the last paragraph, reads, "An Industrial Research '100' Award is to applied research what a Nobel prize is to basic research. You should be proud of the research and development achievement of your company." Never having won a Nobel prize or anything close to it, the McLaughlins decided that they would *make* the time necessary to attend the banquet.

Among the fellow recipients of this honor were such goliaths as General Electric, Westinghouse, RCA, Union Carbide, Bell Laboratories, General Telephone, Hewlett-Packard, Honeywell, IBM, and Bendix. At the banquet, the featured speaker indicated that the average cost of development of the items that had won awards that year was $240,000. Since such a figure represented ten times the total assets of Laser Technology, McLaughlin offered his listeners assurances that development cost for the Wire Saw was substantially less than $240,000.

Today, seven years after start-up, Laser Technology employs a staff of twenty, most of whom have regular eight-hour-a-day jobs in the aerospace industry. To accommodate such a staff, Laser Technology runs two shifts, and McLaughlin works from 7:00 a.m. to 10:00 p.m., five days a week and puts in substantial additional time every weekend. As I sat in McLaughlin's office surveying the shelf-lined walls and the storage racks suspended from the ceiling and listening to the clicking of an automatic wire-processing machine in the background, McLaughlin beamed and said, "I am now seventy years old and I have a place to work. In fact, I'm working seventy hours a week and enjoying every minute of it. I'm so happy in my work that I wouldn't trade my opportunity here for a berth in heaven." Amen!

North Hollywood, California—1984
A decade later, H. B. McLaughlin and Laser Technology are still going strong. At the age of eighty-four, when most people have long since retired, McLaughlin still works sixty hours a week in his business, which has grown to half a million dollars in annual sales and boasts twenty-three full-time workers plus several part-time employees who staff the evening shift. Wire saws are still the core of the business, but the product line has expanded from four to eighteen models over the past ten years, and a new computer-driven saw is scheduled to be unveiled soon. The company's customer list includes such government and corporate giants as NASA, General Electric, and IBM.

Laser Technology continues to be a unique operation. Many people are still unaware of the endless variety of applications for the company's products. In McLaughlin's own words: "Ninety percent of the engineers and people who ought to know about wire saws have never heard of them." Often, customers only discover them as a last resort, so the jobs Laser Technology wins are not of the everyday variety. As McLaughlin puts it, "after everybody else has tried everything they could ever think of and couldn't do it—*then* we get the job."

McLaughlin recognizes the importance of advertising his unique product line. He distributes a booklet, *Cutting with Diamond Wire,* to potential customers, which includes a discussion of forty-three suggested applications for his products and case histories of successful applications, including the moon rock story.

Each day when McLaughlin arrives in his office at 6:30 a.m., he reviews completed questionnaires from potential customers and forwards the wire saw booklet to them. He follows this up a few weeks later with a phone call. These early morning exercises generate three to six "hot prospects" daily.

McLaughlin feels that the key to selling is for the customer to have confidence in the seller. Once this trust has been established, the customer "will just order by phone, and that's all there is to it."

Not quite all. McLaughlin prides himself on maintaining the most exacting standards of quality and customer service. The gemstones that Laser Technology continues to sell via direct mail still come with an unconditional money-back guarantee. Faulty equipment is replaced at no charge to the customer. When a certain supplier sold the company diamond wire which subsequent testing proved to be faulty, replacement wire was immediately provided for all the affected equipment. When I spoke with McLaughlin, he was about to send an engineer to North Carolina to help out a customer who was having difficulty operating his wire saw properly; Laser Technology paid for the trip. It's this philosophy that has created, according to McLaughlin, "good will with our customers like no company I ever was with."

Over the years, McLaughlin has continued to finance the growth of his company out of revenues generated. He chuckles as he recalls the one and only time he got "carried away," which was a few years ago when he decided to take out a bank loan to help expand the business. The interest rate on the loan was less than ten percent, barely over prime. However, interest rates skyrocketed to twenty-one percent not long afterwards. McLaughlin withdrew money from his savings account and loaned it to the company, which promptly turned around and paid off the bank loan.

After that episode, the company never turned to outside financing again. McLaughlin admits that his insistence on generating funds internally has kept the company from growing as fast as it might have otherwise, but he says he'd "rather go a little slower" and is quite satisfied with the size of the business that has provided him with a "good living for twenty years" and allowed him to squander money on inventing new gadgets, his passion.

Most of the company profits do get "squandered" in this way. Laser Technology plows back twenty-five percent to thirty percent of gross income into research and development, a substantial figure even for the most research-oriented firm. The net result of this commitment to R & D is a stable of twenty-four proprietary products, including the wire saw that won McLaughlin the coveted "Industrial Research '100' Award" back in 1967.

The commitment to research has also made possible a new computer-driven saw, which McLaughlin considers to be the company's biggest technical achievement to date. Most saws are capable of cutting movement in one direction only. This new computer-driven saw can be programmed to cut in two different directions simultaneously. Using it, a properly trained operator could make anything from precision jigsaw puzzles out of plate glass to graphite electrodes for the manufacture of steel extrusion dies. Only the user's imagination limits the applications for this technological breakthrough. (If you would like to know more about this remarkable device, simply write to Laser Technology and ask for their descriptive booklet referred to earlier in this story.)

McLaughlin's wife no longer works with him at the business. She retired three years ago for health reasons. "I kind of miss her, too," McLaughlin admits, and the emotion in his voice is unmistakable. Nevertheless, she keeps involved from the homefront, and dinner discussions invariably revolve around what happened at the office that day. As McLaughlin puts it, "When I go home, I'm still reporting to the Chairman of the Board."

At eighty-four, McLaughlin feels he's "four years past" when he should have retired, and reports he's thinking about selling the business. There are a number of capable men on his staff who could take over the operations successfully. What would McLaughlin do if he sold Laser Technology? His not surprising answer: "I'd open up another little shop!"

The fact that McLaughlin has developed a staff capable of taking over for him attests to the success of his philosophy in selecting associates. What's the one thing he looks for in hiring a new employee? "Enthusiasm. If you can talk to a fellow and get him steamed up and enthused about something—why, he'll work miracles for you."

McLaughlin knows all about miracles. And enthusiasm. You'd think you were listening to a teenager daydreaming about career possibilities rather than a man basking in the glow of his twilight years, as McLaughlin pauses to reflect on all the ideas he has up his sleeve for new inventions. "I've got a written list of forty-five more things that I want to develop if I live long enough and the money holds out."

I'm betting on both!

2

What Motivates
the Entrepreneur?

Many academic treatises have been written for the purpose of identifying and analyzing the factors that motivate the entrepreneur. In this chapter, we will address the subject in a style with which you personally may identify or which may closely relate to the situation of someone you know well.

A Sunny Day

Dear Boss,

I, Jack B. Nimble, hereby give notice of my formal resignation, effective two weeks from today.

I've been a designer with the Gargantuan Growth Group, Incorporated (G Cubed) ever since I finished college. My work here has been very educational, although I do confess to occasional bewilderment regarding big business management decisions. This example should illustrate what I mean: Once at a gripe session, the Director of Manufacturing responded to a question of mine by telling a story about the "Mushroom" Theory of Management. He said that you should always keep your employees in the dark, feed them lots of manure, and, when they grow up, cut them off at the ankles and can them. Everybody thought it was a funny story; but by the time the meeting was over I still didn't have an answer to my question.

41

However, I'm not writing this letter to complain. I'd like to take this opportunity to thank you and the company for all you have done for me.

That $100 bonus I got last Christmas in exchange for patent rights on my fourteenth invention was a welcome addition to my son's college fund. And I get a real kick out of seeing the Production Department turning out thousands of my little gadgets every day, even if my name isn't on the label. I only regret that I had to spend two years and write three fat proposals before persuading you and the division manager that it was a good product idea in the first place.

In case you think that my decision to leave has anything to do with the layoff of Lucy Longtimer last week, I want to put your mind at ease. I had been wondering why Lucy was still on the payroll. Her enthusiasm and drive really went to pot after she was promoted to Vice President of Historical Planning. I just didn't feel she was doing the company any good in that new position. Confidentially, though, something has been puzzling me. Why did the top brass transfer her out of the Stockholders' Delight Division she started twelve years ago, especially right after they racked up their tenth straight record year? The new manager, Mr. Presidentson, isn't doing nearly as well.

At Lucy's farewell luncheon last Friday, I was really moved by the company's generosity in giving her a solid gold twenty-five-year service pin with a real diamond in it. It's too bad Lucy couldn't hold out until she was eligible for retirement next year, though. I guess it couldn't be helped, what with the big losses this year in the Stockholders' Delight Division. Anyway, that check for two weeks' severance pay should tide her over until she qualifies for unemployment compensation. I understand you can get as high as $100 a week nowadays.

I'd also like to say that my resignation is in no way related to my having to terminate those "summer-hire" students last year just two weeks after they started working. (Remember how long it took me to persuade you to let me hire them in the first place?) I guess the company's sudden realization that it was in a cash bind and required immediate layoffs couldn't be helped. I sure had a tough time explaining it to those students, though. They went away grumbling some terrible things about their first introduction to big business.

Boss, I remember your explaining that the last six percent raise you gave me was the largest in the whole department, that I'm the youngest person in the company's history to have the responsibilities I hold, and that my salary is the highest in the company for my job classification. I also recall that to be eligible for my next promotion to Novice Manager, I have to put in at least two more years with the company.

Boss, you've gotta understand! Each month, I get a copy of the *Alumni Review* from my *alma mater*. My wife reads me the class news at bedtime every evening after that darn thing comes in the mail. You wouldn't believe the jerks I used to have for classmates and lab partners who have started businesses of their own and are now making out *very* well. One has launched a successful magazine with an international circulation; another has his own real estate development corporation. Still another has a computer peripheral company with 500 people on the payroll and grossed $25 million last year while our "most likely to fail" is a *bona fide* magnate in the alfalfa exporting business. Phil Anthrope, my former class president, just made a $100,000 Alumni Fund donation to establish a perpetual scholarship bearing his name. With competition like this, you can understand why I was too ashamed of my career progress to go to last year's reunion. I *know* I'm at least as good as most of these guys, and I've got to prove it to my wife, my friends, and most of all, *myself*. G Cubed timetables just don't hack it!

By now, I'll bet you're wondering what my plans are. I want you to know that I am not going to work for a competitor. You remember that new electromechanator Willie Whizbanger recently finished an eighteen-month development program on? You know, the one you circulated a memo about, saying the company was going to abandon it because there was no market for it? (You even let Willie buy the sole patent rights for $1). Guess what? The Vice President of Corporate Development at Upward Spiral Industries read Willie's recent professional society article about it and called our Marketing Department to see if he could buy some electromechanators from G Cubed. When he learned we weren't going to make any here, the Upward Spiral man asked if they might buy the patent rights. That's when Marketing referred the call to Willie.

Later that evening Willie telephoned me at home to say that if I wanted to start a company with him to make electromechanators, Upward Spiral had indicated they would be our first customer. Willie said that the man at Upward Spiral even told him that he could help us get some venture capital if we would prepare a business proposal. He mentioned the possibility of our being a subsidiary or some such thing, but Willie and I are going to get more details after we finish working on our business plan. Incidentally, we will probably be calling our new company Nimble Whizbanger Laboratories. I'm going to be the President and Willie is going to be the Vice President of Engineering.

The main reason Willie and I feel so confident about our prospects for success is the way Fred Faithless and his group made out when they spun off to start Levitation Laboratories two years ago. They were just acquired last month by Colossal Conglomerate in a stock swap deal, and we understand that Fred has now retired to a cattle ranch in the Canadian Rockies at the tender age of thirty-seven.

Of the seven or eight companies started by former G Cubed staff members, the only one we know of that has failed was started by Stanley Spleen and Gilda Gall. As near as we can reckon, their difficulties were basically due to walnut paneling, palace revolts, and the thirty-five-hour work week.

Willie and I have built a new prototype of our electromechanator at my uncle's auto repair shop using parts we bought at the Spleen and Gall bankruptcy sale. Also, we went to one of these new seminars on how to get started. Willie and I have talked to our wives about this, and last night we came to our final decision. Boss, it has been a pleasure working for you, and if you decide you might like to join us in about six months, we'd be glad to talk it over.

Sincerely,

Jack B. Nimble

A Clear Day

Dear Readers,

If I have been successful, Jack's letter should sum up most of the factors that prompt some people to consider starting businesses of their own. There are two categories in which these factors can be classified:

1. Those elements outside the corporation walls that irresistibly lure entrepreneurs to test their mettle in their own enterprises. They include:

    a. The desire for personal autonomy
    b. The desire for fame
    c. The desire for personal fortune
    d. The pure joy of winning

2. Those elements in the corporate experience that provoke the entrepreneur to run screaming for the exit. They include:

    a. Inadequate corporate communications
    b. Inequity between major contributions and financial rewards
    c. Promotion and salary policies
    d. Absence of employment security
    e. Corporate politics and nepotism
    f. Red tape
    g. Orphan products
    h. Questionably relevant educational requirements

Let's examine each of these in detail.

Factors External to the Corporation

The Desire for Personal Autonomy

When corporate decisions and fortunes appear to be most capricious, people may feel an ungovernable desire to do their own thing. They want to feel that, if they fail, it was their doing and their doing *alone*. The essence of entrepreneurship is the charting of one's own course on the high seas of tomorrow's business world.

Obviously the degree of autonomy entrepreneurs can enjoy depends largely on their stockholders or partners (if they have any), their customers, their financial condition, and even their products. With careful planning, entrepreneurs can weigh autonomy against their other entrepreneurial objectives and arrive at an acceptable compromise *before* they commit their financial, physical, and emotional resources to the enterprise.

A very important aspect of being your own boss is the freedom to choose those projects to which you will devote your efforts. Should you wish to spend part of your time literally building sand castles at the beach, this option may be yours to pursue, *if* you work things right. The satisfaction in *doing* instead of *proposing* or *justifying* can be quite liberating. Successful entrepreneurs derive some of their greatest satisfaction from nurturing their ideas and concepts until they flower and bear fruit *without* first having to perform a ritual dance for the corporate demigods of fertility.

The Desire for Fame

I have no statistics on the number of companies that bear in some form the names of their founders, but a look through any business directory suggests that companies that do include founders' names substantially outnumber those that do not. And consider that a large percentage of those that do not are the result of the desire for trademark protection not possible or practical with the use of the founder(s)' name(s). For example, the familiar name of the Kodak film company was specifically selected, in the words of its founder, George Eastman, "because I knew a trade name must be short, vigorous, incapable of being misspelled to an extent that will destroy its identity, and, in order to satisfy trademark laws, it must mean absolutely nothing."[4]

I seriously doubt that the desire to see one's name on a billboard is the sole reason for the inception of any corporation, but the opportunity for obtaining some degree of fame certainly enhances the attractiveness of the "my-own-business" undertaking. The identification of the founders with their creations is a major incentive in goading them to superhuman efforts. They often feel that both their reputations and that of their families depend on the success of their efforts. Significant achievement in the business and social community, with its attendant prestige and honor for the entrepreneurs and their families, serves as justification for undertaking the risks involved.

The Desire for a Personal Fortune

There are other financial factors at work in the motivation of an entrepreneur apart from score-keeping of rewards for work performed. For example: In school, a perfect mark is 100 points out of 100 possible points. Measuring the worth of an idea without access to such a simplistic yardstick is a fundamental enigma. Obviously, 100 percent of all the money there is in the world (or in the company treasury, for that matter) is an impractical prize for perfect business performance. Some slightly smaller apportionment will have to make do. The amount of money available with which, then, to "keep score" is usually in grossly inadequate supply, particularly if corporate structure has the key to the counting house. As the expression goes, "you'll never get rich working for somebody else."

Accordingly, after working several years in industry, potential entrepreneurs simultaneously begin to discover that their salary growth *and* their promotion rates are running along with very short steps. And they begin to recognize that people who launch their *own* successful businesses often make a *lot* of money in the process. The realization comes to them about the time when: the FHA-financed tract house with its tar and gravel roof is beginning to need repairs; the property taxes have doubled in the last five years; the kids are reaching school age or are far enough along so that college tuition has ceased to be a nebulous future concern; the balancing of the family budget requires more and more time and proves less and less encouraging a task than it was when the expense/income ratio was a lot more reasonable.

And suddenly other symptoms of latent entrepreneurship begin to manifest themselves. Instead of devoting all of the evening reading to trade and industry publications, the stricken entrepreneur-to-be makes time for a review of *The Wall Street Journal* and *Business Week*. Here to dazzle the reader are success stories of new glamour companies with fifty-to-one price/earnings ratios (Chapter XI obituaries seem to appear on a space-available basis as column fillers, if they appear at all). As the captivated company founders of the future continue to grapple with their personal finances, they begin to visualize how much more they could be enjoying life if they had no money worries. They begin to evaluate their own potential in comparison with the examples they have been reading about. And they decide that they've got as much success serum in their veins as the people in those articles they've been reading. Why shouldn't they, also, enjoy a new house, a yacht, that great new sports car, a Paris-designer wardrobe, Ivy League colleges for their kids? They could even set up charitable foundations, like the Fords and the Rockefellers. All they've got to do is put together a company and hire a good tax accountant to keep Uncle Sam from taking all of the profits. Right? Well, not quite, but such decisions are rarely reached on a rational basis, anyway.

The Pure Joy of Winning

It's pretty tough for a corporation to supply continuing opportunities that can satisfy the consuming, emotional need to *win* that possesses the soul of the embryonic entrepreneur. Dr. Stanley F. Kaisel, founder of what is now the MEC division of Teledyne, once addressed a group of young MIT alumni by stating, with the authority of the business veteran, "Victories come from doing things *better* than other people. Victories are what provide the fun in having a company of your own."[5]

And indeed the *élan* of intense competition and the heady feeling of victory *is* a very significant motivational factor in the creation of new companies. As a member of a large corporation, the soul of the entrepreneur often feels like a handicapped race horse, bearing a greater burden than less able counterparts. In the case of race horses, handicapping ostensibly provides for an "equitable" contest; it gives the older, albeit more feeble, a crack at the finish line. How frustrating to watch the trophies and glory accrue only to senior or better-entrenched colleagues! Conversely, excessive competitive zeal has no place in either a large *or* small company. A delicate balance between internal cooperation and external competition is an essential element of long-term survival in any corporate entity. Recently a fourteen-month-old company *and* $350,000 of an investor's money were almost totally dissipated by the disaster of internal competition. Today, only one of the six founders (not the president) remains to administer intensive care to the corporate dream turned nightmare.

Fortunately, I have observed far more business success stories than I have instances of failure. These successes have resulted in no small degree from the ability of the members of each founding group to constructively channel their competitive energies. The point I'd make is that there was enough *room* in their new corporate structure for them to expend their energies to the limit without colliding with ceilings *or* colleagues. A story that magnificently illustrates this theme is that of Thomas Alva Edison. Because he was his own boss, he was free to devote his enormous inventive talent to just about any project he wanted to work on. As a result, he became one of the most prolific technological creators of all time. We are indebted to him for his work on such diverse products as the radio, the phonograph recording, the motion picture camera, the telephone, and the electric light. Edison also left us his statement on the subject of winning: "I don't care so much about making my fortune as I do for getting ahead of the other fellows."[6]

Factors Internal to the Corporation

Inadequate Corporate Communications

Entrepreneurs are often impatient with and confused by the typical communications problems of the large corporation. The only viable solution to this problem (as far as people like Jack B. Nimble are concerned) is for Jack to call the shots himself. But his lack of patience with The System makes it highly improbable that he will stick around long enough to gain the vantage point in the corporate hierarchy where the visibility is 100 percent. What Jack must do, then, is build his own corporate structure beneath him (where, ironically, if the enterprise is successful, the ponderous insensitivity of the large corporation will reassert itself to annoy the frustrated entrepreneurs in Jack's employ). The Gordian knot of corporate communications has been the subject of many books and many studies. There is only one conclusion, however, upon which everyone agrees—the sword is most efficiently wielded from the *top* of the knot.

Inequity Between Major Contributions and Financial Rewards

When Jack's new product is commercially successful, all the diamonds in Africa wouldn't represent sufficient compensation for his efforts. Totally his is the product—memories of budget over-runs in research and development; projects written off as failures; tens of thousands of dollars invested in capital equipment; the assisting small army of purchasing agents, production workers, machinists, technical writers, draftsmen, stockroom clerks, sheet-metal workers; the librarian; and the secretary who every Friday faithfully watered his philodendron fade from consciousness. They were, he rationalizes, only doing their jobs. But the invention, the idea that became a successful *thing*—that, thinks Jack, is a horse of a different color, and he should be the one to receive first and foremost consideration in the distribution of the rewards.

In the typical corporate structure, the Jacks of this world may expect little more than a relatively comfortable salary plus a token bonus in recognition of their occasional and unpredictable inventive output. The company attitude seems to be: "We're paying you to invent, so why should we give you additional incentives simply because you manage to do what we hired you to do in the first place?"

On the other hand, companies are rarely equipped adequately to reward the innovative and pioneering achievements of genuinely creative minds. Company standards are established on the expectation of mediocrity in innovation. Often, incentives are structured to provide bonuses based solely on the number of patents applied for, regardless of commercial or scientific merit.

However, in the hands of a resourceful entrepreneur, a worthwhile innovation may provide a sound basis for a new enterprise. The resulting financial rewards may be a more realistic quantification of the merit of a genuine contribution to the industry and may provide entrepreneurs with substantially greater returns for their efforts than they could ever have expected from a corporation.

As I see it, if creative people (be they inventors, scientists, marketing innovators, or manufacturing geniuses) are really willing to take a chance on the commercial merits of their output, if they are willing and able to *risk,* then founding companies of their own can provide them with a well-deserved return. On the other hand, if they are comfortable only with the resources of a large corporation backing their longshot ideas, then, like the race track tipster's, their "equitable" return is the price of a tout sheet.

Promotion and Salary Policies

My friends, you got trouble. Right here in Corporation City. Trouble starts with a "T" and that rhymes with "P" and that stands for Prejudice—*age* prejudice. Yeah!

Are expressions like "time in grade," "Yes, but he's too young," or "She ain't old enough to be makin' that kind of money" creeping into your vocabulary? Are you set on keepin' these young whippersnappers down in their proper place? My friend, you got trouble, trouble, Trouble! That Music Man's gonna lead 'em right down Route 128 (or Silicon Valley, or any other hotbed of opportunity) to the first vacant shop they can find. I've seen plenty of young engineers who "weren't ready" for increased corporate responsibility resign and subsequently succeed in mastering far more demanding problems in starting their own company. These young cockerels simply said "Forget the incubator! Let me at the hen yard!"

When it comes to the compensation of exceptional young talent, corporate practice is baffling. Why is it that companies are so reluctant to flex their salary guidelines for promising, productive young men and women? Ultimately, such people quit in frustration to take a higher-paying position elsewhere or to start their own businesses. Then—and this is the grabber—the first company often will pay their replacements *higher salaries* to fill the opening and pay the head-hunters a ten-percent-of-annual-salary (or more) bounty to boot! (Remember, the bump you get when you hit your head on a salary ceiling injures more than just your cranium.)

Employee Security?

There is no such thing. Security comes from keeping your skills sharp enough; up-to-date enough; and versatile enough to weather the fickle winds of corporate fate. Personal resourcefulness is far more valuable an asset than any narrow skill. (What do you do when they stop making anything resembling the only computer you know how to operate?) Furthermore, it is hard to conceive of any endeavor that can tax your personal resourcefulness more than running a company of your own and that has the potential for rewarding you more handsomely with the kind of reward that means the money-in-the-bank security *most* people have in mind when they talk about security.

This security thing is a slippery concept. To paraphrase the late producer, Michael Todd: "I've never been insecure, only broke. Being insecure is a frame of mind, while being broke is only a temporary situation." For the spirited entrepreneur, reversals and setbacks are only bumps and detours on the road to success. Security results from the self-knowledge that *you* and not some impersonal corporate entity are responsible for your own destiny. Security results from positive personal action to insure that you acquire and maintain skills and attitudes for which there is a continuing demand. *Real* personal security is measured by the confidence with which you undertake difficult new challenges and the ease with which you adjust to adversity. Hand-wringing worry-warts will *never* be secure, with or without a company job.

In summary, as long as you have a skill or talent for which there is a professional demand, you may look forward to "security." To expect to be retained in *any* position after you cease to be able to contribute effectively toward the goals of an organization is to pay a terrible penalty in terms of self-respect and the real security that comes from knowing that your contributions are important.

Corporate Politics and Nepotism

Most companies, and particularly the small ones that people like J. B. Nimble start, are patterned in the image of their creators. From what I've seen, the Laws of Relativity (Nepotism) and corporate politics are at least as virulent in the small, closely held corporations as they are in their larger counterparts. The expression "Blood is thicker than water" must surely have emerged from the small-company milieu. As long as companies are run by people, politics will have to be reckoned with as a factor of corporate reality. Therefore, you may as well be the nepotor instead of the nepotee.

Red Tape

No matter how you hack at it, red tape is a royal pain! It is a disease endemic to large corporations, being symptomatic of procrastination and indecision. The originators of red tape, called "corporate cowards," are characterized by a fear of making decisions. Their *modus operandi* is an insistence on including any and all steps effective in producing delay. The problem is thereby dissipated until it is too vague to require a decision and, thus, the risk involved in general decision-making is brought to its nadir. Progress-minded employees find it necessary to negotiate the complex administrative labyrinth that *their ideas*—the bureaucracy's *problems*—have become, which frustrates their efforts to advance their programs and destroys or seriously impairs their initiative. And, as may be expected, their productivity is similarly affected.

Red tape also includes the corporate cowards' ability to insulate themselves from responsibility. The insulating material is in the form of voluminous data from various studies and reports; any decision that they reach limps forth from under the crush of background material and is ready at any moment, should its efficacy be questioned, to scuttle again beneath the bulging dossier as the corporate cowards mumble "Well, we did everything *we* could to insure that the decision was correct." (In effect, they are only saying, "Don't we deserve an 'A' for effort?")

I am reminded of a situation I experienced while in the military service, when I ran a one-man office in a records-retirement warehouse. (Obviously, this was not a job for which I volunteered!) The lighting in the building was terrible, and I felt that my efficiency could be considerably enhanced (*and* my eyesight preserved) if I had the benefit of fluorescent lighting. I discussed the problem with my boss, a Chief Warrant Officer of many years' experience. Although he indicated that my suggestion was worthwhile, he pointed out that it would be necessary to document the merits of my request in order to secure approval to have the work done. I therefore spent the next hour carefully preparing a concise, half-page report to justify the installation of the lighting and submitted it.

Approximately one week later, I received notification that my request had been turned down for insufficient supporting information. At this point, I revised and resubmitted the request, giving an elaborate discussion of the savings in time and money and the increased efficiency which would result from the added lighting. Naturally, many of the figures were slanted to obtain the necessary approval. Later, I was told that the second request I had submitted was one of the best the authorizing officer had ever seen. He further indicated that if every request that came to his attention was as carefully documented as the one representing my second attempt, every one of them would qualify for his approval. Needless to say, I did not dare question him as to what impact this rationale might have on his budget or the manpower available to him.

In the preparation of this kind of justification, I was, in effect, placed in the position of making the decision *for* the responsible individual; and, thus, the desired goal was achieved. I got what I wanted, and he didn't have to make the decision.

I was quite appalled, however, when subsequently it took two men one and a half days to install the two fluorescent lights in my small office. It turned out that they had very little to do; their backlog was very low, and they were simply stretching out their work to fill in the hours on their time cards.

Orphan Products

Let's take a closer look at Willie Whizbanger, the engineer to whom we referred above. Willie was an enthusiastic soul, very bright and very creative and very involved with his projects. Whenever he was assigned a particularly challenging task, he would jump up and down (discreetly, mind you) and rub his hands with glee! His eyes would twinkle and his customary mask of deep preoccupation with theoretical considerations would give way to an earlobe-to-earlobe grin. He would even be polite to the company sales representatives when they annoyed him with questions about when he might finish his project and how much the end product might cost to make.

Often the night watchman would wonder about this man who stayed up until it was nearly dawn fiddling with the knobs on his expensive instruments and marking strange symbols in his notebook. Now and then, the watchman would write little notes to the day-shift Security Officer, seeking assurances that all was well.

Willie, working until dawn, was very happy. He was doing just what he spent six years in college studying to do.

Finally the prototype was complete. Every design objective had been achieved and the final reports had been painstakingly written. All that remained was to tool up in Production and turn out thousands more just like the first. Willie offered cigars around. "Willie," his boss said, placing his arm around the young man's shoulders, "you've done a fine job; I'm really proud of you. Now let's go into my office for a few minutes. I want to bring you up to date on a few changes we've just made in the Marketing Department."

Minutes later, Willie and his boss were luxuriating in the fine aroma of Jamaican tobacco and the comfort of heavy leather chairs. "Willie, I know how much this latest project has meant to you. I personally feel it represents the most creative work you've done for me to date.

"However, I've spent the last two days in discussions with our new Vice President of Marketing and the Controller, reviewing the new product promotion budgets. Now I know the previous Marketing Honcho was looking forward to a big campaign to introduce your new product; but, as you know, he recently resigned—another company offered him a salary we couldn't meet. Anyway, the new marketeer just isn't convinced the market is ready for your product. His budget is tight, so he's asked us in Engineering to put the idea on the shelf for a year or two. I hope you'll understand, Willie. If you want to, take the rest of the day off, and we'll talk about a new project tomorrow morning."

In a blue funk and with a lump in this throat, Willie dumped the remaining cigars into his briefcase and prepared to go home. Just then, his phone rang. The switchboard operator said, "Mr. Vector of Upward Spiral Industries is calling."

It is unreasonable to expect one or two entrepreneurs to personify *all* of the reasons people have for starting businesses of their own. Therefore, the next section will cover additional motivations not mentioned in Jack's letter.

Questionably Relevant Educational Requirements

Within the corporate compound, manager candidates lacking a college degree (a "mustang," in Navy parlance) have the deck stacked against them. In many cases, degree snobbery is so great that less-capable college-educated recruits will refuse to work for very capable mustangs. The college graduates have spent four years preparing for their careers; evidently they don't want to let anyone else into the circle of the elite unless they too ante up the four-year membership fee. Like the old days of fraternity hazing, the attitude seems to be "I had to put up with it; why should the new candidates get off any lighter?" Given such a set of circumstances, degree-deficient candidates either take the time to complete their college educations, resign themselves to mediocre career progress, or start businesses of their own.

Everyone knows of individuals who have studied several years in night school for an advanced college degree. Have you ever noticed the large salary increase they often receive after they finish the last three lousy units needed to complete the degree requirements? Ask yourself: Are they being paid for capability or for a slip of parchment?

Unfortunately, a college education serves too often as a ball and chain, preparing individuals for lifetime careers as corporation employees. Listen to the graduate speak: "I've spent four years of my life getting this degree in Esoteric-Synergistic Technology, and I'll be darned if I'm going to give that up to go into any *new* field, *regardless* of how promising it may appear to be. So what if I haven't had a raise in two years? I've got security."

Contrast this with the talented high-school graduates who go into fast-food franchising, real-estate development, or garment retailing. If they are modestly successful, their incomes will be comparable to those of college-educated corporation employees. If their success is more than modest, their lifetime earnings will exceed the corporation employee's by several times over.

Without a doubt, the reader can conjure up a list of entrepreneurial motivations twice as long as mine. To treat this topic exhaustively, however, would be the subject of an entire book. The references at the end of the book should be of help to those wishing to study this fascinating phenomenon further.

3

Personal Resources Checklist

"The single most important factor in the success or failure of a new enterprise is the *people*."[7] Do *you* have the personal resources necessary to successfully withstand the rigors of starting a business of your own? Measure yourself and see.

Many of the topics to be covered below are just plain common sense. Yet, within the past ten years the failure rate more than doubled, and the number of failures has been climbing sharply during the 'eighties (see the following graph). From a thirty-year low of

Business Failures, 1951–1981

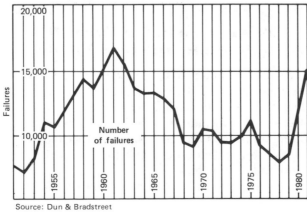

Source: Dun & Bradstreet

57

6619 annually in 1978, the number of failures nearly quadrupled, to more than 25,000 by 1982.[8]

The single greatest underlying cause of business failure, or *bankruptcy,* is simple managerial incompetence, which accounts for approximately forty-six percent of the total failures. Before you take the chance of being added to this burgeoning casualty list, consider *your* personal capabilities.

Competence

None of us can be completely objective in evaluating our own levels of competence. Competence constitutes a measure of one's ability to gather information, evaluate it, and arrive at operational decisions with a high percentage of right answers quickly, in order to render these decisions maximally effective. Generally, the information that must be evaluated is less than complete. Accordingly, imagination, an ability to "read between the lines," the maturity of judgment necessary to recognize when a decision *must* be made (with or *without* all the facts), and the guts to say "We'll do it this way," are the marks of the competent manager.

Fear of making a wrong judgment causes the administrative paralysis that is a sure sign of incompetence. Consider this story of a baseball player: It was the bottom of the ninth inning. The score was six to five. Runners were on second and third. Any base hit would bring in two runs and win the ball game. There were already two outs. The count on the batter was three and two. The crowd in the packed stands watched with pounding pulses and bated breath as the pitcher delivered a hard, fast ball right down the middle. "Strike three," the umpire roared. The game was over.

"Why didn't you swing at that last pitch?" the red-faced coach demanded of his retired batter.

"Well sir," responded the batter, "I was afraid I'd miss it."

Motivation and the Three D's: Desire, Determination, and Dedication

Starting a new firm is not a recommended pastime for the dilettante. Desire, determination, and dedication, the three ingredients in my personal definition of motivation, are essential qualities that enable the entrepreneur to continue to function effectively in the face of crushing disappointments and reversals. Motivation is the catalyst that facilitates the application of one's talents to the resolution of seemingly insoluble problems.

There is a vast literature that has popularized the subject of motivation. We have all heard of people such as Norman Vincent Peale, Robert Schuller, Wayne Dyer, and Maxwell Maltz. In the writings of all of these men, one theme prevails: You get more satisfaction out of life by deciding what it is you want and then pursuing that goal with single-minded devotion. One businessman of my acquaintance is so motivated that he has prepared a formal, written life plan. This plan includes all of the major goals he has scheduled for himself and a listing of the carefully thought-out steps necessary to enable him to obtain his life's objectives. People contemplating businesses of their own must decide what it is they hope to achieve by their actions. (A review of the earlier section that discussed "What Motivates the Entrepreneur" should be of some help in making your personal evaluation.)

To illustrate the power of motivation, consider the tale of the young swain out one evening in the family car with the girl of his dreams. As the lovers admired the twinkling lights of the city below from their mountaintop parking spot, the girl looked deeply into her escort's eyes and said, "I'd feel much more in the mood for love if you'd put the top down." He did.

The next day, when the young man was talking with a buddy, he mentioned that it took him nearly twenty minutes to get that car top down. "How come?" his friend asked. "On my convertible, I can put the top down in about *three* minutes." "Well, you see," our friend replied, "my car isn't a convertible!" *That's* what I mean by the power of motivation!

First-hand Knowledge of the Product or Service to be Offered

The concept of apprenticeship is older than recorded history. Although someone may learn the ropes the hard way by starting in a new field without any relevant experience, the knowledge gained at the knee of a master is worth a full-tuition scholarship in the School of Hard Knocks.

I recall the time between my freshman and sophomore years in college. Summer jobs were scarce; and, after several days of fruitless searching, I finally managed to secure a promising position as an ice cream vendor. The work entailed hawking my wares from a small refrigerated truck in the finest tradition of the Good Humor Man. Based on my second week's sales, I judged my competence level to be pretty high. In spite of the fact that my training consisted of verification of my driver's license and the posting of a $50 bond, I was selling a lot more than many of the guys who had been "in the business" for a much longer time than I had.

Also, my motivation was of the most basic kind—I needed the money to pay rent on my $46.50-per-month basement apartment. And I wanted to have the highest weekly sales volume in the organization by the end of the season. But, despite working seven days a week, twelve hours a day (counting the routine three-hour round trip from Boston to my Cape Cod resort market), I found that my sales were peaking out at a level that brought me a net before taxes of about 75 cents an hour.

Then Fortune smiled upon me. Papa Fortune. Papa Fortune was five-feet-six and 250 pounds. (He liked ice cream.) Winters he sold heating oil from his own truck (*not* his *ice cream* truck), and summers he was the Assistant Manager at the ice-cream vending plant. Papa decided that any kid who worked as hard as I did should be able to sell a lot more than I was managing to sell.

One night as I was plugging my refrigeration unit into the outdoor receptacle after another grueling day's work, Papa called me aside for a consultation. "Wad chew take in terday, kid?" When I told him, he said, "Tamarra, I'm goin out wit cha. I'll show ya da ropes."

When we arrived at the "front" the next day, I watched and listened and was stupefied by what I observed. "Lady, yew don't want yer kids to rot dere teeth on them color'd water sticks (5 cents) when dey could be injoyin de healt-given goodness of a frozin oringe jooce bar wit Vitamin C (10 cents), do ya?"

"Sonny (quarter in hand), you'd rather have a choclit sundy (25 cents) dan an ice creem bar (10 cents), wooden ya? Dey lass fibe times longer, an' yewl still hav yers wen de udder kids finish deir ice creem bars."

"Mister, yew doan wan ate ice creem bars (80 cents total) fer yer kid's birfday pardy. Make it a reel treat an git um a haff gallin ($1.75) of de bess ice cream money kin by!"

To a little girl loitering around the truck: "Hi, Sis, watt wood yew like?" Answer: "I don't have any money, Mister." Rejoinder: "Well, run ast yer Mommy fer sum. We'll cetch yew at the nex block." (In most instances, this nonbuyer would become a huffing-puffing, beaming little tyke dropping a dime in Papa's pudgy paw on the next street stop. Not only that, but on future days she would be prepared for my visit with a dime tied inside a corner of the handkerchief pinned to her dress.

Our sales for the day were about double my previous average; and the next day (the one that really counted as far as I was concerned), my sales were fifty percent higher than they had been before my "apprenticeship." I seriously doubt whether I could have come close to realizing those sales results by the end of the summer had it not been for Papa's training. He had enabled me to obtain a substantial gain in *first-hand knowledge* of my job.

Ability to Manage People and Resources

We've all heard of or seen cases where craftsmen, salespeople, designers, or other nonmanagers were promoted to a position of managerial responsibility and failed miserably. Clearly, the optimum time for entrepreneurs to test their capabilities as managers is *before* they go into businesses of their own.

Management weaknesses in a large firm are generally remedied by what is known as the "horizontal promotion," where, in Peter-Principle[9] terms, people who have reached their Level of Incompetence are simply placed aside the pathway of progress and into a new but nonfunctional position. Usually this ploy involves no cut in salary and ostensibly no change in prestige; rather, it is like removing a barnacle from the hull of a ship and stowing it in the cargo area so that it can enjoy the voyage without continuing to slow the vessel. In a firm of your own, however, stowaways are unwelcome regardless of the circumstances, and they must be promptly excised to protect the corporate ship from foundering without hope of salvage.

In the framework of a new enterprise, the availability of people and resources is usually extremely limited. The ability of the president to initially achieve dramatic results in output per manhour and per invested dollar will profoundly affect the ensuing rate of company growth.

When the amount of information available on a fledgling company is scarce (and this is typically the case), the evaluations made by customers, suppliers, bankers, investors and even prospective employees tend greatly to magnify any slight indications of trouble. The willingness of customers to buy a company's products, the order size to which they are willing to commit themselves and the frequency of their reorders, the amount of credit a supplier is willing to extend, the willingness of bankers to lend money (and the level of risk reflected in the interest rate charged), and investor confidence reflected in stock valuation all reveal a careful review by the parties concerned of the early performance of the new company. Deficiency in the specialty of managing people and resources currently ranks as the third largest cause of business failure. Thus, an objective evaluation of these management skills is of crucial importance.

Broad, Well-rounded Experience

As mentioned earlier, the founders of new companies rarely have the good fortune to start out with a large, seasoned staff. Not only, then, must they possess substantial expertise in at least one business area (preferably that which represents the main thrust of the operation) but they should also be familiar enough with the other areas to insure survival and growth of the firm until additional staff can be added to bolster any weaknesses.

The new business will probably demand that the founder possess *some* experience or knowledge in sales, purchasing, manufacturing, engineering, and certainly finance. The *degree* of expertise required will obviously depend on whether the business deals in a product or in a service. Furthermore, the nature of the products or services will also determine the skills required. The manufacturer who supplies products, such as motors, to other firms has markedly different problems than the manufacturer of, say, household furniture, who offers goods for sale to the public. The hairstyling salon operator with a staff of six beauticians also has problems quite unlike those of the president of a drayage concern with a fleet of trucks.

If possible, prospective entrepreneurs should structure their work experience prior to starting their own businesses so that they have an opportunity for exposure to those key areas that will dramatically influence the success of the enterprises they launch. The minimum requirement is the development of an ability to communicate effectively and intelligently with people who are experts in their specialties.

Should the presidents-to-be decide, after careful analysis, that they need a partner or two to complement their skills, they have probably done themselves and their businesses a great favor. There is only one thing worse than new company presidents with serious deficiencies in key areas of operation, and that is individuals who fail to recognize these deficiencies so that they can compensate for them. Cultivation of the ability to identify personal deficiencies and, further, to be able to recognize and evaluate other individuals who have the desired expertise is the mark of a person who has a high probability of building a company from a garage-shop operation into a major competitor in its industry.

For contrast, consider the unfortunate case of the corporation that had an excellent product concept, a fantastic marketing capability, a manufacturing organization that was the envy of all the competition, and a record of timely deliveries that made it the darling of the marketplace. The product pricing afforded the company a very nice profit, but it still failed. How could such a thing happen, you ask. Quite simply: If the accounts receivable don't turn quickly enough to provide the necessary cash flow for meeting the payroll and giving the government its pound of flesh, the sheriff will soon visit with a padlock for the door. It's happened to thousands and thousands of businesses in the past, and it will continue to happen. Failure in this one critical area can cost the company its life and the founders their jobs, their dreams, and quite possibly their personal financial solvency. The time-worn but time-honored cliche about a chain being only as strong as its weakest link has justifiably earned its place in business parlance.

One more observation before moving on: In the operation of a small, new company, there is precious little time. If you are contemplating starting a business and if you recognize a deficiency in a given area and if you decide that you can brush up by referring to a textbook or some other source once the clock starts running, forget it. The race will be over before you remove that pebble from your track shoes.

Stamina and Physical Well-being

If you ever have an opportunity to meet with a group of entrepreneurs shortly after they have started their business or if you see a photograph of such a group, take note of their eyes. If they are true entrepreneurs, their eyes will be bloodshot; and large, black rings will have taken up residence just underneath.

Starting a business and handling the hundreds of details necessary to get it firmly established is probably one of the most grueling tasks anyone can undertake. A work week of 80 to 100 hours on the job is quite common for the dedicated entrepreneur. One president told me that his weekly work record, attained during the first weeks after the start-up of his second company, was 135 hours. This man, needless to say, had a cot in his office.

The justification for working such long hours stems from the requirement that every dollar invested in the business has to do the work of at least three. This is partly the result of the excessive optimism so common in forecasting the cash requirements of the new firm. (Typically, money is the most limited resource of all in any new enterprise.)

Until products are delivered or services are performed to generate accounts receivable, the young company must sustain itself with its meager cash reserves. The fixed expenses, which include taxes, rent, utilities, and the payroll for the hourly workers (if things are going well, the founders *may* also get paid), provide a steady drain on the financial reserves of the enterprise. What the firm's treasury lacks must be compensated for by the stamina of the founders.

Stamina requires two things: excellent physical health and an inflexible determination to drive your body to whatever lengths are necessary to meet the demands of the moment. It is not my intention to peddle physical culture or promulgate pious platitudes regarding the virtue of having a healthy body. This is a no-nonsense subject that warrants the serious consideration of all those contemplating businesses of their own.

One of the occupational diseases of entrepreneurship is the duodenal ulcer. Having one can be a nasty, miserable experience. The entrepreneur cannot afford the inefficiencies that favoring such a problem requires; nor can a fledgling business endure, without serious penalty, the burden of a bedridden president. To overlook the importance of proper diet (a supper of candy bars from the vending machine is not exactly the ideal meal), adequate regular sleep (insomnia is a common problem of young presidents), and regular exercise is foolhardy. You can demand far more of a robust, healthy person than of one who is run down and out of shape. Giving their bodies the proper attention they deserve is one of the wisest investments entrepreneurs can make.

An added benefit of good physical health is the forceful, dynamic image you project of your company when speaking with customers, suppliers, or investors. No matter how good your product is, it's tough to dazzle a buyer when fatigue has you bushed, beat, and befuddled. I have heard more than one venture capitalist tell of a company president he knew who had to spend time in the hospital every time things got rough. This is not an undertaking for frail frames or tender tummies.

Financial Resources

Even a shoestring operation requires a shoestring for a start, and we all know that shoestrings today cost a lot more than they used to. For most entrepreneurs, the process of starting a business will probably entail making the largest cash investment they have made thus far in their lives.

A start-up situation in which a significant amount of funding is not provided by the founders themselves, from their personal resources, is quite rare. Thus, people contemplating businesses of their own should consider the economic demands such a decision will make upon them and their families. If they have been particularly successful in corporate careers, with the attendant handsome salary and expense-account travel, they are going to have quite an adjustment to make in the early years of operating their new business. This change in lifestyle may prove to be quite traumatic for the entrepreneurs and even more so for their families. (But canned beans aren't nearly so bad as they're made out to be. Try the B&M brand Brick Oven variety.)

When and if the new enterprise needs financial assistance from outside sources, a record of personal fiscal responsibility will be most helpful. Almost invariably, any investor contemplating a major equity position in a new company will very thoroughly investigate the financial circumstances of the officers of the company. At the outset, modest salaries and even more modest expense accounts should be programmed as a matter of company policy.

In those instances where a very small-scale beginning is planned and the initial capitalization is modest, only minor adjustments in lifestyle will be necessary. However, the rate of return one can reasonably expect from such limited financial commitment will also be modest.

First-hand experience with members of the financial community is of considerable value and importance to anyone in business. At the very least, entrepreneurs should cultivate an association with the commercial bankers where they maintain their checking accounts. If the bank has been properly chosen, its bankers should be able to provide considerable assistance later on in locating additional financing, if needed. A substantial part of this book is devoted to an in-depth analysis of the many sources of financing available to the young business, including commercial bankers.

4

Increased Responsibility— The Price of Success

With the founding of new companies, entrepreneurs will discover a small army of interest groups and individuals making heavy demands on their time and resources. The price of neglect of any of these groups can be a catastrophe. One of the easiest to overlook when formulating your business plan is the interest group represented by your spouse and children. Yet your family represents a host of things which give meaning and substance to your personal life.

To the entrepreneur, the founding of a successful company represents the fulfillment of a life-long dream. Frequently, entrepreneurs have failed to recognize that many of the glowing stories they have heard regarding the concept of "working for yourself" are fictional. Let's explore for a moment these complex relationships between the family, the new firm, and the founder.

One company president of my acquaintance has devised a near-perfect situation. His company is in the manufacturing business and in recent years has grown steadily; today he has a staff of about fifty employees. His products are proprietary in nature, thus giving him a unique competitive advantage—his products lend themselves well to distribution in regional markets. One factor this company president is considering is the possibility of opening subsidiary plants (carbon copies of the parent plant) in these regional areas.

It is the president's feeling, however, that at this time he is not personally disposed to making the personal sacrifices in time and effort to make this expansion. He believes that it will take several years for him to develop a cadre of capable lieutenants who he can send into the field to open the subsidiaries and that his responsibilities to his family are of sufficient importance that he is unwilling to apportion more of his own energies to his company.

One unique factor in this man's situation is that the company of which he is president is one he totally owns. He has no other stockholders. Non-family stockholders would probably recognize significant potential for capital appreciation if the company were to expand right now, taking advantage of their technological lead in the proprietary products the company manufactures. Stockholders might feel that, if this particular man cannot handle the responsibilities of an expansion, he should consider stepping aside into an ancillary position, thus permitting the stockholders to bring in a stronger administrator able to pilot a rapidly growing company. But by structuring his company as he has, this president is able to satisfy all of his personal needs. He is deriving from his company all that he wishes. It has reached a size that is satisfying to him and he does not wish to compromise his marital responsibilities at the altar of greater corporate success.

The Extramarital Affair

Whenever the subject of entrepreneurship comes up, someone is bound to make the observation that starting a company of your own can be much like getting married. Carrying the analogy further, there is rarely room in a marriage for an extramarital relationship (particularly a full-time affair). There are no statistics regarding how much higher than the national average is the divorce rate among new company founders. However, the difference is significant; and it has two causes. Early in the formation of a company, if a spouse works 100 hours a week there will be very little opportunity to nurture and nourish a marital relationship. It takes a very strong, devoted partner indeed to withstand the rigors of being married to a near stranger.

To manage successfully the demands of marriage and possibly a growing family while simultaneously meeting the insistent demands of a young company requires a very deep personal understanding of the relative importance of these two elements of life. The wise founder includes ample provision for continued marital happiness in planning for business success.

One alternative is for your spouse to join your staff. But this is difficult to manage successfully, particularly if your company grows to a large size very quickly; and few couples are equal to the challenge. The jealousy of other employees and the vulnerability to charges of nepotism pose too great a potential corporate morale problem. Furthermore, once you hire your mate to work in the office, the task of dismissal (should the need arise) can prove to be a most unpleasant bit of housekeeping.

A partial solution to the problem may take the form of mini-vacations or mini-honeymoons. Several entrepreneurs of my acquaintance successfully manage this feat by setting aside a full day at least once or twice a month that is the exclusive property of the spouse. Once established, this commitment should be honored faithfully; worrying about company problems during this break is not allowed. No note paper or tape recorders are permitted for catching the elusive solutions to work problems; escape the telephone, if you can. You're not *supposed* to be thinking about work on these days off.

Close on the heels of the neglected-spouse syndrome comes the problem of handling newly acquired riches. A thrice-married friend of mine advised me that the number of gold-diggers in the world is legion. (Having followed the "Milestones" column in *Time* magazine for years, I have been intrigued by the regularity with which the wealthy shed and acquire mates.) This matter is obviously a highly personal one, but it should certainly be considered before embarking on a career of entrepreneurship.

Contemplating this problem from the corporate point of view provides still another perspective. Divorce is almost invariably a traumatic experience for all parties involved. Consider new company presidents who give every last iota of their resources to the new operations to make them successes. Should they subsequently find their marriages breaking up, their effectiveness in handling corporate problems will suffer. Their ability to give their companies their all will be severely compromised, and their subsequent handling of corporate problems will reflect the difficult personal adjustments they have made. The workload they managed to handle on a sixteen-hour-a-day regimen cannot possibly receive satisfactory treatment from half-hearted, listless, and dispirited presidents. Late shipments, forgotten commitments, and neglected staff can only bring about unavoidable and possibly irreparable corporate financial problems. To protect the companies, the marriages, and the well-being of the presidents as well, they *must* give due regard to the delicate balance to be struck in handling the sometimes unreasonable demands of the two rivals in their lives.

Sesame Street May Be Fine, But Kids Need Parents, Too

After spouses comes another special group that frequently suffers from the ambitions of new company presidents—children. Many sociological studies have been conducted on children who are reared in a fatherless or motherless household. Unfortunately, too little study has been done to document the problems of youngsters caught in a situation where father or mother is always at work.

It has been suggested that the entrepreneur's spouse actively cultivate the friendship of the spouses of other company founders. Consideration might also be given to the possibility of moving the family to an area where there is a high percentage of families whose husbands or wives have their own businesses. In this way, the children will have playmates who share their parental situation. When all of Tommy's friends have parents who are home by six o'clock, Tommy may feel a sense of deprivation due to his parents' work habits. If, however, most of Tommy's friends have parents who are similarly engaged, the circumstances are regarded as normal and the childhood trauma is somewhat diminished.

The solutions entrepreneurs devise to cope with their family obligations are as varied as the founders themselves. Some insist on spending at least two days a week with their families, engaged in communal recreation. Some adamantly refuse to discuss anything with their families regarding the pressures of their business. Others spend less time with their families and frequently talk about nothing during those infrequent reunions but their business problems.

Doing justice both to a marriage and a company is one of the most commonly overlooked difficulties of starting a business. Yet many people who contemplate businesses of their own would state without hesitation that the success of their marriages is very important to them. Reviewing the divorce statistics, one can only conclude that either these people understand themselves poorly or the price of honesty is something they would rather put on their credit card.

The Myth of Working for Yourself

Another commonly overlooked pitfall in establishing a business of your own is the mistaken idea that as a company president you will enjoy a heretofore unimagined degree of independence. Consider the following list for a few minutes and then analyze once again your expectations for independence.

Interest Groups Which Compromise the Independence of the Entrepreneur

- Stockholders
- Members of the Board of Directors
- Partners
- Landlords

- Customers
- Suppliers
- Key Staff Members
- Manufacturer's Representatives
- Service Agencies
- Consumer Protection Groups
- Certifying Entities (such as Underwriters Laboratories)
- Governmental Agencies, including city, county, state, and federal jurisdictions
- Trade Associations
- Creditors
- Unions

In his book, *The Small Businessman and His Problems,* lawyer-author L. Charles Burlage illustrates the entrepreneur's dilemma with the following letter, reproduced here with the author's kind permission.

Dear Creditor:

In reply to your request to send a check, I wish to inform you that the present condition of my bank account makes it almost impossible. My shattered financial condition is due to Federal laws, state laws, county laws, brother-in-laws, sister-in-laws, and outlaws.

Through these laws I am compelled to pay a business tax, amusement tax, head tax, school tax, gas tax, water tax, sales tax, liquor tax, income tax, food tax, furniture tax, excise tax, and now the Princess Anne County tax. I am required to get a business license, car license.

I am also required to contribute to every society and organization which the genius of man is capable of bringing to life.

For my own safety, I am required to carry health insurance, life insurance, fire insurance, earthquake insurance, tornado insurance, unemployment compensation insurance, and old age insurance.

My business is so governed that it is no easy matter to find out who owns it. I am expected, inspected, suspected, disrespected, rejected, defected, examined, re-examined, informed, required, summoned, fined, commanded, and compelled, until I provide an inexhaustible supply of money for every known need, desire, or hope of the human race.

Simply because I refuse to donate to something or other, I am boycotted, talked about, lied about, held up, held down, and robbed, until I am almost ruined.

I can tell you honestly that except for a miracle that happened, I could not enclose this check. The wolf that comes to my door nowadays just had pups in my kitchen; I sold them, and here is the money.[10]

5

Recruiting Partners

I don't know of any sector of the business community in which it is possible to develop a large sales volume without having to rely on the services of others. This reliance involves relinquishing to your assistants or associates the necessary controls to enable them to effectively discharge their responsibilities. One former company founder (now a venture capitalist) says that, in distilling his years of experience, the best advice he had to offer is: "Pick your partners as carefully as you would pick a spouse. Furthermore, insofar as possible, choose people who complement your business and personal strengths." Now this book does not presume to tell you how to pick a marriage partner. But it will give you some ideas on partner selection that you will find of value.

Former Business Associates

The most common candidates for partnership are former business associates. Management consultant John L. Komives, former Director of the Center for Venture Management, speculates that at least eighty percent of all new multiple-founder businesses involve circumstances where two or more members of the founding team were employed by the *same* firm prior to starting their own company. If you have previously been associated with your proposed partner, you will have had an opportunity to test your ability to work to-

73

gether and to arrive at as objective an evaluation of the person's capabilities as is possible before adding another name to your payroll.

Friends

Depending on the kind of talent required to produce a well rounded, broadly experienced management team, it is possible that a new company president may find one or more friends suitable for the role of co-founder. Objectivity in the evaluation of a friend's capabilities is, however, frequently difficult. Furthermore, subsequent performance appraisals of those staff members numbered among the president's friends becomes difficult and sometimes unpleasant. This kind of relationship warrants very careful scrutiny *before* it is entered into.

You must also consider the possibility that your circle of business acquaintances and friends may not be large enough to include the full management team you require to staff your company adequately. Recruiting your partners from a group limited to friends and acquaintances is a little bit like marrying your high school sweetheart. When you get to college you may discover a dating pool the likes of which you never imagined.

Business Consultants

A number of entrepreneurially inclined professionals set themselves up as consultants in their specialty fields. Frequently, this role of consultant is an interim one, halfway between working for a corporation and finding a position as a corporate founder. Often these people can be employed by a new business on a limited contract basis, receiving payment in cash, stock warrants, or other negotiated forms of compensation. Should this "trial marriage" prove satisfactory, the consultant can be smoothly integrated into the staff. In the event the trial marriage does not prove satisfactory, the relationship can be terminated neatly without recrimination and without the trauma commonly associated with partnership upheavals in a small firm.

Competitor's Staff

Qualified experts for the new enterprise may often come from the staff of a competing firm. The recruiting of these employees is commonly referred to as "raiding," and this practice entails some risk of legal action. However, in most instances, judicial shenanigans are limited in their effect and can usually be disregarded. (Fortunately, serfdom went out of vogue some time ago.) Nowadays the courts don't take very kindly to limiting the freedom of individuals to pursue any legitimate careers and employers of their choosing.

Referrals

By letting your friends and business associates know of your requirements in rounding out your staff, you should be able to obtain a prescreened list of qualified contenders. This list can be an extremely helpful source of information in your quest for a competent team.

Classified Advertising

Every day the major metropolitan and financial newspapers serve as clearing houses for people with a broad range of skills, qualifications, and interests. I prefer to group the classified headings into two categories: (1) Those listing people who are looking for positions or situations, and (2) those listing situations that are looking for people.

An intriguing array of apparently gifted people regularly appears under the headings: Positions Wanted, Situations Wanted, or Business Opportunities. Entries range all the way from a disenchanted super-corporation vice president looking for a position as a general manager, through the inventor with a new product for you to help manufacture and exploit, to the Harvard MBA with $50,000 or $100,-000 cash who would like to become a partner in some new enterprise. In the other category, Positions Available or Business Opportunities, you will find ads placed by companies that are offering a handsome salary-stock option package to the right person who is willing to take the position of vice president of manufacturing and ads placed by companies that are seeking a marketing manager with a track record and money to invest in the chance of a lifetime.

An Owl, a Goose, and the Little Red Hen

In closing this section on how to recruit partners, I am reminded of a story from my childhood. As I recall, it went something like this . . .

Once upon a time in Pawtucket, Rhode Island there lived a Little Red Hen who decided that she would like to go into business and make a lot of bread. She surveyed the market and decided that public demand for the whole-wheat variety was inadequately served by the present suppliers. So she called a meeting of several of her friends to try to interest them in helping with her project. She started off the meeting by saying, "Friends, I have quite a proposition for all of you today. How would you like to go into business with me and really make a lot of bread?"

"I think that's a swingin' idea," said a little banty from his perch on one of the rafters.

The cock-of-the-walk puffed up his chest and said to the group, "My missus is always complaining about a shortage of dough in our house. I think the Little Red Hen really has something here. Count me in." And so it went; every one of the Little Red Hen's friends volunteered to participate in this bread-making venture.

The next meeting of our little group was held two weeks later, and the first thing on the agenda was the selection of the company name. After much debate, everyone decided that the "Doughty Dough Makers" was a real pip. So with that important item of business concluded, it was time to assign responsibilities to various members of the new firm in order to get the enterprise under way.

However, from this point on, very strange things began to happen—the new founders became restless and fidgety. Every time the Little Red Hen asked one of her partners to undertake a certain task toward implementing their plans, problems arose.

The bantam rooster indicated that his regular job as a night club bouncer made him too tired to work on anything else. He needed the daylight hours to rest up for the next night's work. Furthermore, he said that his lifestyle was such that he simply couldn't afford the financial risk of quitting his steady job and waiting until the Doughty Dough Makers could pay him a regular salary. However, once the company got rolling, he'd be glad to work as the night watchman. Salarywise, he said he'd be content with a stock option *plus* the same money he was getting now at the night club. "After all," he said, "you're entitled to some kind of a raise when you change employers, aren't you?"

The cock-of-the-walk complained that his duties as president of the Strut and Show-Off Marching Band Society were getting very hectic because of a convention the Society was planning. He wouldn't really be able to help out until this event was over, about eight weeks from now.

The brooding hen said that she had decided she couldn't spare the time away from her babies; but later on, when the company needed someone to assist with counting the profits, her chicks would be old enough to stay by themselves and she would try to find time to come out and lend a helping wing.

By this time, the Little Red Hen was in a foul mood; and she bit the cock-of-the-walk right on the tail. His screech sharply brought the attention of the bickering attendees back to their leader, who requested that only those founders able to start working for the new company immediately remain at the meeting. The rest of the founders (the really chicken-hearted) were asked to leave and told that they would later be notified about the future role they might play in the company.

Well, as you might have guessed, everyone left the meeting coop except the Little Red Hen. However, don't despair, dear reader. Our heroine teamed up with a Wise Owl on the East Coast and an Old Lady Goose on the West Coast, and now they're all making a bundle selling potato chips.

6

A Training Program
for Success

The decision to start a company of your own will have as profound an effect on your life as your marriage or the arrival of your first child. It is not a matter that should be taken lightly. Just as athletes preparing for a major contest must condition their bodies for the stress ahead, just as scholars contemplating year-end examinations must force-feed their minds with facts and information, just as medical doctors must undergo a period of internship before entering into formal practice, prospective entrepreneurs must plan and pursue a program of self-improvement so that they will be in optimum condition for the demanding, challenging experiences they will encounter in the formation of their own businesses. In planning your own program for success, take time to consider each of the following points.

Physical Conditioning

The importance and value of stamina and good physical condition to the founder of the new firm was discussed earlier. The regular programs that are offered by YMCAs and various health clubs, spas, and gymnasiums are ideal for this purpose.

Now I'm not suggesting that you approach this regimen with the expectation of becoming the next International Bodybuilding Champion. Endurance and stamina are the objectives, and the conditioning might even improve your social life!

Acquiring the Proper Mental Attitude

The concept of motivation is a very important element in business success. Reference was made earlier to the vast body of literature on the subject of personal motivation; the would-be entrepreneur should read one or two of these books in order to vicariously experience the success of others. If you don't come away from this reading with the conviction that you've got at least twice as much going for you as some of those other seemingly ordinary people who made it to the top of the heap, then ask yourself what kind of dynamite it *takes* to get you excited.

If your "Hot Button" isn't in the full-on position, there's an excellent possibility that the stuff of which company presidents are made does not lie dormant in your breast. You let it die there when Daddy gave you a spanking for taking the alarm clock apart with your little screwdriver, and you might as well sign off. But, if you're among the *living,* read on.

Make Your Spouse the Head Cheerleader in Your Rooting Section

Earlier, we discussed the importance and value of marital stability in enabling the entrepreneur to devote his or her attention to the problems of the business. Remember the popular observation that "Behind every great man, there stands a woman." The converse is also true. With this thought in mind, if you've got domestic fence mending to do, do it *before* you start your business.

Investigate Seminars

One of the most convenient and readily assimilated forms of education is the seminar. Typically, such courses are of short duration (one or two days is the rule); and, since most seminar speakers have a reputation to maintain (and a handsome income to preserve), their talks are not only informative but they are also usually entertaining. Unlike many of their academic counterparts who deliver a lecture designed to fill the allotted fifty minute hour, a seminar speaker is confronted with the problem of distilling and refining a vast amount of knowledge in an effort to convey the very essence of it in an hour.

A large number of different groups and organizations sponsor seminars. The following are just a few of them.

The U.S. Department of Commerce

Most regional branches offer short courses, lecture programs, and movie presentations of primary interest to businesses involved in international trade. A surprisingly large number of small businesses are active in the import-export field, handling products of their own manufacture or acting as brokers or agents for other manufacturers. The limited amount of capital necessary to get into selected areas of this fascinating industry makes it ideal for the small entrepreneur. Advance notice of U.S. Department of Commerce seminars may be obtained by contacting your nearest District Office and requesting that your name be added to their regular mailing list. Admission fees, if any, are nominal. (Listed in your telephone book under the heading, U.S. Government.)

The Small Business Administration

Regular programs including short courses, conferences, problem-solving clinics, and workshops tailored to the needs of small businesses are offered by all major field offices of the SBA. Offerings cover, for example, personnel problems, taxation, sales, marketing, manufacturing, and inventory control. In some cases, special topics of concern to businesses in a particular geographic or industrial sector are scheduled in areas where interest level warrants their discussion. Session speakers include lawyers, accountants, bankers, university professors, and management consultants. As in the case of Department of Commerce offerings, admission fees, if any, are nominal. (Listed in your telephone book under the heading, U.S. Government.)

Trade Associations

Every trade association I know of has a big wing-ding of a convention at least once a year. At these gatherings, conferences, seminars, panel-discussions, guest lecturers, movie and slide programs, and other such presentations are profusely provided. Convention programs generally are planned to include sessions dealing with engineering, marketing, manufacturing, and financial problems as they relate to the needs of the industry sponsoring the convention. Many conventions, particularly those sponsored by associations serving high-technology industries, offer seminars dealing specifically with the problems of starting a new business.

It is customary that convention registration fees provide not only for admission to the main exhibits but also for admission to any or all seminars. Since trade associations are almost always non-profit organizations, convention admission fees are typically quite modest.

For a comprehensive directory of trade associations, your library should have a copy of the *Gale Research Company Encyclopedia of American Associations,* a guide to the trade, business, professional, labor, scientific, educational, fraternal, and social organizations of the United States. Another helpful directory, *National Trade and Professional Associations,* is published by Columbia Books and can also be found in your library.

The American Management Association

This association is a non-profit, educational membership organization devoted to developing and sharing better methods of management throughout the management community. Every year, the AMA presents more than 2000 seminars, conferences, briefing sessions, and courses treating almost every conceivable topic of management concern. A representative list of the Association divisions includes:

- Manufacturing
- Marketing
- Packaging
- Personnel
- Purchasing
- Research and Development
- Finance
- General Management
- General Services
- Insurance
- International Management
- Information Systems and Technology

Programs are offered in most principal cities in the United States and Canada. For the latest information on scheduled presentations and membership benefits and fees, write to the AMA Membership Department, The American Management Association Building, 135 West 50th Street, New York, New York 10020.

Colleges and Universities

Many colleges and universities offer business programs for alumni; others extend their hospitality to the community at large. Most of these institutions send out advance announcements of course and seminar offerings to individuals who have asked to be placed on their mailing lists. A letter or phone call to the appropriate school office should insure your receiving future mailings.

The admission fee for these seminars covers a very broad range, depending on the school. Usually, privately supported institutions charge more than schools supported by the taxpayers. Based on my recent experience, fees for a two-day seminar may run from a low of $295 to a high of more than $1000. Some private universities conduct regular seminar series as a supplementary source of revenue.

Other Seminars

There is an industry made up of private companies that offer seminars purely for profit as well as public-minded non-profit entities created to further the public good. Some of the most professional and worthwhile presentations in the seminar field are conducted by these groups. Often, the program offerings of these "seminar companies" include speakers who have garnered world renown in the business and financial community. A few of the many firms active in this field include:

Control Data Institute
8100 34th Avenue South
Minneapolis, Minnesota 55440
(612) 339-8282

Dale Carnegie & Associates, Inc.
1475 Franklin Avenue
Garden City, New York 11530
(516) 248-5100

Dible Management Development Systems, Inc.
1125 Missouri Street
Fairfield, California 94533
(800) 556-7500

The Institute for Advanced Technology
(A Division of Control Data Corp.)
6003 Executive Building
Rockville, Maryland 20852
(202) 468-8567

Institute for the Advancement of Human Behavior
4370 Alpine Road, Suite 208D
Portola Valley, California 94025
(415) 851-8411

New York Management Center
30 - 30 Borden Avenue
Long Island City, New York 11101
(212) 392-9441

Penton Learning Systems
420 Lexington Avenue
Suite 2846
New York, New York 10017
(212) 953-1001

For a comprehensive listing of seminars on a wide variety of topics, you may wish to subscribe to *Seminars: The Directory of Continuing and Professional Education Programs,* which contains information on approximately 200 organizations sponsoring more than 2000 seminars and workshops throughout the United States and Canada. The directory includes program titles, descriptions, listing of speakers, fees, location, and dates; it is published three times a year. For subscription information, write to: Seminars, 525 N. Lake Street, Madison, Wisconsin 53703.

In weighing the decision to attend a particular seminar, the problem of determining cost-versus-value will eventually steal into your mind. Cost is not limited to registration fees, transportation, and food and lodging. Another very real cost is the *time* you spend in attending the seminar. In other words, if your job is real-estate development or personnel problems in manufacturing, what are you doing at a seminar on nuclear physics?

To derive the greatest value from a seminar, you should determine the suitability of your education, experience, and interest relative to the subject matter to be presented. (Of the dozens of seminars I have attended, I have never been to one from which I didn't get at least five valuable new ideas that I was subsequently able to employ for my personal advantage.) It is your responsibility to obtain value from a seminar. The speakers will do their part to convey knowledge and experience; absorbing and applying this knowledge and experience is up to you.

Three other factors to be considered in evaluating the merits of seminar attendance are these:

1. Seminars should afford you an excellent opportunity to meet large numbers of people with interests similar to or complementary to yours. You should make a concerted effort to interact with other attendees during the intermission and break periods for the purpose of cultivating new and potentially rewarding acquaintances.

2. In many cases, the sponsor of the seminar will provide all registrants with a listing of other attendees, frequently including their company affiliation, address, and telephone number. This courtesy list significantly enhances your opportunity for developing valuable contacts.

3. Seminars should also serve to stimulate new ideas. Information delivered by the speakers should produce a synergistic, catalytic interaction with the knowledge and experience you already possess—in other words, you should end up with a $1 + 1 = 3$ result.

Rediscover Books

Entrepreneurs are typically mavericks, more interested in *doing* things than in thinking about them, studying them, or planning them. No bookworms are they! Probably these poor souls found schoolwork something to be endured rather than enjoyed. Thus, the process of learning the business of business from books is not something they anticipate with delight. The midnight oil they burn is far more likely to illuminate their sweating brows than a treatise on how others solved their problems. They like to be in the thick of things, where the action is. Their attitude is, "Why be content with Front Row Center when you can be the Star of the Show?"

Overlooked is the fact that the Star studies; even the understudy studies. So forget the klieg lights and get your hindquarters down to the library, the repository of *Mistakes to Avoid, Dragons I Have Slain,* and *Accounting for the Simpleton* (for when it comes to accounting, most entrepreneurs are just that). Let your education commence!

The wealth of information contained in books and the opportunities that this packaged knowledge represents remind me of a story that Zig Ziglar,[11] one of America's super-salesmen, delights in telling. Back in the days of the general store with its cracker barrels and kegs of black-strap molasses, there was a storekeeper who had a vexing problem. A mischievous little boy took to loitering in his shop; whenever no one was looking, the lad would lift the lid on the keg of molasses, dip his fingers into the sweet sticky mess, and get himself a hand-to-mouthful. One day the suspicious proprietor caught the lad in the act, and said "Sonny, if I ever catch you doing that again, I'm going to dunk you, clothes and all, into that very keg."

It wasn't long afterward that temptation overcame the boy and he was back to the store and into the molasses. The storekeeper had a hunch as to what was going on and snuck up on the little thief.

"I've caught you again, you rapscallion," the proprietor said, picking him up by the seat of the pants and the scruff of the neck. He gave the little shaver a mighty shake and then said to him, "Do you have any last words before I drop you into this-here keg? Remember, the Lord has mercy on those sinners who repent."

Wide-eyed, the lad looked at the nearly full keg, then gazed into the proprietor's eyes and said, "Yes, sir, I do. Lord, please grant me a tongue large enough to equal this opportunity."

I hope that all entrepreneurs will feel a little of this anticipatory delight when they discover the opportunities in the world of books. I know of very few *successful* entrepreneurs, college-educated or not, who have failed to avail themselves of the wisdom of their predecessors, those who have taken the time and trouble to record what they have learned for the benefit of their "heirs" who have been stricken with the do-your-own-thing malady. Let's have a look at a few of the more common types of libraries and bookstores available to you.

Community Libraries

Do you live in a community so intellectually impoverished that it doesn't have a library? If that's the case and if your criterion of success is more than mere economic survival, then the burg you live in is probably a terrible location in which to open your business. However, if yours is a more typical situation, there will at least be a county and/or city library to which you will have access. The extent of the library collection that is of specific interest to small businesses largely depends on the support of the citizenry. The composition of the collection is one of the most important responsibilities of the library staff. Rather than make their acquisition decisions in a vacuum, libraries greatly appreciate hearing specific requests and recommendations from their patrons. Provided that there is sufficient demand for the type of information included in the books you request and that the library budget permits, the staff will be glad to order them for you.

College and University Libraries

Although these libraries are primarily intended for the use of the faculty and student body, most institutions make provision for the use of their facilities by the community at large. Depending on whether or not the institution is privately or publicly supported, the cost of library privileges will vary widely. (In spite of the fact that the practice is frowned upon, a few of the more pragmatic and resourceful entrepreneurs I have known have been successful in persuading some of their student friends to take out university library books for their use.) If you are fortunate enough to have access to a business school library, you should find their collection to be an enormously valuable resource.

Professional and Trade Association Libraries

Many trade associations and professional organizations maintain book collections that are specifically related to subjects of primary interest to the association members.

Provided there exists such a library to serve your industry and access to it is practical from a geographical standpoint, you should not fail to investigate the services the facility has to offer.

One facility which should be of particular interest to the entrepreneur is the American Management Association Library and Management Information Service, available at no additional charge to members of the AMA. A free brochure describing these services may be obtained by writing to the Management Information Service, American Management Association, The American Management Association Building, 135 West 50th Street, New York, New York 10020; or telephone (212) 903-8165.

Bookstores

First cousin to the library is the bookstore, and you will find that there are a surprising number of bookstores that limit their stock to a particular subject area. Some shops specialize in religious books, some in legal or medical reference works, others in best sellers, and still others in foreign language works. Fortunately, a few of them concentrate their efforts in the field of business books. In spite of this penchant for specialization, however, most bookstores are in business to provide their owners with a livelihood. Thus, they are usually quite accommodating in ordering books in print from any trade publisher whose offerings you request.

In the event you encounter difficulty in obtaining a particular book, there is a process you can employ to bring results. First, consult a copy of *Books in Print*,[12] a 14 volume reference published by the R. R. Bowker Co. and available in most libraries and bookstores. Obtain the author's name, title, and publisher of the book you wish. Then contact a major metropolitan bookseller to place your order. The cost to you will probably include the regular list price plus postage, sales taxes where applicable, and nominal handling charges. (Please note that most public libraries carry a selection of telephone books for major cities. Consulting the Yellow Pages should enable you to find a suitable bookseller.)

Book Clubs

Many book clubs (and some trade and professional associations) provide their members with a wide selection of offerings, usually at a cost discounted below the normal publisher's list price. Once you get on the mailing list of some of these firms, you'll be hearing from them regularly for a long, long time.

One business-book seller that has been recommended to me by a satisfied customer is The Executive Program, Riverside, New Jersey 08075. A trade association that offers business books at special membership prices is the American Management Association, American Management Association Building, 135 West 50th Street, New York, New York 10020. Write a letter of inquiry to either or both of these firms for a brochure describing the services they offer.

Still another source of information on book dealers who are offering volumes at prices lower than retail may be found in the "Book Exchange" section of *The New York Times Book Review,* a feature section of the Sunday edition of this newspaper.

Periodicals, Too

Unending sources of information on the subject of small business are the periodicals. Presently, there are more than 67,000 different periodicals offered for sale in the United States and Canada. These publications afford the entrepreneur an excellent opportunity for acquiring the latest information available in any subject area that may be of interest.

Several directories that list business periodicals exist; with luck, you should find at least one of them in your library. Three of the more commonly available directories are:

- *Business Publication Rates and Data,* published monthly by Standard Rate and Data Service, Inc., contains a descriptive listing of business magazines and is indexed by name of magazine and by business fields covered.

- *Standard Periodical Directory,* published by the Oxbridge Publishing Company, Inc., gives comprehensive coverage to periodicals in the United States and Canada. It contains over 67,-000 entries, including magazines, journals, newsletters, house organs, government publications, advisory services, directories, transactions and proceedings of professional societies, yearbooks, and major-city daily newspapers.

- *Ulrich's International Periodicals Directory,* published annually by the R. R. Bowker Company, covers 65,000 current periodicals throughout the world, in 55 subject areas, indexed both by title and name of the organization that publishes the periodical.

Another publication *any* information seeker should treasure is the *Readers' Guide to Periodical Literature,* published semimonthly in September, October, December, March, April, and June, and monthly in January, February, May, July, August, and November with a bound cumulation yearly, by the H. W. Wilson Company. This guide provides a complete, up-to-date index of all articles, listed by subject, in leading periodicals including *The New York Times*

Magazine, Time, Newsweek, Fortune, Business Week, Forbes, Harvard Business Review, and *Nation's Business.*

To obtain specialized information on business periodicals serving any particular industry, additional assistance may be obtained by corresponding with one of the following organizations:

IMS Press
426 Pennsylvania Avenue
Ft. Washington, Pennsylvania 19034

American Business Press, Inc.
205 East 42nd Street
New York, New York 10017

R.R. Bowker Company
1180 Avenue of the Americas
New York, New York 10036

Many organizations offer subscriptions to leading magazines at discounted prices. One such firm is Publishers Clearing House, 382 Channel Drive, Port Washington, New York 11050. A free bulletin is available on request.

Trade Journals

Trade journals are some of the most authoritative sources available of timely, specialized industrial information. Announcements of the latest commercial products, analyses of major innovations in marketing, and discussions of manufacturing and research and development activities are regular editorial subjects. Invaluable market survey and market forecast information is frequently printed in these publications before it is reported by any other news medium. Meeting and convention calendars are also commonly included as a convenience to the reader.

A study of trade journal advertising affords the marketeer and designer one of the most valuable sources of information about industry competitors. These advertisements typically extol the virtues of new products and provide the entrepeneur with useful information on the sort of competition one may expect to encounter.

Bank Publications

Several major banks offer free of charge or at nominal cost publications of interest to small businesses. A particularly fine service is offered through the Bank of America publication *Small Business Reporter.* Information on subscription rates and reprints may be had by writing to *Small Business Reporter,* Department 3120, Bank of America N.T. & S.A., San Francisco, California 94120. A description of the publication, from the *Small Business Reporter* Publication Index follows.

> The *Small Business Reporter* provides straightforward, practical information on owning and operating a small business. It is for all those who need information about small business—the business owner, of course, but also bankers, attorneys, accountants, consultants, industry trade associations, schools, and libraries.

Financial Papers

Such periodicals as the *Wall Street Journal, Barrons,* and the financial sections of major metropolitan dailies provide small businesses with an excellent source of up-to-date information on events of interest in the financial community. In addition to providing up-to-date information on stock prices and trading volume, business papers also serve as a source of information with regard to broad, national economic trends; and they regularly provide analyses of selected industries.

Business Magazines

Magazines such as *Inc., Venture, Business Week,* and *Forbes* provide the entrepreneur with considerable information on the condition of the business community that is useful in determining, in a broad sense, the availability of capital in capital markets; also published occasionally are in-depth stories on selected industries.

Newsletters

There are more than 6000 different newsletters currently published in the United States. Almost any subject you can conceive has a voice through the medium of a newsletter. There are newsletters dealing with automotive parts retailing, and newsletters dealing with zoo management.

The survival of any newsletter depends on the ability of its editors to address their special subject with authority, consistency, and a timeliness usually not found in any other information source outside of a full-time staff consultant.

Newsletters, typically, are *not* low in cost. They rarely include paid advertising; thus, the full cost of research, preparation, and distribution must be borne by the readers. Usually the no-advertising policy assures a minimum of bias and a maximum of objectivity in the material covered. In addition, when the cost of hiring consultants or maintaining the staff necessary to acquire the specialized information made available in newsletters is weighed against the subscription rate, most people would agree that the newsletter editor is the lowest paid "employee" on the staff. For a direct pipeline into virtually any commercial field, newsletters are hard to beat for being the "firstest with the mostest" at the lowest practical cost. The *National Directory of Newsletters and Reporting Services,* published by the Gale Research Company of Detroit, lists every major publication and can be found in most major library reference collections.

Community Newspapers

The editors of most community newspapers pride themselves on being the first to offer their readers news of recent developments on the local business scene. Therefore, community newspapers eagerly solicit newsworthy items regarding product development, contract awards, and personnel changes from businesses in and around their major area of circulation.

Businesses also recognize the public relations value of keeping the local newspaper informed of significant developments. Furthermore, by keeping their local editors up to date and providing news releases to community newspapers, these businesses avail themselves of free advertising and succeed in enhancing their corporate image.

When a local paper has an aggressive staff, even information unfavorable to a local business may be ferreted out and served up to the voracious appetite of its readership. Regardless of the circumstances, community newspapers represent an informative and inexpensive source of business intelligence within a limited geographical area.

Computerized Information Services

There are a number of computerized information services that allow you, if you have a computer terminal with communications capabilities, to plug directly into vast databases to find selected information on an endless variety of topics. Dialog Information Services in Palo Alto, California, is one of the better known of these companies. Typically, you subscribe to these services and pay only for the time you are connected to the database. A brochure describes the extent of Dialog's services:

> Dialog provides you with immediate access to more than 100 million items of information, including references to books, patents and directories, journals and newspaper articles. More than 200 databases pro-

vide comprehensive coverage of such fields as science, technology, business, medicine, social science, current affairs, and the humanities. Thousands of information users in business, industry, government, and all types of libraries find searching for information online to be quick, precise, cost effective, and easy.[13]

You may contact Dialog at 3460 Hillview Avenue, Palo Alto, California 94304.

While these services are becoming more popular, I should point out that initial access methods can be difficult to learn, and unless you need access to information on a regular basis, you may be better off engaging the services of an information broker or fee-based information service that will do the research for you. The Directory of Fee-Based Information Services, listed in Appendix 1, will help you find the correct resource for your needs, or you may ask your librarian for assistance. Many community and university libraries also offer computerized search services.

Uncle Sam Wants (To Help) You

Many government agencies produce enormous quantities of timely, worthwhile information of interest to the entrepreneur. One remarkable aspect of this service is that the government publications are available free of charge or for a very nominal fee. The U.S. Department of Commerce and the Small Business Administration are the front-runners in the race to suppy entrepreneurs with all the tools-in-print that they can effectively use in launching and operating their own businesses. Consider the following publications these two agencies offer.

The U.S. Department of Commerce

In 1970, the Department of Commerce established the National Technical Information Service (NTIS) to coordinate and consolidate the Department's business and technical information activities and to serve as the primary focal point within the federal government for the collection, announcement, and dissemination of technical reports and data. The NTIS makes available reports summarizing the research work supported by federal funds in agencies throughout the federal government. Material covered in these reports ranges through all levels of business, scientific, social, and economic research.

In addition to making announcements and distributing information, NTIS maintains a specialized reference service. A staff is maintained to assist the public in locating specific literature and information on specialized centers of expertise.

The NTIS information system includes more than a million technical reports on completed government research. It is a permanent information source, and each title is available on film, paper or magnetic tape.

Key announcement services of the NTIS include:

- 26 *Abstract Newsletters,* grouped by subject and published weekly, which provide timely information on the latest research being done.

- *Government Reports Announcements and Index,* a biweekly publication that covers current report titles and includes additional abstracts not published in the newsletters.

- *U.S. Government Research and Development Reports Index,* companion to the *Bulletin* that indexes each issue by subject, corporate and personal author, and contract and report numbers.

The amount of information available through the NTIS is truly vast, and a detailed discussion of its resources is beyond the scope of this book. For a free forty-page catalog describing the services of NTIS, write to them at 5285 Port Royal Road, Springfield, Virginia 22161.

The Small Business Administration

Every year the Small Business Administration literally gives away millions of leaflets and pamphlets relating to various topics of interest to small businesses. The SBA form "Free Management Assistance Publications" (SBA Form 115a) includes a listing of more than 150 different publications available free from SBA. These publications include such series as Management Aids, Technical Aids, Small Marketers Aids, Small Business Bibliographies, and Starting Out.

The SBA form "For Sale Booklets" is SBA Form 115b. This form includes the Small Business Management Series, the Starting and Managing Series, Business Basics Series, and several nonseries publications.

Taken as a whole, the publications offered by the SBA present encyclopedic coverage of just about every major problem a small business can expect to encounter. The cost of the "For Sale Booklets" is often no more than $4.00; no booklet costs more than $7.00.

Another valuable service the SBA provides is a group of retired executives organized under the label SCORE (the Service Corps of Retired Executives). SCORE volunteers provide small businesses with managerial assistance at no charge. Contact your local SBA office in order to avail yourself of their services.

In addition, Small Business Institutes (SBIs), located on hundreds of college campuses across the country, offer free guidance and assistance to small businesses. SBIs are staffed by senior business administration students working under the guidance of faculty advisors in conjunction with the SBA. Any of the SBA district offices can provide you with the name and phone number of the SBI nearest you.

Public Speaking

Entrepreneurs who have the ability to express their thoughts effectively before an audience possess an extremely valuable asset. This ability is part of the "charisma" that so many venture capitalists and other members of the financial community look for in the people in whom they consider investing money.

People who say they are not capable of addressing a large group generally lack confidence in their ability to do so. Formalized programs of instruction afford the bashful orator the opportunity to overcome this fear. Public speaking is an ability that readily lends itself to cultivation through practice and experience. Participation in a formally structured program of public speaking repeatedly forces students to test their wings. Pretty soon they are saying "Look, Ma, I can fly!" and another one of life's problems has been turned into a talent of substantial worth. There are many ways in which the entrepreneur can cultivate speaking skills.

Toastmasters Clubs

According to a Toastmasters International brochure, "Even experienced speakers have butterflies in their stomachs—this is natural—but the Toastmasters program will help you make them fly in formation." To be maximally effective in discharging their newly assumed responsibilities, entrepreneurs should develop the ability to present their ideas and thoughts persuasively and confidently. One of the finest and least expensive programs for attaining this goal is that provided by Toastmasters International, which is an organization devoted to helping its members master the art of effective oral communication and dynamic leadership.

Meetings are usually held once a week; they afford the members opportunities for delivering prepared speeches and extemporaneous monologues and for cultivating the hard-to-master ability to *listen* to what other people say while making critical evaluations of their ideas. A typical Toastmasters meeting is charged with an air of camaraderie as the members share their experiences and enjoy the pleasure and satisfaction of helping one another.

As you progress through the Toastmasters program, you will overcome the nervousness common to most inexperienced speakers and progress via a series of projects toward the development of techniques, speech preparation, voice modulation, the use of word pictures, and enhancement of your vocabulary.

The enthusiasm with which Toastmasters graduates describe their experience is testimony to the high caliber of the program. The solid foundation I established as a member of Toastmasters years ago helped pave the way for a very rewarding public speaking career—I heartily recommend that you give them a try! For a descriptive brochure and further information on how to become a member, write to Toastmasters International World Headquarters, 2200 North Grand Avenue, Santa Ana, California 92711.

National Speakers Association

Another excellent organization is the National Speakers Association (NSA). According to an Association brochure, the purpose of NSA is to "increase public awareness of the speaking profession, insure and advance the integrity and visibility of professional speakers, and to create an educational program and designation for speakers."

The group is not a speakers bureau or a booking agency for speakers. Rather, it functions as a resource center for professional speakers and anyone interested in becoming involved in the speaking profession.

Through workshops and annual conventions, members learn more about public speaking and have the opportunity to exchange ideas and establish relationships within the professional speaking community. A bimonthly "Educational Bulletin" provides insight into business aspects of professional speaking. For more information about this organization, write to them at 4323 N. 12th Street, Suite 103, Phoenix, Arizona 85014.

International Platform Association

Still another organization devoted to the cause of public speaking is the International Platform Association. Members of this group are professional lecturers, musicians, actors, and any others who appear in public before live audiences to inform or entertain. The Association's purpose is to increase the scope of contacts of the members, and to sponsor workshops on various topics of interest to the members. For more information you may write to the Association at 2564 Berkshire Road, Cleveland Heights, Ohio, 44106.

Community Colleges and University Extension Courses

Many educational institutions offer courses of instruction in public speaking at very low cost. On the college campus, one can expect experienced, professional assistance in the development of one's oratorical talents.

Commercial Institutions

Schools devoted to the teaching of public speaking, sales techniques, and "personality improvement" can be found in every major city. Probably the best known of these is the Dale Carnegie Institute, which offers the famous Dale Carnegie courses in cities around the world.

I have spoken to many people who have availed themselves of some form of organized public speaking instruction through Toastmasters International, university evening programs, and commercial schools such as the Dale Carnegie Institute. Invariably the comments I have received have been extremely favorable. The people involved indicate consistently that their public speaking ability and their self-confidence have been significantly enhanced as a result of participation in the programs' regimens.

7

Many People are Glad to Help You— Just Ask Them

When I started writing this book, I could hardly wait to get to this section because I wanted to share with you my discovery of how unselfish other people were in their willingness to help. I used to feel, as most of us do, that my pride would not let me ask for help. Asking for other people's assistance struck me as being much like seeking charity. But as I see it now, other people are usually delighted to help, that is, if they are convinced that you will make effective use of their advice. You must project to others your capability and willingness to implement their suggestions. You must convey the spirit of your worthiness to receive the benefits of their knowledge and experience. This is the *real* measure of pride: *The self-knowledge that you are worthy of other people's help.*

Have you ever heard of getting a hernia while pulling yourself up by your own bootstraps? I haven't. First, you must make a sincere effort at getting started in your chosen business. Then, when you need help, when you really start looking for help, when you are in a position to turn help to good use, you *will* find it. And bear in mind: It is highly unlikely that anyone is going to seek you out to spoon feed it to you—you've got to go prospecting for it on your own.

One crackerjack entrepreneur I know states that there are two qualities never found lacking in the president of a successful new business: *persistence* and *audacity*. When it comes to getting the help you need—help to turn your business idea into a commercial enterprise—these characteristics are musts. You should find them extremely valuable when seeking advice and guidance from the suggested sources listed below.

_____ Entrepreneurs Who Have Already Gotten Started _____

Men and women already active in businesses of their own represent one of the best possible sources of general, first-hand information on what it is like to have your own show. As a rule, they are most willing to discuss the mixed blessings their work affords them.

A typical conversation might start with a question like, "What was it like when you got your initial big contract? How did you finagle it?"

"Well, I had all my relatives come down early in the morning the day my best customer came to town for his first plant tour. They all put on white smocks and sat on folding chairs in front of door panel/saw-horse work benches. This quadrupled the size of our assembly line. Next, I borrowed some test equipment for the day from a friend of mine who owns a TV repair shop. We also brought in half a dozen job-shop draftsmen just for the occasion. Needless to say, our customer was satisfied with our capability because we got the contract and our bank loaned us the money we needed to do the job."

"What happened after you finished that order?"

"Well, we didn't get another big one for six months, so we had to let half our people go. My nerves got so bad I could hardly sleep and I started working on an ulcer. Once we got our second big job, though, things settled down. We've had a very encouraging sales growth ever since, and I've been careful not to hire more people than our order backlog would justify."

This example is merely representative of the typical nitty-gritty insight such interviews can offer. Another way you can benefit is through referrals. Usually, successful entrepreneurs have a wide circle of colleagues and can suggest several who might take an interest in helping you along. Other business contacts may be cultivated at community service clubs, such as the Junior Chamber of Commerce, Rotary International, and Kiwanis International. The members of such clubs are dedicated to helping others and to serving society constructively. Frequently, a club officer can direct you to someone willing to take a personal interest in you. Fraternal organizations such as Elks, Moose, Odd Fellows, Masonic Groups, Knights of Columbus, and B'nai B'rith have served as meeting grounds for developing business contacts over many years. College fraternity and alumni associations, professional and trade associations, political organizations such as the Young Republicans and Young Democrats, and church groups also fill the bill. In fact, whenever and wherever people meet, an opportunity usually exists for the development of business relationships.

Others in Your Trade

Other people in your trade are also fine sources of information and assistance. These include the suppliers, customers, manufacturers' representatives, and distributors in your chosen industrial field.

Suppliers

In prospecting for information, you will undoubtedly discover that suppliers are very much interested in helping a potential customer develop and grow. And their assistance won't be limited only to market savvy, either. It may also include piece-part and subassembly quotations for use in your business proposal, free parts and material samples, and contracts and customer leads.

Customers

While you're at it, don't overlook potential customers as another source of help. You must understand that customers desire greater competition among their suppliers. It is their hope that competition will spur suppliers on to better quality, lower prices, and more timely deliveries. When it comes to new product specifications and market forecasting, customers can provide really valuable advice. New order downpayments or deposits and progress payments constitute another area where customers can be of help. Tens of thousands of companies owe their starts to a good-sized contract from an understanding customer who was willing to gamble on the new firm on the block.

Manufacturers' Representatives

Another group in the cheering section is made up of manufacturers' representatives, usually an entrepreneurially inclined bunch themselves. "Reps" often operate as sole proprietorships or partnerships and earn their bagels and butter hustling products for small- and medium-sized companies. Usually their principals (companies whose products they sell) can't afford a large network of direct sales offices, so a marriage of convenience is contracted. You pay the Reps a commission on each order they get; and, with proper factory support, they'll do wonders for you.

At the outset, though, even before your company gets started, the Rep can be a big help. Most Reps are constantly on the lookout for principals offering new lines to complement (not compete with) the products they already handle. The opportunity to "sign up" a promising new firm with a hot product line is a powerful attraction.

Since Reps work with small- to medium-sized companies constantly, they can often provide a whale of a lot of information on market size, product pricing, and desirable product characteristics. Their income is almost entirely dependent on their business contacts and a perpetually renewed supply of "leads." In my own experience, I have found Reps to be a congenial, hardworking, and helpful group with a first-hand knowledge of the markets they serve.

Distributors

Distributors comprise still another unique group that may be of help to you. Usually operating as wholesale outlets specializing in a particular industry, distributors tend to have much larger organizations than manufacturers' representatives have. Distributors typically maintain inventories of finished merchandise; the Reps, on the other hand, act primarily as marriage brokers in placing customer contracts directly with manufacturing suppliers. Inventory maintenance incurs substantial costs in the operation of a distributorship. Understandably, then, distributors must operate on a larger commission or discount than does a Rep.

Distributors can be of help to the new business in providing product, pricing, and marketing suggestions. From the point of view of the small business, the distributor is a hybrid—part sales representative and part customer.

In essence, the difference between Reps and distributors is in the type of product handled. Most Reps specialize in the custom or job-shop field, where substantial supplier-customer liaison is necessary. Usually the product sold is tailor-made to the customer's specifications. Most distributors handle standardized products which (hopefully) are not overly vulnerable to obsolescence while in the warehouse.

Bankers

An often maligned and much misunderstood group of new-business helpers is the banking community. Banks don't spend millions of dollars every year advertising their services solely to get their message across to the Ford Motor Company and Bethlehem Steel. They really do have an interest in working with the "small time operator." Several of the larger institutions have developed extensive literature in brochure and pamphlet form for this express purpose. In recent years there has also been a sharp increase in the number of *small,* growth-oriented banks that are actively seeking small businesses, with good growth potential, as customers.

When it comes to juicy industry "insider" stories, bankers' ethics forbid them from divulging any information about their clients. However, they can serve as a valuable reference point in evaluating the business climate in almost any area of commercial specialization, be it beauty salons or ecological systems manufacturing. Bankers deserve a section of their own later on, so for now let's move on to the next source of help.

Stockbrokers

Stockbrokers spend five days a week functioning as croupiers in the nation's largest game of chance—the investing public's confidence level in the future of American Business. Many of them have wealthy clients or business contacts who can either help in locating private investors for a new company or can commit funds themselves. Your broker can be an excellent contact in furthering your plans.

All of the major brokerage firms maintain research departments to provide the latest information on pivotal companies, "market indicators," and key industries. Although you may find their augury a little heavily spiced with *ifs, ands,* and *buts,* their expertise in this wizardry is probably a lot better than yours or mine.

College Faculty Members

The next group of baby-business boosters may be found in our universities. College professors and teachers, particularly those in business schools, colleges of pure and applied science, and engineering schools, are often veritable clearing houses of information for new companies. Many professors have extensive consulting practices in addition to their teaching duties. They are thus afforded a firsthand look at new applications of technology to commercial markets. Most professors sincerely enjoy their vocation of communicating knowledge to people, including entrepreneurs. Some teachers have gone to great lengths to assist and encourage their graduate students and research associates in starting small companies. In fact, for years a number of large university laboratories have served as spawning grounds for high technology companies.

In most cases, it is safe to say that your request for a conference with a former professor to discuss your new enterprise plans will be greeted with warm enthusiasm. Over a luncheon at the faculty club, you will be pleased and delighted to discover how poorly you had estimated your old prof's interests outside of the classroom. You will probably find yourself committed for days simply to the task of following up on leads and suggestions you receive. Furthermore, it's likely you won't even be permitted to pay for the meal—"Club rules, you understand," says the prof with a grin, signing the chit.

Would you have believed there was such a mighty reservoir of willing, qualified assistance ready to respond to your needs for help? Let me tell you, it was a welcome surprise to me. These broadly defined groups operate largely with the expectation that some day you may be able to return or pass on the favor. This may take the form of your future patronage or of a spirit of "Go thou and do likewise."

On the assumption that the typical small business does not often suffer the burden of a surfeit of cash, the preceding list purposely omitted such service groups as attorneys, certified public accountants, and business consultants. *I do not intend to suggest that professional services are unnecessary.* To do so would be foolhardy of me and a disservice to you. I simply have chosen to discuss paid services as a separate group.

Let's take a moment now to catalog, for ready reference, the many helpers that tomorrow's businesses can turn to:

1. Other entrepreneurs, who can be reached through
   a. Community service clubs such as
      (1) The Junior Chamber of Commerce
      (2) Rotary International
      (3) Lions International
      (4) Kiwanis International
      (5) Junior Leagues
   b. Fraternal organizations such as
      (1) Elks
      (2) Moose
      (3) Odd Fellows
      (4) Masonic Clubs
      (5) Knights of Columbus
      (6) B'nai B'rith
   c. College-related organizations including
      (1) Fraternities and Sororities
      (2) Alumni Associations
      (3) American Association of University Women
   d. Professional and Trade Associations

    e. Political organizations typified by the

        (1) Young Democrats

        (2) Young Republicans

    f. Church groups

2. Tradesmen, broken down into groups of

    a. Suppliers

    b. Customers

    c. Manufacturers' Representatives

    d. Distributors

3. Bankers

4. Stockbrockers

5. College Faculty Members

8

The Conception and Protection of a Product Idea

Having made the decision to go into business for yourself in spite of the hardships and pitfalls discussed in preceding chapters, you must next give consideration to your business vehicle: a product or service to be offered for sale. This chapter will treat the subject of product selection and its protection.

Mommy, Where Do Product Ideas Come From?

Contrary to the teachings of our wealthy friends from Chapter 5, the Wise Owl, the Old Lady Goose, and the Little Red Hen, I must point out that the Stork does *not* bring product ideas. These ideas originate in many different ways and places, including:

Former Employers

Very often, product ideas are "adopted," bought, licensed from former employers. Now it may interest many of you to learn, in passing, that the body of law which treats the relationship between employer and employees comes under the legal heading of "Master and Servant." (Remember our *Olde English* heritage!) This section of the law covers those things that an employer *may* require of employees (such as patent agreements and employment contracts) and those things which guarantee the rights of an employee to earn a livelihood in any *reasonable* area of choice. Under the safeguards in our Constitution, employers may not make indentured servants of their employees.

An employer may not, for instance, extract a promise from a plumber on his staff that would preclude that plumber from working for another employer if he chose to do so. Such a covenant would be unenforceable. However, if the plumber-employee were taught by his former employer, in confidence, a "secret" way of clearing stopped-up drains and agreed in writing not to use this technique when working for any other employer, he could be obliged legally to honor his commitment provided it did not stop him from earning a livelihood as a plumber.

To illustrate this point further, employees may resign from their jobs and legally set up businesses of their own to manufacture products identical to, and in competition with, those made by their former employers provided that (1) the products are not protected by patents, (2) the elements of the manufacture and operation of the product are evident from an examination of the finished product (dismantled if necessary) by anyone reasonably skilled in that product discipline, and (3) the employees had not previously consented, as a consideration of employment, not to compete with their former employers for a specified period of time after termination of employment.

On the other hand, employees who take "trade secrets" from their former employers when their former employers have followed the necessary procedure for communicating these secrets in confidence are vulnerable to legal action. A few examples of trade secrets are (1) the formula for, or ingredients in, Coca-Cola soft-drink syrup, (2) the technique used to cut sheets of plastic film into thin strips (called *slitting*) for use in tape recorders or as gummed tape, and (3) a process for annealing the steel alloys used in ball bearings to attain the desired hardness.

Note: The foregoing is not intended to serve as a substitute for competent legal counsel. In any case where vulnerability to legal action from a former employer may exist, the services of a skilled attorney should be retained. *As a bare minimum,* where a signed employment or patent agreement was a condition of hire demanded by a former employer, counsel for the entrepreneur should be given the opportunity to examine the document.

One further note on this subject: Individual states regulate their own corporate laws, and practices regarding trade secrets and their protection *do* vary from state to state. Again, competent legal counsel is a must!

On a friendlier note, many companies are willing to sell patent rights on certain products to former employees or, in some cases, even to make them available to *any* interested buyer. Alternatively, various licensing agreements may be drawn up providing for the use (exclusive or nonexclusive) of the patent on a royalty basis. An example of the transfer of trademark rights by an employer to an employee is the Pert-O-Graph discussed in Chapter 1.

In recent years, a number of employers have decided to "join them (the entrepreneurs) rather than fight them," and they now encourage spin-offs in the form of subsidiaries. In this way, the entrepreneur receives the help of a large company in getting established; and the parent company retains a stock position in the new firm. Thus, the parent company realizes a gain where otherwise there would have been a net loss of employee talent and product revenue.

In those instances where the form of company organization is a sole proprietorship or partnership, entrepreneurially inclined employees may succeed in persuading the company owner(s) to make them partners rather than let them resign to start their own companies. In the position of partners, entrepreneurs should then have greatly increased latitude in promoting the products in which they are especially interested.

New Partners

There is an increasing tendency today for *teams* of entrepreneurs to found new companies. Thus, the product idea may have originated with only one of the partners, but it provides the revenue-producing article for exploitation by all of them. In this context, I will long remember a graduation-time bulletin board notice I saw at MIT when I was an undergraduate there. It went something like this:

> Two Harvard MBA candidates wish to discuss partnership possibilities with MIT degree candidate or laboratory assistant with a commercial product concept. Purpose: Join forces and start a new company.

Similar advertisements may be found regularly in the classified section of *The Wall Street Journal.*

New Product Periodicals

Many periodicals offer specialized information of considerable value to those searching for new product ideas. Several are listed below.

1. Idea Source Guide publishes a monthly newsletter dealing with the newest products in the sales incentive and premium field. The newsletter is designed to "trigger an idea, improve a promotion, add excitement to a contest, enhance a mailing, reveal a new, more profitable source." For subscription information, write to Idea Source Guide, P.O. Box 366, Devon, Pennsylvania 19333.

2. *The Journal of Product Innovation Management* is a quarterly publication of the Product Development and Management Association, an international organization devoted to research and education in the area of new product management. Articles focus on both theoretical and practical concepts and are selected on the basis of originality of ideas and freshness of presentation. For subscription information or to request a sample copy of *The Journal*, write to: Elsevier Science Publishing Co., Inc., P.O. Box 1663, Grand Central Station, New York, New York 10163.

3. The U.S. Patent and Trademark Office publishes the *Official Gazette* in two parts every Tuesday—one for patents, the other for trademarks. Each issue contains a claim and drawings of each patent granted on that day, notices of lawsuits pending, indexes of patents and patent holders, and a variety of general information. Since this publication is large and may contain many entries of no practical interest to you, a visit to one of the numerous libraries around the country which subscribe to the *Gazette* may serve to satisfy your curiosity. Copies of desired patents may be obtained from the Patent Office for a nominal fee.

4. Newsweek, Inc. publishes a monthly bulletin entitled *New Products & Processes*, which covers all phases of new products and technology throughout the world, reviewing them for suitability, improvements, uniqueness, and a host of other characteristics. There is a detailed report on a different trade show in each issue, along with information on technical trends and international trade fairs. For subscription information write to the publisher at 444 Madison Avenue, New York, New York 10022.

5. The New York advertising agency of Dancer Fitzgerald Sample publishes a monthly newsletter, *New Product News,* which carries information on new products and services sold in supermarkets and drug stores throughout the country. Subscriptions may be obtained by contacting the publisher at 405 Lexington Avenue, New York, New York 10174.

Regular review of any or all of these publications should unleash a flood of commercially viable new product ideas in the mind of the entrepreneur, any one of which could be adapted to business plans or vice versa.

Doctoral Dissertations

Every year thousands and thousands of bright young men and women compose dissertations as part of the requirement for the doctoral degree. These dissertations represent original work in almost any subject area you can imagine, from accounting to zoology.

Since several hundred thousand doctoral dissertations have been written in the last thirty years, there is an excellent probability that a student has labored for years doing research on a subject of interest to your business and has summarized the findings in a doctoral dissertation that may be available to you for the mere cost of reproducing it.

Many corporations today recognize the value of doctoral dissertations as resource material in locating new products and ideas. The cost of doctoral dissertations is modest; as a business resource, such papers are often, unfortunately, neglected. Here are two particularly useful ways of determining the availability of doctoral dissertations covering subjects relevant to your business.

Various University Libraries. Copies of doctoral dissertations are often available through the library services of universities that offer doctoral programs. Either by corresponding with or by visiting a university that has a particularly strong department in the subject area of interest to you, you may buy copies of the doctoral dissertations you want.

University Microfilms International. This organization, a Xerox company, offers microfilm or photocopies of approximately 500,000 dissertations in all fields, representing the work of graduate students from more than 500 North American and European universities.

Because of the enormous amount of information represented in this library, a specialized information retrieval system called Datrix Direct has been implemented. The Datrix computer's memory is enriched with a constant input of key words selected from the titles, authors, subject headings, and other relevant portions of the paper. A University Microfilms client simply provides the company with a list of key words that are matched against a list of the entries in the Datrix computer. The computer subsequently prints out a listing of all dissertations containing the key words supplied, and this list is forwarded to the client for evaluation. Titles of desired manuscripts may be selected from this list and copies of the dissertations may be ordered from the company. For further information on this unique resource service, write to University Microfilms International, 300 North Zeeb Road, Ann Arbor, Michigan 48106.

Idea Books

Another wellspring of embryo businesses is idea source books. You may not necessarily use one of the ideas in these books "as is," but you may add your individual novel twist to it to provide the basis for your new enterprise. Several such books follow.

1. *Profitable New Foreign Products* is a regularly revised compilation of entries taken from *The Journal of Commerce.* This pamphlet, published by one of the leading newspapers of business and international commerce, includes listings of hundreds of new products originating in Australia, Denmark, England, Japan, West Germany, and many other countries. Copies of this publication are available only to subscribers of the *Journal of Commerce.* For subscription information write to them in care of their Promotions Department at 445 Marshall Street, Phillipsburg, New Jersey 08865. *The Journal,* which is published every weekday, also carries a column on domestic "New Products and New Sales Ideas," usually twice weekly. Most major libraries and all business libraries should carry copies of this newspaper.

2. *Design News* is a set of five directories of interest to engineers, each covering a different topic, including "Materials," "Electrical/Electronics," "Power Transmission," "Fluid Power," and "Fastening." A different directory is issued every two and a half months, and all are revised annually. They contain product and supplier data as well as distributor locations. *Design News* is available from the Cahners Books Division of the Cahners Publishing Co., Inc., at 221 Columbus Avenue, Boston, Massachusetts 02116.

3. *100 Sure-Fire Businesses You Can Start with Little or No Investment,* by Jeffrey Feinman, provides a nuts-and-bolts approach to starting businesses that lend themselves to part-time, office-at-home, small capital operation. Copies may be secured by writing to Jove Publications, 200 Madison Avenue, New York, New York 10016.

4. *184 Businesses Anyone Can Start and Make a Lot of Money*, by Chase Revel, is a gold mine of ideas for business start-ups written by a man who started more than a dozen successful ventures. It is a very readable and practical guide that includes start-up manuals, which readers can order, for each business described. Revel recently came out with a sequel, *168 More Businesses Anyone Can Start and Make a Lot of Money,* written in the same style. Both books can be obtained in bookstores or by writing to Bantam Books, Inc., 666 Fifth Ave., New York, New York 10019.

5. *The Student Entrepreneur's Guide* by Brett M. Kingstone, goes through all the fundamentals of starting and running a small business based on the experiences of students and young people across the country. This book can be obtained by writing to the Ten Speed Press at P.O. Box 7123, Berkeley, California 94707.

Trade Shows

Every year many millions of dollars are spent by major trade association members to exhibit their products at national and international shows. These shows afford the alert visitor unique opportunities to identify and recognize new product ideas and marketing trends. Provided the entrepreneur does not have to spend an inordinate amount of money in traveling to the location of the trade show, the expense of attending should prove to be quite nominal. If a new trade show is sponsored by an industrial sector with which the entrepreneur is not intimately familiar, it is a good idea to take advantage of the many opportunities that will be available for discovering new products and concepts that may be applicable to fields not obvious to the trade show sponsors and exhibitors.

Your local library should have a copy of *Exhibits Schedule: A Directory of Trade and Industrial Shows*. This semi-annual directory of trade and industrial shows is produced by *Successful Meetings* magazine. In the event your local library does not have a copy, further information may be obtained by writing to Exhibits Schedule, 633 Third Avenue, New York, New York, 10017. This publication covers trade, industrial, and public shows throughout the world, arranged by industry and/or profession. It is also indexed by geography and show site, in chronological order.

Your library may also have copies of *World Meetings: United States and Canada* and/or *World Meetings: Outside United States and Canada*. Each of these directories provides a two-year registry of future scientific, technical, and medical meetings. They are published quarterly by *World Meetings Publications,* Macmillan Publishing Company, Inc. Professional Books Division, 866 Third Avenue, New York, New York 10022. Further information, including a descriptive brochure, may be obtained by writing to this organization.

State Invention Expositions

A unique opportunity awaits the product-seeking entrepreneur at annual state invention expositions. These expositions, which generally run for two or three days, are attended by inventors, patent owners, manufacturers, distributors, and investors interested in negotiating patent licenses, patent sales or puchases, manufacturing services, and commission sales of new products.

These events are generally sponsored by each state's Department of Economic Development, Commerce Department, or their equivalents. The National Association of State Development Agencies (NASDA) publishes a directory of state agencies that sponsor these expositions, but it's rather expensive. If you are interested in events held in just a few states, you would be better off contacting each state individually. For information about NASDA's directory, write to them at Hall of States, Suite 526, 444 N. Capitol Street, N.W., Washington, D.C. 20001.

Patent Brokers

A patent broker makes the patents or ideas of inventors available for examination by individuals who are seeking new products for commercial exploitation. Patent brokers operate in much the same way as real estate brokers. They bring together the patent owner (usually the inventor) and the prospective buyers or licensees of the patent rights. Patent brokerage firms may operate in any number of the following ways.

Seller's Agent. An inventor or patent-holding client may engage the services of a patent broker in order to locate a buyer for the patent or salable idea.

Buyer's Agent. An individual or corporation wishing to purchase or license rights to a patent or idea may engage the services of a patent broker to locate the desired patent idea or process.

Independent Dealer. In some instances, a patent broker or a patent brokerage firm may elect to purchase patent rights outright from the inventor or patent holder, with the intention of subsequently selling or licensing the patent rights to a buyer. The patent broker then takes legal possession of the patent. (In the case of the seller's agent or the buyer's agent, the broker merely acts as an intermediary to introduce the buyer to the seller or vice versa.

Patent brokers may be of considerable help to inventors in marketing their patents. A good patent broker will be able to assist inventors in preparing marketing plans that will enable inventors to obtain the highest possible prices for their patents.

Patent brokers may receive remuneration for their services in any combination of the following ways.

Simple Fees. The patent broker may exact a fee, either a fixed amount or a percentage of the cash transaction involved, from the buyer, the seller, or both. The patent broker is often paid in much the same way that a stock broker is paid—by receiving a commission on both the purchase and the sale of any given item.

Royalties. In some instances, a patent broker will receive compensation in the form of a royalty levied against the licensed or sold patent or process.

Retainers. The services of a patent brokerage firm are sometimes permanently retained by industrial clients. In these instances, the industrial concern may simply indicate to the patent broker a particular area of interest. Thus, the patent broker will be on the alert for any products or processes that might be useful to clients. Conversely, a client company may periodically provide the patent broker with a listing of the latest products and processes that the corporation is interested in licensing or selling.

The patent broker receives a retainer for performing marketing services regardless of whether or not they prove effective. Obviously, the long-term failure of a patent broker to effectively perform a service for a client may result in discontinuance of the relationship.

National Information Referral and Exchange Centers

Two little-known national services of particular interest to the information and idea seeker are offered by the National Referral Center and the National Technical Information Service (NTIS).

National Referral Center. The Center, a division of the Library of Congress, is a clearinghouse for information in any field related to science and technology. And in these days of heart transplants and space exploration, that covers *plenty* of subject matter. A brochure offered by the Center indicates that it is

> ... a free referral service which directs those who have questions concerning any subject to organizations that can provide the answer.
>
> The referral center is not equipped to furnish answers to specific questions or to provide bibliographic assistance. Instead, its purpose is to direct those who have questions to resources that have the information and are willing to share it with others. Some of these resources exist within the Library itself.[14]

In discussing the interpretation of the term "information resource," the Center explains that its extremely broad definition includes

> ... any organization, institution, group, or individual with specialized information in a particular field and a willingness to share it with others. This includes not only traditional sources of information such as technical libraries, information and documentation centers, and abstracting and indexing services, but also such sources as professional

societies, university research bureaus and institutes, Federal and state agencies, industrial laboratories, museums, testing stations, hobby groups, and grassroots citizens organizations. The criterion for registering an organization is not its size but its ability and willingness to provide information to others on a reasonable basis.[15]

Requests for information from the Center should be limited to one topic in order to facilitate prompt, efficient handling. Inquiries should also include reference to information resources already explored in order to avoid needless duplication of effort. It is also helpful if the inquirer states any special qualifications, such as researcher, member of a professional society, etc., to assist the Center staff in assessing the potential utility of recommended information sources to the end-user.

I have personally made use of the Center's services on two occasions and was pleasantly surprised and quite pleased with the prompt, efficient, and helpful assistance rendered by their fine staff. Best of all, the service is provided free of charge. To avail yourself of this service or to secure a copy of the Center's descriptive brochure, write to the Library of Congress, National Referral Center, 10 First Street S.E., Washington, D.C. 20540.

Federal Research in Progress (FEDRIP). This is a service of the National Technical Information Service (NTIS). It is a huge database that contains information about ongoing research projects funded by the federal government in the physical sciences, engineering, and life sciences. Currently 72,000 records are included in the database, which is updated semiannually by NTIS.

The FEDRIP database includes details about research currently in progress or initiated and completed during the previous two years. Records include title, principal investigator, performing and sponsoring organizations, and usually a description. FEDRIP can be accessed online through Dialog Information Services, Inc., 3460 Hillview Avenue, Palo Alto, California 94304. You may call them toll-free at 800-227-1927 (in California, dial 800-982-5830).

Protection

The mortality rate for new businesses is consistently and alarmingly high. One primary cause of business failure is the inability of a new company to cope effectively with vigorous, well-entrenched competition. Here is where the concept of *protection* comes into play.

In formulating a business plan, the entrepreneur should give very careful consideration to questions such as: "What unique characteristics do my products have that will prompt customers to give them preferential consideration in a competitive market?" and "What can I do to *protect* this advantage?"

The most commonly recognized form of product protection is a patent. In other instances, protection can be obtained through possession of trade secrets such as special manufacturing processes, "secret formulas," or the use of exotic materials. Still another form of protection can be realized through the use of proper timing: being the first entrant with an innovative concept into a new (but *ready*) market. This latter case requires swift establishment of the new product as "*the* one to buy" in the target virgin market before the competition has an opportunity to develop and obtain distribution for a rival product.

Patents

When reviewing any business proposition, professional, experienced investors will always want to know what means entrepreneurs intend to use to protect their products and, at the same time, safeguard investors' money. The entrepreneur certainly has an obligation to do everything possible to secure the competitive advantage a patent affords.

Although it is far beyond the scope of this book to offer an in-depth study of patent law and procedures, a brief discussion of the subject is certainly in order. The following material was obtained from the Patent and Trademark Office publication *Q & A About Patents*. For further information on patents, consult the references indicated at the end of this chapter.

> A patent is a grant issued by the United States Government giving an inventor the right to exclude all others from making, using, or selling his invention within the United States, its territories and possessions.
>
> The term of a patent is seventeen years from the date on which it is issued; except for patents on ornamental designs, which are granted for terms of 3½, 7, or 14 years.[16]

And, finally,

> A patent may be granted to the inventor or discoverer of any new and useful process, machine, manufacture, composition of matter, or any new and useful improvement of these items. A patent also may be granted on any distinct and new variety of plant, other than a tuber-propagated plant, which is asexually reproduced, or on any new, original, and ornamental design for an article of manufacture.[17]

Ordinarily, the services of a competent patent attorney should be obtained to assure maximum protection for any valuable idea, patentable or not. However, lawyers usually prefer to work on a cash basis instead of taking a "piece of the action" or working on a contingency arrangement. Therefore, the entrepreneur with a patentable idea and severely limited resources who wishes to establish a record of the time or origination and nature of an idea may do so by making use of the Patent and Trademark Office's "Disclosure Document Program." The following excerpt is taken from a Patent and Trademark Office brochure:

> A paper disclosing an invention and signed by the inventor or inventors may be forwarded to the Patent and Trademark Office by the inventor (or by any one of the inventors when there are joint inventors), by the owner of the invention, or by the attorney or agent of the inventor(s) or owner. It will be retained for two years and then be destroyed unless it is referred to in a related patent application filed within two years.
>
> The Disclosure Document is not a patent application, and the date of its receipt in the Patent and Trademark Office will not become the effective filing date of any patent application subsequently filed. However, like patent applications, these documents will be kept in confidence by the Patent and Trademark Office.
>
> This program does not diminish the value of the conventional witnessed and notarized records as evidence of conception of an invention, but it should provide a more credible form of evidence than that provided by the popular practice of mailing a disclosure to oneself or another person by registered mail.[18]

In closing this section on patents, I should quote Thomas A. Edison, who opined, "A patent is a license for a lawsuit." Quoting the Patent Office publication *General Information Concerning Patents:*

> The Patent and Trademark Office has no jurisdiction over questions relating to infringement of patents. In examining applications for patent no determination is made as to whether the invention sought to be patented infringes any prior patent. An improvement invention may be patentable, but it might infringe a prior unexpired patent for the invention improved upon, if there is one.[19]

For the typically under-financed entrepreneur, these words simply mean that if you get a humdinger of an idea for a product and protect it with a patent, you must consider the possible expenses of protracted litigation to defend your patent property. Now it may turn out that some industrial colossus decides that your patented product would make a very nice addition to its line. A not uncommon practice is for such companies to employ highly skilled patent attorneys on a full-time basis for the purpose of suggesting ways of "designing around" a particular patent. I have heard several attorneys assert that unless the subject of a patent represents a truly new and basic innovation, it is virtually impossible to prevent infringement either directly or as a result of this "designing around" process.

Any attorney can acquaint the legal neophyte with facts on the expense of protracted litigation and the frequency with which some large corporations resort to this ploy as a means of circumventing the rights of a patent holder. It is not an uncommon thing for small patent holders to simply abandon the defense of their rights due to an inability to afford the necessary legal fees.

In this country, we have an elaborate legal system for the enforcement of our laws and the apprehension and prosecution of offenders. In the case of patent infringements, however, the expenses of protecting and enforcing patent rights must be borne by the patent holder. The primary deterrent to patent infringement is the award of triple damages for provable losses *provided* the patent holder can afford the time and expense of the necessary litigation. One of the more practical solutions I have repeatedly heard suggested is the licensing or outright sale of the patent to a large corporation that can afford to exploit, promote, and *protect* this valuable property.

Another risk the holders of patents may encounter has to do with the possibility that, after spending substantial sums of money and considerable time fighting alleged infringement of their patents, a court may decide that the patents are invalid. Any monies spent on litigation and even on the acquisition of the patent are thus lost.

This aspect of patent law can be likened to other areas of law as well. Simply because a law is on the books does not mean that it is necessarily constitutional or enforceable. Its verity *may* hinge on the results of an actual test in the courts.

Unpatentable Ideas

Unfortunately, many ideas and concepts of potential commercial value are not readily protectable (if they are protectable at all) by a patent umbrella. They may, however, be turned to profitable use at some future date. In the meantime, steps must be taken to protect them from careless disclosure until the opportunity arrives for exploitation by the originators or their designees.

The publication *Small Business Profits from Unpatentable Ideas,* referenced at the end of this book, treats this problem in detail. In that publication, the author explains that:

(1) An idea made public, either by word of mouth or in writing, immediately becomes common property, and unless the plan is revealed under contract or by confidential disclosure, anyone can make use of that property without infringing any rights;

(2) The voluntary submission of an idea does not set up a contractual relationship between the originator and the other party;

(3) Because of the lack of contract, no action of any kind can be brought by the originator for breach of trust or contract;

(4) Ideas can be protected, provided the originator follows certain procedures governed by the law of contracts.[20]

In the same publication, the following form is suggested for the submission and review of an idea while affording the originator protection of the law of contracts:

John Doe Co.
123 Fourth Street
Anytown, U.S.A.

Gentlemen:

I have developed a new idea for the packaging of your product which I believe would greatly increase your sales and profits. The new method of packaging would not raise production costs.

If you are interested in details of the idea, I shall be glad to forward you complete information if you will kindly sign the enclosed agreement form. Promptly upon receipt of the signed form, I shall forward to you all information I have regarding the idea.

                                        Sincerely,

                                        Robert Roe

Agreement to Review Idea

We, the undersigned, agree to receive in confidence full details about an idea for product packaging to be submitted for our consideration by Robert Roe.

It is further understood that we assume no responsibility whatever with respect to features which can be demonstrated to be already known to us. We also agree not to divulge any details of the idea submitted without permission of Robert Roe or to make use of any feature or information of which the said Robert Roe is the originator, without payment of compensation to be fixed by negotiation with the said Robert Roe or his lawful representative.

It is specifically understood that, in receiving the idea of Robert Roe, the idea is being received and will be reviewed in confidence and that, within a period of thirty days, we will report to said Robert Roe the results of our findings and will advise whether or not we are interested in negotiating for the purchase of the right to use said idea.

Company_____

Street and Number _____

City_____ Zone _____ State _____

Official to receive disclosures (please type)

_____ Title _____

Date _____ Signature _____

Accepted: _____

Robert Roe, Inventor

Warning to Inventors

Inventors typically are poor business decision makers and even worse managers. The eccentricities and volatile temperament that usually characterize the creative genius are almost invariably irreconcilable with the unflappable personality and judgmental constancy required of a good manager. Thus, inventors who would realize financial reward from their mental offspring would be well advised to give serious thought to the following alternatives to founding a company with the intention of single-handedly presiding over the enterprise.

Outright Sale. The inventor may sell a patent for a fixed amount, thereby formally assigning the right, title, and interest in the patent to the buyer. The inventor may assign either the patent itself or the patent application, in the event the patent is still pending. Upon proper notification, the U.S. Patent Office will then take the necessary steps to record the assignment on the patent document.

License for a Flat Fee or Royalty. The inventor who does not wish to sell the patent interest outright may license its use to another individual or firm in consideration of a flat fee or royalty. In the case of a flat fee arrangement, the patent "renter" agrees to pay a negotiated sum in exchange for the right to use the patent for a fixed period of time on an exclusive or nonexclusive basis. In the case of a royalty arrangement, the patent "renter" agrees to pay the inventor a piece rate for the number of items manufactured or the number of items sold. Alternatively, the "renter" may pay the inventor a percentage of the manufacturer's wholesale price or a percentage of the retail price. In other instances, an agreement may include flat fees *plus* royalties. In the case of patent licensing, the Patent and Trademark Office makes no provision for registering the licensee on the patent document.

These two alternatives may prove to be much more financially rewarding to inventors than the launching of businesses they are psychologically, educationally, and emotionally ill equipped to handle. If the inventors *must* start a business, then they would be wise to consider hiring qualified general managers to "run the store" while isolating themselves in the laboratory where they can most effectively apply their creative talents for the benefit of the enterprise. (Remember that qualified general managers are far more plentiful than truly creative inventors.)

9

Projecting a Good Image

Every year, untold millions of dollars are spent by the nation's leading firms for the purpose of enhancing and perpetuating their corporate images. Generally speaking, the factors that motivate these companies to consider such enormous expenditures stem from the simple desire that they be thought well of. The idea is to persuade the customers, suppliers, creditors, employees, and stockholders that the XYZ Corporation is progressive, is technologically and professionally capable, provides products and services of the highest quality, and has a fundamental concern for the well-being of the community it serves. Hopefully, the result of such a campaign will be increased sales, creditor confidence, improved profits, *and* job security for the corporate officers and directors.

A favorable corporate image typically has a profound effect on stockholder confidence and, hence, on the trading-price of a company's securities. In economic terms, the difference between the aggregate market value of the outstanding stock in a company and its net worth is defined as "goodwill." This balance-sheet term uniquely identifies stockholder confidence and is an excellent measure of the effectiveness of a company's public-relations efforts. A high price to earnings ratio or a high stock valuation to net worth ratio simply means that the company is successful in projecting a good *image.*

The Importance of Image to the Entrepreneur

In the case of entrepreneurs eager to establish businesses of their own, the concept of projected image is of enormous importance. Usually, none of the company founders will have had first-hand experience as the president or founder of another company. In other words, they don't have "track records." In lieu of this, they must possess and/or perfect the ability to communicate their enthusiasm and professional capabilities to investors, suppliers, and customers alike. In short, they must project a *good image*.

Image is the "wrapper" in which you present your product or service. The quality of this product or service is far from being the only element important to the customer: The customer wants and *expects image* with the purchase. If a customer is considering the merits of competing offers, it is impossible to eliminate the subjective factors that obscure objective comparison. Velvet and satin lined boxes for precious jewelry, artistically designed crystal flacons for exotic perfumes, "imported" gifts (probably made in a garage in Germany instead of a garage in Hoboken), "secret" ingredients in franchised fried chicken, tuxedoed headwaiters, and a host of other examples attest to the importance of image in the marketplace. *This is a fact:* You can sell very nearly anything if you surround it with the right image!

What I am driving at is this: If the entrepeneur has something *worthwhile* to offer, an image must be built around it merely to compete *unhandicapped* against the lousy service and crummy merchandise the other image builders are successfully marketing. What's more distressing, the buyers *know* they're paying for image. False front stores are older than our Old West; and any society that will countenance annual automobile model changes for as long as ours has isn't about to scuttle image overnight. Honest, that's the way it is. Those are the house rules. If you don't like them, you'll have to look for another table or maybe even another casino.

Consider Alexander Graham Bell. The poor guy had a terrible time persuading people that his telephone gadget had any merit. Had he been a better image builder, he would have found it much easier to garner the support he needed to get his idea off the ground.

I don't care how good your product is; I don't care how wonderful your service can be. If you can't sell it, it won't benefit you *or* the public. Who knows how many worthwhile products and services society has been deprived of due to the promotional ineptitude of their champions? If it takes image to get the buyers to try a good thing, then give it to them. With both barrels. Don't hesitate simply because promotion is a bad word. Sell! Then you'll have the opportunity to show what you can really do. *But* you gotta get the order *first!*

Summary:

1. Ya gotta be a Barnum to get 'em into the tent.

2. Then give 'em their money's worth, or you'll louse things up for everybody else in the biz.

Selection of a Company Name

Having decided on the initial product or service to be marketed and gone through preparation necessary to solicit customers or investors, the entrepreneur is very quickly going to experience the need for a company name.

In those instances where a new company will be serving the fields of science and technology, the founders will often select a company name with endings that include scientific or technological "buzz words." The staff of companies serving the consumer market may select names such as "Quality Gismos" or "Superior Widgets Company." Still other companies in the service fields may stress speed of performance or low-cost services. Typical names for such enterprises might be "Speedy Spade Gardening" or "Economy Photographic Service."

Another factor to be considered in the selection of a company name is the possibility that the one chosen may resemble, or be identical to, the name of a previously established business. The company attorney can arrange to have a search made to insure against the possibility that the proposed name is currently being used by another firm.

Having selected a name that is both satisfactory to the founders and legally acceptable in that it neither duplicates the name of an existing company nor misleads the public (for instance, you cannot establish a business suggesting that you are a doctor or a lawyer without having the appropriate credentials), the next step involved is the registration of this name with some public agency. Again, the company attorney can provide the appropriate assistance in handling this matter. Since licensing regulations vary between different municipalities, counties, and states, the assistance of a lawyer in handling this formality is usually advisable. Alternatively, information on business licensing can be obtained by getting in touch with your local municipal or county clerk's office.

Pointers on Business Stationery

With the formality of name selection and registration completed, the entrepreneur is ready for the next step in public relations. Business stationery is a *must* in image building. A well-executed logotype ("logo") and its embellishment upon your business cards, letter-heads, and envelopes does much to enhance the initial impression a new company and its founders make on a prospective customer or investor.

Often the founders will know an artist who would be willing to design a company trademark or logo for a nominal charge. An artistically gifted founder might also take on the task of designing the logo. Otherwise, many commercial art firms (and a few souls in the printing trade who still qualify to do more than merely reproduce *other* people's art work) will be able and happy to undertake the task.

A number of local printers advertise their services in the classified section of major metropolitan newspapers and in the ubiquitous Yellow Pages of the telephone book. Still others offer highly specialized printing services (business cards only or envelopes only) by mail. A few sources of supply and ideas are listed below. Samples and catalogs may be obtained by addressing your inquiries to:

Idea Art
799 Broadway
New York, New York 10003
(212) 533-6622

Hammermill Paper Company
1475 East Lake Road
Erie, Pennsylvania 16500
(814) 456-8811

Goes Lithography Company
42 West 61st Street
Chicago, Illinois 60621

Commentary by Robert Townsend

I disagree with this chapter. It seems to me that image is one of the most dangerous concepts in modern organizations. One of the great advantages that a small, new company has over a big, mature one is that the small, new company knows the difference between form and substance, between appearance and reality. Image is not a goal. It's a by-product. A good image has to be earned by performance.

Now, having said all this, I could be pushed into letting a small, new company spend a little more for embossed letterheads, for example; but I can't be pushed much further than that. In any event, there ought to be some kind of a tickler file in the chief executive's desk that comes up every thirty days and says "Image is a by-product. Let's not chase image any more. Let's go earn one by our performance and by chasing the real goal of customer satisfaction, employee satisfaction, and shareholder satisfaction."

As a service to those entrepreneurs who have never worked in a gigantic business, or as a reminder to those who have and might otherwise be tempted to forget their experience, I'd like to give you a reading list of books which show in one light or another the enormous triviality, waste, and phoniness of the big organization.

Arnold, Thurman. The Folklore of Capitalism. *New Haven, Connecticut: Yale University Press, 1937.*

Ayers, Edward. What's Good for GM. *Nashville, Tenessee: Aurora Publishing, 1970.*

Bannock, Graham. The Juggernauts: The Age of the Big Corporations. *Indianapolis: Bobbs-Merrill Co., 1971.*

Dahl, Robert A. After the Revolution: Authority in a Good Society. *New Haven, Connecticut: Yale University Press, 1970.*

Galbraith, John K. The New Industrial State. *New York: Signet, 1967. (With the proviso that he is all wet on the inevitability of large organizations.)*

Goodman, Paul. New Reformation: Notes of a Neolithic Conservative. *New York: Random House, 1970.*

Goodman, Paul. People or Personnel *and* Like a Conquered Province. *New York: Vantage Press, 1965 and 1967. (Two titles in one paperback.)*

Harrington, Alan. Life in the Crystal Palace. *New York: Alfred A. Knopf, 1959.*

Jay, Anthony. Corporation Man. *New York: Random House, 1971.*

Lundberg, Ferdinand. The Rich and the Super-Rich. *New York: Bantam Books, 1968.*

Mills, C. Wright. The Power Elite. *Oxford, England: Oxford University Press, 1959.*

Mintz, M., and Cohen, J. S. America, Inc.: Who Owns and Operates the United States. *New York: Dial Press, 1971.*

Nossiter, Bernard. The Mythmakers: An Essay on Power and Wealth. *Boston: Houghton Mifflin Company, 1964.*

Parkinson, C. Northcote. Parkinson's Law and other Studies in Administration. *Ballantine Books. Boston: Houghton Mifflin Company, 1964.*

Peter, Laurence J., and Hull, Raymond. The Peter Principle. *Bantam Books, New York: William Morrow and Co., 1970.*

Quinn, Theodore K. Giant Business: Threat to Democracy. *New York: Exposition Press, 1954.*

Raskin, M. Being and Doing. *New York: Random House, 1971.*

Slater, Philip. The Pursuit of Loneliness: American Culture at the Breaking Point. *Boston: Beacon Press, 1970.*

(Author unknown; it drifted up in a bottle). Up the Organization: How to Stop the Corporation from Stifling People and Strangling Profits. *New York: Alfred A. Knopf, 1970.*

Whyte, William H., Jr. The Organization Man. *New York: Simon and Schuster, 1956.*

That's a pretty good reading list, which will tend to remind you of what goes on in large organizations and, hopefully, will lead you to fight nonsense, waste, phoniness and triviality.

II
The Business Plan

10
The Importance of a Business Plan

If entrepreneurs combine the marvelous mechanism of persistence with their talent and determination to start businesses of their own, they have a high probability both of establishing their businesses and of succeeding in them. However, by first formulating a thoughtful, carefully prepared plan of their objectives, entrepreneurs can economize in the use of their financial resources and personal efforts. A well-prepared business plan is like a scholarship in the School of Hard Knocks; it reduces what might otherwise be a prohibitive tuition to a manageable one.

The Business Plan is a Sales Document

Fundamentally, a business plan (sometimes used as a proposal, a prospectus, or if capital is to be raised using the plan, an offering circular) is the primary vehicle for giving credibility to an idea. In order to effectively organize the resources required for the establishment of a new business, it is usually necessary to persuade a great many people that the business concept is viable. Oftentimes the willingness of suppliers to extend credit, the willingness of customers to place orders, and, usually most importantly for the young business, the willingness of investors to invest will depend on the care with which the business plan has been prepared.

Often, a business plan will outline a process for "combining your money with my brains so we can both get rich." A properly prepared plan, then, will clearly outline the process for the efficient exploitation of the business concept and explain the attendant multiplication of those monies invested. The plan is a scenario briefly describing the principal characters and the marketplace in which they will function.

A business plan prepared for the scrutiny of a professional, seasoned venture capitalist should be able to provide all the answers *any* investor, from your rich aunt to a Wall Street underwriter, might ask. The business plan as a sales document must be prepared for the most sophisticated investor and must communicate such subtle characteristics as credibility, authority, and ingenuity.

Credibility

The plan must convey a sense of optimism regarding the success of the intended venture tempered by the realities of the marketplace. Obviously it would be foolhardy to propose a venture in which the principal participants did not anticipate a substantial measure of success, but the concepts embodied in the plan should be sufficiently documented in order to inspire not only optimism but also confidence.

The use of professionally prepared market surveys and reports that discuss present demand and provide detailed projections of future requirements for the proposed product or service are of great value in communicating a sense of credibility to the reader. Relating your planned enterprise to such factors as population growth (for predicting an agricultural market), far-reaching legislation on environmental pollution (for predicting a water- or air-filtering process market), or a new but accepted technological breakthrough such as television (for estimating the demand for TV antennas) enormously enhances the believability of a proposed business idea.

Authority

The plan must convey the image of the founders as possessing an unusually sophisticated knowledge of the market they intend to serve and the maturity of judgment necessary to respond to the challenges of a dynamic marketplace. Ordinarily, such a characteristic is established by having a "track-record" in a related field of business or an unusually distinguished educational background. For instance, if the success of the new enterprise will be heavily determined by the excellence of its engineering talent, one or more of the founders must have a record of numerous successful and profitable innovations in products or processes. Presumably this background would have been obtained while in the employ of some other company, while at a university laboratory, or under some other set of circumstances that would afford the individuals the opportunity to simultaneously gain experience and demonstrate their creativity.

Obviously, excellence in the areas of marketing, sales, finance, and manufacturing is also expected of the founders in a measure proportional to the demands of the business areas they contemplate exploring. A background in cosmetics marketing would be ideal for an entrepreneur planning to supply the beauty industry, but it might very probably be wasted on a company planning to make custom parts for the automotive industry.

Ingenuity

Invariably, the entrepreneur who solicits constructive criticism will encounter the question "What have you got that nobody else has got that will make you, your company, and its products and/or services outstanding in the marketplace?" Your idea must have *pizzazz,* that exciting ingredient that inspires the imagination and fires the enthusiasm of all who behold it.

A low-cost computer that works five times as fast as the best one currently being sold on the market, an economical new process for softening household water, and a genetics research team with a promising new development are all characterized by the pizzazz that is bound to win the heart and the purse of some investor or underwriter. The application of a proven idea, technique, or product to a new, previously unrecognized but waiting market might also qualify for financial support.

Most investors, to summarize, are looking for a ground-floor, ten-cents-a-share shot at the next Xerox or Polaroid. It is up to you to demonstrate that your idea has at least a little of the potential of ideas such as these.

The Business Plan and the Responsibility of the Founder

In organizing the resources necessary for the formation of a new enterprise, the founders take upon themselves a very great responsibility to every individual and every business that their plan may affect. A conscientious, responsible effort including careful research and investigation in the preparation of the plan will do much to insure against financial injury to employees, suppliers, customers, investors, and even the founders themselves.

A properly researched business plan will represent a "dry run" of the early years following the formation of the business and should expose the founders to every major problem they can reasonably expect to encounter. Obviously, not all problems can be foreseen. But, by anticipating and preparing for *some* problems, more of the energies and resources of the founders will be available for solving the hidden difficulties. Entrepreneurs who take the time and trouble to conscientiously prepare a business plan can know that they have done their best to honor their responsibilities to the business community. They will also, because they have familiarized themselves with every aspect of what they propose to do, acquire the self-confidence that is so essential in persuading others that their proposed endeavors will be successful.

None of the sources of assistance listed in the next section are suggested as substitutes for your own hard work. Your business plan should, again, represent your finest efforts and capabilities. You are the one who is going to manage the new enterprise. In doing so, you will have available to you the assistance and counsel of many individuals. However, the responsibility for the results of your actions rests solely upon your shoulders. The business plan, like your business, must represent an extension of your ideas, molded and modified by the most competent assistance you can acquire.

You properly expect to enjoy a substantial percentage of the rewards of success in your venture; therefore, you must also be prepared to bear the brunt of the blame and hardship in the event of failure. As Harry S. Truman, once the president of a very large organization, was fond of saying, "The buck stops here."

Sources of Assistance in Preparing Your Business Plan

There are a number of ways in which an entrepreneur can acquire a first-hand knowledge of the characteristics of a well-prepared business plan. The following list includes many of them, but your own imagination will provide you with many others.

Public-Offering Prospectuses

Any time a public offering of stock is made, the document that describes the offering (called a prospectus) must be registered and approved either by the Corporation Commissioner, or a similar agency within the state in which the offering is tendered, or the Securities and Exchange Commission. Since the offering of stock for sale to the public is a rather common occurrence, most stockbrokers have a ready supply of prospectuses describing current offerings. Your broker will be happy to give you one or two samples, which will give you a number of ideas regarding the kind of information you should expect to provide in your business plan.

The Business Plan of Another Company

Your attorney may have had recent experience with other clients successful in starting their own businesses. If so, there is a possibility that copies of the business plans of these companies can be found in the law office files. In those instances where no possibility of a conflict of interest exists and where the subject company gives its permission, your attorney may afford you an opportunity to examine copies of these plan. It is unlikely, however, that you will be permitted to remove them from the attorney's office.

Business Consultants

A number of individuals billing themselves as business consultants may be of assistance to you in the formulation and preparation of your business plan. Provided you rely on their services only as advisors and insure that the finished business plan is truly a representation of your *own* concepts, such assistance can prove to be quite worthwhile.

Lawyers and Certified Public Accountants

A competent attorney can provide a critical, objective evaluation of your business plan. Furthermore, if there are elements of the plan that may make you vulnerable to a lawsuit, your attorney's counsel is valuable insurance.

Another professional who can assist you in obtaining an objective evaluation of your business plan is the Certified Public Accountant. Of course, the CPA's comments will be particularly appropriate in evaluating the merit of your financial projections.

Public Relations Firms

Some public relations firms occasionally undertake the task of preparing business plans. Provided the entrepreneur recognizes that such firms may be tempted to oversell the potential of the business and inject excessive optimism into the business plan, their services can be of value.

Books on Writing Effective Sales Letters

Your business plan may be regarded as a sales letter of sorts. That is because new businesses grow from ideas that can be effectively *pro-*

moted, first in the investor's office and later in the marketplace. Assuming that your business idea has merit, the very least you can do for it is to learn how to properly promote it. A number of books exist on the subject of writing effective sales letters; your local library undoubtedly has several. If you have not already been exposed to such books, you will find them quite educational and informative.

Trial Runs

Although you feel that your initial written plan is ready for exposure, you may find after your first few contacts that it needs some revision. Incorporation of new ideas that have resulted from suggestions and criticism offered during what otherwise might be termed "false starts" can prove to be beneficial in producing a polished, professional plan.

Packaging the Business Plan

The business plan is of critical importance in establishing your corporate image. Depending on the nature of the intended recipient, the business plan may range all the way from a neatly typed presentation bound in a manila report folio all the way up to a four-color, heavy-stock pamphlet printed on the finest coated paper. In the cosmetics of the business plan as well as in the content, the judgment of the entrepreneur will be evident. Too lavish a format will frighten off a penny-pinching millionaire who made his money the hard way or an ulcer-prone banker just as quickly as will a sloppily typed, mimeographed document.

Shopping in the Financial Marketplace

The entrepreneur who is seeking capital with which to start a business will very quickly discover that most investors want to be the first on the planet to cast their eyes upon your proposal—to feel that they are having the first crack at a great, new opportunity. A number of seasoned venture capitalists will invariably inquire after the names of other investors who have been afforded an opportunity to review your business plan. Some may even ask you to fill out a form listing the members of the investment ccommunity to whom you have already presented the plan. In the event these other investors have declined to participate in funding the plan, the interviewing investor may also be expected to ask *why* they declined. The business plan that has been reviewed and rejected by a number of venture capitalists is referred to as a "shopped" or "shop-worn" proposal. The fund-raising entrepreneurs, then, must develop the capability for shopping their proposals *discreetly.*

Busy Investors May Unintentionally Waste Your Time

Busy investors will spend anywhere from two weeks to two months making a preliminary review of your business plan. Obviously, approaching investors on a one-at-a-time basis can prove extremely costly in terms of time; in addition, a small minority of the investing community may not even accord you the courtesy of responding to an inquiry. Therefore, you must learn how to distribute many copies of your plan both simultaneously and discreetly, without over-exposing and hence "shopping" it.

In order to keep track of the proposals that you have distributed, it is advisable to number each copy. However, investors will not be flattered if they receive copies numbered 97 or 132. These investors may not give your proposal more than a cursory review on the assumption that, if it has merit, some other investor may have already initiated action to finance the company or on the alternative assumption that, if the other dozens of knowledgeable investors have already rejected the proposal, it certainly does not warrant the expenditure of their valuable time.

Note: Before presenting *any* copies of your business plan to potential investors, *see your attorney*. If you distribute it indiscriminately, you may be guilty (knowingly or otherwise) of making a *public offering* without proper registration, a crime under civil law punishable by fines *and* possible imprisonment!

Forget Everything I've Said!

Regardless of the subject, exceptions to the rule almost invariably exist.

Back-of-the-Envelope Advocates

The president of a particularly successful electronics firm I know of has his own approach to fund raising and investor solicitation—the "back-of-an-envelope" philosophy. This individual perfected an excellent prototype of a new device; and, with nothing more than his track record as a scientist and manager, unbounded enthusiasm, and a great product, he was able to raise more than $100,000 with which to launch his enterprise. In his fund-raising campaign, he conveyed the attitude, "If you don't like my approach, I'll find someone who does. I don't have time to fool around with elaborate proposals; I want to get into high gear *now!*"

The problems he has encountered since commencing operation have been handled as they arose by the growing cadre of capable lieutenants he has been able to attract. He concedes that he had a number of problems early in the game due to inadequate financial planning, but his business volume is now such that he can afford the full-time services of a professional financial staff.

The Unbelievers

The investment community has more than its fair share of cynics. In my own fund-raising efforts, I had the dubious honor of having a seasoned venture capitalist compliment me on the excellence of my business plan and then inquire regarding the name of the public relations firm that I had hired to prepare it for me. To this day I don't believe I was successful in persuading this particular gentleman that the proposal represented my own work exclusively, although it was extremely well received in the rest of the financial community. If you have never had a business of your own and your business plan looks too good, you might run the risk of this kind of rejection.

"We Want to Help, Too!"

A number of investors (entrepreneurs themselves) are unwilling to become involved in any new business that does not at the outset exhibit a definite need for their special talents, whether in the area of finance, engineering, manufacturing, sales/marketing, or management. The entrepreneur, in dealing with such a situation, should seek to locate investors with whom a long-term, harmonious relationship may be anticipated. The investor who insists on telling you how to run the store before the doors are even open may later insist on personally running it not long after you get operations started.

On the other hand, there is a good chance that you have a lot to learn in running your first business. And it doesn't hurt to have someone handy who knows some of the answers and is willing to give you help over the rough spots.

Super-Serendipity

As has been stated earlier, careful planning can prove to be of enormous value in the founders' effort to guarantee the success of the new venture. Furthermore, by securing the services of a good insurance underwriter, the founders may take steps to minimize the effects of unanticipated and possibly catastrophic occurrences. However, a very significant element that cannot be integrated into the founders' plans is the ability to *recognize* and *exploit* unexpected opportunities when they present themselves. This element I call *super-serendipity*.

Take the case of the lucky person who wins the Irish sweepstakes or a state lottery. Given this substantial windfall, a winner unaccustomed to and unprepared for a life of wealth may squander all of the winnings within a short time. Nevertheless, the good fortune in winning the sweepstakes *is* serendipity. But, if the winner were to take that prize and suitably invest it in a growth opportunity, the same windfall might become super-serendipitous.

As another example of super-serendipity, consider this story taken from my own past. An inventor acquaintance solicited my services to assist him in marketing one of his latest creations. Subsequently, while attending a seminar, I heard a venture capitalist indicate that one of his portfolio companies was engaged in the manufacture of products related to the invention I had recently been asked to market. This is an example of serendipity. Had I then simply forgotten about this potential opportunity, I would never have realized the return the situation potentially offered. However, by asking the speaker what the name of the portfolio company was and by subsequently tracking down the founders of this company, I was able to successfully market the invention and thus realize a commission. It is virtually impossible to plan for super-serendipity in the preparation of a business proposal or in formulating the growth projections for a proposed venture. However, it would serve the founders well to emphasize their ability to exploit new opportunities, for it is the recognition of unanticipated opportunity that has resulted in the substantial success of many businesses.

In summary, a group of founders capable of demonstrating that they have the sophistication and maturity necessary to recognize and exploit unanticipated opportunities enjoys a unique advantage when trying to inspire investor confidence in a highly competitive capital market. After all the "hard data" has been favorably evaluated, it is the hint of the existence of this founder quality that gives rise to the "gut-feel" upon which many investors ultimately base an affirmative investment decision.

11
The Mini-Proposal

The mini-proposal typically serves as a brief introduction summarizing a business plan. It is designed to help potential investors ascertain at the outset whether or not they have interest in participating in the financing of your enterprise. In many instances, investors develop a high degree of specialization within their portfolios. A properly executed mini-proposal can produce a number of highly positive results: (1) it saves investors a considerable amount of time by enabling them to determine—without having to wade through page after page of introductory material—whether or not the investment opportunity is within their areas of interest; (2) it saves the entrepreneur the substantial delay normally encountered while an investor carefully reviews an elaborately executed proposal; (3) it reduces the likelihood that your full-blown proposal (maxi-proposal?) will become shopped. There is far less stigma associated with the rejection of a mini-proposal than with the rejection of a detailed, formal plan.

Oftentimes, investors keep lists of basic requirements any proposal must have before they will consider it. This chapter is devoted to an analysis of these important factors.

Investor Preferences

Investors can be crap shooters looking for a fast buck or conservative banker types who aren't satisfied unless they can secure significant

equity in a "sure thing." Some investors are willing to bankroll almost anything that offers the potential for substantial capital gains
in a short time frame. Others restrict their investments in many
ways, thus carefully formalizing the process of analysis to which any
new business plan is subjected. An investor engaged in the initial
screening of your mini-proposal will probably be concerned with all
of the following categories.

Initial Capitalization Required

Many investors—in fact, the majority of investors—have relatively
low ceilings on the amount of money they are willing to invest in any
one particular project. In the case of private individuals, the figure
may be as low as a few thousand dollars; more adequately capital-
ized investors or agencies might prefer ceilings between $500,000 and
$1 million. Professional money managers may not want to get in-
volved in the financing of any business requiring less than $1 million
or $2 million. Some of the most successful members of this category
have expressed the attitude that it takes as much time, effort, and
money to monitor a $50,000 investment as it does to monitor a $1
million investment. Commonly, investors will have a preference for a
particular range of invested dollars; and, while they don't wish to
become involved with the problems of a small, penny-ante enterprise, at the same time they may be unwilling or unable to underwrite an entity requiring substantial financing no matter how
appealing its prospects may be.

Maturity of the Enterprise

Closely related to the *amount* of financing sought is the matter of
the *maturity* of the enterprise. This is often a primary consideration
in the willingness of an investor to participate in any new round of
financing. Generally speaking, this maturity is defined as a company's degree of development and is described in terms of the type of
financing sought by the company. Although there are several additional, more mature financing levels commonly recognized in the investment community, I will concentrate on the following five.

   Seed. In this case, all that exists is an idea for a product, possibly a plan, and possibly a proposed company team. This represents
one of the highest possible risk investment opportunities.

   Start-up. Here there is usually a prototype product (or a well-
defined service); a plan and a team exist; but no operating history
has been established. Since visualization of the business concept is
easier here than it is in the case of seed financing, this situation is

more attractive to investors. However, risk is still considered quite high, and the cost of equity financing is also usually substantial in terms of what the founders must surrender to obtain backing.

Mezzanine. In this stage, a company has withstood the rigors of start-up, usually has a record of service billings or product shipments (including an adequate manufacturing capacity and capability), a customer list (albeit a small one), and a financial record (whether profitable or not) that will permit an analysis of progress to date versus dollars spent.

Growth. At this stage, a business has usually established its viability as a commercial operation, but it is unable to generate sufficient cash flow or to attract adequate debt financing at manageable interest rates to permit the rapid growth possible with its proven products (or services) and available staffing. Characteristically, this problem is typified by an inability to handle the cash differential between accounts receivable (on orders shipped) and accounts payable (on raw materials and parts in inventory) while trying to increase sales volume.

Bridge. This type of funding frequently takes the form of debt instruments with warrants or options attached (called "kickers" or "sweeteners") for the later purchase of company stock at a price established at the time the debt is incurred. The term "bridge" derives from the fact that this form of financing is generally used to provide funds to sustain operations while the company is in the process of securities registration for a public offering of stock.

Preferred Industrial Sectors

Many investors prefer to participate in the development of corporations in sectors of the business community where they have established expertise. Thus, you find some investors who will invest in nothing but computer-related industries. Others have a preference for the retail-clothing industry. Still others seek to specialize in those areas that seem to be in vogue in the "initial public offering" category in the stock market.

Emphasize the Highlights

Provided your business plan successfully passes the investor obstacle course in that the amount of capitalization you require, the nature of the market you intend to serve, and the maturity of your enterprise are consistent with investors' objectives, you should next give consideration to providing a brief, accurate, and appealing discussion of each of the following highlights.

Niche in the Market

To improve the chance of success of their new business, the founders should identify a well-protected niche in the market they plan to serve. Ideally, they will provide a needed product or service unlike any currently offered by competitors. Their concept should enjoy the protection of patent coverage, unique founder know-how, trade-secret exclusivity, and/or proprietary characteristics. For example: The Polaroid camera and film development process represent excellent examples of products enjoying the protection of extensive patent coverage. The early processes involved in the manufacture of semiconductor devices (transistors and their descendants) enjoyed both patent and founder know-how protection, which enabled their originators to operate profitably and relatively free from competition for a number of years before other suppliers appeared on the scene. The syrup formula for Coca-Cola is one of the most famous examples of trade-secret protection. Although this drink is bottled at plants in most of the major countries of the world, the syrup is manufactured exclusively by the parent Coca-Cola Company, and its preparation remains a very carefully guarded secret.

Superior Qualifications of the Founders

A brief outline of the qualifications and major accomplishments of the founders is a valuable piece of information to include in the mini-proposal. Patent and/or publication activity, unusual academic or professional standing, sales records, previously successful marketing plans, merger or acquisition negotiation experience, profit-and-loss or product-line responsibility, project managership, and a substantial background in personnel supervision all exemplify the type of information appropriate for this section. Only superior qualifications and major accomplishments, however, should be indicated here. A more extensive discussion of founder background belongs in the formal business plan.

Market Characteristics

A brief description of the market to be served should include the following information: (1) Description of initial products or services. (Although all investors are interested in owning part of a corporate giant of the future, most new companies generally begin with a limited number of products or services. The primary features of these items should be mentioned briefly and objectively.) (2) Information on the growth rate of the market for this product or service. (3) A statement indicating the anticipated percentage of market capture. (Ordinarily, to be attractive to an investor, a new company must be in an industry that is growing significantly faster than the gross national product; and the founders should plan for a company growth rate faster than that characteristic of the planned market.)

Keep It Short and Sweet

Some large venture capital organizations process more than 100 business plans each month. Typically, one or possibly two of each 100 plans ultimately receive the investor's backing.

In light of the substantial work load involved in processing these many proposals, you can appreciate the importance of stating your case succinctly and alluringly—the mini-proposal is to the formal business plan what an hors d'oeuvre is to a sumptuous repast. Ideally, the mini-proposal should not exceed two pages in length. This will enhance the probability that it will receive prompt attention. Investors are human beings and are just as susceptible to procrastination as any other mortal. The thick proposal that will require hours to read is going to find its way quickly to the bottom of a very large pile. On the other hand, a one- or two-page summary is likely to be read as soon as the envelope is opened.

In essence, the mini-proposal must be detailed enough to cover every major factor, written well enough to communicate the professionalism of the founding team, and brief enough to invite immediate attention. If you can crank in these three factors, you'll be off to a good start.

12

The Formal Business Plan

When the founders have managed to sufficiently interest the investors in their mini-proposal, the investors will request that the founders provide them with a formal business proposal. This is the document that in most cases will determine whether or not the investors and founders will reach a point of serious negotiation in the financing of the new enterprise.

Every key aspect of the proposed business should be covered in detail in this document. The founders should endeavor to communicate a sense of thoroughness and a feeling that "We're ready for anything!" This chapter is devoted to a discussion of each of the many items that should receive consideration in preparing the proposal. (You can also refer to the checklist provided in Appendix 4 as you are developing your business plan).

Introduction

A one-page (two if you must) summary of the business proposal should state substantially the same information included in the mini-proposal. Some venture capital organizations are staffed with a number of capable assistants. It is likely that your proposal will be reviewed by one of these staff members. Possibly the reviewer did not have an opportunity to study your mini-proposal (some other staff member may have read it). Thus, a restatement of the mini-proposal information in your introduction will serve to familiarize the reader with your basic plans. The sequence in which material appears in the proposal should follow that of the exposition in this chapter unless the founders have a strong desire or a good reason for preferring some other arrangement.

Table of Contents

Depending on the length of your proposal, you may wish to include a table of contents to give reviewers ready access to any parts of the proposal they may wish to find quickly. Some analysts with a penchant for accounting may want to look at your financial projections first of all while others may be more concerned with the resumes of the founders. The table of contents is a convenience and a time-saver for the busy analyst, and it also gives another bit of professional polish to your proposal.

The Management Team

In the "old days," solo operations were very common in the business community. Even now, this fabric of the business community has not changed too much. However, when the launching of a business concept requires substantial funds, the sophisticated investors of today are generally reluctant to invest in a one-man show. Typically, every key management function—marketing/sales, manufacturing, engineering, and finance—must be covered by someone who has demonstrated exceptional capability in previous business assignments and who has suitable academic credentials. This section of the business plan should give some consideration to each of the following seven subjects.

Capsule Resumes of the Founders

Condensed resumes of the founders, including name, age, education, major accomplishments to date, and recent employment history, will serve to introduce the management team to the investors. The resumes should be limited to a brief exposition of those career highlights that would have an impact on the success of the proposed venture. More detailed information can be included in the resume section of the Appendix.

References

Where possible, each of the founders should obtain anywhere from one to five letters of reference from respected individuals attesting to their character and their business and/or technical expertise. The investor will be less interested in letters written by friends and clergymen than in references from customers, sales representatives, former employers, and other *business* acquaintances. College professors may also provide such letters if they would be appropriate to your circumstances. Ordinarily, the references should not be included in the main body of the proposal. Instead, following the capsule resumes mention that letters of references are included in the Appendix.

Organization Chart

A diagram showing the proposed organizational structure for the new enterprise serves neatly to convey this important information. Each block on the diagram should include a description or title appropriate to the indicated function. The name of the individual occupying each position should also be indicated.

Who Does What, with Which, and to Whom

This section should include a discussion of the primary duties of each member of the founding team. This discussion will serve not only to communicate to the reader the role of various team members but also to promote a clear understanding on the part of the team members of what their functions are in making the corporate machine go.

Kenneth Olsen, the founder of Digital Equipment Corporation, feels very strongly about the value of job descriptions and clearly defined responsibilities in a new enterprise. In his keynote speech before a group of several hundred would-be entrepreneurs, he emphasized that the early operation of his company was significantly improved when he recognized that the problems he was having were due to a general misunderstanding on the part of his team members regarding their functional responsibilities. Almost all of his staff members expressed surprise when they were formally notified by Ken as to the nature of their responsibilities.

Synergy of the Founding Team

One of the most exciting phenomena in business is that interactive result we call synergy. When the productivity and creativity of a small group of uniquely compatible people is equivalent to the output of a much larger organization, synergy is at work. The business plan should suggest that the talented individuals selected for the business team are capable of working together harmoniously, obtaining inspiration and motivation from each other, and being tremendously productive.

Management Assistance Required

As we mentioned earlier, some investors enjoy and look forward to the opportunity to actively participate in the operation of a new enterprise. If the founders know of their investor's nature in advance and do not object to it, provision may be made in the business plan for the services of the investor or a designee.

In most instances, however, leaving a key position unfilled is the kiss of death for an otherwise excellent business plan. Many investors are fond of the truism, "A chain is only as strong as its weakest link." Therefore, failure to designate key positions can prejudice investors against your plan.

A more common problem, which you will surely encounter, is that of filling every executive position with highly qualified personnel without at the same time burdening the new enterprise with such a heavy overhead that an unrealistic first-year sales forecast would be necessary to support it. Arranging for part-time professional services may prove to be a satisfactory alternative to a full-time high-priced staff member.

Watch the Birdie

As an added fillip, you may wish to include photographs of the founding team. The practice is not a common one, but it could prove helpful in early contacts with investors who are located some distance from the founding team and the proposed site for the new company.

The Board of Directors

If a business is organized in the corporate form, statutory provisions will require that the company's stockholders elect a Board of Directors. It is the duty of this Board to represent the interests of the stockholders because, if the number of stockholders is large, it is impractical for them to regularly attend meetings of the company executives to monitor the operations of the business. The Board of Directors has a responsibility to the stockholders to meet on a regular basis with the officers of the company to review corporate progress, to assist in the formulation of policy decisions, and, where necessary, to influence the makeup of the staff of company officers. The Board of Directors, then, is the conduit through which wishes of the stockholders are channeled to the company officers.

Let's clarify the corporate flow of authority. Each company shareholder enjoys voting rights in determining the makeup of the Board of Directors of any company. The distribution of votes to the stockholders is in direct proportion to the number of shares of "voting stock" they own. Thus, a stockholder who personally holds more than fifty percent of the stock in a given corporation may very significantly influence the operations of the corporation through the Board. The company officers—the President, Chief Executive Officer, and Vice Presidents—are responsible to the Board of Directors for the day-to-day operation of the company. If a majority of the Board of Directors decides that it is necesary to effect a change in the management of the company, changes *will* be implemented.

A Board of Directors is also responsible for establishing the salaries of the company officers and for providing for the succession of company officers in the event of resignations, firings, or death.

One of the least-appreciated sources of information and guidance available to small businesses is this same Board of Directors. In launching a new enterprise, the founders can use all the help they can get. By establishing an effective Board of Directors, the founders may avail themselves of the objective advice of the knowledgeable group of seasoned business executives and professionals who will have a continuing interest in the progress of the enterprise.

Since some members of the Board of Directors may be elected who are not officers of the company, they should be able to maintain a perspective on the business different from that of the company officers. Company officers too often cannot see the forest for the trees. The "outside," or noncompany, members of the Board may provide a continuing remedy for this visibility problem.

An effective, active Board of Directors may also offer good management counseling services. Ordinarily a small business is not able to afford a large staff of specialists to provide advice and directive guidance to the corporate staff. But members of the Board who are from outside the corporation can be of valuable assistance. Frequently, if a Board member has some unusual proficiency that is of particular interest to the company officers, private consultations outside of the Board meetings may be arranged.

Fortunately, experienced business executives are often eager and willing to serve on the Boards of small new companies in order to further broaden their own experience, enjoy greater variety in their work routine, and be of service to the business community. In many cases, they are equipped to provide insight into areas of business with which the founders may not be intimately familiar.

In planning for the Board, the entrepreneur commonly asks these questions: How many members should it have? Who should serve on the Board? What qualifications should they have? How are members recruited? What sort of compensation should these Board members receive?

How Many?

No matter how many members there are on the Board of Directors, statutory provisions and common sense suggest that the number be odd. When the Board transacts official business, key decisions must be submitted to the entire group for a vote. Since a majority vote of the members of the Board is usually sufficient to effect or to ratify any resolutions, the odd number of members ensures that there *always* will be a majority. In most states, the minimum number of Directors required by statute (where there is more than one stockholder) is three. Ordinarily, the Board will include a Chairman, a Treasurer, and a Secretary. The President of the company serves on the Board of Directors. It is not uncommon to have one or more of the company Vice Presidents serve on the Board. As the size of a corporation grows, it may become necessary to enlarge the Board to provide the company with as broad a range of experience and assistance as is financially and administratively practical.

Again, bear in mind that the members of the Board of Directors of a small company are in a position to provide specialized services to that enterprise, which might otherwise require the services of full-time employees. The number of individuals on the Board of a small business should be sufficient to provide the company officers with guidance and consultative assistance in those administrative areas in which they have the least capability or in which an independent, objective appraisal is desired.

Composition—Who?

Philosophically, the stockholders must decide whether they want a Board that will simply "rubber stamp" the recommendations of the company's senior officers, or whether the advice and counsel of outside Directors will benefit the company. Even if all of the stockholders are company officers, the decision regarding the possible benefits of outside Director participation on the Board is of no small importance.

If the decision is made to limit Directorship to company officers, no further discussion is warranted. However, if outside advice and counsel are perceived to be of potential value, then who should be chosen? And why?

Furthermore, assembling a prestigious Board should not only result in the rendering of sage counsel to the company officers. A well-chosen Board may also significantly influence the attitudes of present or potential investors, lenders, customers, vendors, and possibly even government regulators—domestic and foreign.

To begin with a selection discussion, it may be easiest to discuss who should *not* sit on the Board. A good rule of thumb is that no *supplier of services to the company* should sit on the Board. That means attorneys, CPA's, bankers, advertising agency executives, consultants, etc. Aside from conflict-of-interest concerns, it is simply unwise to have as Board members individuals who (or individuals representing organizations that) are vendors to the company. Pricing of vendor services or termination of vendor services simply gets to be too sticky an issue.

In deliberating selection criteria for Board members, one might include consideration of the following questions:

1. Will the candidate complement or supplement strengths of the officers or compensate for weaknesses of the officers?

2. Does the candidate have time to prepare for—and attend—all Board meetings?

3. Will the candidate be reasonably compatible with the other board members?

4. Does the candidate have a genuine interest in the business of the company?

5. Can the candidate be relied upon for candor and integrity and not shrink away from the "creative tension" that sometimes surrounds consideration of key policy issues and often results in the identification of significant growth opportunities?

6. Is the candidate "well connected" as a part of a larger network that may be of help to the company?

There is still one more question asked all too infrequently when deliberating the issue of Board composition:

7. Are both genders represented on the Board, and are there special reasons for seeking a particular racial, ethnic, age, political, or religious mix in Board composition?

Compensation

Board members are generally compensated for their services in the form of a fixed payment for each meeting in which they participate. Board members of small companies may receive fees as low as $100 per meeting. However, fees of $500, $1000, and more are not at all uncommon. One should bear in mind, however, that the assistance of a Board of Directors should represent an *economy* to the small business. Therefore, the fees of the Directors should not represent a greater drain on the company coffers than would the retention of a full-time staff of qualified executives or the retention of the services of professional consultants on a contract basis.

Remember that the individuals who will serve on the Board must have a sincere desire to assist the enterprise and to take a personal interest in it. Therefore, if the proposed Board members seem overly concerned with the fees they will receive for their services, there is an excellent probability that the company would do better to seek the services of other candidates.

Supporting Professional Service Agencies

Regardless of the kind of business you plan to start, your enterprise will require the services of a law firm, an accounting firm, a bank, and an insurance agency. To be more precise, you will need the services of professionally qualified *individuals:* a *lawyer,* an *accountant,* a *banker,* and an *insurance agent.* In this section, it is imperative that entrepreneurs recognize that in dealing with service organizations, they are dealing with individuals. Select them carefully.

How to Select a Law Firm

Based on the reading I have done, the discussions I have had with other business executives, and my own personal experience in acquiring the services of several different law firms to assist me in business ventures of my own, I have concluded that it is no small task to locate a qualified law firm—one staffed to meet your special business needs. Although many local Bar Associations have established Lawyer Referral Services, which may be found listed in the Yellow Pages of the telephone book under the heading "Attorneys," I would not advise the entrepreneur to attempt to locate satisfactory corporate counsel using such services. According to a statement made in the *ABA Journal* (reprinted here with permission), "The Lawyer Referral Service is the Bar's only organized effort at making competent legal service available to people of moderate means . . . . " In other words, the Lawyer Referral Service exists primarily to assist *individuals* in locating legal counsel to help them with their personal problems. It is hardly a suitable resource to use in attempting to locate satisfactory *corporate* counsel.

If you had a medical problem and wished to locate a specialist, you would probably inquire of your friends and acquaintances to determine the name of someone they knew who had had a similar medical problem. You would then contact the person who had the problem, obtain the name of the attending physician, and ascertain whether or not the service obtained was satisfactory. In the selection of corporate counsel, the same process appears to be useful: Locate a relatively new business engaged in an activity similar to but not in direct competition with the one you contemplate. The management of the company should be flattered to have you ask their advice and may be quite willing to provide you with whatever information you ask for regarding their legal counsel. By asking the same questions of several companies, you should be able to compile a list of several competent firms.

Next, make appointments with representatives of each firm. Since it is likely that the attorney will enjoy a worthwhile financial return if successful in obtaining you as a client, there is generally no charge for such an introductory meeting. However, this matter should be discussed at the time the appointment is arranged to insure against any misunderstandings.

At the first meeting with a new attorney whose services you are considering, be prepared to discuss in some detail the plans you have for your new enterprise. You should also consider in advance the type of questions you wish answered in order to satisfy yourself that the law firm can provide the service your enterprise will require. You should make certain that the firm represents no clients who are competitors of yours, and you should not hesitate to openly discuss the lawyer's fees.

Other factors to be considered have to do with the firm's work load. If the firm is inadequately staffed, it is unlikely that you will receive the kind of service you require. On the other hand, if the firm appears to be seriously lacking business, there may be a very good reason for it. You should determine the experience of the staff, their ages, education, and legal qualifications. Finally, you should determine to your own satisfaction whether or not there is empathy between you and the attorney. If you get the feeling that the attorney is doing you a favor in taking you on as a client, it is doubtful that any ensuing relationship will be mutually satisfactory.

Finally, entrepreneurs should make a point of talking with more than one firm to satisfy themselves that they have a basis for comparison and will thus be able to pick the firm with which they feel most satisfied. Additional information on each firm considered may be found in the individual listings in the *Law Directory,* the publication that many recent law school graduates consult in seeking information on possible firms with which they may seek an affiliation as a junior partner.

In discussing your requirements with a candidate attorney, you should attempt to learn whether or not the firm has had extensive experience in dealing with new companies. Determine if the firm has seen many companies through the incorporation phase, if they have drawn up many partnership agreements, if they can be of assistance in locating private sources of venture capital. In other words, you should attempt to learn all of the services that the firm can offer you.

How to Select an Accounting Firm

An accounting firm can provide many necessary and worthwhile services to a new enterprise. Assistance may include but is not limited to:

1. Helping in establishing and maintaining a sound accounting system.

2. Reviewing the company's books in order to advise the company officers regarding their financial progress and the possibility of improving corporate financial performance. Independent analysis of inventory, budget and working capital problems, and cost accounting and management studies are all within the understanding of a good accountant.

3. Proper handling of tax matters. This service is of the utmost importance to a new company. In many instances, policies regarding the handling of tax matters are very difficult to change later on. For example, determining whether accounting will be on a cash, accrual, or modified accrual basis, and arranging techniques for depreciating assets require a very careful evaluation.

4. Assisting a client company in securing additional financing through a bank or other financial source. The accounting firm is uniquely qualified to help the company prepare a financial presentation for use in a fund-raising effort.

Locating a suitable accounting firm for the new business is handled in much the same way as locating corporate legal counsel. There are three primary factors to be considered in the selection of an accounting firm:

1. The firm should have a well-established reputation for integrity and competence. The names of such firms may be obtained from established businesses by requesting that they refer you to firms with which they are familiar and which they regard as reputable and competent.

2. Interviews with candidate accounting firms should be arranged. During these interviews the entrepreneur should determine whether or not the experience, professional knowledge, training, and skill of the staff of the firm is sufficient for the needs of the new business.

3. By checking with major clients of the accounting firm and by discussing the subject with representatives of the accounting firm, the entrepreneur should determine if the firm will be in a position to provide the time and service that the new business will require. Accounting firms range in size from small local organizations all the way up to the "Big Eight." Typically, the fees required by a large firm may be higher than the fees charged by a smaller firm, and the matter of fees may not be a trivial consideration in the selection of an accounting firm for a small new business.

Auditing is one of the most frequently overlooked services that an accounting firm can provide. Whether the company anticipates a need for additional financing at a later date, whether the company founders anticipate the possibility that they will seek to be merged with or acquired by another corporation, or whether the founders wish to make sure that the company is not being subjected to the handiwork of an embezzler, a regular independent audit will prove to be of enormous value. If only for the reason of this audit, a new firm *must* give serious consideration to engaging the services of an accounting firm.

How to Select a Commercial Bank

When looking for a banking firm, one of the most important considerations a small new company should bear in mind is this: Will the bank be there when you need their help? Consider that any bank can provide the routine services of maintaining accounts, clearing checks, and providing traveler's checks and safe deposit boxes. As the founder of a new business, you should consider each of the following factors in your evaluation of a commercial bank.

Credit and Loan Policies. You should determine how much credit the bank is prepared to extend to you. You should also determine the interest rates you may be expected to pay, the extent to which your credit may have to be collateralized, the requirements of the bank regarding compensating balances (i.e., if you borrow $10,000 and the bank requires that you maintain a minimum balance of $2000 in your account, that $2000 represents a compensating balance; you are in effect borrowing only $8000 while paying interest on $10,000).

1. Is the bank familiar with your type of business? Typically, bankers are conservative people. They are much less likely to be liberal in their loan policies when dealing with industries with

which they are not familiar than they would be when dealing with industries they understand well. Therefore, it would be wise for the entrepreneur to determine what industries are represented by the bank's existing clientele.

2. Is it the bank's announced policy to encourage small businesses, or does the bank appear to be primarily concerned with the financing of automobiles and appliances?

3. Does the bank make provision for extending credit against accounts receivable?

4. A bank's financial statement can provide a considerable amount of information about its management attitudes. If most of the bank's assets are in the form of readily liquidated securities, it is probably safe to assume that the bank management is ultra-conservative. Should you require a loan from this bank under marginal circumstances, it is unlikely that you would receive it. On the other hand, if many of the bank's assets are represented by assets not readily liquidated, you may assume that the bank's attitude toward loans is quite liberal. The offsetting factor may be that the liberal bank does not represent as secure a repository for the new company's funds as does the more conservative bank. It is also difficult to get a loan from a liberal bank that is in trouble because of too many bad loans.

Empathic Management. You should attempt to determine whether or not the bank officers have any basic empathic interest in you and the needs of your business. Do the bankers appear to be at least willing, if not eager, to render whatever assistance they can to the new enterprise? Are they young tigers, eager to build new accounts through the encouragement of entrepreneurship in hopes of cultivating the Xerox of tomorrow? Or are they sedate executives on the verge of retirement, who don't want to try *anything* that might jeoparidze their imminent pension? Alternatively, are they young lambs who have no idea as to what they can get away with, who are afraid to try anything? Or are they old pros who will bend as far as the law will allow, fully confident of their ability to assess the prevailing economic climate and the willingness of the bank to rely on their seasoned judgment? How willing are the bankers to assist the entrepreneur in obtaining credit information on customers and suppliers? How willingly do they supply other information that will be of help to the new enterprise?

How knowledgeable are the bankers? Do they have a good understanding of the broad services available in the financial marketplace? Do they appear to have insight into private financing? Are they in a position to recommend an accounting firm, a legal firm, or other business services? Are they in a position to provide you with the kinds of business contacts that will assist your company in growing rapidly?

Looking at the financial needs of your own small business through the eyes of your banker can give to you an appreciation of the banker's perspective. Consider the investment position of a bank. The bank's main source of income is the interest received from loans. Therefore, the loan interest rates the bank charges represent a very real ceiling on the investment returns. The risk, however, on the types of loans a bank generally makes is necessarily also very low due to strictly enforced federal and state standards—the bank makes low-risk investments and must content itself with low returns. Another reason for this conservatism is that most bank deposits are placed on a "demand" basis—bank patrons may withdraw their funds whenever they wish. Therefore, bankers must make allowance for the possibility that a significant number of depositors may request the withdrawal of their funds within a short period of time. (This is called a "run on the bank"—no laughing matter.) The bank must thus maintain low-risk investments that can be easily liquidated; equity in a company or a high-risk loan to a new business clearly is not such an investment. Relative, then, to the other options available, bankers may find lending to your business too risky. They may, however, be able to assist in locating other financing for you—for example, though a bank-owned Small Business Investment Company or the Small Business Administration.

In summary, banking is an industry, a competitive one. Therefore, it is to the entrepreneur's advantage to select the one institution that is in a position to offer the greatest and most flexible resources in satisfying the financial needs of the new enterprise. The entrepreneur should select the most progressive banker to be found, one who can also satisfy the unique requirements of the company.

How to Select an Insurance Agency

In today's complex business community, providing broad insurance coverage for any enterprise requires the attention of the trained and knowledgeable staff of a professional insurance agency. The following is a list of some of the services you may wish to have provided by your insurance agency. There are several different types of business life insurance, each one serving a specialized function.

Key-Man Insurance. Any new enterprise depends very heavily on the unique talents of its founders. The death of any one of them could prove a mortal blow to the foundling business or result in serious financial loss due to the interruption of business or the subsequent retardation of growth. Key-Man Insurance provides an allowance that will enable the company to recruit and train a successor and reduce the loss in profitability during the training period. (Although this type of coverage has always been called Key *Man* Insurance, you may be sure that it is available without regard for the gender of the people involved.)

Partnership Insurance. Unless legal provision has been made to the contrary, a partnership automatically dissolves at or shortly after the death of any partner. With foresight, the members of the partnership can make appropriate arrangements to avoid the consequences of this disaster. Their business attorney and insurance agent can work together to draw up a partnership insurance policy in which provision can be made to retire a deceased partner's interest in the business. Thereby the continuity of business operations is ensured, and the beneficiaries are provided for with an equitable recompense for the deceased partner's share of the business.

Shareholder Insurance. If a single stockholder retains a substantial equity in the small business, the company officers and remaining stockholders may wish to take steps to protect their interest against the possibility that, should this major shareholder die, a new stockholder whose interests are prejudicial to those of the remaining stockholders and company officers would gain a controlling interest in the company. An insurance policy on the life of a major stockholder can provide for the outright purchase of that stockholder's interest in the event of death, thus insuring that the company will maintain its continuity.

Sole Proprietorship Insurance. Approximately seventy-five percent of the businesses in this country are sole proprietorships. Such businesses often provide regular jobs for many employees. The death of the proprietor can cause significant inconvenience and even hardship for the surviving employees. Sole Proprietorship Insurance can provide for a lump-sum payment to the family or beneficiaries of the deceased while simultaneously insuring the continuity of the business for the protection of the staff.

Other Types of Insurance. Other types of insurance include public liability insurance; comprehensive, personal injury, broad-form property damage, blanket contractual, and products insurance; security and theft insurance, including robbery, safe, and alarm system insurance; surety bonds for employees; Directors' and Officers' liability insurance; plate glass insurance; accounts receivable insurance; fire insurance, including extended coverage, special extended coverage ("all risk"), and sprinkler damage insurance; automobile insurance, including physical damage and nonownership of automobile insurance, boiler insurance; earthquake insurance; business interruption insurance; disability insurance; and medical/hospital/surgical insurance. In these days of terrorist activity, even kidnap ransom insurance can be purchased for the top managers of the firm.

Having reviewed this bewildering array of various insurance options available to businesses, it should be readily apparent that so complex a field warrants the attention of a qualified specialist—the business insurance broker. As was the case with the law firm, accounting firm, and bank, the insurance broker must be empathic with the client. The most effective means of locating such a broker is by obtaining referrals and then investigating them. Bear in mind when looking for the services of an insurance broker that you are not merely buying insurance, you are buying a service. Just as you would not seriously consider acquiring the services of a physician merely because you know this doctor to be the least expensive practitioner whose services are available, you should not evaluate the services of a particular insurance broker solely on the basis of the price of the coverage offered. Insurance is critical to any business, and the entrepreneur should be very sensitive to the difference between an order-taking insurance clerk and a bona-fide broker equipped with the education, background, and desire to serve clients effectively.

Remember also that the founders can anticipate and make allowance for everything but the unexpected. Insurance provides blanket protection against the unexpected; the insurance broker assists the founders in making provision for what they cannot anticipate and, thus, for what many new businesses overlook. Proper insurance coverage for a new enterprise thus results in a significant reduction of financial risk. Therefore, financing may be obtained much more easily for the well-insured new enterprise.

The Market To Be Served

In this section of your formal business plan, you should provide a detailed analysis of the market to be served by the new enterprise. Here the founders should provide a showcase of the knowledge and expertise with which they expect to realize substantial competitive advantages in their target market.

Document Your Assertions

The member(s) of the founding team responsible for marketing should investigate every major available source of marketing intelligence. These resources include leading trade, professional, and financial journals, industry and trade associations, the U.S.

Department of Commerce (see *"Uncle Sam Wants* (to help) *You!"* in Chapter 6), and organizations specializing in the field of market analysis. Several of the primary information sources in this latter category include:

Stanford Research Institute
333 Ravenswood Avenue
Menlo Park, California 94025

Arthur D. Little, Inc.
25 Acorn Park
Cambridge, Massachusetts 02140

Battelle Memorial Institute
505 King Avenue
Columbus, Ohio 43201

Frost and Sullivan, Inc.
106 Fulton Street
New York, New York 10038

Predicasts, Inc.
200 University Circle Research Center
11001 Cedar Avenue
Cleveland, Ohio 44106

For a comprehensive annotated guide to statistical and informational material about business trends and consumer and industrial markets, see *Data Sources for Business and Market Analysis* by Nathalie D. Frank and John V. Ganly (3rd ed., 1983). This book covers government publications, university programs, research institutions, trade associations, and many other sources. Copies are available from the Scarecrow Press, Inc., 52 Liberty Street, Box 656, Metuchen, New Jersey 08840.

Finally, the U.S. Department of Commerce, Bureau of the Census, offers an extensive selection of current industrial reports including data on the production, inventories, and orders for 5000 products representing forty percent of all U.S. manufacturing. To obtain additional information on these government reports, request Form POF 386 from the Bureau of the Census, Washington, D.C. 20233.

List Major Potential Customers

A valuable aid to inspiring confidence in a potential investor is a roster of potential customers, complete with estimated annual sales to each and a brief justification for this prediction. However, forecasts of the length of time necessary to cultivate customers and to establish the flow of new purchase orders are frequently overly optimistic, and the investor will be understandably suspicious of them. Thus, wherever possible, actual purchase orders or letters of intent expressing the customer's willingness to purchase the products of the proposed new firm should be included in the Appendix of the business plan.

Analyze Major Competitors

A listing of the new firm's major competitors should be included in the business plan, along with a brief discussion of their strengths, weaknesses, estimated market share, and profitability. Provide also an analysis of how your company plans to cope with this competition—and your plans for capitalizing on competitor weaknesses and for meeting the challenges represented by your competitors' strengths. Much intelligence on your competitors' marketing programs can be had by examining their annual reports (if the stock is publicly traded) or by obtaining a report from one of the major independent credit rating services (your banker or accountant can normally assist you here).

Estimate Market Share

If a new business is to be viable, it must plan to control a certain minimum share of its market. To be a significant force within its market, the volume of its business must be such that its actions are "felt" by the rest of the market. Otherwise, the business is just another "Me, too" company and is subject to the mercy of those firms that dominate the market. Your business plan, then, should include an estimate of the share of the market you plan to capture.

Polish Your Crystal Ball

Anyone involved in the launching of a new enterprise is interested in an assessment of the projected annual growth rate for the market the company will serve. Most investors find the prospect of financing a company that may capture a small percentage of a rapidly growing market far more appealing than the prospect of underwriting a company likely to secure a substantial share of a market with a diminishing annual volume and an uncertain future growth. Sources of such information were suggested earlier in this chapter.

Discuss Product Timing

In these days when accelerated obsolescence is commonplace in almost any new market and when half the products we will be using five years from now haven't been invented yet, *timing* occupies a position of considerable importance in evaluating the prospects for success of a new product. Almost every industry has its own hula hoop, but remember that today's demand for vacuum-tube hi-fi sets is just about as great as its demand for washboards.

The subject of product-timing invites hours of discussion and pages of exposition. The dilemma is this: You must be neither too early nor too late with your product. The automobile industry provides us with two excellent examples—decades ahead of its time was the Studebaker *Avanti;* born too late, and subjected to much ridicule, was the Ford *Edsel.*

The Products and/or Services

This section of the business plan should provide an in-depth review of the product and/or service to be marketed—the revenue-producing item on which the company founders are willing to stake their future. The following discussion will highlight the major features to consider in the introduction of a new product or service. The discussion is intended to be comprehensive and practical. However, the peculiar characteristics of any innovative product or service may demand highly individual treatment.

Competitive Features

In preparing a business plan, one must give careful consideration to those factors which will prompt a prospective customer to try your new product or service in preference to the product or service of your competitors.

Size. In many products, size is a factor of considerable importance. Consider, for example, the modern-day transistor radio, which is small enough to fit on your wrist or in a set of earphones. This reduced size was responsible for a substantially new market for radios.

Advances in modern electronics and materials technology have resulted in other new billion-dollar markets that did not exist before the prefix "mini." Portable two-way communications devices, pacemakers for cardiac patients, and contact lenses are just three examples of how size reduction due to advancing technology has opened new markets. Bigness, too, is a successful market by-product of technology. Today we have ships and airplanes with payload capacities undreamed of decades ago, and each new skyscraper seems taller than its older neighbor across the street.

Weight. The modern-day invention of lightweight products and materials has also resulted in the creation of new markets, the expansion of old or existing markets, and the conferral upon various innovators of an encouraging, satisfying share of a new market. Aviation and space exploration were particularly affected by all of this weight-reduction technology—modern-day feats obviously would not have been possible without it. The huge consumer markets have seen the by-products of this new technology in the form, to give one example, of very sturdy, lightweight luggage. Innovation in the freeze drying of foods has eliminated the necessity for carting the proverbial—and heavy—can of beans in your back-pack when you go camping. The agricultural industry provides us with another example of technology's attempts to alter weights—poultry producers have worked for years to produce turkeys and chickens that have more meat per animal and thus a higher weight per bird. Increased weight is also attractive in synthetic diamonds, and a major industry has rapidly emerged in the production of these and other synthetic gemstones.

Durability. As consumer interest groups come of age, federal regulation of product durability is becoming increasingly likely. Consumers are almost always concerned with durability in the products they buy. The entrepreneur who has a product to offer the market that is more durable than a competitors' product has a fair chance of enjoying substantial market acceptance. Recent years have seen new products such as five-year-lifetime light bulbs, chip-resistant dinnerware that is replaced free of charge if it sustains damage, and hardware designed to last for years in outer space.

At the other extreme, there is also an increasing demand for products intended for limited use. We have seen the emergence of paper garments, camera flashbulbs, and disposable containers. Today's marketplace, despite its fondness for durability, is enamored of ingeniously designed "throwaways."

Convenience. Convenience has become a highly marketable concept in this age of affluence and opulence. The automation of toothbrushes, pencil sharpeners, egg beaters, blenders, lawnmowers, hedge trimmers, industrial screwdrivers and wrenches, etc., afford the mechanically inclined entrepreneur with product and market opportunities limited only by the ingenuity of the Engineering Department. Consumer willingness to embrace new products which mechanize formerly manual operations appears to be nearly limitless.

Convenience is one of the primary features of any service enterprise and should be given particular attention in a business proposal that is concerned with a service industry. Factors such as location, hours of business operation, and/or availability of personnel may prove to be of the utmost importance. Obviously a beauty or barber shop that is open sixteen hours a day, seven days a week is providing its clientele greater convenience than is the shop that operates five days a week on a nine hour day. The same also applies to food services.

Quality. Where price remains constant, there is always a market for a properly promoted product that has a higher quality than the product offered by the competition. The convenience food industry, which has always afforded those with a yen for their own businesses the opportunity to earn a living as franchisees, serves as an example—to this day, the term "homemade" is almost irresistible to consumers. In virtually every sector of industry, there is room for new companies that can provide higher quality products at a price equal to or lower than the prevailing price. Typically, however, the concept of quality is not easy to sell; a reputation must be established over a period of time. The assertion that one's goods or services are of superior quality must withstand the test of time. Therefore, although quality in the product is extremely important to the *survival* of any business, the reputation for quality cannot be depended upon to leap full-blown from the business plan. *Some* degree of quality is a necessity, but it is *not* a significant competitive advantage for a new enterprise. Maintaining a high level of quality over a sustained period of time will, however, enhance growth of the new enterprise.

Price. Price is a fascinating topic. Everywhere there are markets where one particular product is priced over a broad range. In the food industry, one can pay 39 cents for a hamburger or $75 and up for a dinner in some swank supper club. One can buy a pair of shoes for $10 through a mail-order catalog or have a pair custom-made for more than $1000. Considerations involved in the establishment of a price for a given commodity or service are subtle indeed. Even in industries that are highly competitive, such as the cosmetics field, one finds products representing a wide variation in price. Even in the area of governmental procurement, where product specifications are typically very clearly delineated, one frequently finds intense price competition. Entrepreneurs preparing their business plans should find an interesting and demanding challenge in their efforts to persuade investors that their pricing will be such as to promise significant market share while simultaneously providing a satisfactory return on the invested dollar.

Customer Service. Where products are offered, some consideration must be given to customer service. Provision must be made for the repair of broken or defective products either through a nationwide network of repair agencies or by means of a special department at the factory to which customers can return products for replacement, repair, or servicing.

In formulating the business plan, entrepreneurs should give careful consideration to the warranty program they plan to offer with their products. They must also determine what office procedures will be needed to monitor such programs. The long-term success of any business rests heavily on the reputation it is able to establish in the area of customer service.

If the product is a new one, the entrepreneur must plan for the expense and effort necessary to educate the customer in the use of the product. For example, the introduction of a new computer may require the development of an educational program to instruct the purchaser or lessee in its use.

Standardization and Compatibility. In those industries where the major competitor's product is firmly entrenched, an entrepreneur may successfully compete by offering a line of products compatible with the popular product on a replacement basis. One example of this approach may be seen in the computer industry, where literally hundreds of manufacturers now offer products that are designed to replace parts of the system provided by the original supplier. Viewing this subject from a different point of view, it may be possible to offer to the market a product so designed that it may be readily repaired by removing an easily accessible part and replacing it with a new one.

In a service, standardization is of primary importance. If California-bottled Coca-Cola were to taste differently from Florida-bottled Coca-Cola, there might be some serious problems in the marketing of the product. The means for securing and maintaining standardization in a service industry (which relies heavily on the vagaries of regional labor markets) is of the utmost importance.

Patents. This subject has been covered at length in previous sections of the book (see Chapter 8). Suffice it to say that possession of a well-drawn patent, coupled with the financial resources to defend it properly, will provide any new business with a significant advantage in the marketplace, provided that the new product concept itself is a viable one. (A patent, you will recall, is a license for a monopoly affording protection to the holder for a period of seventeen years.)

Proprietary Content. In some instances, a product, although not protectable with a patent, may be afforded the protection of *covenants of secrecy.* Manufacturing processes and secret formulas often have protection of this kind. If the proposed business is in the food industry, for example, certain recipes—like that for Colonel Sanders' Kentucky Fried Chicken—can prove to be of enormous long-term value.

Pictures

In order to better communicate the idea for your product or service to the investment community, it is wise to include illustrations of the product to be offered. If drawings or photographs of individual parts would assist the reader in visualizing the proposed product, include them. Depending on how elaborate the business proposal is, these illustrations may either be in black and white or color. However, it must be borne in mind that the quality of the illustrations is quite important. Poorly rendered drawings may do more harm than good in your efforts to interest a prospective investor.

Manufacturing Process

This section of the business plan should be devoted to a discussion of whatever steps are necessary to actually produce items for sale. If specialized machinery is required in the manufacture of the product, this machinery should be described in detail. Features of the product should be discussed from the standpoint of ease of manufacture. If the product requires the assembly of a number of component parts, some of which may be procured outside the company, an analysis of these factors is most appropriate. If the procurement of parts, equipment, or raw materials may pose problems, a plan for handling each of these problems should be presented.

Cost Breakdowns

Where appropriate, a list of every part that goes into the product should be prepared. Such a document is commonly referred to as a "Bill of Materials." Pricing on each of these parts in small and large quantities should be indicated. Where practical, a step-by-step sequence of drawings should be prepared to illustrate the various phases in product assembly and testing, all the way up to and including packaging and shipping. Ideally, each step in this process will be separately identified and characterized in terms of the time required to perform indicated operations, cost in terms of raw materials and direct time (the real wage rate paid the person performing each individual step), and overhead and administrative charges. Since this figure varies widely from industry to industry, more specific references are included in the recommended reading list.

A breakeven analysis, which simply shows the point at which total sales revenues will equal total costs, should be included in your analysis. The breakeven point should be shown both in terms of units of goods and dollar volume. (Any basic cost accounting text will provide you with a simple method of computing the breakeven point.) This is a particularly helpful calculation for a manufacturing firm to present, since costs per unit of goods produced can drop significantly as the volume produced increases.

State of the Art

In many industries characterized by rapid growth, there is a concept called the "State of the Art," which refers to the condition of the industry in terms of technical advancement or present status and rate of change. In preparing the business plan, entrepreneurs should give consideration to an analysis of their industry and their product. If they are proposing a venture into an industry where products may be obsolete within a short period of time, the proposed venture may turn out to be a disaster. The proposal should contain a realistic evaluation of these factors and a discussion of the founders' plans for dealing with the eventualities of product obsolescence and for keeping up with, or ahead of, rapidly changing technology. In concluding your discussion of the State of the Art, be certain to identify individually those factors that characterize the new company product and those factors that will serve to protect it from a competitive contest with the product of a larger and better-financed corporation.

Marketing Strategy

No doubt many of you have already heard that the days have passed when the world would beat a path to your door if you invented a better mouse trap. Well, they have. A new product today must receive the benefits of careful marketing strategy in order to be accepted and to be successful. Failure to implement proper strategy may provide a capable competitor with an opportunity to produce a similar product that *is* assisted by a superior marketing plan, with the result that the product originators are deprived of any advantage they might have enjoyed had they properly marketed their product in the first place.

Promotional Methods

This section of the business plan should include a discussion of the promotional methods to be employed in bringing the product or service to the attention of the end user. These methods may include trade-journal advertising, direct-mail advertising, or newspaper and television advertising. A new-product news release and news releases announcing the formation of the company are musts in providing inexpensive media coverage. Additional sources of publicity for the company, its founders, and its products are technical articles written for publication in trade and professional journals. Whether or not the founders decide to use the services of an advertising agency depends on the financial resources of the founders and the magnitude of the advertising campaign they wish to undertake. Advertising agencies do not always obtain fees directly from their clients; instead, they obtain commissions from the media in which they place the advertising material. In other cases, however, retainers and/or fees are demanded.

Advertising Efforts

When contemplating a promotional campaign, the entrepreneur may be confronted with a bewildering array of communications media including radio, television, newspapers, magazines, billboards, direct mail, and even those (to my mind) unwelcome intermission spots at the local theater. When an advertising campaign is crucial to the success of a business, the business plan should discuss the proposed campaign in detail. It is suggested that the services of a competent advertising agency be engaged to assist with the preparation of such a plan.

Distribution

The subject of product and/or service distribution is fascinating. There are an enormous number of channels available if the individual with marketing responsibility simply exercises ingenuity in discovering them. The following list is intended merely to suggest a few of the avenues open to the imaginative entrepreneur.

Point-of-Sale Manufacturing. This is the most basic form of product or service distribution. The man or woman operating a beauty salon is engaged in the business of direct selling. The same is true of a restaurant that prepares food to order for its clientele. Any situation in which a product or service is prepared and supplied at the point of sale is referred to as a direct sale. Variations on this approach are represented in the two following sections.

Direct Mail. In those instances where customers are far removed from the supplier, direct mail may afford entrepreneurs a satisfactory means of marketing their products. For example, a major manufacturer of vitamins in this country manages to sell a large volume of merchandise by distributing copies of its catalog to potential clients, who then mail their orders to the manufacturer. Computer dating is an example of a service that has been successfully distributed through the mails. Literally billions of dollars worth of products are sold annually by direct mail, according to the Direct Marketing Association.

Direct Sales Through Salaried or Commissioned Salespeople. A company can also bring its products to its customers through an organization of company sales representatives. In some instances, these sales representatives receive compensation not only in the form of wages or salary but also in the form of commissions and bonuses. An example is the sale of Allstate Insurance by Sears, Roebuck and Company—the sales reps who offer this service to the marketplace are employees of Sears. Many large manufacturing organizations, such as Hewlett-Packard, an electronics equipment manufacturer, offer their products for sale through their staff of salaried sales representatives.

In each of the above instances of direct selling, middleman fees (commissions or discounts offered to persons or organizations outside of the company) are either minimized or eliminated. However, in many instances the products of a new company require a more elaborate distribution organization. The following examples discuss some of these channels.

Wholesalers (Jobbers). It is often customary for a manufacturer of consumer products to sell goods at a discounted price to wholesalers or jobbers, who in turn distribute their purchases to retail outlets within their territory.

Industrial Distributors. These organizations or individuals function in relation to their industrial clients as wholesalers function in relation to their retail clients. An industrial distributor typically purchases products for resale to industrial clients. An example of an industrial supplier is the modern-day steel service center. A steel service center may purchase raw materials from a large number of geographically dispersed suppliers and offer them for sale to local industrial clients.

Private Label. A number of the major retailing organizations in the United States, such as Sears and Roebuck and Montgomery-Ward, regularly sell products that are manufactured by independent suppliers. These independent suppliers build products for major outlets on a contractual basis. A set of product specifications is usually drawn up by the retailer, who then solicits bids from various manufacturers who are qualified to manufacture the desired products. Subsequently a manufacturer is selected to produce the desired products that will bear the label of the retail organization.

Premiums. A number of products are marketed today as premiums. For example, computer dealers may offer a free software package to the consumer who purchases more expensive, often newer, software the dealer really wants to sell.

Manufacturers' Representatives. In the instances where much contact with the customer is required and the company finances are such that a full-scale company-employed sales force is not practical, the manufacturers' representative provides a very convenient solution. Typically, a manufacturers' representative or a manufacturers' representative organization will carry a broad line of products representing the offerings of several manufacturers. Ideally, these products will complement each other. As an example, a manufacturers' rep or agent supplying manufacturing machinery may carry one manufacturer's lathes, a different manufacturer's drill presses, and still another manufacturer's milling machines.

Some of the advantages of using a manufacturers' representative organization accrue from the fact that the agents work exclusively on a commission basis. Ordinarily, when a sale is completed, the manufacturer bills the end customer and, after receipt of payment from the customer, forwards a commission check to the manufacturers' representative. As a result, if sales are slow, selling costs are also reduced. Thus, manufacturers are able to determine in advance a significant part of their costs. Manufacturers' agents will generally cover a relatively small geographical area with a broad line of products. They are thus in a position to uncover new markets for your product while they try to interest a potential customer in the purchase of some noncompeting product in their lines.

Terms of Sale

In times when money is in short supply (and for new companies this is most of the time), the determination of the terms of sale of the products can be of primary significance in market penetration and in the company's ability to survive financially. To achieve significant market penetration, a new company frequently may find it necessary to resort to financing techniques that will benefit the customer in order to induce them to try the new products. Commonly, two techniques in financing the sale of new products are used.

Net Thirty Days. The most common form of sale financing is the maintenance of a thirty-day accounts receivable credit basis. Typically, a small discount is offered the customer in return for full payment within a ten-day period. Unfortunately, when the money markets are tight for the customers as well as the new companies, customer credit can extend to sixty and even ninety days or longer. The diligence with which the new company plans to pursue collection of overdue accounts receivable will rest in part on recognition of the fact that some customers may not regard paying their bills as something they care to do. Therefore, a new company may find itself at a competitive disadvantage in insisting on prompt payment of all accounts receivable. Not uncommmonly, although sale terms will dictate a thirty-day turnover in accounts receivable, a new company must realistically plan on a sixty- to ninety-day turnover period unless it is prepared to lose those potential customers who make a practice of stretching credit terms.

Product Leasing. In today's marketplace, product leasing is becoming increasingly common as a means of financing the sale of "big ticket" items. Mainframe computers and other expensive equipment are rarely sold on a cash basis. Ordinarily, customers are very reluctant to part with a large amount of capital for the purchase of such equipment. Thus, it has become common for the customer to be afforded the option of leasing the desired equipment. In some instances, manufacturers may be able to make leasing arrangements with a bank or other financial institution. Then the manufacturers sell their products for cash to the financial institution, which in turn leases the products to the end users.

Delivery/Performance Timing

Since the beginning of recorded business history, the customer has demanded "delivery yesterday." A new company planning a program of rapid market penetration must give considerable attention to the problems of supplying customer delivery requirements on a consistently reliable basis.

When a new company is supplying parts to a major user, the importance of delivery cannot be overemphasized. Consider a situation of a major manufacturer-customer who has hundreds of thousands of dollars tied up in in-process assemblies. If the assembly lines and the delivery of large products or systems are held up due to a shortage of relatively inexpensive parts, suppliers of the late parts will find that the welcome mat for them has been withdrawn, possibly on a permanent basis. And in those instances where a service is to be provided, customers generally have little patience with agencies that do not live up to their delivery commitments.

The characteristics of the market to be served should also be analyzed to determine whether or not it makes economic sense to provide customers with a line of products available from inventory or whether the market demands constant flow of custom-made devices. The latter case can prove to be particularly challenging for a small company. Nevertheless, this kind of market is one in which a new small company may typically find ready acceptance because of the inability of large corporations consistently to supply custom products in a short period of time. Unfortunately, as a small company grows, speed of custom product delivery typically suffers.

A New Twist

In some instances, acceptance of a new product may depend heavily on the ability of the supplier to provide a new gimmick to the intended market. Consider if you will the famous case of King C. Gillette, inventor of the first safety razor. Gillette found market acceptance of his new concept practically nil in the age of the straight-edge razor until he got the idea of giving away the blade holder with the sale of each packet of blades. Since the largest market he intended to reach was the market created by the introduction of his disposable blades, his purpose was served and customers accepted the product—a profitable result of Gillette's judgment! More recent examples can be found in the soft drink industry, where caffeine-free, sugar-free drinks with no preservatives and no artificial colors have been introduced to capitalize on the current wave of health-consciousness in American society.

Research and Development Program

In order to interest investors and to attract a well-qualified and capable staff, the company founders must give serious consideration at the outset to their plans for growth. A company that offers products to a market must anticipate having to refine their existing products and to develop new products. A company that offers a service must anticipate and provide for growth opportunities. A clearly written statement that describes a program for analyzing and exploiting new opportunities will do much to inspire confidence in the growth potential of the proposed enterprise. A discussion of possible anti-obsolescence programs and sources of funding for such programs follows.

Product Improvement

When the average enterprise begins operation, the products it offers to the marketplace are only one step removed from their prototypes. In other words, these early products are not particularly sophisticated. The products will no doubt successfully perform the function for which they were designed; however, details such as the cost of the individual parts, the materials used in the fabrication of these parts, and the aesthetics of the product will not have received much attention. The business plan for the new enterprise should include a program of product improvement within the master plan for corporate growth.

Process Improvement

Often, when a business is small, products are built in small quantities. The labor content in each product is typically high and the manufacturing process is usually inefficient. The formal business plan should include some discussion of how the company founders plan to increase their manufacturing efficiency, improve their delivery schedules, and reduce the unit cost of their product. Greater automation in the manufacturing process might be considered. In-house facilities for the manufacture of certain parts might also prove economical. In fact, the development of a brand-new manufacturing technology might result from a suitably planned research and development program, which should be discussed in this section of the business plan.

Development of New Products

The preceding two topics considered product and process improvement. In this section of the business plan, the founders should discuss their plans for the development of new products and new service ideas. Failure to plan for the development of new products is one of the primary factors in arresting the growth of a new enterprise.

After a new business offers a new product or concept to the marketplace, it has a limited period of time in which to enjoy its monopoly. If the company is successful and its product accepted in the market, the founders may be confident that their competition will make a vigorous attempt to copy their product. Therefore, it behooves the growth-minded founders to plan a program for the exploration and development of new products in order to retain whatever lead they may achieve at the outset.

Who Pays?

Plans for product improvement, process improvement, and new-product exploration and development are all well and good when one wishes to enlist the enthusiastic support of a prospective investor. However, the cost of carrying out these plans can prove to be quite substantial. If the *company* is to underwrite the cost of its internal research and development programs, then substantial profit margins must be realized on the original products in order to sustain the programs. Alternatively, outside capital must be obtained to finance the risky and expensive search for new products.

If the company's staff is well noted for excellence in a particular field, customer contracts may be obtained for development programs. In fact, many research organizations exist today for the exclusive purpose of developing new products for major clients. Your company, if you are lucky, can hitch a ride on this kind of gravy train. For example, if you have a contract to develop a new kind of plastic material that will satisfy the specialized needs of a particular customer, it may be possible for you to retain all rights to the manufacturing process and to the new material, both of which were developed with the customer's money. In return for its investment, the customer may receive a guaranteed price for the material for some contractually specified period of time.

In addition, the favorable tax treatment of R & D partnerships has led to a huge increase in the number of these arrangements in recent years. Cash-rich companies looking for tax shelters and hoping for substantial returns represent a large pool of potential financing that new businesses should not overlook. (For an informative discussion of this topic, contact the accounting firm of Arthur Young & Company at 800–344–8234 and request their booklet, "Research and Development Arrangements.")

The federal government has, throughout its history, been a major source of research and development funds for businesses. Although the government usually insists that all information resulting from such programs be disclosed, a company fortunate enough to develop a new product or process with federal money still enjoys a unique competitive advantage. They have developed an in-house know-how that their competitors do not have. A description of the manufacturing process is one thing; mastering the techniques of the process is another.

Plant Location and Related Considerations

In selecting the location for a new business, many factors must be evaluated. The determination of the location for a retail store is a highly specialized subject and will not be discussed here. However, material treating this subject is included in the recommended reading list. The following discussion concerns factors influencing the location of industrial enterprises.

Founder's Back Yard

There is often good reason for locating a new business in the founder's "back yard." For example, a new business should be located close to the founder's residence so that precious working time spent commuting to and from the business will be minimized. In addition, starting a new business places many stresses upon the founder's family; they should not be further burdened with adjusting to a new locale. Also, the founder will have cultivated a number of useful contacts within the community, which might get lost in the shuffle of a move to a new residence.

Customer Proximity

There are those business advisers who maintain that it is best for a new company to develop a local clientele, thereby eliminating travel expenses in sales campaigns. For example, if a company is located on the West Coast and attempts to cultivate new customers on the East Coast, it may cost the new company in the vicinity of $2000 every time a sales representative or other company representative has to visit customers.

On the other hand, there are those business advisers who maintain that it is very difficult for a new company to cultivate local customers when the staff may be very small and the building in which the company is located may be nothing but the residence of one of the founders. Customers who are far removed from the plant site cannot know what it looks like; and thus its frailty, which might frighten customers away, is successfully concealed.

However, the best procedure is probably the most obvious one. The new company should first attempt to develop local customers. If obtaining local customers proves difficult or impossible, then the radius of the company sales efforts should be expanded until customers are obtained.

Supplier Proximity

Many of the factors discussed under "Customer Proximity" are applicable to the topic of supplier proximity. The ability of the new company to maintain an adequate inventory of parts and raw materials and its ability to operate effectively without being in close proximity to major suppliers will determine whether or not the founders will wish to locate the facility close to their suppliers. If highly specialized supporting services are required (such as the fabrication of exotic materials) or, if occasional access to machinery representing prohibitively high capital investments for the small company is required, it may be *necessary* to locate the enterprise near a major supplier. If the new company uses raw materials that are expensive to transport, economy may also require that the plant be located close to the supplier.

Personnel Availability

In formulating plans for the new business, the founders must consider the availability of personnel resources. If a large number of hourly semi-skilled or unskilled workers is required, then the founders would be wise to locate in an area noted for its low labor rates. Conversely, if the company products demand the services of highly skilled scientists, engineers, and technicians, the company founders would be well advised to establish their business near a leading technical college or university.

Transportation Services

The availability of adequate transportation facilities may be very important in the success or failure of the business or in the determination of its growth rate. For example, a major importer of electronics equipment of my acquaintance has his warehouse located in an industrial park adjoining a major international airport. This location permits him to process all shipments while minimizing transportation delays.

Another company I know of is located next to a railroad siding. This firm manufacturers coil springs for mattresses. Although the raw material (wire) for these springs is delivered by truck, the company receives a freight car rate on the wire it buys because the supplier's standard price list reflects a lower rate for all customers, large or small, having access to railroad sidings.

Still another entrepreneur of my acquaintance operates his business within two miles of a small country airport. This founder happens to be an avid pilot, and he makes frequent use of the company aircraft in conducting his electronics business. Thus, he is able to enjoy the comforts and style of residing in the country simultaneously with the financial benefits of operating a high-technology electronics company.

Educational Facilities

High living costs, availability of skilled personnel, and proximity to a university all seem to go hand in hand. In many instances, a nearby university may provide a source of qualified staff members. Furthermore, if the university offers courses that are related to the activities of the new enterprise, professors and other learned people may be available to sit on the company's Board of Directors.

Investor Preferences

Some investors prefer to "plant" their money some place that is close enough so that they can drive their car down to the garden and watch the sprouts. Other investors are content to permit the founders considerable latitude in the utilization of their funds and merely require periodic reports on company progress. But the founders must be prepared for the possibility that the only way they can obtain funding is to locate the enterprise far from the place where they had originally intended to locate it.

Tax Climate

There are many economically depressed areas of this country and there are many foreign governments that are willing to give new industry a very favorable tax advantage to induce it to locate there. Where such opportunities are not inconsistent with the plans and expectations of the company founders, they may find that they will enjoy significant economic benefits from accepting such a government's offer. Details of the inducements that some countries, states, and towns use will be discussed in Section III.

--- **Concept in a Capsule** ---

While attending a seminar on venture capital at the University of Toronto, I had the great pleasure of hearing a seasoned entrepreneur extol the value of a well-prepared PERT (Program Evaluation and Review Technique) diagram as a tool to help visualize the process of launching a new venture and planning its subsequent growth. The speaker claimed that the PERT diagram was, in his opinion, one of the most important documents in his business plan.

Initially, this entrepreneur prepared an extensive list of his major corporate objectives in terms of product development programs, sales campaigns, establishment of a manufacturing facility, and so forth. Then he prepared another list itemizing all of the steps necessary for its realization. Subsequently, these steps were placed in little blocks on the PERT diagram; the blocks were connected with lines to demonstrate the sequential character of the development process. For example, a step requiring completion of a set of product specifications would have to precede a step calling for the initiation of a development program for the design of that product. The diagram might also show the development steps that can be completed independently rather than sequentially, thus demonstrating a savings in total elapsed time.

In addition to providing the management team with a valuable, worthwhile planning tool, the PERT diagram served another extremely useful purpose: It made a very favorable impression on the financiers! ($2.5 million worth!) On one large sheet of paper, it was possible to see every major step in the planned growth of the new company and to observe the relationship of each of these steps to every other step. The ease with which each phase of the planned corporate development could be studied inspired enormous confidence in the minds of the investors, and the founders' presentation of the concept was accepted for what it was: a carefully formulated strategy designed to minimize investor risk and maximize prospects for success. Considering the magnitude of the required funding and the conservatism of the participating investors, this proposal was financed in a remarkably short time. I have made a point of following the progress of this company. After two years of operation, growth has been substantial and prospects for continued success are excellent.

In summary, a PERT diagram, a flow chart, or another graphical representation of the steps involved in corporate growth serves two very important functions: (1) it is an invaluable planning aid and (2) it can be an extremely effective sales tool.

One of the foremost authorities in the country on this subject is James L. Halcomb, whose company was profiled in Chapter 1. For further information on the subject of PERT, the reader is invited to contact Jim or to consult some of the books referenced in the Recommended Reading List.

13

Appendix to
the Formal Business Plan

While the bulk of the formal business plan should suffice to enlist the interest and enthusiasm of the investor and provide entrepreneurs with an opportunity to place all of their thoughts regarding the business concept together on paper, the Appendix to the formal business plan should include a substantial part of the basic documentation necessary to support information presented in the main body of the proposal.

Sales Forecast

The most basic financial document in the entire business plan should be a conservatively prepared sales forecast. From the standpoint of presentation of the information, it may be displayed in either graphical, chart, or tabular form.

It is reasonable to expect that the founders will be able to project with some accuracy the sales they anticipate during the early months of company operation. Estimation of sales several years into the future will obviously have to be based on more speculative assumptions.

One of the least imaginative sales presentations or sales forecasts is represented by a simple "straight-line" sales growth pattern. It is preferable, however, to indicate sales figures on a monthly basis

179

for the first quarter of company operation, on a quarterly basis for the next seven to eleven quarters, and semi-annually or annually for two years beyond that point. Where possible, specific customers should be identified in the sales forecast. Particularly desirable would be the inclusion of firm customer orders or letters of intent from key future customers indicating their willingness to buy the company's products, along with some estimate of what dollar volume this would represent. Otherwise, or in addition to this, a list of the names of potential customers should be provided to support the sales forecast.

Also to be included with this information is any other material drawn from market research that describes the total market available in the industry to be served. Such a description places the founders in a position to offer data on their anticipated market share. This is not, however, the place for excessive optimism. For example, a projection of a market position equivalent to between five and ten percent of the total available market for a period of four to five years should appear perfectly creditable to a potential investor. However, when the founders of a new company assert that they expect to enjoy well over fifty percent of their available market in such a short period of time, the investor may laugh and toss the business plan into the wastebasket.

To repeat: The sales forecast is one of the most important documents in the entire business plan. It is the basis for all financial projections. In its preparation, the founders must compromise between the optimism necessary to insure an aggressive assault on the marketplace and the sensible projection that will interest the investor.

Pro Forma Financial Statements

Translated literally from the Latin, *pro forma* means "as a matter of form." However, in the context of contemporary accounting practice, the words pro forma indicate that the information presented is a representation of how things *might* be during some future period covered in a document. Therefore, a pro forma financial statement, for example, is a financial statement that represents projections into the future of current assumptions and information. The information for the pro forma financial statements should always be presented in tabular form. Commonly, the information is placed on spread sheets, which are forms designed especially for the presentation of financial information. Your local business stationer should be able to provide you with a supply of these forms.

If you have access to a microcomputer, you might use one of the many computerized spreadsheet packages available on the market, such as VisiCalc® or Lotus 1-2-3® and Symphony®, which will greatly simplify the process.*

To assist individuals in the preparation of pro forma financial statements, Bank of America publishes sample worksheets in its publication "Steps to Starting a Business," part of the Small Business Reporter series. Copies of this booklet may be obtained by writing to the Small Business Reporter, Bank of America, Dept. 3120, P. O. Box 37000, San Francisco, California 94137.

It is recognized that this section on pro forma financial statements is far from detailed. However, the subject of preparing financial statements is beyond the scope of this book. It is my intention here simply to describe these statements and indicate why they must be included in the business plan. Mention of several elementary texts is made at the end of this book under the heading, Recommended Readings. Finally, it is not a bad idea for the founders to acquire the services of an accountant to assist with the preparation of the financial materials.

Cash Flow Statement

The cash flow statement is fundamentally a presentation of two types of information: the sources of company funds and an indication of the uses to which these funds are put. Typically, sources of funds include equity money received from the sale of stock, from founder investments, from sales, and from loans. Under the heading "Uses" should be included information regarding purchase or rental of capital equipment, salaries, provision for taxes, cost of materials, etc. The cash flow statement should, in other words, provide the reviewer with a quick picture of the company liquidity. To determine in advance how stable a picture your pro forma cash flow statement presents of your proposed company, it is recommended that you consult books on ratio analysis and also information made available through Dun and Bradstreet on various operating ratios in different industries. It is desirable that your cash flow statement exude a rosy glow of financial health and demonstrate that the new company will always have a comfortable "cushion," or cash reserve, available in the event of unforeseen difficulties.

One of the basic problems with any new company is that a substantial amount of the operating capital may be tied up in inventory or in accounts receivable (orders shipped but not yet paid for by the customer). The young company might be quite profitable, but, if it

---

*VisiCalc® is a registered trademark of VisiCorp. Lotus 1-2-3® and Symphony® are trademarks of Lotus Development Corporation.

does not have enough money in the bank account to pay its own accounts payable when they are due, it is in financial difficulty no matter how great the assets represented by inventory and accounts receivable. A supplier cannot be expected to wait indefinitely for payment from you for goods you have disposed of in one way or another. Your suppliers do not wish to become the creditor for your customers. They are *your* creditors, and it is *your* responsibility to see that they are paid. You agreed upon certain terms and conditions when you made your original purchases from them, and it is unreasonable to expect a supplier to "hold the bag" until you collect from your customers. Thus, it is important for a new company to insure that it has sufficient *working capital* to bridge the gap between a supplier demanding payment now and a customer insisting upon paying later. Alternatively, extended terms from your suppliers and accelerated collections from your customers are called for.

Profit and Loss Statement (also called the Income Statement)

Of fundamental importance to anyone involved in business is company profitability. A company that operates for a sustained period of time without realizing a profit is certainly doomed to eventual financial failure. Profits are essential to long-term corporate survival. The profit-and-loss statement provides the reader with an indication of the financial performance of the business for the period of time covered in the report. For example, if a quarterly breakdown of profit and loss is provided for the first two years, the statement will indicate the profit (or loss) the company earned in each quarter.

An investor will be particularly concerned about how long after company start-up it will be before the enterprise shows a profit. It would be a gross understatement to say that a company with a sustained record of losses and no periods of profitability is financially unattractive. However, once a company starts realizing profits, its attractiveness to new investors is considerably enhanced.

In this context, the concept of "turn-around" (the point at which the company stops losing money and begins earning money) is of considerable importance. "Turn-around" is the time in the future when the company may look attractive to new investors. The value of the company may subsequently be established by applying the prevailing industry price-to-earnings multiplier to the earnings reflected in the profit-and-loss statement after "turn-around." Thus, the original financial backers may be afforded an opportunity to sell out their interest and realize a substantial capital gain—their reason for investing in the first place!

Balance Sheet

The balance sheet provides a running summary of the a[...]
liabilities of a business as of each date specified in the state[...]
investor may ascertain the net worth of the company by su[...]
the liabilities from the company assets. Evaluation of the [...]
entries in the balance sheet will enable the investors to visualize the
growth of their investments as the company develops and matures.

Projected Staff and Plant Requirements

Head Count

A tabulated presentation indicating the total number of employees
the company will have during the first five years of operation should
be prepared. The time period represented in such a tabulation
should correspond to the breakdown provided in the pro forma financial statements. The presentation should include a head count of
the number of employees in each specialized category within the
corporation—for example, managers, engineers, secretaries, machinists, and sales staff.

Floor Space

As it grows, the new company will need more and more floor space.
This section of the business plan should demonstrate that management recognizes the additional demands that business growth will
put upon company facilities.

Leasehold Improvements

In most instances, a new or growing business finds that it is necessary to make modifications to the buildings it occupies in order to
tailor these facilities to its own specialized requirements. For example, it may be necessary to install additional electrical outlets, walls
for offices, modified lighting, and air conditioning. The business plan
should offer some discussion of these needs and an estimate of the
cost involved in providing for them.

Major Capital Equipment

As the company grows, it will be necessary to acquire additional capital equipment. The decision to purchase this equipment or to lease
it should be discussed in this section of the business proposal, along
with the primary factors considered in reaching the decision. Mention should be made of the cost of the equipment, and these ex-

penses obviously should be included in the pro forma financial statements.

Legal Structure of the Company

The three most common legal structures for a business are the sole proprietorship, the partnership, and the corporation. The differences among these three basic legal structures involve the personal financial risk to which the participants are vulnerable, the requirements of federal, state, and local tax regulations, and those arrangements necessary to make investment in the enterprise attractive to investors who may not necessarily wish to participate in the day-to-day operation of the business. The basic legal structures are compared below. Obviously, the information presented here is merely intended to serve as an introduction to the subject, and the importance of the retention of qualified legal counsel cannot be overemphasized!

Sole Proprietorship

Approximately seventy-five percent of the more than ten million businesses in the United States today are of the legal structure known as a sole proprietorship. In the case of a sole proprietorship, all net income of the enterprise is taxable as the proprietor's personal income. The proprietor maintains individual and personal liability for all financial and legal obligations of the enterprise, and, under most circumstances, the only source of outside financing available to the enterprise is in the form of loans. No one other than the proprietor participates in a distribution of the net income of a business organized under this legal structure.

Partnership

In the case of a partnership, the key individuals in the organizational structure fall into either of two categories: the general partners (there must be at least one) and the limited partners. The general partners typically are responsible for the day-to-day operation of the enterprise, whereas the limited partners exercise no control whatever over routine operations. The general partners must carrry the burden of the financial liabilities of the entire enterprise and the personal financial liability of each general partner is virtually unlimited in regard to the business. Furthermore, the general partners are, individually and jointly, completely liable for the financial obligations incurred in the name of the partnership by *any one* of the general partners.

From a fund-raising standpoint, the partnership may wish to re-cruit limited partners who typically will invest money, land, build-ings, patents, etc. (anything except services) in exchange for the right to enjoy a share of whatever profits and/or assets may be gen-erated by the enterprise. Because they do not participate in the management of the partnership, limited partners are sometimes re-ferred to as "silent" partners. Unlike the situation with the general partners, the liability of the limited partners *is* limited—to the amount of their investment. The extent to which the general and limited partners participate in the distribution of the net profits and assets of the partnership is ordinarily specified in the Limited Part-nership Agreement, a formal document ordinarily drawn up by the attorney who represents the organization. From a tax standpoint, any income the partnership enjoys is taxable to the individual part-ners, both general and limited, on a pro-rata basis established in ac-cordance with the partnership agreement and is taxable as ordinary income to each of the designees *whether or not these profits are dis-tributed to the partners.*

Corporation

A corporation is a legal entity separate and distinct from its stock-holders, officers, and employees. The corporate legal structure af-fords the stockholders and officers the greatest possible legal protection against financial vulnerability. In the event the corpora-tion is unable to meet its expenses and its assets are less than its lia-bilities, bankruptcy may be forced upon the corporate entity without exposing the stockholders and officers to any personal financial lia-bility beyond their investment in the stock of the enterprise. (How-ever, if there are any unpaid *taxes,* the Directors may be personally liable if other corporate assets are not sufficient to cover these liabi-lities.)

Depending on the tax bracket in which the corporate stock-holder falls, significant tax advantages may be gained through par-ticipation in a corporation rather than participation in a partnership.

From the standpoint of attracting additional financing, the legal structure of the corporation is typically the most attractive of the three discussed herein. The vehicle of stock distribution provides the corporate entity with an opportunity to obtain well-dispersed own-ership in the company. Most of the *major* business entities in this country are organized as stock corporations.

In the event additional financing is required by the corporate en-tity, such financing may be secured by issuing additional shares of stock. A more detailed analysis of stock offerings will be presented in Section III.

In summary, the three most common legal structures for a business enterprise are the sole proprietorship, the partnership, and the corporation. This sequence represents increasing financial and legal complexity. In general, the personal liability of an individual who is both an investor and a participant in the day-to-day operation of a business enterprise is greatest for the sole proprietor and least for the stockholder-officer of a stock corporation.

The type of organizational structure most suitable for a given business entity is in no small way influenced by the financial and other circumstances of the primary participants. Therefore, the services of competent legal counsel should always be retained to provide for a knowledgeable analysis of all the appropriate factors.

Founders' Resumes

In the Appendix of the business plan, complete dossiers on the founders, including every vital piece of information in each individual's background, should be presented. A minimum presentation would involve the names of the individuals; their addresses; their birthdates or ages; their marital status; their number of children, their places of birth; their formal educational history, including special course work completed; any society memberships; any special honors and awards they have received; any patents that have been awarded them; their national security clearance (where appropriate); and their full employment history, including major career accomplishments and a reverse chronological exposition of all employment. Of course, the length of the employment history in relation to the rest of the business plan should be short, but, for completeness, it must be thorough.

When preparing these resumes, remember that the founders are attempting to persuade the reader that they have particular capabilities that will enable them to effectively function in the positions of responsibility outlined in the business plan. Therefore, it would seem only reasonable that the material in the resumes must be presented in a manner that effectively persuades—that is, in a manner that emphasizes the factors important to the proposed enterprise and minimizes the factors that are only peripherally related to it.

"To Whom It May Concern:"

In this section of the business plan, the founders should include letters from various references regarding the technical and managerial competence, character, and integrity of each member of the new team. Such letters may be obtained from former colleagues, managers, members of the banking and financial community, the clergy, etc. In seeking these testimonials, the entrepreneur should make a careful evaluation as to the suitability of each reference source and the appropriateness of each letter as a means of enhancing the image the team wishes to project.

Key Articles by Members of the Founding Staff

If members of the founding staff of the new enterprise have written or published technical, financial, or management articles in fields related to the activities of the new enterprise and if these articles would serve to enhance the author's image in the mind of the reader, include them. In those instances where founders have been so prolific that inclusion of all of their articles or publications would prove to be unwieldy, use only the most representative writings.

Founders' Personal Financial Statements

Before any knowledgeable investors will commit substantial funds to a new enterprise, they will want—and are entitled—to know the financial condition of the individuals whose plans they are being asked to back. Blank forms for the presentation of such personal financial data may usually be obtained free of charge from the credit department or loan department of your local bank.

Founders' Compensation

When the time comes for the founders to prepare this part of the business plan, one may truly say that they confront the moment of truth. When venture capitalists get together for tall drinks and taller stories, they often share their own accounts of the "young hustler syndrome," wherein an entrepreneur walks into their offices seeking a million dollars with which to start a new business and a salary that represents twice the current figure. Soon such "hustlers" are confronted by reality for, in most instances, entrepreneurs who are serious about their new businesses must be prepared to accept a fairly significant *reduction* in income. Usually the salaries founders draw from their enterprises during the early stages of operation will range from no salary at all up to a salary merely sufficient to meet the minimum normal operating expenses of their families. Obviously, if the founders invest all of their liquid assets and go into personal debt in order to contribute to the capitalization of the enterprise, they will have to draw higher salaries than the founders who have made a minimal personal investment in the business and can afford to maintain themselves and their families with previously accumulated savings or other resources.

Company founders may derive compensation from the enterprise in several ways. They may draw salaries, take compensation in the form of stock, or, in the case of a partnership or a proprietorship, participate in the appreciation of the value of the enterprise due to the accumulation of profits retained in the business. The following discussion is intended to cover the primary topics related to founder compensation within a new enterprise.

Tax Aspects

Since the establishment of a new business is frequently intended to provide the founders with substantial long-term financial rewards, it is wise to consider tax planning at the outset of the operation. It is at this point that the company founders should seek the advice and services of tax accountants, tax attorneys, insurance agents, tax consultants, and anyone else who can assist with tax problems.

Salaries

As was discussed earlier, the founders of a new business must be prepared to draw salaries substantially lower than those they might have enjoyed with a former employer in a much-less-risky job situation. The higher, safer salary was also one that offered much less long-term potential. One of the important considerations in the financing of a new company is the expectation that monies invested will appreciate substantially within a period of three to five years. Thus, it would seem reasonable that the founders would avoid drawing out substantial amounts of capital when, by leaving the capital in the company coffers, they can enjoy through their ownership a substantial appreciation in the value of the company.

In addition, one of the very significant factors any potential investor will consider when approached for additional financing is the amount of income the founders have withdrawn from the business in preceding years or, alternatively, the amount of money the founders anticipate drawing from the company in the form of salaries in the future. If the founders demand substantial salaries from the outset of the new business, an investor may reasonably conclude that their psychological commitment to the enterprise is probably less than it should be. The likelihood of securing new financing when the founders are not prepared to satisfy themselves with modest salaries is small indeed.

Equity Formula

A stock company is financially attractive primarily because of the prospect of substantial capital gains in the value of the stock. Accordingly, the founders are concerned about control of the company and capital appreciation.

Control of the Enterprise. In most instances, entrepreneurs who start companies do so because they desire to exercise substantial control over their own business careers.

Substantial Capital Appreciation. Through the successful development of a corporation from start-up to cash-out (the time when much or all of the founders' stock holdings are converted into cash by sale to a private investor, public offering, merger, or acquisition), the entrepreneur hopes to create a substantial personal estate. Not surprisingly, the objectives of the investment community are quite similar. They also wish to enjoy substantial capital appreciation and to build a substantial personal estate. Furthermore, it is not uncommon for investors to wish to exercise sufficient control in the operation of a new enterprise to guarantee the safety of their investments. Thus, it can be seen that equity participation represents the two primary areas for negotiation between the founders and the financial backers—financial gain and the control of the enterprise. Realize, in addition, that, in any typical financing, neither the financiers nor the founders will be entirely satisfied with the final arrangement. The following discussion will treat some of the considerations in the determination of an equity formula.

The founders must recognize that in all cases it is better to have thirty percent of the future Xerox or International Business Machines than to secure one hundred percent of a financially static business entity that has had its growth permanently stunted due to a deficiency of expansion capital and its profits limited due to a lack of the capital assets necessary to achieve a viable business volume.

When the founders attempt to determine how much equity they are willing to exchange for invested capital, they should recognize that it is possible to surrender the majority of the outstanding stock to an investor without surrendering voting control of the company. Voting control can be maintained by issuing nonvoting shares to the investors, thus giving them a status similar to that of the limited partners discussed earlier in this chapter under the heading "Legal Structure of the Company."

In almost every instance, the final arrangements necessary to bring about the capitalization of a new enterprise are *negotiated* between the founders and the financial backers. Therefore, in this section of the business proposal, the founders should simply indicate their position regarding whether or not they intend to demand majority ownership of the outstanding stock and/or voting control of the new enterprise. Stating their position at this point may save considerable negotiating time later, for many financiers will not *con-*

sider investing in a new enterprise unless they can exercise control *and* enjoy majority ownership of the stock.

Finally, the entrepreneur should recognize that there are tens of thousands of different financing arrangments that may be suitable for financing a new enterprise. These arrangements are almost always worked out between the founders and members of the financial community. On large deals, legal counsel frequently participates.

Since the subject of corporate finance is admittedly quite complex, the entrepreneur would do well to learn some of the highly specialized terms in the financial jargon. An excellent glossary, "Understanding the Securities Market," may be obtained by writing to the Commodity Research Bureau, Inc., 75 Montgomery, Jersey City, New Jersey 07302.

A Standard and Poors publication, "How to Invest," containing a more abbreviated glossary of financial terms, is available on a complimentary basis by writing to Standard and Poors Corporation, 25 Broadway, New York, New York 10004.

Supporting Documentation

Formally prepared materials from sources outside the founding staff should be included in this section.

Market Surveys and Reports

If the founders have arranged for a market survey to be prepared by an independent agency, it should be included in the business plan under this heading in the Appendix. Additionally, if marketing surveys and reports have been purchased from agencies that regularly provide such services to the industry, they should also be included in the business plan in this section of the Appendix.

Newspaper and Magazine Articles

Any recently published articles that relate to future prospects for the industry in which the proposed company wishes to participate will enhance and support the authenticity of material presented elsewhere in the business plan. They should therefore be included in this section.

Credit Reports and/or Annual Reports on Competitors

Where possible, financial data that reflects the economic conditions of the major competitors in the proposed industry should be presented. If information is available on similar companies that are only one or two years old, include it also for the purpose of affording the reviewer of the business plan an opportunity to scrutinize the economic condition of a company that has recently preceded the proposed enterprise into the marketplace. Credit reports may be obtained by subscribing to the services of some of the leading national credit information agencies, such as Dun and Bradstreet. An alternative source of credit information would be the annual reports (where available) of your competitors.

III

Ali Baba and
the Forty Money Sources

14

Introduction to Money Sources

Small business owners often forget that the position of preeminence enjoyed by this nation in the world of commerce is fundamentally due to our capitalistic system of economics. Through a process whereby public, private, and institutional *capital* sources provide industry with money in exchange for equity or interest, business as we know it is made possible. The material presented in this final section of the book is intended to show entrepreneurs how *they* may join the ranks of the rugged and colorful individualists we refer to as *capitalists*—the hearty souls responsible for building and sustaining our land. (*Note:* In this section, I have chosen to define venture capital in very loose terms; i.e., any monies, regardless of the source, that may be used for the purpose of financing a new or young enterprise.)

Money Concepts

This material is intended to provide the reader with a review of basic economic concepts as they relate to the financing of enterprise.

Salt, Beads, and Grain

In primitive times, *barter* was the only means of securing goods and services from others. The farmer would give so many measures of grain to the blacksmith in exchange for services, thereby satisfying the farmer's needs for blacksmithing and the blacksmith's need for grain. The blacksmith similarly might offer services in exchange for the weaver's cloth, again directly satisfying the needs of both individuals. Here, each individual is a seller *and* a buyer offering goods or services (selling) and receiving in exchange (buying) the goods or services provided by another person. As commerce expanded, a more universally acceptable method of transacting business became necessary. Gradually, various *media of exchange*, or forms of *money*, came to be accepted as having a more or less standard value. Thus, the farmer could sell grain to a grain merchant and receive some form of primitive "money," such as salt or beads, as payment. With this "money," the farmer could buy services from the blacksmith without resorting to barter. The blacksmith could then buy cloth from the weaver *even if the weaver did not need any blacksmithing services!* In turn, the weaver could hire a carpenter who might be unwilling to build the weaver a house if the only medium of payment was cloth.

As the demands of commerce increased, the use of money and credit expanded enormously, making business as we know it possible. Commerce soon needed experts in the handling and utilization of money—the money-changers Christ booted out of the temples were the forerunners of contemporary financial specialists. Today, money and its management constitute our single largest industry.

Supply and Demand

Regardless of the medium of exchange—whether it is salt, beads, grain, or some other commodity—its "value" in terms of what it will buy is subject to variation due to supply and demand. In an economically primitive society where wheat might serve as the medium of exchange, handmade pots hammered out of sheets of metal may have commanded a price of two bushels of wheat prior to the advent of metal stamping equipment. However, with the high volume and low unit labor content made possible through mechanization, similar pots might command a price of only a fraction of a bushel of wheat.

On the other hand, recognize that mechanization has evolved quite slowly through history while the quantity of wheat harvested in any given year is subject to very great fluctuations depending on the weather, parasite damage, or the acreage committed to the crop. Thus, when wheat is plentiful, it may take many more bushels to buy a pot than it would take if the wheat supply were limited. The *medium of exchange*, therefore, is sensitive to the law of supply and demand in a way quite similar to that of the articles and services it buys.

This law of supply and demand applies to money—dollars, for

instance—also. Contrary to popular belief, the value of money changes dynamically in terms of what it will buy and the interest rate that must be paid in order to "rent" it. It is extremely difficult to find any commodity to which the value of any kind of money can be related over a long period of time. Thus, when money is in short supply and borrowing demand exceeds reserves available for loans, the cost of money is high. Conversely, when the supply of money is plentiful and loan availability exceeds borrower demands, the cost of money is low.

From the standpoint of entrepreneurs, the cost of money is reflected in the interest rate they must pay in order to borrow it. Similarly, the cost of money may be reflected by the price the common stock of many corporations is able to command. When market conditions result in low price-to-earnings ratios for securities traded on the stock exchanges, you may be certain that the value of shares of stock in small corporations *not* publicly traded will also be adversely affected. Accordingly, the amount of equity in their companies that the founders must surrender in exchange for a given amount of capitalization is directly related to prevailing investor psychology as manifested in the level—and the rising or falling—of the Dow Jones Industrial Average.

Summarizing, entrepreneurs raising funds with which to start a business during a bull market may have to relinquish a mere thirty or forty percent of the equity in their firms to raise X number of dollars. In a down or bear market, the same entrepreneurs may have to relinquish sixty to eighty percent of the equity in the same company for the same X number of dollars.

Leverage. The concept of leverage is an important one, particularly for businesses starting out with a minimum of capital. In financial terms, leverage is simply a measure of borrowing, or the extent to which a purchase is made without cash. On a small scale, good examples of leverage can be found in the real estate market in the form of second mortgages, home equity loans, and seller-financed home purchases where little or no cash is produced when the deal is struck. On a larger scale, leveraged buyouts of businesses have become increasingly popular in recent years. In a leveraged buyout scenario, a company is purchased with very little money down. Usually a long-term loan, secured by the assets of the company being bought out, pays for the purchase, although equity financing may also be secured.

Whether leverage takes the form of debt or equity financing, the entrepreneur should be aware of the many ways in which a company can expand its limited capital resources by making use of this concept.

Debt Versus Equity Financing

In financing *any* business, it is important to understand the advantages and disadvantages of debt and equity capital.

Debt Capital. In its most common form, debt capital carries with it the obligation for a periodic payment of interest and a lump-sum payment of the principal at maturity. Alternatively, a mortgage-type arrangement may be agreed upon wherein regular fixed payments are made. Mortgage pyaments made early in the contract period will reflect a *greater* percentage allocated for interest charges than for the reduction of the loan principal. Toward the end of the contract, this same fixed payment will reflect a *smaller* allocation for interest payment than for retirement of the principal.

There are a number of disadvantages in the use of debt financing to meet the financial needs of a new enterprise. Typically, a new enterprise will weather a period of several months or even years before profits are realized. In the case of debt financing, interest and quite possibly payments to reduce the amount of the principal are required on a regular basis. A new enterprise can usually ill afford the cost of "servicing" a large amount of debt. Debt financing also represents a corporate liability, which adversely affects the appearance of financial solvency any company is interested in maintaining.

On the plus side, interest payments represent a business expense and are, therefore, tax deductible. Furthermore, it is not necessary to surrender equity in exchange for ordinary debt. Finally, should your business encounter severe financial difficulties, there is a certain leverage that can work in your favor *if* you've borrowed heavily; at a certain level of debt, lenders become *partners* rather than mere creditors. Since their stake in your survival is large, they will be reluctant to see your company's name added to the business casualty list. The most striking example of this concept can be found in the recent restructuring of International Harvester's *multibillion* dollar debt. Rather than face the substantial losses that dissolution of this gigantic firm would bring about, International Harvester's lenders agreed to a complicated restructuring of the company's debt into equity and medium-term loans and notes in order to maintain solvency and keep operations moving. Hopefully *your* company will never reach such a critical stage, but you should be aware of this concept of creditors as partners.

Equity Capital. To secure equity capital, it is always necessary to give up a percentage of the ownership in the enterprise. Thus, the operations of the company become subject to the wishes of *all* of the owners, including those "outsiders" who supply equity capital. Depending on the emotional and financial needs of the founders and of the backers, equity financing may or may not be a desirable means of financing.

One of the major advantages of equity financing is that there is no requirement that monies so invested be repaid. Furthermore, in the eyes of suppliers, a company having a high stockholder equity should be financially sound, representing a good credit risk. And customers will think it unlikely that such a company will be unable to perform any given contract because of a financial inability to assemble the necessary materials and resources.

Convertible Debt. In the money markets of today, it is becoming increasingly common for suppliers of debt capital (especially non-bank sources) to insist on equity "kickers" or "sweeteners" as part of a financial package. Thus, a supplier of debt capital may be able to recover an investment in the enterprise through foreclosure should the business encounter financial difficulty. On the other hand, the supplier could take the option of converting his debt into stock in the enterprise should the company prosper and its stock increase in value.

Comparison Shopping

When contemplating the purchase of a house, an automobile, or any other expensive item, people usually attempt to evaluate as objectively as possible the value of their purchase relative to its cost. The same attitude should govern the selection of a money supplier. A thousand dollars borrowed from your Aunt Minnie may cost much less in terms of interest than a thousand dollars borrowed from your commercial banker, which in turn will cost less than a thousand dollars borrowed from the neighborhood hoodlum. Not only that, in the event you have difficulty repaying the debt when originally promised, your Aunt Minnie may be quite forgiving, your banker may drive you to bankruptcy, while the hoodlum may get violent.

Just as a commercial banker may charge less for a loan than a finance company, one supplier of equity capital may be willing to pay a much higher price for stock in a new enterprise than another. Unfortunately, just as many people expend very little effort in shopping for loans for their personal needs, many entrepreneurs are equally remiss in their efforts to secure debt and equity financing at the most economical rate for their business. Don't *you* be guilty of this! Remember though, shop discreetly—as I have said before, many bankers and financiers like to feel that they are the only ones with whom you are negotiating.

Are Venture Capitalists *Really* Thieves?

Contrary to the feelings expressed by many of the entrepreneurs with whom I have spoken, venture capitalists taken as a class are *not* thieves. However, one venture capitalist I know who is the president of a California-based business development firm—and a self-appointed industry spokesman—offers the observation that "most venture capitalists are driven by greed and fear."[22] I have had the misfortune of meeting several for whom his description is quite appropriate. However, I share with equal conviction the feeling that the vast majority of them are not! The most objective evaluation of the industry would suggest the the typical venture capitalist defies simple classification just as stubbornly as does the ideal vacation. Bear in mind while reading what follows that generalizations regarding venture capitalists are expedient at best.

What to Look for in a Venture Capital Partner

In looking for venture capital partners, entrepreneurs must realize that the relationship they *should* seek to establish will be long term. The following discussion is intended to suggest a number of factors that entrepreneurs would do well to consider in evaluating a potential capital source.

Money

The most obvious test venture capitalists must meet is whether or not they have funds available for investing in the proposed venture. I have personally had the unfortunate experience of spending several weeks in preliminary talks with a venture capitalist who, a short time later, went bankrupt because of an inadequate supply of working capital. In his desire to participate in every worthwhile proposal that came his way, he had stretched his own credit and that of his company beyond the breaking point. The price of his greed was not only his own bankruptcy but the creation of very serious economic difficulties for the several portfolio companies in whose financing he had participated.

There are some venture capitalists who syndicate private partnerships (see below) for the purpose of financing almost any good deal they may have the fortune to examine. In other words, they organize an investing partnership in which they are the general partner; the other investors participate as limited partners for the express purpose of providing capital for one enterprise. In such situations, the resources of the partnership are only as plentiful as the combined assets of the partners. When working with venture capitalists such as this, the financing of the deal is fundamentally dependent on their ability to secure the bulk of the required capital from *other* investors.

More Money

The new company that is able to follow its business plan without needing more capital than the founders originally anticipated is the exception, not the rule. Not only do things typically cost most than anticipated, not only do a plethora of unexpected and unanticipated minor expenses manifest themselves until their sum represents a significant percentage of the initial capitalization, but also everything *invariably* takes longer to accomplish than the original schedules planned for. The development of a prototype, the creation of a manufacturing capability, and the penetration of a market consume time with a mystifyingly voracious appetite. Since we all know that time is money, the problem of schedule slippages soon manifests itself on the bottom line of the income statement, and the business is in trouble. If the individual or organization providing the initial capitalization has had extensive experience in working with new enterprises, this need for additional capital will come as no surprise, and provision will have been made for it. However, when dealing with less-sophisticated capital sources (the general public is probably the worst), the ability of the enterprise to secure a capital transfusion when the income statement is having a red-ink hemorrhage may be difficult indeed, if not impossible.

Realistically, however, it is unlikely that an entrepreneur with a high-risk/high-potential package will be successful in securing financing from a venture capital organization that has significant cash reserves. Significant cash reserves generally reflect a conservatism that rules out investment in all but the safest of business propositions. In most cases, this conservatism completely excludes start-up situations.

Availability of Managerial Assistance

One of the salient motivations of entrepreneurs is the desire to call the shots themselves, to crack the whips in their own circuses. However, the more mature entrepreneurs will have an unusual awareness of their own shortcomings and will not be so proud as to refuse to seek assistance in any area of their business operations if and when they need it. In Henry Ford, the unschooled industrial genius of yesterday, we have an excellent example. Ford gathered around himself a formidable staff of experts in fields as diverse as metallurgy and mass production methodology to compensate for his own shrewdly acknowledged educational deficiencies. Harvard-educated Edwin H. Land, brilliant physicist, applied scientist, and inventor of the Polaroid camera (now retired), attracted an enviable stable of astute business talent, expert in marketing, financial planning, patent protection, and other areas that are so essential to substantial business success. Obviously, entrepreneurs who have limited financial resources are not in a position to attract and retain such a staff at the outset. They may, however, through judicious selection of venture capital partners, avail themselves of a very substantial reservoir of talent for the purpose of complementing their own unique qualities.

Among the larger and more sophisticated venture capital firms, a staff of seasoned, "graduate" entrepreneurs—those who have met a payroll themselves—is available for the purpose of counseling the officers of the new enterprise on an "as-required" basis, provided the enterprise is successful in meeting or exceeding its originally stated objectives. This group may provide nothing more than applause unless the founders request their assistance.

In such a situation, the potential for having too many cooks in a kitchen is obvious, and it must be carefully guarded against; similarly, the nonavailability of competent counsel when it is required can prove to be of grave consequence to the survival of the enterprise. Seasoned entrepreneurs will make a sincere effort to determine the complementary nature of the skills and services their venture capital partners-to-be are in a position to provide.

Compatibility of Objectives

It is most important to ascertain whether or not the objectives of the investing parties are compatible with those of the founding team. If capital is provided through noninstitutional channels, such as customers, suppliers, etc., that are possibly motivated by the desire to create or groom an acquisition candidate, catastrophe is only a matter of time if it is the desire of the entrepreneurs (openly acknowledged or furtively concealed) to build a corporate monument for their personal, financial, and psychological aggrandizement. The pacifist entrepreneur who wishes to make fireworks for holiday celebrations will obviously be at loggerheads with an investor who wishes to make explosives for an upcoming war. The entrepreneur who is sold on the value of employee profit-sharing and stock-option plans will reach an impasse with an investor who desires income through dividends.

If more than one individual or capital-supplying firm participates in the syndication of the financial package, it is imperative that the investors' objectives be similar. Whether these objectives have to do with determination of the geographic location of the firm or whether they have to do with the magnitude of the anticipated return on the investment, investors' objectives must be compatible in order to ensure a harmonious relationship between the financial backers and the company officers and to preclude the needless dissipation of the energies of the founders in the refereeing of boardroom brawls.

Investors Who Can Keep Their Cool

In his excellent book, *Starting and Succeeding in Your Own Small Business,* Louis L. Allen states:

> The nervous investor who packs up and runs at the sound of trouble is almost always content to take a loss of some kind in order to extricate himself. . . . The nervous investors are the losers in the venture capital game. They stay in it because they somehow have the idea that they can make their money work for them. They do not know that making the investment should be the first and easiest work they will undertake with their small business client.[23]

It is unfortunate that many investors, particularly those without significant experience in the funding of new enterprises, tend to be nervous about their investment and are prone to abandoning it *and* the unfortunate individuals whom they chose to back when they are most needed—just when financial recovery is imminent but when unprofitable operating history makes the enterprise unattractive to new investors unfamiliar with the extent of the problems the founders have *already* overcome. This abandonment may range all the way from a refusal to supply additional funds up to and including liquidation of the company assets at auction or forced sale. If the only financing that may be secured for the launching of an enterprise is from gutless, spineless, self-fancied investors such as these, the entrepreneurs would be best advised to delay the start of their business until a more propitious time when other sources of financing become available.

Wise investors who have the courage of their convictions and who are satisfied with the integrity, commitment, and business acumen of the company founders will fully appreciate the long-term financial rewards for sticking with *their* commitment as the founders strive to achieve profitability in the face of unexpected difficulties.

Confidence in Team and Concept

It is not enough to satisfy the investors that the proposed venture idea has significant market potential. The investors must also feel confident that the management team is able to achieve the originally proposed objectives. Investors who participate in the financing of a new enterprise simply as a lark, to make a quick buck, or because they happen to have some spare cash lying around are not in a position to provide the encouragement and understanding the entrepreneurs will require as they weather the storms that batter their corporate vessel in its early years of operation. When the going is rough, an expression of confidence from your investors can prove enormously encouraging.

Reasonable Expectations Regarding Capital Appreciation

Investors who will only be happy if their money quadruples every year can be a real pain to a hard-working, highly motivated group of aggressive entrepreneurs; investors who moan and groan about the fact that they only tripled their money in two years when the original company plan intimated that they would quadruple it are people whom the founders can do without. I have personally heard a number of Wall Street gun-slingers explain that because of the tight money market and the competition for available capital they are not interested in looking at any deals that don't project at least quadrupling the original investment every year for the next five years. It is wild and unrealistic expectations such as these that prompt unsuspecting novice entrepreneurs to prepare the wildly optimistic financial forecasts that cause them to be laughed out of the offices of the more conservative investors in the capital community.

Knowledge of the Market to Be Served

The investor in the new enterprise should have more than a passing familiarity with the nature of the market the entrepreneurs intend to enter. Thus, if the company is not doing quite so well as expected but the market is doing better than expected, the investor can remain optimistic in regard to the future of the business because of the favorable market conditions. In the event the enterprise is not doing well due to serious market reversals, the investor is in a position to appreciate that the company's inability to realize its original projections is due not to operational deficiencies but to the vagaries of the marketplace, over which the company officers have no control.

Terms of the Deal

Depending on how many attorneys are involved, depending on the number of years the investor has participated in financing new enterprises, and depending on the sophistication of the entrepreneur, the written deal may take one to two pages or one to two *hundred* pages. You would be wise to acquaint yourself with such terms as notes, preferred stock, common stock, leases, convertible leases, warrants, options, debentures, subordinated debentures, hypothecation, and other jawbreakers you will probably encounter in your negotiations with investors. Your library should have one or two glossaries of finacial terms for reference. The following are four considerations normally encountered in structuring the deal.

Reward-Risk Ratios

Whenever the subject of gambling odds comes up, a discussion of the reward-risk ratio is inevitable. To provide a simple illustration of the concept, consider the game of roulette. On the American roulette wheel, there are thirty-eight cups into which a little ball may fall. Thus, in the simplest case of one bet on one number, there is one chance of winning and thirty-seven chances of losing out of thirty-eight possible chances. This establishes the risk. In the event you were a player and won, you would receive thirty-five times the amount of your bet. If you were to play the game long enough, your winnings would average out to $35 for every $38 played. Thus, the reward risk-ratio is slightly less than one. The amount by which this ratio differs from one represents the house winnings.

In the financing of new or unproven enterprises, many money suppliers evaluate investment opportunities in gambling terms. Risk is evaluated as objectively as possible in terms of market projections, capabilities of the founders, excellence and uniqueness of the proposed business concept, and the prevailing whims of the investing public. (For instance, companies in the computer software field are hot issues today; in the previous decade, companies in the pollution control field were the darlings of the market; and, much further back, railroads had their day on Wall Street.)

In addition to considering the risk *before* they become involved, astute venture capitalists endeavor to make expert assistance available to the enterprise to reduce the risk *after* they put their money into the venture. In some instances, venture capitalists may insist on majority ownership of the stock so that they may assert themselves and impose their own management style upon the enterprise in the event they feel the operational techniques employed by the company officers are jeopardizing their investment.

In assessing the reward for taking the risk, the investor will determine the projected value of the company at some point in the future (typically three to five years) in terms of annual sales per share, profits per share, and the stock price-to-earnings ratio prevailing in the industrial sector served by the enterprise. For instance, most "growth" companies (firms experiencing rapid increases in sales volume and profitability, which make a practice of plowing back all of the earnings into the enterprise for the purpose of sustaining this growth at the expense of dividends to stockholders) are valued at large price-to-earnings multiples in the marketplace, offering investors very attractive vehicles for capital appreciation. By conservatively estimating the projected value of their holdings at some point in the not-too-distant future, investors can determine the anticipated reward such an investment would offer. Naturally, investors are concerned with maximizing rewards and minimizing risks. Thus, they hope to gamble in a situation where the reward-risk ratio is large.

Regardless of the reward potential, the more conservative investors are, the less willing they will be to invest in high-risk propositions. A conservative investor is accustomed to a yield on an equity investment that is not substantially greater than a small multiple of the prevailing prime interest rates. On the other hand, the crap shooters may be willing to take on a proposition that has five times the minimum risk a more conservative investor would consider. However, they expect—even demand—a potential reward of *ten* or more times greater than the reward that will satisfy their more conservative colleagues. In other words, risk-takers accept the risk in exchange for rewards that are as close to being unlimited as possible.

Return on Investment

A concept invariably considered in evaluating the merits of financing a new enterprise is that of return on investment (ROI). It is remarkable how often members of the financial community make reference to ROI and subsequently fail to point out that it is meaningless unless it is considered in the context of risk. Thus, venture capitalists who contend that they are not interested in participating in the financing of deals that offer an ROI of less than an annual doubling of their investment also mean to convey the range of risk they are willing to take.

To give you an idea of the differences in expected ROI prevailing among different members of the financial community, I offer the following quotations for your consideration:

E.F. Heizer, Jr., Chairman and President, Heizer Corporation:

> You might wonder what our objectives are. First of all, in terms of that portion of our money invested in venture capital, we feel that we should earn year in and year out, to be doing our job at all, a fifteen percent compound rate of return on our money. Our goal is actually forty percent compounded on our money that is invested in venture capital. Overall as a corporation, we hope to earn ten to twenty percent a year.[24]

Charles B. Smith, Former Partner, Venrock Associates:

> Our goal like everybody else's is to make wads and wads of money for the [Rockefeller] family. If we like a situation, but have to change our critieria to fit, it goes something like four times [our investment] in three years and five times in four and so forth, based on a plausible set of projections, not the entrepreneur's but our own. It never happens but if that sort of gain is at least possible, perhaps you will have a chance of coming out across the board on your portfolio.[25]

Mark Rollinson, President, MR Associates:

> We are looking for a compound return on investment, somewhere between twenty-five and thirty percent. We don't care how we arrive at that, but we want to have a reasonable opportunity of achieving that sort of performance.[26]

G. Stanton Geary, President, Gemini Associates:

> In the venture capital business, the downside risks are very substantial, so the upside potential must be commensurate with this risk; i.e.— there must be an opportunity to make at least ten times the original investment in five to seven years.[27]

Benno C. Schmidt, Managing Partner, J.H. Whitney and Company:

> After balancing the homeruns against the strikeouts, a venture firm . . . should be able at least to double its money every four years. Not an easy goal. Few have achieved it.[28]

Earned Equity

In Section I, I tried to make the entrepreneur aware of the difficulties of building a business. The novice may have begun to think that the task of securing venture capital is the biggest obstacle to be surmounted in starting and building a successful business. Unfortunately this is not the case. Although imagination and ingenuity are necessary to persuade someone to invest in your enterprise, *building* a successful company is the real test of the entrepreneur's mettle.

At the many seminars I have attended on starting and financing a new business, I have never failed to hear the question posed from the floor: "How much equity may I retain when I am financed by a venture capitalist?" There is no simple formula. Not only does the answer depend on the entrepreneur and the venture capitalist reaching a satisfactory compromise, but also considerations such as founder salary, founder investment, founder investment *as a percentage of personal net worth,* patents, copyrights, trademarks, prototypes, capital equipment and other "hard" assets provided by the founders, the business plan, size of the founding team, reward-risk ratio, return on investment, management assistance required, total financing required, competence and maturity of the founders, and many other subjective and objective considerations characteristic of each individual situation must be evaluated.

There is probably nothing wrong with the entrepreneurs wanting all of the equity they can possibly get at the outset, particularly if the investors with whom they are working are unsophisticated. However, the more astute investor will require a deal wherein the founders initially own only a modest degree of equity, although they may be provided with the very great incentive of a sliding scale of equity ownership based on successful performance. For example, a founding team may start out owning a mere twenty or thirty percent of the company; if they are successful in building a viable enterprise, they may ultimately obtain significantly more than majority interest. The point I am trying to make is that, since starting a business is much easier than building a *successful* business, the astute investor will insist on a financing package that requires entrepreneurs to *earn* their equity. I feel that this is a fair and reasonable requirement.

"Getting Out"

In almost all cases, investors participating in the financing of new enterprises have as their major objective capital appreciation. Investors specializing in medium- to high-risk situations characteristic of financing new enterprises recognize that within a period of three to seven years the new business will begin to mature and will be unable to sustain the rapid early-years growth in the worth of its common stock. Thus, the investors will be interested in converting their equity to cash so that they may go on to invest in other new, promising, cash-hungry businesses or to retire to a life of mountain climbing or fishing.

There are two common techniques investors may use to convert their holdings to cash. One is the process of taking the company public (possibly offering some new stock for sale as a means of securing additional capital for the business while at the same time offering most or all of the investor's stock for sale to the public so that he may "cash-out"). The second technique for cashing-out is to arrange to have the enterprise acquired by another firm. In many such instances, the investor may be paid off with common stock in the acquiring company. Usually this new stock is publicly traded and has a value that may be readily ascertained through a phone call to a stockbroker or by consulting the financial pages of the daily newspapers.

In rare instances, the company founders may find it possible to buy out the investors themselves, thus retaining 100 percent ownership of the company. I have a strong personal preference for seeing a deal so structured that the founders may buy out the investors at *any* time, in accordance with a schedule established when the financing was originally arranged. Many investors will balk at having a ceiling on their return. But there are few investors who are willing to put their money into a situation where they might suffer unlimited losses; therefore, I see no reason why those same investors should be afforded the opportunity for unlimited *gains*, particularly when the gains are built on the sweat and the ingenuity of the founders.

15

Forty Money Sources

Mr. Ali Baba worked for the Automaton Personnel Agency, an executive-search firm catering to the nation's top 500 corporations. He had decided several months ago that his conscience could no longer bear the burden of his being a party to sending capable, qualified men and women into dull, dead-end careers with these faceless frustration factories. In spite of his high income, Al had decided to risk starting a nationwide network of personnel agencies of his own, using resident owner-managers who would cater to small companies, "where the action is." He had spent most of the summer working out a business plan and had just begun what looked like several months' work in reading about the many different sources of funding that might be appropriate for his business.

One weekend, feeling the need for a well-deserved rest, he decided to head for the mountains. Sunday afternoon he was riding his Honda down a remote trail near the end of a canyon when he noticed the faint outline of what looked like a huge door in the canyon wall. Recalling the childhood story of his namesake, he decided to give the Arabian Nights' "Open Sesame" bit a try. Well, sure enough, a loud rumbling was heard, the earth trembled, and a gaping hole appeared in the canyon wall where the outline of the door had been.

He scooted his bike inside, uttered the magic words once again, and the opening closed behind him. However, unlike the cave in the old story, *this* cave appeared at first glance to be devoid of any treasure. Neither the glitter of gold nor the sparkle of precious gems was in evidence. However, as his eyes became accustomed to the dim light, he could make out a set of forty large tablets inscribed upon the cave walls. At first, he thought they might be some primitive art work. But as his vision cleared, he saw that he had found the key to the treasure he sought—financing for his business. Inscribed on the panels was the following information—complete with footnotes.

Closed-End Investment Companies

For our purposes, we define an investment company as an organization, registered under the Investment Company Act of 1940, which

1. Is engaged *primarily* in the business of investing, reinvesting, or trading in securities;

2. Is engaged in the business of investing, reinvesting, owning, holding, or trading in securities *and* owns or proposes to acquire investment securities having a value exceeding forty percent of the value of such issuer's total assets (exclusive of government securities and cash items).

The two most common types of investment companies are the closed-end companies (also termed "publicly traded investment funds") and the open-end companies, the latter being popularly known as mutual funds. (A discussion of mutual funds is offered in a separate section below.) The technical distinction between open-end and closed-end companies depends upon the redeemability of the company's shares. Those companies that stand ready to redeem shares whenever called upon to do so (generally at net asset value per share) are classified as *open-end*, and presently about ninety-seven percent of all investment company assets are held by these open-end companies.

Those companies having a relatively fixed capitalization and a normally static number of shares outstanding are classified as *closed-end*. New shares in a closed-end company may, however, be created for the acquisition of additional equity capital or for the payment of capital gains distributions; and occasionally rights to purchase additional shares of stock may be issued to stockholders. Thus, closed-end companies do *not* stand ready to redeem outstanding shares. Instead, new buyers of closed-end shares usually must arrange to purchase them from existing stockholders.

Of the ten *major* closed-end companies, six are listed on the New York Stock Exchange, and the shares of the other four are traded over the counter. Thus, the prices of closed-end investment company shares are subject to the regular supply-and-demand influences characteristic of any publicly traded stock.

For the most part, the portfolios of major closed-end companies are concentrated in equity-type, common-stock investments. According to *Wiesenberger Investment Companies Service,* the portfolios of the major companies are broadly diversified, and the management, objectives and policies are similar to those of many mutual funds.[29] Only in rare instances do they buy the securities of new or relatively young—and, therefore, unproven—businesses.

One group of closed-end investment companies does, however, make a specialty of providing venture capital for such companies, usually by taking equity in the form of common stock. Often this stock is not registered for public sale and thus cannot be readily liquidated. Arriving at a value-per-share figure for the securities of a young company is a highly subjective process, which serves to magnify the risk of such an investment.

The first closed-end investment company to enter the venture capital field was American Research and Development (ARD), located in Boston. Now a division of Textron, ARD was listed on the New York Stock Exchange until 1972. Today, ARD continues investing in the start-up and later stage financing of companies with high potential, pursuing the philosophy upon which the firm was founded in 1946 by "a group of farsighted men who recognized the degree to which American prosperity would depend on venture capital astutely directed toward promising new ideas."[30] More recently, the Nautilus Fund was established in 1979 with the express purpose of investing in emerging companies as a means of maximizing capital growth.[31]

For those desiring additional information on the subject of closed-end investment companies, many libraries subscribe to the publication *Investment Companies,* offered by Wiesenberger Investment Services. Further information on this publication may be found in Appendix 1.

Colleges, Universities, and Other Endowed Institutions

An endowment is money or property given to an institution such as a college, university, hospital, or foundation for the purpose of providing that institution with income. When an endowment takes the form of real estate, the endowed institution may derive income from the lease or rental of the land. (Ordinarily, sale of this land is precluded by the terms of the endowment.) In those instances where cash or securities constitute the endowment, income is derived from dividends and interest on securities in the original portfolio and on new investments. In a growing number of cases, these institutions are investing in venture capital situations, but participation is usually through a professionally managed partnership or some other investment organization of the sort discussed elsewhere in this chapter.

A good example of venture capital participation by universities can be found in the Stanford University Endowment Fund. The Fund takes an active role in providing seed capital and early stage financing of start-up enterprises (usually acting as a coinvestor in deals created by other venture capital firms.)[32] While such direct participation by universities in the venture capital arena is still the exception rather than the rule, the fact that the endowment fund of a highly distinguished institution such as Stanford has become an active participant in the area attests to the growing acceptance of venture financing as a viable investment option, even for traditionally conversative capital pools.

University-sponsored "incubators" have become a popular investment vehicle for colleges that want to support entrepreneurial endeavors without committing large amounts of capital. Under the incubator concept, the university provides facilities, advice, inexpensive labor, and/or equipment to promising entrepreneurs (often students or alumni) to help them get their companies off the ground. The university may agree to rent out campus-owned facilities to help the entrepreneurs develop prototypes of their inventions. Access to faculty advisors and student labor may also be part of the package. The university's hope, of course, is to grow the next "Apple" on campus, with the university owning a piece of the pie.[33]

One of the best-known of such incubators is Rensselaer Polytechnic Institute (RPI) in Troy, New York. RPI not only provides facilities and advice but it has also allocated $5 million of its endowment fund as a pool of venture capital to support its incubator operation.[34]

Still other universities are forming partnerships with local venture capital firms. A case in point is The Wharton Innovation Center, an arm of the well-respected business school, which agreed to assist in forming a $20 million venture capital partnership with a Philadelphia venture capital pool. The Wharton Center serves as an adviser to the venture pool, evaluating proposed deals and helping start-ups with business plans and marketing strategies in exchange for a retainer fee and a share of profits.[35]

While most colleges and universities may not be willing to serve as incubators or venture capital partners, they sometimes own industrial parks that provide rental income to the institution. (An industrial park is a tract of land developed exclusively for nonresidential and usually nonretail business use. Ordinarily, very high standards for building construction and grounds maintenance are observed and a concerted effort is made to insure that the industrial park will remain as attractive as possible.) An endowed institution *may* be of assistance to a new enterprise by providing it with buildings that are within its industrial park.

Also, many university faculty members are, as individuals, in a position to assist the founders of a new enterprise. This assistance may take the form of technical/business consulting or of simple investment in the enterprise. If the vehicle for a new business is to be a product developed as an offshoot of a research activity conducted under the supervision of the university's faculty, their interest in encouraging the success of this enterprise may be quite significant. They may be more than willing to provide their consulting services in exchange for stock in the company.

In other instances, faculty members who are well acquainted with former students and who feel optimistic about their chances for business success may wish to participate in financing the new enterprise. (In one of my own business ventures, I was successful in persuading two of my former professors to participate as investors. A third professor was of considerable help in persuading a businessman of his acquaintance to invest in this same venture.)

Commercial Banks

Until recently, the commercial bank was uniquely identified as being the department store or the supermarket of the financial community. While deregulation has brought competitors to their doorsteps, commercial banks are still prime sources of the following financial services of interest to the entrepreneur.

Short-Term Loans

Short-term loans generally constitute credit that is extended for one year or less for the purpose of augmenting working capital. Loans may be used to take advantage of often significant trade discounts offered for prompt retirement of accounts payable, to permit a buildup of inventories in preparation for a seasonal increase in sales volume, to cover peak payroll demands, and to satisfy other temporary cash needs. Ordinarily, the funds with which to repay short-term loans are derived from the sale of the goods or services that originally precipitated the need for the loans. Short-term loans are typically unsecured, although the personal guarantee of one or more of the company officers may be required. The bank representative considering the loan request will have to feel reasonably certain that there is a high probability that the loan *will* be repaid. Therefore, the applicant should be prepared to give any information necessary to assure the loan officer that the financial health of the firm is excellent.[36]

Intermediate-Term Loans

An intermediate-term loan, or simply *term loan,* provides the small business with capital that typically is repaid over a period of from one to ten years. The use of intermediate-term financing is an alternative to equity financing (sale of stock in the company) that many small business owners prefer since they do not have to relinquish ownership in their firms in order to secure it. (See discussion of debt versus equity financing in Chapter 14.)

For example, an entrepreneur may wish to purchase a piece of machinery for the manufacture of salable goods. Suppose a five-year loan is secured to facilitate the purchase. Since the working life of the machine may be substantially longer than five years, there is a high probability that the loan will be self-liquidating over the loan period from the sale of goods manufactured through the use of the machine. This self-liquidating aspect is typical of many intermediate-term loans.

> Intermediate-term loans are also used to purchase existing businesses, to help establish new ones, to provide additional working capital, and to replace long-term indebtedness that may carry a higher rate of interest. These loans may be either secured or unsecured. Payment may be made monthly, quarterly, semiannually, or annually, often with small early payments and a large final payment called a balloon payment.[37]

Long-Term Loans

Apart from making real-estate loans, commercial banks traditionally have not made a practice of providing long-term credit to the smaller business. However, your bank's loan officer should be in a position to assist you in securing a nonbank long-term loan in the event the circumstances involved justify such an approach to your financial problem. If nonbank long-term loans are arranged, the lender may require "sweeteners" or "kickers" in the form of options or rights to purchase equity in the company at a later date and at a predetermined price. For example, if you are securing first-round financing, you might issue preferred stock. For second-round financing, long-term debt in the form of a convertible debenture is often used. If you are seeking third-round financing, you could negotiate a loan with options or warrants for purchase of stock in your company at a later date.

There is a growing trend, however, for small, growth-oriented banks to specialize in lending to small businesses. There has recently been a dramatic increase in new bank formation across the country. Many of these banks are targeting middle market, or smaller, companies. Small banks, entrepreneurial themselves, are better equipped to handle the needs of the entrepreneur:

> "The incompatibility between giant bank culture and entrepreneurial business suggests that small and medium-sized banks will continue to offer special advantages to growing companies, despite the belated efforts of large banks to get into the market."[38]

Entrepreneurs may be wise in seeking out these smaller banks as a source of long-term financing. These banks have a special incentive to invest in young, growing companies since this represents a way for them to expand their *own* assets and realize substantial growth.

Equity Financing

The banking industry is subject to very strict regulation by federal and state agencies. Bank records are subject to regular scrutiny by bank examiners, and the banks are not permitted to commit depositors' funds to speculative ventures. However, by exercising considerable ingenuity, members of the banking community *have* devised ways of getting a piece of the action in new enterprises that offer the possibility of significant capital appreciation through equity growth.

Small Business Investment Company (SBIC) Subsidiaries and Affiliates. There are at the present time approximately seventy SBICs that are wholly owned by banks. A few examples are First Capital Corporation of Chicago, owned by First National Bank of Chicago; Small Business Enterprises, owned by the Bank of America; First Capital Corporation, an affiliate of First National Bank of Boston; and Citicorp Venture Capital, Ltd., owned by Citicorp, the holding company of Citibank in New York. In addition to those banks having wholly owned SBIC subsidiaries, there are a number of banks that are minority shareholders in SBICs.

Finders. Banks sometimes function as finders or brokers in bringing, for a fee, carefully screened investment opportunities to the attention of customers who are interested in providing venture capital. This is only one of the many services banks may offer their corporate clients.

In conclusion I wish to emphasize that banks are *not* in a position to directly provide equity capital to a new enterprise. *However,* your banker may be of enormous assistance in helping you *locate* this type of funding.

Commercial Finance Companies

Commercial finance companies finance receivables, inventory, and equipment in virtually all types of industry. In fact, commercial financing today represents a multibillion dollar industry. Commercial financing is often used when a company is short of working capital and cannot qualify for unsecured bank loans, especially if the company is already burdened with heavy taxes and inadequate depreciation allowances. However, it should *not* be assumed that all firms using this source are in trouble! Commercial financing is also used for settling estates, providing funds to enable one partner to buy out another, or enabling a business to make acquisitions. It is valuable, too, for firms having large fluctuations in borrowing requirements due to the seasonality of their businesses. It provides substantial financial leverage for the promotion of growth and profit at a time when a business may need it most.

Commonly, a commercial finance company provides for regular financing of accounts receivable on a revolving basis. Many companies find that they have large amounts of capital permanently tied up in accounts receivable. The commercial finance company provides cash in exchange for the assignment or hypothecation of these accounts. As fast as goods or services are invoiced, funds can be loaned against the receivables thus created (usually sixty to ninety percent of the face amount of each invoice). The collections in this instance are made by the seller, who pays the commercial finance company on receipt of customer payment. Thus, the financial burden of carrying accounts receivable is reduced, and the money derived in this way can be put to profitable use in financing those activities in which the small company has the greatest capability.

Commercial finance companies offer a wide range of financing services in addition to accounts-receivable financing. Some of these services include inventory financing, field warehousing, equipment leasing, and the making of collateral loans on existing capital equipment and machinery. Commercial finance companies provide more working capital for businesses on a continuing and flexible basis than almost any other source. However, there are many other advantages commercial financing offers, including: "The increase of capital turnover, a greater return on invested capital, the ability to make advantageous purchases requiring cash, and the improvement of credit standing by discounting suppliers' bills."[39] Furthermore, it may eliminate the undesirable alternative of seeking additional equity capital or taking in partners and diluting the owner's stake in the business. Since many commercial finance companies secure their funds through banks, you will certainly pay more interest on this form of financing than with bank financing.

Consumer Finance Companies

Consumer finance companies, also known as small loan companies, are not commonly regarded as a source of capital for business. However, in a study conducted several years ago by the National Bureau of Economic Research, it was found that a major small loan company had made approximately ten percent of its loans to the owners of small businesses. Nothing has occurred in subsequent years to alter this pattern materially, and major consumer finance companies today continue to provide a significant percentage of their loan volume to small businesses.

Frequently, a loan may be secured from a consumer finance company when no other legally authorized lending agency is willing to provide it, particularly if the amount of the loan is under $10,000. However, administrative and handling charges are often high in relation to the size of the loans, and, in light of the higher risk generally evident in lending to individuals with less than ideal credit ratings, the effective interest rates—or financing charges—are substantially higher than those levied by commercial banks.

Corporate Venture Capital Departments or Subsidiaries

Today, an increasing number of large corporations are creating departments or subsidiaries exclusively devoted to investment opportunities in new or relatively young ventures. To give you an idea of how extensive this corporate interest in venture capital is, a listing of several of the involved companies, including their investment subsidiaries (where a subsidiary has been established), follows:

1. Control Data Corporation (Microtechnology Investments Ltd.)
2. Cooper Laboratories, Inc. (Palo Alto Ventures, Inc.)
3. Davis, Skaggs & Company, Inc. (Davis Skaggs Capital)
4. General Electric (General Electric Venture Capital Corporation)
5. SRI International (Commtech International)
6. W. R. Grace & Co. (Grace Ventures Corporation)
7. Xerox Corporation (Xerox Development Corporation)

The elements that motivate a large corporation to enter into financing of new businesses are as complex and varied as the goals and markets of the corporations involved. The following is an analysis of some of the major motivational factors.

Diversification. By supplying equity capital for the formation of a new company or the expansion of an existing small company, a large corporation may cultivate a potential acquisition candidate that specializes in a field of business in which it is not already engaged.

Growth. As a result of their merger and acquisition activities, many large corporations have come under increasing pressure from the Justice Department. However, by appropriately structuring the financial package that launches a new venture, a major corporation may acquire a minority ownership at the outset, with provision through warrants for the acquisition of majority control in the event the new business is successful and the corporation chooses to exercise its stock options.

Capital Gains. In a number of instances, major corporations enjoy more cash surplus than they can profitably use for expansion in their present product areas. Participation in the financing of new enterprises may afford a large corporation unique opportunities for substantial capital gains, with their attendant tax advantages.

Acquire Technological Leadership. As a result of the considerable interest in entrepreneurship on the part of many of today's highly capable technologists, many large corporations have found it difficult to attract the services of these people because mere salaries do not satisfy them. In addition, the stock in major corporations is not apt to undergo substantial increases in a short period of time, regardless of how hard the young technologists work; therefore, stock options in a major corporation are not particularly attractive. However, if the technologist-entrepreneurs are given the opportunity to start new businesses that are financed by major corporations and that have the potential, tied directly to their efforts, for substantial financial success, they may be induced to associate with those major corporations as presidents and part-owners of corporate subsidiaries or affiliates.

The investment activity of corporate venture capital groups is primarily designed to produce prime acquisition candidates for the future, and the methods used to provide financing reflect this fact. Compromises often subordinate entrepreneurs' desires for independence through majority equity control to their desire for personal wealth. Accordingly, deals can be structured to provide the founders with thirty percent of the equity and the corporate venture capital group with forty percent, allocating the remaining thirty percent for a "public offering" (see "Investment Bankers" later in this chapter) in order to arrive at an equitable valuation of the stock. Initial arrangements may set forth the requirement that the founders make their stock available to the investing corporation at some future date at a price equal to that of those shares publicly traded.

Another means of structuring the deal is to establish a buy-out formula that is tied to annual sales, profits, or other performance criteria. Here, the question of majority ownership of equity in the new firm is moot because the founders are committed to relinquishing ownership at a later date. The primary area of negotiation is the way in which the buy-out price relates to the performance of the enterprise.

Even though the major corporation may insist upon owning a majority interest in the business, its financial assistance can offer the entrepreneur many advantages. For example, a large corporation can be expected to show much greater patience with the development of a new enterprise than will a financially oriented investor who is interested merely in a quick return. A large corporation can also provide marketing channels, manufacturing assistance, accounting support, and general bolstering in every weak area outside the entrepreneur's area of expertise—the expertise that made the venture attractive to the corporation in the first place.

Credit Unions

There are two basic kinds of credit unions—those chartered by the federal government and those chartered by state governments. Since the federally chartered credit unions substantially outnumber the state-chartered credit unions, this section will be devoted primarily to a discussion of federal credit unions.

The present definition of a federal credit union is "a cooperative association organized . . . for the purpose of promoting thrift among its members and creating a source of credit for provident or productive purpose."[40]

The creation of federal credit unions was authorized by Congress under the Federal Credit Union Act of 1934, which underwent major revisions in 1959 and again in 1977, resulting in expanded powers for the credit unions and greater opportunities for their members. Under the amended act, all federal credit unions are regulated by the National Credit Union Administration (NCUA), an independent agency of the federal government. The major activities of the NCUA involve the chartering, supervising, and examining of federal credit unions. The administration's activities are exclusively financed by fees and assessments paid by the credit unions under its jurisdiction.[41]

Of particular interest to the entrepreneur is the lending function of the credit union. *Eligibility for credit union loans is exclusively restricted to their memberships.* In order to become a member, one must subscribe to at least one share of stock in the corporation and must pay an entrance fee. Additionally, credit union membership is "limited to groups having a common bond of occupation or association, or to groups within a well-defined neighborhood, community, or rural district." However, recently the NCUA amended its guidelines to authorize the granting of charters to credit unions serving multiple occupational groups.[42] In general, the operational definition of common bond is expanding, meaning that more and more people have the opportunity to find a credit union to which they can belong.[43]

A variety of federal legislation in recent years has expanded the powers of credit unions. Among other things, credit unions can now issue interest-bearing share drafts, authorize lines of credit *and* make thirty-year mortgages. In addition, new laws allow for an upward adjustment of the interest rate ceiling on credit union loans to fifteen percent. (Unfortunately for the borrower, this removes one of the great traditional benefits of credit union borrowing, the ability to secure a loan at rates significantly below the competition).[44]

Under recent regulations, restrictions on loan sizes have been relaxed. Unsecured personal loan limits typically vary from $1,000 to $2,500, depending on the state, and secured personal loans can be offered to a maximum of ten percent of share capital.[45]

Entrepreneurs may avail themselves of the benefits of credit union membership and borrow money as a personal loan, which will be subject to the reasonable requirement that there be a high probability that the loan will be repaid in accordance with the terms of the original loan agreement. Such loans may prove quite helpful in financing the purchase of equipment for use in a new enterprise.

While credit union lending is still primarily confined to personal loans, these institutions are authorized to make commercial loans. This activity may increase in the future, according to a recent study which indicates that

> While credit unions have not generally used their authority to make commercial loans to members, legislation enacted in 1979 allowing participation loans with other financial institutions may eventually lead to an increase in business lending by credit unions.[46]

The national trade organization and outspoken advocate of credit unions is the Credit Union National Association, Inc. (CUNA). For more information about this subject, write to them at P.O. Box 431, Madison, Wisconsin 53701.

Customers

In a number of instances, customers are able to provide some of the financing needed for the launching of a new business. A customer may have a number of reasons for offering financial assistance to a new supplier, and there are many ways in which this assistance may be extended. The following are but a few of the factors motivating customer assistance to a new enterprise.

Encourage Supplier Competition in Virtually Every Industry. A fact of economic existence is that increased competition invariably results in lower pricing. Therefore, customers are almost always happy to see new competition, and some are willing to offer financial encouragement to a new supplier with the expectation that lower prices will result. This heightened competition may also provide better service in the form of more timely deliveries, higher quality standards, and more diverse product offerings.

Obtain "Backyard" Supplier. If the customer is geographically remote from its present suppliers, it may wish to encourage a new supplier to establish a facility in a nearby location. The customer may also wish ultimately to acquire the supplier as a subsidiary.

Obtain Supplier Where None Existed Before. If a market need exists and there is no supplier to satisfy it, the founders of a new venture may be able to persuade a customer that in order to obtain the products it needs, it should assist in the financing of their venture.

Some of the techniques through which financial assistance may be furnished by customers are listed below.

Advance Payments or Deposits. Depending on the product and the market, a new supplier may be in a position to secure deposits or advance payments (partial or full) before any actual work on the order commences. While this is a common practice in many sectors of industry, it is particularly evident where products are specially manufactured to customer specifications.

Progress Payments. In industries as diverse as highway construction and technical research and development, it has become accepted practice for suppliers to demand periodic payments from their customers for work satisfactorily performed to date. Such a financing schedule can significantly reduce the amount of working capital the suppliers need in order to function effectively and solvently.

Loan Guarantees. If a customer desires to purchase a product or service from the lowest bidder in a highly competitive market, the lowest bidder is often a new company trying to enter the marketplace. In some cases, a customer may be willing to guarantee a bank loan to the small supplier in order to obtain the lowest possible price for purchases.

Direct Loans. Customers may also make an outright low-interest loan to a supplier as a means of insuring prompt delivery of their orders. Usually, in a situation of this kind, the customer hopes to realize very significant benefits from providing the loan—either in the form of low-cost purchases or in the establishment of a geographically convenient new supplier.

Purchase of Stock in the New Company. In some instances, a customer may develop a "captive supplier" by investing substantially in the common stock of a new supplier's company. In such a situation, stock options may be arranged at the outset to provide for the acquisition of the supplier by the customer at a later date, when the new business has matured and may no longer provide the founders with the challenges that prompted them to start it.

Lend Equipment. In some highly specialized situations, a customer may provide a supplier with the equipment needed to produce the desired products or to perform the desired services. A common example of this type of support is in the performance of research, development, and manufacturing for the federal government. The government may loan specialized equipment to the supplier to insure the performance of the contracted assignment.

Economic Development Administration

The Economic Development Administration (EDA), an agency of the U.S. Department of Commerce, provides business development loans solely for the purpose of assisting economically deprived areas:

> The legislative mandate of the Economic Development Administration is to generate jobs, help protect existing jobs in economically distressed areas, and promote the capacity of States and localities to plan and conduct economic development programs.[47]

It is the policy of the EDA to make loans in order to establish viable businesses with the expectation that new jobs will be created and the local citizenry may enjoy higher personal incomes. Since the economic health of different regions will vary depending on many business and nonbusiness factors, EDA offices maintain regularly revised listings of all eligible communities.[48]

EDA Loan Terms

The EDA may guarantee up to ninety percent of the loans made to private borrowers for fixed asset purchases and/or for working capital, for projects in areas eligible for EDA assistance.[49] The EDA will finance the purchase or development of land and facilities (which includes machinery and equipment) for industrial or commercial use, including construction of new buildings, rehabilitation of abandoned buildings, and conversion or expansion of existing buildings. This financing comes in the form of guarantees on loans made to borrowers by private lending institutions. The *lending institution* is the applicant for EDA financing guarantees.

EDA will not normally guarantee revolving type or open-end working capital loans, nor will it refinance existing debt for borrowers.

Loan Eligibility Requirements and Conditions

The major conditions for EDA borrowing include the following:[50]

1. Applications can only be submitted by private lending institutions.

2. The project must show a good possibility of alleviating unemployment or underemployment in the project area on a long-term basis.

3. There must be "reasonable assurance" that the loan will be repaid.

4. The maximum lending period is twenty-five years. Working capital loans ordinarily are limited to five years.

5. The interest rate of the applicant (the bank) must not be excessive, in EDA's estimation.

6. Loan amounts requested must be greater than $550,000 and cannot exceed $10 million.

7. For guaranteed fixed asset loans, EDA requires an equity contribution of at least fifteen percent; for working capital loans, at least twenty percent.

There are a number of other restrictions on EDA loans. For example, EDA will not guarantee a loan unless there is evidence that funds cannot be found elsewhere without hindering the accomplishment of the project. Also, under current regulations, EDA expects that each $7,500 loaned will create an additional job.

For a detailed description of EDA loan requirements and restrictions, contact any one of the regional offices of the EDA listed below. You may also wish to discuss the possibility of obtaining an EDA loan with your banker, who may provide a good indication of the likelihood of obtaining this type of funding.

EDA Regional Offices

- **Philadelphia Regional Office** (325 Chestnut Street, Room 401, Philadelphia, Pennsylvania 19106) serves Connecticut, Delaware, District of Columbia, Maine, Maryland, Massachusetts, New Hampshire, New Jersey, New York, Pennsylvania, Puerto Rico, Rhode Island, Vermont, Virginia, Virgin Islands, and West Virginia.

- **Atlanta Regional Office** (1365 Peachtree Street, NE, Suite 700, Atlanta, Georgia 30309) serves Alabama, Florida, Georgia, Kentucky, Mississippi, North Carolina, South Carolina, and Tennessee.

- **Denver Regional Office** (Tremont Center, 333 West Colfax Avenue, Denver, Colorado 80202) serves Colorado, Iowa, Kansas, Missouri, Montana, Nebraska, North Dakota, South Dakota, Utah, and Wyoming.

- **Chicago Regional Office** (1755 West Jackson Boulevard, Suite A-1630, Chicago, Illinois 60604) serves Illinois, Indiana, Michigan, Minnesota, Ohio, and Wisconsin.

- **Seattle Regional Office** (Lake Union Building, Suite 500, 1700 Westlake Avenue, North, Seattle, Washington 98109) serves Alaska, American Samoa, Arizona, California, Guam, Hawaii, Idaho, Nevada, Oregon, and Washington.

- **Austin Regional Office** (Suite 201, Grant Building, 611 East Sixth Street, Austin, Texas 78701) serves Arkansas, Louisiana, New Mexico, Oklahoma, and Texas.

Employees

A very significant—but often overlooked—source of venture capital for the new enterprise is its employees. Employee ownership in the business may provide significant benefits to the firm beyond the obvious easing of corporate cash flow shortages. These benefits to the firm are best analyzed by considering some of the factors that motivate employees to purchase an interest in their firm.

Pride in the Company. Employees can be encouraged to identify with the goals and image of their company if they have a personal interest in its success. Employees who feel a close identification with the objectives, productivity, standards of quality, and all the other characteristics ordinarily associated with pride can benefit both the company *and* themselves.

Security. Employees who own stock in their company usually find their feelings of personal security enhanced. Through ownership of stock, they are guaranteed a position from which they can make their wishes known to the company management through the Board of Directors, the corporate entity established exclusively for the representation of stockholder interest.

Build an Estate. Stock ownership can make it possible for employees to build personal estates. If they recognize that their own efforts can be effective in furthering the objectives of the company while thus enhancing their equity in the company, they are motivated to work harder. Not only will they be able to realize growth in their financial worth, but they are also in a position to directly affect the rate of this growth.

The channels available for employee participation in financing the new enterprise are many and include the following five.

Direct Loan. Employees may provide capital to their company through the vehicle of a direct loan. As employees, they are in an excellent position to assess the risk involved in making such a loan. The parent company should, of course, make provision for regular payment of interest to the employee. A separate fund for the purpose of retiring the loan (called a "sinking fund") should be established, and, most importantly, the loan should be documented with a formally authorized note and with a lien on company property if it is secured by tangible assets.

Loan Guarantee. In some instances, an employee of substantial personal net worth may not wish to make a direct loan or to purchase stock in the company but may be willing to guarantee a loan obtained by the company from an outside borrower.

Outright Purchase of Stock. An employee may acquire a stock interest in the company in a number of ways. The simplest of these is the outright purchase of stock through the company treasurer. Through the mechanism of a *qualified stock option plan,* executive employees meeting certain qualifications established by the Internal Revenue Service may be eligible for stock options that permit them to buy stock in the company at various times in the future at a price established at the time of the initial award of the option. Still another way of obtaining capital from company employees is through the mechanism of the *employee stock purchase plan.* The terms under which this plan is ordinarily administered afford quali- fying employees the periodic opportunity to purchase stock in the company at slightly less than fair market value of the stock and in amounts usually proportional to their annual income. (The specifics of the plan can vary significantly from company to company.)

Accept Stock in Lieu of Wages. In some instances, com- pany management may wish to pay certain of its employees with stock in the company instead of with cash. Such a compensation scheme requires the establishment of an escrow account for the ac- cumulation of cash that would otherwise be payable to the em- ployee. This account is maintained until such time as permission is granted by the appropriate government regulatory agency for the is- suance of stock to said employees. Subsequently, the money in the escrow account can be returned to the corporate treasury cash ac- count. (An example of compensation provided under this plan was covered in Chapter 1 in the story about Laser Technology.)

Provide Tangible Assets. It is possible for the employees of a new business to provide tangible assets to the company in ex- change for stock. Such assets may include land, buildings, raw mate- rials, parts, and equipment, which are exchanged for stock in amounts based on the fair market value of the goods provided and the nominal value of the stock as approved by the appropriate state regulatory agency.

Equipment Manufacturers

In the face of increasingly stiff competition, many equipment manu- facturers have come to appreciate the value of assisting their cus- tomers in securing financing for the purchase of their products. Confronted with two potential suppliers who offer comparable equipment in terms of quality and specifications, a small business contemplating a major purchase will favor the firm offering the most attractive financing arrangements. Therefore, it is commonplace for many of the large and financially sound suppliers of high-cost equip- ment, such as computers, road-building machinery, lathes, end mills, drill presses, dry-cleaning equipment, or printing presses, to provide their customers with intermediate-term, mortgage-type loans se- cured by this equipment. Under such an arrangement, customers may realize tax write-offs on both interest expenses and accelerated depreciation allowances while they acquire equity in the equipment purchased. Often, a major equipment manufacturing corporation will establish a wholly owned subsidiary exclusively for this purpose.

Although chattel mortgage and installment financing is often provided, it is also common practice for equipment suppliers to lease equipment to their small business clients. This last arrangement has the advantage in that 100 percent of the rent is a customer expense for income tax purposes.

From the standpoint of the equipment supplier, there must be a reasonable assurance that the equipment will be a self-amortizing investment: (1) through the revenue produced by the sale of products made with it, or (2) through the increased profitability due to higher efficiency resulting from its use.

From the standpoint of the entrepreneur, equipment suppliers may prove to be an extremely helpful source of financial assistance. Information on the availability of such assistance should be secured well in advance of actual need in order to permit proper preparation of cash flow projections.

Factoring Companies

Factoring companies, or *factors*, as they are sometimes called, perform many financial services for the business community. They trace their origins in this country to a time roughly 150 years ago, when factoring was concerned exclusively with the import of textiles from Europe. Factoring houses represented European textile mills, sold goods, and collected the money from buyers in this country. They assumed the entire responsibility for collections and possible credit losses while at the same time making discounted cash payments to the European mills. Thus, the mills were able to obtain prompt cash payment for goods supplied to customers in this country, and the factoring houses made their profits on their ability to evaluate the credit worthiness of their buyers and to collect fees and interest charges.

Today, factoring companies provide similar, although greatly expanded, services to a large number of industries as diverse as electronics, heavy machinery, durable consumer goods, and many businesses in the service field. The most commonly known advantages of factoring follow.

1. Factoring frees the capital ordinarily tied up in carrying accounts receivable. The sellers do business for cash while their customers get the terms they require, which permits sellers to use their capital more productively.

2. Factoring eliminates the expense of a credit department.

3. Factoring provides full credit protection and eliminates all risk, as the factor absorbs credit losses.

4. Factoring reduces bookkeeping expenses, maintains accounts receivable ledgers for the client, and absorbs all collection expenses.

5. A factor will usually provide money prior to the shipment of goods to finance a pre-season build-up of inventory [by the seller].

6. A factor may finance machinery.[51]

Through factoring, a service or manufacturing company can substantially increase the volume of business it can handle in relation to the net worth or equity valuation of its enterprise; it can plan cash needs with confidence because it collects receivables whether the customer pays or not; and it is in a strong buying position through the short-term availability of cash, should cash be required to make a purchase on unusually favorable terms. In effect, the firm is selling for cash while the factor provides the firm's customers with credit. In this way, companies are relieved of what might be substantial financial risk and of many of the time-consuming involvements normally associated with the collection process. Thus, the entrepreneurs are in a position to devote all of their time to those elements of the business in which they are qualified.

In addition, factoring may replace the need for additional equity capital, thus avoiding the dilution of the owner's equity in the business. It can also be used to buy out partners and to finance an acquisition. In this manner, factoring can provide substantial leverage to a small capital base.

There are two basic kinds of factoring. In nonrecourse, or "old line" factoring (rarely used these days), the factor purchases the accounts receivable outright (at a discount from face value), subsequently notifying the customer that it has assumed the legal position as a creditor and that payment of the accounts should be made directly to it.

A second form of factoring has come into general use—accounts receivable are purchased *with* recourse. Although a cash payment is made to the manufacturer at the time of assignment of the accounts receivable, a reserve is set aside against the possibility of default. After the customer retires the accounts receivable, the manufacturer will receive the balance due, minus the factor's discount and interest on the funds advanced. If the customer defaults, the factor, having recourse to the manufacturer, may demand full recovery of the funds originally advanced. In this instance, since the risk to the factor is reduced, the amount of the discount reflects this diminished risk.

The expense involved in using the services of a factor can be significantly higher than bank rates since receivables are sold at a discount and, in addition, interest must be paid on the funds advanced. However, the business only pays for the financing it needs—unlike the case of a bank loan where some of the funds may not be used or must be set aside as a compensating balance (see "Commercial Banks" above).

Financial Consultants, Finders, and Other Intermediaries

In the face of the bewildering array of financial sources, the sometimes conflicting requirements of different organizations and individuals supplying venture capital, and a malaise brought about by the apparent mystique characterizing the fund-raising process in general, many entrepreneurs seek the services of financial consultants, finders, and other financial intermediaries in their search for venture capital. Properly qualified finders may be a godsend to the entrepreneur from the standpoint of the services they are in a position to provide.

Determine the Possibility of Obtaining Financing. The initial effort of the financial intermediary will be to determine the commercial viability of the proposed business idea with an eye not only to the prospects for commercial success but also to the probability of locating financing. (In many instances, perfectly valid business proposals go unfunded because the proposed venture is of a type that is currently not in vogue in investment circles.)

Determine the Amount of Financing Required. Experienced intermediaries should be in an excellent position to evaluate objectively the magnitude of the financing required by the proposed venture. They may be of further assistance in evaluating this requirement relative to prevailing capital market conditions (tight money or surplus).

Advise on the Best Financing Technique. The financial intermediary should suggest the best approach to the fund-raising problem. This particular function is especially important in evaluating the pros and cons of equity versus loan financing for the venture.

Assist in Preparation of the Business Plan. In many instances, the intermediary can be of considerable help in assisting the entrepreneur with the preparation of a suitable business plan for the fund-raising effort. One consultant I used to know charged a flat $5,000 fee for this service.

Locate Capital on a Commission Basis. The primary service a financial intermediary renders to the entrepreneur is the location of venture capital. In most cases, this is done on a commission basis, although a fee in the form of a retainer may also be negotiated.

Syndication. Sometimes in the process of securing a large amount of capital, it may be necessary to persuade many individuals and organizations to pool their resources. Financial intermediaries may be of considerable assistance in such a project since their contacts in the financial community will be far more numerous than those of the entrepreneur.

Negotiate the Deal. In most instances, the entrepreneur is a novice in the conduct of financial negotiations. Thus, the services of a seasoned financial intermediary can be invaluable. Although the attitude of venture capitalists toward financial intermediaries is mixed, the involvement of an ethical and knowledgeable financial intermediary is usually welcome in financial circles. A financial intermediary who has previously earned the respect of members of the investment community is in a unique position to provide services of value to investors as well as to the entrepreneur.

Screen Propositions. One of the biggest complaints venture capitalists have is that, of the many hundreds of propositions they regularly review, only a very few are acceptable. A financial intermediary can be of great help in culling out all but the very best propositions for the investor's consideration.

Management Consultant. After financial arrangements have been made, the financial intermediary may serve as a management consultant in a liaison capacity between the new enterprise and the investors.

In general, complaints regarding financial intermediaries revolve around the following three key points.

High Fees in Relation to Services Rendered. If a financial intermediary does nothing more than provide an entrepreneur with a list of venture capitalists whom the entrepeneur is expected to contact directly, it seems reasonable to conclude that the standard finder's fee of five to ten percent of the eventual deal represents excessive remuneration for the efforts expended.

"Proposal Mills." Some of the less ethical financial intermediaries have provoked well-deserved ill will among members of the investment community as a result of their operation of "proposal mills." The entrepreneur should be quite leery of any financial intermediary who expresses the attitude "I don't care *what* your product is, kid! We'll work up a good proposal and get financing for you, anyway!"

Some unethical financial intermediaries may also *promise* their clients that they will be successful in locating financing for the proposed venture. However, unless these financial intermediaries are personally furnishing the required capital, they are not in a position to make such a guarantee. They can only do their best to secure funds from others.

Disappearing Act. If financial intermediaries successfully arrange funding for new enterprises, it is desirable to structure their compensation in such a way that they have a personal stake in the ultimate success of the new venture, possibly through ownership of stock. All too often, intermediaries successful in locating financing are never seen nor heard of again once the capitalization arrangements have been completed and their fee has been paid. Again, this minimum level of effort is not in consonance with the five-percent-or-more charge that is normally levied under such circumstances.

Financial intermediaries are particularly unique in venture capital financing as a result of their visibility. In the New York City telephone directory Yellow Pages, there are more than 150 financial consultants listed. Other Yellow Page headings under which financial intermediaries may be found include Financing, Business Consultants, Business Development, and Investment Management.

Founders

With rare exceptions, the founders of a new company make a personal capital investment that represents a substantial percentage of their individual net worth. The elements that prompt entrepreneurs to invest their personal assets in their companies are largely the same as those which prompted them to launch the venture. (These elements were discussed in some detail in Chapter 2 and will not be repeated here.) Some of the more commonly employed financing techniques follow.

Make Direct Loans. Ordinarily, company founders do not make funds available to their company on a loan basis. However, if one of the founders has substantially greater personal assets than the rest of the founders have, some of these funds may be supplied on a direct loan basis. For example, if Mr. Brown and Ms. Smith each have $20,000 to invest in the new venture while Mr. Jones is prepared to invest $100,000, they may all agree to receive an equal number of shares by each investing $20,000 in an equity position. Jones may then agree to provide an additional $80,000 in exchange for a long-term, interest-bearing note. Thus, each of the founders will own the same amount of stock in the venture. Ordinarily, Jones would further agree to subordinate his note, meaning that any other lenders would have priority should it become necessary to liquidate the assets of the corporation.

Guarantee Loans. In some instances, founders may have assets of substantial value such as unimproved real estate that cannot readily be liquidated or that they do not wish to turn into cash. In such cases, an outside lending agency may accept these individual founders as the guarantors of a loan to the new firm.

Purchase Stock. The most common form of founder investment in a new enterprise is through the cash purchase of common stock. Frequently, this cash is obtained through the sale of previous investments and through substantial individual borrowings. Common secondary sources for loans include:

1. Life insurance policy loans.
2. First or second mortgage on home. Refinancing of home furnishings, automobiles, pleasure boats, etc.
3. Personal loans (signature or character loans).

It is interesting to note that in many cases a banker may be willing to lend someone several thousand dollars for the purpose of making a vacation trip around the world, but he may be *un*willing to lend this customer the same amount of money for the purpose of starting a business. A leading Chicago-based manufacturer of cosmetics created for black Americans got his start under just such a set of circumstances—turned down on a loan request for $500 with which to start his business, he reapplied indicating that he wanted the money for a vacation trip. The loan was granted. However, the hero of our piece was unable to bring himself to squander this money on anything so frivolous as a vacation. Instead, he started a company. Regardless of the circumstances surrounding the loan application, personal loans are *not* an uncommon source of capital for financing a business.

Supply Tangible Assets. Very commonly, company founders are in a position to contribute assets to the new venture in exchange for stock. Such assets may include capital equipment, land, buildings, raw materials, and supplies.

Pool Resources. Another technique for raising money when the number of founders involved is large is to establish an organizational chart where the key positions to be filled may number as many as ten or more. The idea is to persuade each of these potential founders to invest a nominal amount of cash in the company—for instance, $1000, $2000, or $3000 each. Thus, sufficient resources may be accumulated to permit the development of a prototype. The founders who do this early work may be the engineering members of the staff. The others may plan to join the venture at a later date. Subsequently, members of the financial community may be approached when the founders are in a much better bargaining position because they have hardware to exhibit. It stands to reason that it is much easier to sell an investor with a piece of hardware than with an eloquent word description of an idea.

One of the fundamental factors any venture capitalist, private investor, relative, friend, neighbor, or other potential source of funds will want to know is the degree of commitment the founders have made to their new enterprise. (Bear in mind that it is extremely difficult to measure, in terms of dollars and cents, the value of hard work and long moonlight hours.) Thus, a consideration of enormous significance is documented evidence that the founders have made a substantial cash investment. This investment does not necessarily have to represent *large* cash amounts; however, it must represent a major percentage of the founders' personal assets. If your car is not in hock, if you don't have a second mortgage on your home, and if you have not borrowed all you can possibly raise from your friendly banker or neighborhood loan company, you may have difficulty convincing *some* investors that you are serious. Fortunately, such an attitude is not held by *all* investors, although *resasonable* evidence of financial commitment is universally expected.

Franchising

Once you have developed a business concept and have a viable operation in place, you might consider franchising as an option for financing additional growth of your business. Under a typical franchising contract, the franchisor grants someone a license to duplicate a business operation under the franchisor's name, in exchange for an initial fee and a percentage of the profits. By employing this concept, the small business owner can conserve capital while expanding the business at the *franchisee's* expense.

While a discussion of franchising conjures up images of McDonald's and Kentucky Fried Chicken, there has been a trend in recent years towards innovative new franchises with low start-up costs.

Business and professional franchises, computer-related businesses, and a wide variety of service operations are springing up as franchises across the country. One pioneering example in this area is Century 21, the successful real estate brokerage chain.[52]

There are disadvantages to franchising as a financing source. The most obvious is the loss of control over the operations of the business. Then, too, there is always the unpleasant possibility of contract disputes. During the past decade there have been extensive abuses of the franchising system in this country. Major court battles have been waged between franchisors and franchisees over infringement of contract rights. As a result, many states have enacted strict laws regulating the sale of franchises.

Nevertheless, despite the problems inherent in this financing method and the need for caution, franchising remains a viable and sometimes very attractive option for expanding a business without putting additional strain on capital reserves. For information about franchising opportunities, refer to the directories outlined in Appendix 1.

Industrial Banks

Industrial banks—which include institutions referred to as Morris Plan banks—are sometimes difficult to distinguish from ordinary commercial banks, while in other respects they appear to be more like consumer finance companies. The lines between commercial and industrial banks are becoming more and more blurred. In some areas of the country you can hardly tell the difference between them.

> Industrial banks, which originally operated in much the same way as finance companies, now offer many banking services, including accepting time and savings deposits and lending to consumers and small business.
>
> In addition, in recent years a number of states have expanded the commercial lending powers of industrial banks and allowed the institutions to offer the check-like negotiable order of withdrawal, or NOW, accounts.
>
> Consequently, in many states there is very little difference between industrial and commercial banks.[53]

Industrial banks have become popular acquisition targets in recent years. A number of large commercial bank holding companies, including Citicorp and Mellon National Corporation, are purchasing industrial banks as a means of getting around laws that prohibit interstate banking by commercial banks. There are no such restraints on industrial banks.[54]

State laws regulating industrial banks vary, as do loan limits and typical maturities. Depending on loan competition with commercial banks, interest rates charged by industrial banks range from slightly above the prime lending rate charged by commercial banks all the way up to the maximum permitted under the state law. In almost all instances, loans are retired on the installment basis.

One of the major differences between industrial banks and consumer finance companies is that industrial banks are authorized to accept savings certificates of investment from businesses as well as from private individuals. Policies governing the availability of loan funds from industrial banks are very much like those of consumer finance companies (discussed above), although industrial banks typically handle larger notes than do commercial finance companies.

Although there are pronounced differences in the investment postures of industrial banks and consumer finance companies, it is interesting to note that in early 1971 the American Industrial Bankers Association merged with the National Consumer Finance Association. The surviving organization, now called the American Financial Services Association, was known as the National Consumer Finance Association.

Insurance Companies

Historically, insurance companies have been a major source of long-term debt capital for American industry. Life insurance companies in the United States, as of the end of 1982, had combined assets that exceeded $600 *billion*,[55] while property and casualty insurance company assets exceeded $230 billion.[56] Life insurance company investments traditionally have been primarily in public utility and industrial bonds and in real estate mortgages, but they have been branching out in other areas as well. For example, for a number of years insurance companies have sponsored mutual funds.[57] Investment standards are typically quite high, and new or speculative investment opportunities are rarely considered. Furthermore, life insurance company investments are very carefully regulated by *each* of the fifty states in which they operate. The strictness of these regulations varies sharply from state to state, though, and a number of companies have allocated a small percentage of their assets to the venture capital field. Since a "small percentage" of billions of dollars *is* millions of dollars, this is not an inconsequential source of capital. The property and casualty insurance companies, subject to less stringent state regulation, have pioneered in the venture capital field. One of the companies to lead the way was the Allstate Insurance Company, a division of Sears, Roebuck and Company, under the direction of Edgar F. Heizer, Jr., former Assistant Treasurer at Allstate in charge of the Private Placement Division. As a result of Heizer's remarkable ability to pick winners, Allstate Insurance was an early participant in the financing of such stock market favorites as Teledyne, Memorex, Control Data, and International Industries.[58] The Allstate venture capital pool invested $60 million in 1982 alone, and was the second most active source of venture capital in the country in that year.[59]

Another insurance firm active in the venture capital field is Aetna Life & Casualty Company. Aetna committed $8 million of its $20 billion loan portfolio to venture capital in 1982, and intends to continue putting more money into the area in the future. As Alan Mendelson, assistant vice president of the bond investment department puts it: "Aetna is not saying it's going to outplay the Hambrecht & Quists, but if we can even come close to the standard return on investment, twenty-five percent, that's good."[60]

Other insurance companies now active in the venture capital field include Prudential Life Insurance Company, CIGNA Corporation, Northwestern Mutual Life Insurance Company, and John Hancock Mutual Life Insurance Company. Still other insurance companies participate in venture capital financing as limited partners in venture capital groups. Insurance companies may also participate in the venture capital field through the use of management advisory services. In such an instance, the insurance company will invest its funds in the venture. It will then engage the services of a management consulting firm or investment management firm, as a representative of the interests of the insurance company, to monitor the investment.

Investment Bankers

Prior to the passage of the Glass-Steagall Banking Act (also known as the Banking Act of 1933), it was the regular practice of banking institutions to provide commercial *and* investment banking services (the purchase and sale of securities) to the business community. However, just as the Securities Act of 1933 (prompted by the 1929 stock market crash) was intended to force corporations and investment firms to adopt higher standards of social responsibility in the solicitation of public financing, the Glass-Steagall Banking Act was devised to insure greater stability and safety in the future of the then failure-plagued banking community. The primary effect of the Glass-Steagall Banking Act was to separate the functions of commercial banking and investment banking. Today the lines between the two functions are becoming increasingly blurred again, and many experts predict the Glass-Steagall Banking Act will be overturned in the near future.

Investment banking as practiced today is primarily concerned with supplying the *long-term* capital requirements of business, while *seasonal* or *short-term* requirements are satisfied through commercial banking and/or other channels. The investment banker functions as an intermediary between businesses in need of permanent working capital or funds for the expansion of plant and facilities and the investor with money to supply.

Since investment bankers operate in a sector of the financial community where competition is keen and rewards are high, great circumspection is observed in the conduct of business transactions. In many cases, investment banking firms have spent decades in establishing a reputation for providing investors with worthwhile investment opportunities. Therefore, the small business owner or entrepreneur must recognize the importance of fully disclosing to the investment banker the details of the new or planned venture. A format such as that described in Section II of this book should be ideal for this purpose.

If the investment banker agrees to assist in financing the venture, the types of notes and stocks to be offered are selected, and the amount, rate, and price are negotiated. Financing through investment bankers may originate in a number of ways.

1. They may provide loan funds from their own account in return for interest and, possibly, stock warrants.

2. They may secure loan funds from outside investors who are clients of the firm in exchange for a fee and/or stock and/or stock warrants.

3. They may make an equity investment through the outright purchase of stock. In recent years, dozens of different investment banking firms have established pools of capital specially earmarked for venture capital use.

For example, Merrill Lynch Venture Capital, Inc., a subsidiary of the prominent nationwide investment banking and brokerage firm, participates in start-up and early stage financing of promising growth companies. The group manages a limited partnership (ML Venture Partners I, L.P.), which was set up expressly for the purpose of investing in young companies with high potential. The investment criteria used by the partnership may be regarded as being typical of the venturing departments and affiliates of large, reputable investment banking firms.

> Prospective venture capital investments are evaluated on an individual basis for their significant growth potential in sales and earnings. ML Venture Partners I, L.P. seeks to invest between $500,000 and $2 million in companies that combine the following critical elements:
>
> - A competent management team with expert knowledge of its business and the ability to work well together. We are prepared at

times to assume a significant role in identifying the necessary management talent.

- A market characterized by favorable relationships among the variables of size, growth potential, and competition.

- Innovative products or services, proprietary technology or specialized expertise.

- Equity participation by ML Venture Partners I, L.P., perhaps in cooperation with other venture capital firms, permitting active, on-going involvement in the strategic direction of the company.[61]

4. The investment banker may undertake to locate equity funds from outside investors—a process commonly referred to as a *private placement*. In discussing this subject in an introductory brochure, the well-established investment banking firm of Bateman Eichler, Hill Richards, Inc. indicates that there are:

> ... certain restrictions on these types of placements. Under present regulations, such a placement can be offered and sold to only a limited number of potential investors unless they are sophisticated financial institutions who regularly purchase such securities in private offerings. It can be quite helpful for a company to obtain financing from such sources since it establishes their credit with institutions of recognized and respected reputations; this can be important to others dealing with the company. It can also assist in future financings, either with the same institutions or with others.
>
> The total cost of such a placement is usually less than half that of a public offering and can be accomplished more rapidly because there is no need to file a document with the SEC. As with the public offering, however, the complexity of the projects is such that the company should deal with only one Investment Banker.[62]

5. They may choose to do an underwriting of a new stock offering for the company. Acting in the capacity of underwriters, the investment banker may be described in terms of the Securities Act of 1933 as a

> ... person who has purchased from an issuer [the new company] with a view to, or sells for an issuer in connection with, the distribution of any security, or participates or has a direct or indirect participation in any such undertaking, but such term shall not include a person whose interest is limited to a commission from an underwriter or dealer not in excess of the usual and customary distributors' or sellers' commission.[63]

Individuals in the latter category are usually stock brokers employed by brokerage houses. (Stock brokerage houses are discussed under a separate heading below). A discussion of the steps involved in the making of a full-scale, SEC registered offering is beyond the scope of this work. It should be noted, however, that public offerings of the securities of new or very young companies are almost always ill advised. The investing public is a fickle supporter. In the event there are operating difficulties (and there are *always* operating difficulties in a small company), the ability to raise additional financing through the vehicle of a new issue will, in all probability, be seriously if not fatally impaired. In only the rarest of rare cases will a major, reputable investment banking firm underwrite a new offering for an unproven, unseasoned enterprise. Invariably, one of the first four financing techniques referred to above will be the preferred choice of the wise entrepreneur.

Investment Clubs

Investment clubs are formed when a group of friends, neighbors, business associates, or other individuals pool limited financial resources or "dues" for the purpose of investing in common stocks or other securities. Such clubs may or may not be formalized through the medium of a written agreement, charter, or by-laws. In many cases, these clubs operate informally, with members pledging regular amounts paid into the club treasury on a monthly basis.

By the fall of 1951, investment club activity in the United States had reached such proportions that the National Association of Investment Clubs was organized by four investment clubs in Detroit, Michigan. Today, nearly 6000 clubs belong to the Association.[64] According to a brochure published by the NAIC:

> The founders were dedicated to the belief that the investment club was valuable to individuals in that it permitted them to learn how to invest wisely while the amount of funds they were using was small, and, at the same time, offered them an opportunity to build a substantial investment account over a longer period of time. The founders believed, too, that the investment club served a vital national function in that it was a way to create many new investors, to train individuals in successful investment techniques, and through the creation of many new investors provide a substantial and regular flow of capital for the needs of growing industry. Consequently, the purpose of the National Association of Investment Clubs was to foster the creation of investment clubs and to take all possible steps to assist these clubs to a successful operation.[65]

NAIC provides a variety of services to its member clubs, including an eighty-page Investors Manual, free Investors Information Reports, low-cost stock purchase privileges, reduced rates to national and regional meetings of the NAIC, and a variety of investment services and educational materials and meetings.[66]

A regular benefit of NAIC membership is its monthly *Better Investing* magazine. Written by individuals with years of successful investing experience, *Better Investing* is full of new investment ideas and practical thoughts that can add many dollars to your investment results.

Each issue points members to a "Stock to Study," a stock that shows the potential for doubling in value within five years. The twelve "Stocks to Study" profiled five years ago, in 1978, have increased in value an average of 141 percent, the seventh consecutive five-year comparison period that NAIC's "Stocks to Study" have outperformed the Dow Jones Industrial Average. Dozens of other investment opportunities are also offered for further study in regular columns in each issue of NAIC's *Better Investing* magazine, columns such as "Spotlight on Growth Stocks" and "An Undervalued Stock."[67]

Club investments over the years have run the gamut from oil wells to race horses, and investment in a new business should certainly be less risky than either of these propositions. The NAIC actively encourages its member clubs to invest in the stocks of high growth companies as one of its four basic investment principles:

1. Invest a set sum once a month in common stocks, regardless of general market conditions. This helps you obtain lower average costs.

2. Reinvest dividends and capital gains immediately. Your money grows faster if earnings are reinvested. This is compound income at work.

3. Buy growth stocks—companies whose sales are increasing at a rate faster than industry in general. The companies should have good prospects for continued growth. In other words, they should be stronger companies five years from now.

4. Invest in different fields. Diversification helps spread both risk and opportunity.[68]

To learn more about NAIC benefits and investment clubs in general write to the National Association of Investment Clubs, 1515 East Eleven-Mile Road, Royal Oak, Michigan 48067. Specific inquiries regarding NAIC should be directed to this address. Telephone inquiries may be made by dialing (313) 543-0612.

Leasing Companies

Leasing companies provide a very specialized form of financing to small businesses. Through a lease agreement, machinery and office equipment may be rented at a contractually specified monthly rate for a contractually arranged period of time. Leasing arrangements are most attractive to small businesses because they provide capital assets without the necessity of a capital investment. This constitutes 100 percent financing. However, it is customary for the leasing company to require the prepayment of one, two, or three months' rental on the equipment as an offset against the very high depreciation commonly experienced in the initial months of equipment use.

In most instances, leasing companies prefer to provide equipment that has the following characteristics.

Long Serviceable Life. Equipment offered for lease usually permits long-term depreciation and guarantees sustained resale value should the lessee not wish to renew the lease upon the expiration of the initial contract.

Universal Marketability. Ideally, the machinery or equipment leased will have a continuing ready marketability. For example, items of universal utility such as desks, chairs, lathes, end mills, paint spray compressors, etc., exhibit the characteristics a leasing agency finds desirable.

Repossessable. If the lessee defaults on the terms of the leasing agreement, the lessor should be in a position to repossess the leased items readily. Thus, it is understood that an oxygen-reduction steel furnace would not qualify under this definition of respossessability, whereas welding equipment, work benches, and laundry and dry-cleaning equipment would qualify quite nicely.

Over the years, lease terms and conditions have become pretty well standardized. Depending on the value of the item leased, its useful life, its repossessability, and its resale value, rent may be arranged on a monthly, quarterly, semiannual, or annual basis. The leasing contract will often make provision for the lessee to purchase the leased item outright on expiration of the lease at a price somewhat less than the fair market value at that time. However, in this instance, the total monies paid over the term of the lease, plus the buy-out amount, typically add up to twice the original simple purchase price.

Leasing affords the small business owner an opportunity to use capital equipment with little or no initial outlay of cash. The productivity resulting from the use of equipment and machinery will provide sufficient cash flow to meet the rental payments. Increasingly, leasing companies are making available to small businesses still another option known as the sale-leaseback plan. Under the terms of such an arrangement, equipment that has already been paid for may be sold to the leasing company and then leased back. In this way, the small businesses acquire cash, which may be sorely needed for working capital purposes, in exchange for the equity in their equipment. Financing arrangements of this sort are very much like the refinancing of a house, where homeowners retire their mortgages in exchange for a brand new mortgage and cash for their equity.

Since the leasing of industrial equipment requires a specialized knowledge of the particular industry to be served, it is not surprising that many leasing companies specialize in different industrial sectors. For instance, one company may specialize in medical electronics equipment, another in metals fabrication equipment, and still others in office equipment. Fleet leasing of vehicles is another special type through which a small business may satisfy its transportation and drayage requirements with a minimum initial outlay of capital.

The long-term leasing of real estate (land and buildings) is one of the oldest forms of leasing and represents a significant economic advantage to small business owners who cannot afford to purchase the fixed assets they require. In many instances, the expense involved in lease financing plans depends on the financial credentials of the small business, the risks involved, the marketability of the equipment or machinery leased, and the value of any land and buildings involved. Although leasing expenses run higher than loans, a small business owner may have no other choice in securing needed equipment.

Mutual Funds

"A mutual fund is a company which combines the investment funds of many people whose investment goals are similar, and in turn invests those funds in a wide variety of securities."[69] Typically, a fund will invest in a number of different common and preferred stocks, corporate bonds, and other securities. These securities, taken as a whole, make up the fund portfolio. Because the value of any particular securities holding is subject to daily variation in the capital markets, administration of the portfolio investments of a mutual fund requires the continuous supervision of professionally qualified investment managers.

Mutual funds are open-end investment companies because they make a continuous offering of shares and redeem outstanding shares on demand. Therefore, the number of their shares outstanding varies as new shares are sold to investors and other shares are redeemed.

"Different mutual funds have a wide range of investment objectives, management policies, and degrees of risk and profit opportunities."[70] One mutual fund may concentrate its investments in high-risk, short-term investment opportunities; others may specialize in investment situations representing modest but sustained long-term capital appreciation opportunities; still others focus their attention and financial resources on income-producing instruments such as corporate and municipal bonds.

If the management philosophy, objectives, and policies allow, a mutual fund may invest a small percentage of its resources in high-risk "special situations," such as new or relatively young enterprises. It is this mutual fund investment area that should be of particular interest to the entrepreneur. There are a number of so-called "aggressive growth" mutual funds whose goal is to maximize their return on investments. They do so by investing in growth companies. The Explorer Fund and the Dean Witter Development Growth Security Trust are two examples of mutual funds that emphasize investments in promising young firms. Reference to the mutual-fund directories mentioned in Appendix 1 should enable the capital seeker to determine the most likely prospects to approach with a business plan.

Mutual Savings Banks

Mutual savings banks (now commonly referred to as "savings banks") are thrift institutions organized for the purpose of providing individuals of relatively small means with a secure repository for their savings. Most mutual savings banks are located in New England and the mid-Atlantic states and until recently were strictly regulated, state-chartered institutions. While these banks are still primarily state-chartered, recent legislation gave them the option of converting to a federal charter if they shifted from FDIC to FSLIC insurance and became permanent members of the Federal Home Loan Bank System. This resulted in a wave of conversions by state-chartered banks that opted for the less restrictive covenants of a federal charter.[71]

All savings banks are empowered to make business loans. Federally chartered mutual savings banks are authorized to make commercial loans to a maximum of ten percent of the bank's total assets. These loans must be made within a bank's home state or within seventy-five miles of its home office.[72]

While savings banks in some areas are moving increasingly into commercial lending, tax incentives still encourage them to invest more of their money in mortgages. Because of this, an entrepreneur is more likely to secure a home loan from this source and use the proceeds for business purposes.

_____ **National Consumer Cooperative Bank** _____

This institution known, as the Co-op Bank, was established for the purpose of providing loans to consumer- and employee-owned cooperatives. Food and housing co-ops, health care, child-care, retail cooperatives and others are serviced by the Co-op Bank.

Created by Congress in 1978 in recognition of the long history of cooperative efforts in the United States and their potential for increasing access to basic services, lowering costs, stimulating the economy and improving local communities, the Co-op Bank is a unique financial institution with a mandate to serve and assist cooperative enterprises. With assets of $230 million and a loan portfolio of $110 million at year-end 1984, a professional staff experienced in cooperative development, banking and financial management, and offices around the country, the Co-op Bank is an increasingly important source of credit for the thousands of existing consumer and producer cooperatives in the United States, as well as for the many new ones that spring up every year.[73]

Loans are originated at the regional offices (listed below). Interest rates are competitive with other financial institutions. The Co-op Bank also participates in loans with other public and private lenders and helps local cooperatives to secure additional funding from other sources.

The Co-op Bank itself is cooperatively owned. As is the case with credit unions, one must become a member of the Co-op Bank in order to borrow from it. For more information about the services provided, contact your nearest regional office:

- **Central Office**: 1630 Connecticut Ave. N.W., Washington, D.C. 20009, (202) 745-4600, toll free (800) 424-2481.

- **Northeast Region**: 1 World Trade Center, #2265, New York, New York 10048, (212) 432-1155.

- **Southeast Region**: 1630 Connecticut Avenue, NW, Washington, D.C. 20009, (202) 745-4755; 41 Marietta Street, #301, Atlanta, Georgia 30303, (404) 525-0759.

- **Midwest Region**: 121 S. 8th Street, #730, Minneapolis, Minnesota 55402, (612) 332-0032; 30 W. Mifflin Street, #401, Madison, Wisconsin 53703, (608) 258-4399.

- **Western Region**: 1800 Harrison Street, #1660, Oakland, California 94612, (415) 268-6850; 114 W. 7th Street, #700, Austin, Texas 78701, (512) 477-3933; 18000 Pacific Highway S., #604, Seattle, Washington 98188, (206) 243-4115; 1011 E. Tudor Road, #210, Anchorage, Alaska 99503, (907) 562-2322.

Parent Companies

Laboratories of large corporations often turn out excellent new products that simply do not fit into the corporations' marketing plans. This circumstance may represent a significant loss in research and development dollars and may also result in an even greater loss to the company—the departure of the skilled but frustrated innovators who developed the product. In many cases, these innovators may open up a business of their own centered around the product they created.[74]

In recent years, some of the more progressive firms have come to recognize that the abandonment of good ideas represents needless waste and have taken steps to remedy the situation. The remedy often involves the creation of a corporate subsidiary, with the innovator as president and the "orphan" product as the market vehicle. At a time when mergers and acquisitions have come under increasingly restrictive government regulation, this "spin-off" of fledgling enterprises may provide a very attractive method of effecting corporate growth.[75]

Entrepreneurs may realize many advantages through having their former employers finance their firms. Many of the administrative services of the parent company, such as accounting, marketing surveys, sales organization, etc., may be made available to the new firm at nominal cost. Also, the parent company may become a key customer for the goods and services of the enterprise. The significant financial resources of the parent company may be made available virtually to guarantee the successful launching of the new firm by providing a steady supply of capital (provided prospects for long-term success remain promising) until profitable operation is achieved. Finally, when the time comes for the parent to acquire full control of the enterprise (should the founders wish to sell), the buy-out medium may take the form of readily marketable securities (usually common stock) in the parent company.

Another common solution is for the former employer to become a minority shareholder in the new business, receiving an equity interest in return for providing the spin-off with management advice and sometimes the use of company facilities. (If the former employer allows the spin-off to use existing R & D facilities, it's tax deductible—an added bonus.)[76]

The list of companies backing former employees in their entrepreneurial ventures includes corporate monoliths like General Electric and Xerox, but smaller firms are in on the game as well.[77] A recent example that typifies this trend is the case of William Sharp. Sharp, head of a research laboratory for Campbell's Soups, quit the firm to start a plant-breeding technology company along with a colleague. He expected to get the cold shoulder from Campbell's when he broke the news. Instead, the company gave him and his partner a $5 million, thirty-two-acre research lab, $8 million in cash, and access to twenty-five employees, in exchange for a thirty percent equity in the new enterprise. Campbell's recognized the value of the founders' experience and saw in the new firm the potential for development of better strains of tomatoes, which would benefit the soup company.[78]

More and more corporate middle managers are coming to feel that the only way to achieve personal satisfaction in business is to start firms of their own. Recognizing the entrepreneurial bent of particular managers, the parent company may decide to underwrite their entrepreneurship—"If you can't beat 'em, join 'em"—and thus avoid the *complete* loss of services and capabilities that the company may have spent years cultivating. In such a situation, the parent company is in a unique position to evaluate the managerial prowess of the potential entrepreneurs, thus reducing investment risk. Instead of watching some opportunistic venture capitalist reap the rewards, the company may also enjoy some of the handsome financial returns participation in a successful new business offers.

Pension Funds

Pension funds provide individuals with cash reserves to be disbursed as retirement income at some future date. There are many different groups involved in pension funds, including labor union members, corporation employees, state employees, and employees of nonprofit entities such as religious and charitable institutions. By mid-1983, pension assets totaled $800 billion, and were growing rapidly.[79] By 1990, this capital source is expected to balloon to $2 trillion, and reach the $3 trillion mark by the turn of the century. [80]

With some corporate pension funds, the employees as well as the employer make contributions. However, whether the employees contribute or not, the *corporation* has the responsibility for administering the funds. This administration is active when a staff is created for the purpose of administering the funds. However, it is more common for the corporation to retain investment counsel or counselors to administer them. Funds may also be turned over to a bank trust department for administration.

Spurred by the spectacular capital appreciation sometimes possible through early investment in growth companies, virtually every individual responsible for money management has become sensitized to the need for *performance*. (As used in financial circles, performance means the rapid appreciation of invested capital.) Now, in many cases, the corporation is obligated to increase the pension fund reserve annually for each eligible employee. The exact amount is based on the number of employees covered, the payments they will receive on retirement, and individual life expectancy. This increase may originate from appreciation of portfolio investments (higher valuation of stocks or other holdings) or corporate contributions. Thus, if funds are so invested that portfolio appreciation is in excess of the 5.5 percent median return on pension fund investments,[81] the magnitude of the corporation contribution may be reduced, and these savings may then be retained as profits. Since the magnitude of the funds tied up in pension reserves is frequently large, the possible advantage of aggressive fund administration is evident to corporate officers and fund managers alike. For example, those responsible for the pension fund at Owens-Illinois, after doing "homework" in the area in 1972, invested in twelve venture capital funds and recently began investing *directly* in entrepreneurial ventures.[82]

The U.S. Labor Department provided a boost in the area in 1979 when it clarified the rules regarding ERISA (Employee Retirement and Income Security Act) accounts, allowing for account funds to be invested in venture situations. Between 1979 and 1983, pension fund commitments in this area mushroomed to $730 million with at least ninety major corporate pension funds active in the area, including American Telephone and Telegraph, General Electric, Honeywell, and Hewlett-Packard.[83]

State pension funds are getting into the venture capital act, too. Colorado, Michigan, Ohio, Oregon, and Washington are among the states that allow pension fund investment in venture capital, and pressure is growing for other states to follow suit. In this case, the investments are more often than not intended to beef up state economies than to reap substantial monetary gains.[84]

Based on this information, it seems reasonable to assume that pension funds will continue to participate in venture capital at a gradually accelerating rate. Many institutional portfolio managers now feel venture capital is as safe as traditional, low-yield investments, especially considering the fact that publicly traded equities have yielded four to five percent over the last few years and some fixed-income assets have yielded negative returns.[85] Participation by all of the many types of funds referred to above is likely as conservative administrators have an opportunity to evaluate the success of more aggressively managed funds.

Private Individual Investors

According to Schedule Y of the 1983 Federal Income Tax Rates, married taxpayers filing joint returns and certain widows and widowers having annual ordinary income in excess of $109,400 must pay fifty cents in federal income tax on every additional dollar of ordinary income earned. Although entrepreneurs are not usually confronted with tax problems of this magnitude at the time they launch their first venture, there are hundreds of thousands of individuals with incomes that push them into this fifty percent tax bracket. Their willingness to invest in interest-bearing corporate bonds or dividend-producing stocks yielding ordinary income is usually less than enthusiastic. The opportunity to retain fifty cents out of every dollar earned is not much of an investment inducement. By investing in situations offering capital gains prospects, these wealthy taxpayers may significantly reduce Uncle Sam's tax bite—income taxable under the long-term captial gains provisions of the Internal Revenue Code is assessed at forty percent of the tax rate on ordinary income in the highest tax bracket.

Prior to June 30, 1958, losses on common stock investments held in excess of six months were deductible in any given year only to the extent by which they could offset capital gains earned in that same year. Thus, wealthy investors who had sustained substantial losses in a given tax year might be obliged to carry these losses forward indefinitely until their capital gains offset them. Needless to say, under these circumstances there was little incentive for these individuals to invest substantially in the high-risk situation, which is the essence of financing a business. But, on June 30, 1958, Section 1244 of the Internal Revenue Code was enacted by Congress to encourage the flow of new funds into small businesses. Although a detailed exposition of the ramifications of Section 1244 is beyond the scope of this book, the overall effect can be summarized this way: Qualified private investors participating in the financing of new, small business corporations meeting certain IRS criteria may elect to have capital losses up to $50,000 in any given tax year (or $100,000 in the case of a husband and wife filing a joint return) treated as ordinary losses for tax purposes, while retaining the right to capital gains treatment on the realized appreciation of such investments.

The federal government offers still another interesting tax vehicle, known as Subchapter S of the Internal Revenue Code, for the encouragement of small business investment. Qualifying small business corporations having thirty-five or fewer stockholders and only one class of stock outstanding may elect to be taxed as a partnership instead of as a corporation. Thus, any losses sustained by the enterprise may be apportioned on a pro rata basis among the stockholders and deducted from their individual tax returns as offsets to ordinary income. Once the stockholders unanimously elect to be treated as shareholders in a Subchapter S corporation, this eligibility is effective for all succeeding taxable years of the corporation until it is terminated, either willfully through a vote of the stockholders or through other circumstances as described under Section 1362 of the IRS Code. (Also particularly attractive to moneyed investors is the fact that an *estate* may qualify for Subchapter S treatment.)

In summary, Section 1244 stock represents an attractive means of maximizing gains and minimizing losses for wealthy investors while they participate in a high-stakes game involving a qualifying small corporation. Section 1244 is an option available to the stockholders of qualifying corporations, whether the Subchapter S election is made or not. Thus, the financing possibilities available in the capitalization of small businesses provide wealthy investors with two very attractive alternatives. Such investors are worth approaching with your business plans, and they can usually be located through knowledgeable lawyers, bankers, accountants, insurance agents, stockbrokers, investment underwriters, financial advisers, and finders of all descriptions.

Another category of private individual investors is made up of financially and managerially successful entrepreneurs who are ready to participate in the launching of their second or third venture and who may run advertisements in leading financial journals offering a package consisting of financial backing *and* management participation. In other instances, these individuals can be located through the same contacts mentioned above. Some of these entrepreneurs have been dubbed "adventure capitalists,"[86] partly because the term "venture capital" is too tame to describe the risky investments in which these bold capitalists are willing to participate.

One distinguishing characteristic of "adventure capitalists" is their willingness to invest in low tech (or "no tech") ventures. Roughly ninety percent of all private venture capital in this country is devoted to high technology.[87] But this hardy breed of investors will put their money into deals that would make the average venture capitalist shake his head in bewilderment. The most notable firm in this area, a pioneer in "adventure capitalism," is the Early Stages Company, which was founded by the creator of Duraflame Logs and which has invested in such nonglamor enterprises as snack foods and shampoo.[88] A team of entrepreneurs successful in persuading a seasoned venturer to participate in their new enterprise should stand a much-higher-than-normal probability of success.

Private Investment Partnerships

Private investment partnerships (or "limited partnerships") provide wealthy investors with a very attractive means of investing their resources in promising new enterprises. By adopting the role of limited partners, these individuals authorize the general partners to represent them in interacting with the officers of the new enterprise in which the partnership has invested. The general partners in such groups usually qualify for their responsibility by virtue of previous experience in new enterprise management or as junior members in other venture capital organizations. In many instances, the general partners, as well as the limited partners, invest their personal resources in the new enterprise. In exchange for their services in managing the resources of the partnership, the general partners often receive salaries or other compensation in addition to their pro rata share of profits resulting from investments of the resources committed by all of the partners.

Participation in such an organization affords the limited partners many advantages. For one thing, they do not have to trouble themselves with monitoring the daily operations of the enterprise in which their money is invested—this is the responsibility of the general partners. Furthermore, because of the tax nature of qualifying partnerships, the individual partners are in a position to treat any losses of the partnership as ordinary losses, while gains receive treatment as long-term capital gains, as explained above in the discussion of Section 1244 of the IRS Code (presented under the heading "Private Individual Investors"). Many wealthy people find participation in limited partnerships a practical, rewarding, and satisfying means of investing their funds in new enterprise—a means that does not demand the time-consuming responsibility of regularly monitoring the investment. They often find such partnerships far more satisfactory alternatives to simple participation in new enterprise ownership through the acquisition of common stock, in which tax advantages are not nearly so liberal.

Some of the most spectacular achievements of a private individual partnership in recent years have been racked up by the San Francisco firm of Hambrecht & Quist, formed in 1968 by the late George Quist, formerly head of Bank of America venture capital activity, and William R. Hambrecht, a former vice president of Francis I. DuPont and Company. In 1978, Hambrecht and Quist formed a $4.4 million limited partnership which has since achieved a rate of return of almost fifty percent per year! Among the partnership's most successful venture investments were ADAC Laboratories, Convergent Technologies, NBI Inc., and Granger Associates (recently acquired for a very hefty price). Each of these companies earned for Hambrecht & Quist a return between six and *twenty-two* times the amount of their original investment.[89]

Privately Owned Venture Capital Corporations

Privately owned venture capital corporations are among the largest suppliers of high-risk capital for new and young enterprises in this country. As a separate class of investors, such corporations typically have more advantages to offer their portfolio companies than does any other capital source.

Substantial Reserves of Risk Capital

Although bank trust departments, pension funds, insurance companies, and university endowment funds represent most of the large pools of capital for investment available today, the bulk of these funds are usually tied up in "high-quality," modest-yield, blue-chip stocks, bonds, or other securities. When it comes to risk capital, a relatively small number of closed-end investment companies (including SBICs), private investment partnerships, and investment affiliates have substantial assets reserved for venture capital use. However, a growing number of privately owned venture capital corporations, also with substantial assets, have been formed for the express purpose of investing in promising young companies. These include family investment companies, one of the oldest sources of high-risk capital for new ventures, drawing on the fortunes of such families as the Rockefellers, the Whitneys, and the Phippses. Typically, investment strategy involves pooling the resources of family members and placing them under the management of one or more financial specialists well qualified in the field of venture capital investment.

To illustrate the importance of these family fortunes in underwriting new American industry, consider that the Rockefeller family figured significantly in the financing of the Polaroid Corporation. Another family venture capital firm, J.H. Whitney and Company, was established in 1946 and has participated in the financing of ventures including the now very successful California-based Memorex Corporation. The Whitney portfolio also reflects its early investments in companies such as General Signal, Minute Maid, Corinthian Broadcasting, Spencer Chemical, Transcontinental Gas Pipeline, and Global Marine.[90]

Privately owned venture capital firms constitute the principal institutional source of venture capital today. There are now over 250 independent venture capital firms, and approximately 150 of them were formed in the last six years.[91] One of the largest of the independent firms—Warburg, Pincus Capital Partners—had invested $350 million in venture capital as of the end of 1983.[92] In general, the capital assets of these funds range from $10 million to $60 million.[93]

The availability of assets of this magnitude provides an excellent "insurance policy" for portfolio companies. Investors with limited assets may be unable to supply promised capital when required, and shortages may occur whether or not the enterprise is meeting projected performance schedules. Thus, the founders may do a splendid job of building their company only to find themselves in financial difficulty because of an investor's inability to honor commitments made. Conversely, large venture capital organizations are generally able to withstand economic vagaries and to continue to support the young company.

Business Development Assistance

Many small investors may pool their resources to "syndicate" the financing of a deal, but they are not in a position to contribute anything else to the enterprise. On the other hand, privately owned venture capital corporations commonly retain a full-time staff for the purpose of monitoring and, where necessary, assisting portfolio companies with whatever problems they may have, financial or otherwise.

Recently, this process has come to be known as *business development,* and investors who offer this service prefer to be called *business developers* rather than wear the more commonly applied label of venture capitalists. As viewed by the Heizer Corporation, business development is the creation of value through the effective combination of people, money, and ideas. It is helping hard-working entrepreneurs with good ideas to be very successful. This is rewarding for Heizer as well as for the entrepreneurs.[94]

Long-Term Objectives

In the words of Edgar F. Heizer, Jr., president and chairman of the board of the Heizer Corporation,

> ... a lot of venture capital outfits are pure dice-rollers. ... It's sort of like going to Las Vegas, except in Vegas you at least know the odds. We're not going into anything on the basis that we might have one winner out of ten.[95] Each company we finance must have the potential of creating an investment quality growth stock.[96]

Thus, for the entrepreneur with a serious desire to build a major corporation over the long haul—as opposed to trying to start a company with the idea of taking it public in one or two years and letting the stockholders hold the bag for a still-green enterprise—the assistance of a privately owned venture capital (or business development) corporation can be of enormous value.

Relatives and Friends

When it comes to having relatives and friends put money into a new and unproven business venture, the matter is largely a case of "you're in trouble if you do and you're in trouble if you don't." Understand that, if you are successful in persuading individuals in this investor group to participate in financing the new venture, and if for some reason the venture fails (whether it's your fault or not), you may spend the rest of your life having to cope with the unpleasantness of intra-family ill will. Conversely, should the venture be financed by knowledgeable risk-taking venture capitalists who are in a position to sustain a substantial loss without experiencing undue personal hardships, the effect on the entrepreneur's relations with friends and relatives will be largely unchanged.

Unfortunately, it is common for friends and relatives to feel that they have rights of first refusal in deciding whether or not to invest in your ventures. In the event the new enterprise is financially successful and the relatives and friends have not been offered the opportunity to participate in the attendant capital appreciation, ill will of still another sort may result. In this situation, relatives and friends may feel that it is unfair of you to give "total strangers" an opportunity to make substantial financial gains through investing in you while at the same time you deprive *them* of a similar opportunity. My personal attitude in this matter is that relatives and friends should be permitted to invest in the new enterprise only to the extent that they would ordinarily invest in other risk propositions. If your great aunt has to hock the family jewels in order to participate in the financing of *your* new venture, she should be discouraged.

A number of other authors on this subject suggest that, whenever relatives and friends are invited to participate in the financing of a venture, their investment should take the form of a simple loan. I feel that such an approach is grossly unfair. Friend- and relative-investors have every right to realize a capital return consistent with the risks involved. My feeling is that the terms and conditions offered to the relatives and friends should approximate those which would be exacted by sophisticated investors. Therefore, the participation of friends and relatives in the financing of the venture should take the form of loans with rights attached allowing for the purchase of stock (at a later date and at a predetermined price), purchase of an equity position, or a combination of the two.

I feel it is safe to say that, in a very large number of instances, relatives and friends play a key role in the financing of new enterprises. Frequently, relatives and friends are the only investors who can be persuaded to participate in the early financing of a business, but too often such investments are made emotionally without the participant having any appreciation of the risks involved. Funds are advanced primarily out of the desire to give a helping hand to someone they know well and to whom they wish the best of luck. However, in such situations people often lose the objectivity that should always characterize financial dealings and often neglect to shore up agreements and understandings with legal documentation. Consider the following two stories which came to my attention a few years ago.

Two bright and very ambitious young men conceived an idea for an exciting new electronics product. The young men decided to organize a company for the purpose of developing a prototype of their product as a prelude to launching a full-scale manufacturing and engineering business. One of these young men persuaded a close friend of his parents, herself a wealthy widow, to provide the necessary seed capital. The financing arrangements were completely informal. Details such as loan interest, the establishment of a corporation, and the creation of equity were not considered at all. Whenever the young men reached a point in the development of their prototype when additional funds were required, they would simply invite the sweet old lady down to their shop to view the progress which they had made to date and then ask for an additional $10,000 or $20,000 loan so they might continue with their work.

One day when the prototype was very nearly complete, the young men learned of the death of their benefactress. Unfortunately, since no contractual relationship had been entered into at any point, this source of funds was cut off permanently. The widow's heirs expressed the feeling that their relative had been bilked and that they were not about to encourage further squandering of her estate.

Had these young men engaged the services of a competent attorney at the outset, a corporation could have been set up and a reserve of equity funds established by selling the woman stock in the business. In this manner, the traumatic effect on the business created by the death of its primary benefactress could have been avoided. With foresight, they could have made their benefactress a stockholder in the business, with a provision that her life be insured with the company as beneficiary. After the woman's death, funds from the policy could have been used for the purpose of buying out the holdings of the heirs to her estate. Instead, these young men spent almost a full year in trying to raise additional funds on terms they regarded as acceptable.

The second story involves a young man who started a company with money he obtained from a wealthy aunt. This young man was well on his way toward creating a moderately successful, although not yet profitable, enterprise. However, the untimely death of the aunt resulted in numerous unplanned-for difficulties. For one thing, the aunt's estate was placed in probate, and the flow of vital funds was suspended indefinitely. In addition, other heirs regarded the entrepreneur with great animosity, feeling that his efforts in launching his own business had significantly diminished the aunt's estate. Because financing of the enterprise was cut off, the entrepreneur found it necessary to secure full-time employment with a major corporation. As of this writing, the company founded by this young man is listed as inactive. Because of the rapid advances in technology, the products which he had spent so much time and effort designing are now obsolete. Thus, the potential returns of his labor and the money invested by his aunt have been irretrievably lost.

In summary, relatives and friends *may* be an extremely helpful source of venture capital. Often they are willing to invest in an enterprise at a time when no sophisticated investor would consider doing so. But, in accepting the financial resources of these investors, entrepreneurs should insure that all financing arrangements are legally documented. They should further satisfy themselves that participating investors invest only those funds that they are in a position to lose comfortably. Wherever possible, arrangements should be made to insure that these investors will function as silent partners to eliminate the possibility that family squabbles may interfere with the day-to-day operations of the enterprises. (To accomplish this, the investors may be limited partners or may hold preferred stock.)

Research Grants and Partnerships

In the early stages of product development, government research grants or private research and development partnerships can be an excellent source of financing to get a business concept off the ground and into the production phase.

Small Business Innovation Research Program. Since 1982, each federal government agency with a research and development budget of $100 million or more has been required to allocate 1.25 percent of its funds to small businesses through the Small Business Innovation Research (SBIR) Program. The program is divided into three phases:[97]

- **Phase 1:** Businesses can compete for awards of approximately $50,000 to explore, over a period of six months, whether an idea is technically or commercially feasible.

- **Phase 2:** The projects that show the most potential in Phase 1 will receive grants of up to $500,000 over a one- to two-year period to develop the products.

- **Phase 3:** Companies must seek additional private funding from venture capitalists or others to put the innovation into commercial production.

There are two key criteria that SBIR funding requests must meet. First, the project must be likely to further federal research and development goals. Secondly, the ideas must be "potentially valuable in the commercial marketplace."[98] The program was begun in 1982, and over a five-year period it is expected that roughly a *billion* dollars will be invested in SBIR funding.[99]

To be put on a mailing list for the agency solicitations that will most likely be of interest to you, contact any office of the Small Business Administration. You can also send specific inquiries about the programs to the Small Business High Technology Institute at 1825 I Street, N.W., Washington, D.C. 20006.

Research and Development (R&D) Partnerships. In an R&D limited partnership, investors can participate in the financing of new product developments while realizing significant tax advantages. This tax shelter feature of research and development partnerships has made them quite popular in recent years. Funds are usually raised through private placements because of SEC rulings, although public offerings (which are more complicated) can be made. The chief tax benefit of a typical arrangement is that the limited partners can deduct most of their investment as an expense in the year they invest, and the income realized from the project in later years may be taxed at capital gains rates rather than the higher rates for ordinary income. (It should be noted that the R & D partnership will retain the rights to the technology and results of the project upon completion.)

Equity R&D partnerships, a variation on the traditional R&D arrangement, have become an increasingly viable source of funding for start-up companies. Unlike the traditional R&D partnership in which investors get an early tax write-off and future royalties on a single product development, equity partnerships are designed to launch entire new business ventures, rather than just a single product.[100] In the early years, investors get the benefit of tax write-offs associated with losses, but as these losses are converted into profits over time, the partners are asked to convert their interests into equity positions in the company. Equity R&D partnerships often fund riskier start-up companies with smaller funding requirements than do traditional R&D partnerships.[101]

Terms of specific R&D partnership arrangements vary widely from case to case. A qualified accounting firm (especially one of the Big Eight) can provide you with specific information about these arrangements and advise you as to the feasibility of such an arrangement for your company.

Energy-Related Inventions Program. The federal government sponsors another program designed to help small businesses obtain financing, in this case for energy-related inventions. A Commerce Department brochure describes the Energy Related Inventions Program which is run by the Department of Energy (DOE).

> The purpose of the program is to provide an opportunity for independent inventors and small businesses with promising energy-related inventions to obtain Federal assistance in developing and commercializing their inventions.[102]

The brochure goes on to state that:

> A description of any new concept, device, product, material, or industrial process may be submitted. The invention need not be patented.
>
> The invention should be well described on paper; drawings are encouraged but need not be done professionally. Claims should be set forth clearly, pointing out how the invention is unique, how performance and costs are advantageous over similar items on the market or in development, and how the invention will affect national energy objectives. The basis for the claims (for example, calculations or test data) must be included.
>
> No models or samples of materials should be submitted unless specifically requested during the evaluation. NBS will not test your invention.[103]

If you want to submit your energy-related invention for evaluation under this program, write to the Office of Energy-Related Inventions, National Bureau of Standards, Washington, D.C. 20234 and ask for an Evaluation Request Form 1019.

Sales Finance Companies

The increasing use of the "installment plan" for the purchase of automobiles, major household appliances, jewelry, furniture, and many other consumer goods has placed considerable demand on the limited resources of the durable goods retailer. Furthermore, consumers do not represent the only sector of the economy that has come to make use of the installment purchase plan. In industry, such durables as office equipment, heavy machinery, and farm equipment are offered for sale on this basis. Again, the sellers of these goods may not have sufficient working capital to permit their resources to be tied up for a long period of time in such contracts.

Enter the sales finance company. The primary activity of the sales finance company is the purchase, at a discount, of installment contracts. For example, a friend of mine who bought some furniture for his home on the installment plan was quite surprised to receive a letter a few weeks later indicating that a sales finance company had purchased his installment contract and that in the future he should forward all of his payments directly to that company. The sales finance company had relieved the seller of all collection responsibilities and the need to maintain a specialized credit department.

Consider this example. A group of entrepreneurs may wish to establish a retail store for the sale of major household appliances. They may make arrangements with their suppliers for sixty-day credit terms. In other words, they have sixty days from the receipt of their inventory until the time they must pay the invoice. Next, the retailers offer these goods for sale to the public. Assume that, within this original sixty days, a customer decides to purchase an appliance at a price representing the normal retail markup over and above the retailer's purchase price. However, the customer's preference is to purchase the appliance on the installment plan. The retailer determines the credit worthiness of the customer through a quick check with a local credit information agency. In the event the customer proves to be a satisfactory risk, an installment sales contract is drawn up. Subsequently, the retailer offers this contract to a sales finance company at a discount and pays the supplier out of these funds. The difference between the amount collected from the sales finance company and the price charged by the appliance manufacturer represents the amount necessary to cover the retailer's operating expenses and to provide a profit as well. Some firms doing a regular business through installment selling often have a *continuous* or *revolving* arrangement with a finance company whereby funds are made available on a constantly renewed pledge of accounts receivable.

Some finance companies, in addition to financing installment sales, also lend on retail inventory, equipment, accounts receivable, and wholesale inventory. Other finance companies will finance major appliances on the "floor plan" basis, where they take title to the inventory, place it on the dealers' sales floor, and take possession of the retail installment contract when the appliance is sold (although this is no longer common). They may even provide financing of major projects such as the construction of production or storage facilities, or for business expansion or working capital. In summary, entrepreneurs who have to provide financing for their customers may find the services of a sales finance company of considerable help in selling their merchandise.

Savings and Loan Associations

Savings and loan associations constitute the second largest type of financial institution in the nation. There are now approximately 4000 such associations in the United States, with combined assets exceeding $700 billion. According to an industry publication,

Savings and loan associations are private institutions, and the development of policy for the conduct of business at the individual association is the responsibility of a board of directors made up of local citizens. Like many financial intermediaries, however, associations work within a comprehensive framework of special state and federal laws and regulations.

The laws set general standards for the chartering of new institutions, govern operating practices and control the kinds of loans and other investments that can be made, while supervisory agencies establish more detailed regulations governing operating procedures.[104]

Although the major financing activity of savings and loan associations is the making of loans for the purchase or construction of homes, other types of loans are also available. Sweeping reforms in the financial service industry have broadened the lending powers of these institutions:

Besides mortgage loans, associations also make a variety of consumer loans. Traditionally, the bulk of these loans were closely related to housing, such as mobile home and home improvement loans. The financial reform legislation of 1980 authorized associations to finance other common consumer needs, such as automobiles and credit card purchases. As yet, however, these nonmortgage loans account overall for only three percent of total association assets.[105]

The Garn-St. Germain Depository Institutions Act of 1982 further expanded association lending powers in the areas of consumer, commercial, and agricultural lending. Savings and loans can now commit up to ten percent of their assets to commercial loans. In addition, federally chartered savings and loans can commit as much as thirty percent of the assets to inventory financing and ten percent to equipment financing.[106] State laws vary. In California, state-chartered savings and loans can invest an unlimited amount of assets in commercial loans.[107]

Although savings institutions can now make a variety of new types of loans, most will remain primarily real estate lenders. As with mutual savings banks, tax incentives still encourage savings and loans to hold most of their assets in long-term mortgages.

Securities Dealers

Under the Securities Exchange Act of 1934, a securities "dealer" is defined to be "any person engaged in the business of buying and selling securities *for his own account,* through a broker or otherwise . . . or any person insofar as he buys or sells securities for his own account, either individually or in some fiduciary capacity, but not as part of a regular business."[108] In contrast, a "broker" is "any person engaged in the business of effecting transactions in securities *for the account of others.*"[109]

In rare instances, where a new or small company has completed a registration of its securities with the Securities and Exchange Commission under the appropriate provisions of the Securities Act of 1933, it may be possible to obtain wide distribution of the securities of the enterprise (almost always a desirable objective for the purpose of limiting the holdings—and power—of any one stockholder) through a network of securities dealers. Thus, it may be possible to sell stock in the company while paying an amount somewhat less than the substantial and customary fees usually exacted by an investment banker for providing this service.

As defined above, a dealer is one who normally buys stocks and other securities for the purpose of later selling them, hopefully at a profit. However, a dealer *may* also function as an *underwriter*. In the securities trade, an *underwriter* is an individual who agrees to market all or part of an issue of securities to the public as a service to the seller (usually a corporation). Underwritings usually take one of the following three forms.

Firm. The underwriters agree to pay the seller a fixed amount of money per share for an entire issue of securities such as common stock within a specified period of time after the offering date. The price paid to the seller always represents an amount discounted below the offering price—a carefully negotiated element in the underwriting agreement. During the offering period, the underwriters attempt to sell these shares at the specified offering price. Although they are ultimately obligated to pay the corporation for the entire issue, technically they take title only to those shares that they are not able to sell.

All or None. The underwriters attempt to sell a specified number of shares within the offering period, and all funds collected are maintained in an escrow account until the issue is fully subscribed. In the event all shares are *not* sold, the money collected is returned to the would-be buyers and the offering is termed a failure.

Best Efforts. The underwriters agree to do their best to sell as many of the registered shares as they can within a specified period of time. Any unsold shares are returned to the company. Because it is possible that the offering may be undersubscribed and the company may fail to raise the amount of funds required to achieve the goals described in the prospectus, this type of underwriting is characterized by the greatest risk to the small firm and is the least desirable of the three here described.

Although the "firm" underwriting is attractive from the standpoint of the new business, it is quite unlikely that *any* underwriters would consider such an arrangement. The certainty of being able to sell the entire issue at the offering price is far from guaranteed and their own risk would be substantial. Since the "best efforts" underwriting is not attractive from the standpoint of the new firm, let's take a closer look at the "all or none" possibility. To illustrate this technique for raising equity capital, consider the public offering a few years ago by Data Recognition Corporation, a California-based high-technology company. A statement in the prospectus regarding dealer fees reads:

> While the offering is not being underwritten, the Company may pay commissions aggregating $52,500 ($.35 per share) [representing 5 percent of the $7 price to the public] to members of the National Association of Securities Dealers, Inc. (NASD), who sell shares of the Common Stock offered hereby. . . . The total commissions are computed on the assumption that all shares will be sold, and that all sales will be made through such dealers.[110]

Additionally, the company had to pay thirty-eight cents per share in other expenses incident to this offering.[111] The prospectus further explains that this

> is a non-underwritten offering, undertaken by the Company through its officers and directors, without payment of commissions except as set forth above. Because such persons are inexperienced in the sale of securities, there is no assurance that all or any of the shares offered hereby will be sold.[112]

It should be pointed out that although the officers of the Data Recognition Corporation and the securities dealers involved were not underwriters *per se*, they nevertheless functioned in this capacity. Incidentally, the offering described here *was* successful and the desired funds *were* raised. For a discussion of the pros and cons of public offerings for small companies, see *"Investment Bankers"* above.

Self Underwriting

In some instances, a company with little or no proven operating history may find that it cannot raise sufficient funds either through lending and credit channels or through a private placement of stock. In such a situation, it is rare that any reputable investment banker will underwrite a new offering of securities. Or if the services of an underwriter are available, the management of the enterprise may decide that the underwriting expenses are excessive in relation to the amount of capital required. Alternatively, a public offering of securities may be attempted through a *self* underwriting. As in the case of *any* public offering of stock, retention of the professional services of a qualified attorney is a *must* in navigating the customary Securities and Exchange Commission and state securities regulations and registration labyrinth. Failure to obtain legal assistance could land you in jail because of the strict enforcement of laws reflecting federal and state governmental concern for the safety of the investing public and the protection of our capitalistic system of private enterprise.

In the event that a small or new company wishes to make a public offering of stock amounting to $1,500,000 or less in any one year, exemption from a full-scale SEC securities registration is available under Section 3(b), as amended, of the Securities Act of 1933 by meeting the conditions prescribed under Regulation A of the SEC regulations. These include the filing with the appropriate SEC regional office of a notification on Form 1-A and the filing and use of a circular that contains basic information about the issues and the security. (In the case of an offering of $100,000 or less, no circular is required.) This filing must take place at least ten working days prior to the date the offering is to be made.

In computing the maximum offerings for any given year, any offerings previously made within that year must be included. Thus, if an offering is contemplated for November and $1,200,000 in securities were sold in July, the new offering may not exceed $300,000. Regardless of how such securities are marketed, the $1,500,000 figure represents *the amount the investing public pays* and *not* the net return after deduction of the legal fees, printing fees, accounting fees, registration fees, postage fees, and any other fees incident to the offering.

Materials filed with the SEC regional office under the Regulation A exemption are carefully examined to make certain that the proposed issue qualifies for the exemption and that all of the required disclosures have been made. Usually, a letter is sent to the offering company indicating areas of noncompliance. If any such areas are present, the offering is suspended until the matter is resolved to the satisfaction of the SEC. If the government determines that the offering circular is seriously misleading or that an attempt has been made to defraud the public, permanent suspension may result. In any event, a hearing may be requested to consider the case, after which a decision will be made regarding retention of the suspension order.

For a complete description of the requirements of a Regulation A exemption status and the filing procedure necessary to qualify, write to the SEC at the address below and request a copy of the publication "Regulation A, General Exemption from Registration under the Securities Act of 1933," SEC document number 1782.

Finally, in considering almost any stock offering, it must be remembered that qualifying for the Regulation A exemption merely satisfies certain federal government requirements. Each sovereign state has its own rules (called "Blue Sky" laws) *in addition to* those of the federal government! *Now*, won't you please go talk to an attorney?

The staff of the SEC is available to small business owners and managers to discuss problems in regard to securities, such as registration and qualification requirements, exemptions, and disclosures. Address inquiries to the Office of Small Business Policy, U.S. Securities and Exchange Commission, 450 Fifth Street, N.W., Washington, D.C. 20549.

Regional and Branch Offices are located around the nation as follows:

- **Zone 1** (New York, New Jersey): 26 Federal Plaza, New York, New York 10278.

- **Zone 2** (Massachusetts, Connecticut, Rhode Island, Vermont, New Hampshire, and Maine): 150 Causeway Street, Boston, Massachusetts 02114.

- **Zone 3** (Tennessee, North Carolina, South Carolina, Georgia, Alabama, Mississippi, Florida, Virgin Islands, Puerto Rico, and that part of Louisiana lying east of the Atchafalaya River): Suite 788, 1375 Peachtree Street N.E., Atlanta, Georgia 30367. *Branch:* Dupont Plaza Center, 300 Biscayne Boulevard Way, Suite 1114, Miami, Florida 33131.

- **Zone 4** (Michigan, Indiana, Ohio, Kentucky, Minnesota, Wisconsin, Iowa, Illinois, Missouri, and Kansas City, Kansas): Room 1204, 219 South Dearborn Street, Chicago, Illinois 60604. *Branch:* 1044 Federal Building, Detroit, Michigan 48226.

- **Zone 5** (Oklahoma, Arkansas, Texas, that part of Louisiana lying west of the Atchafalaya River, and Kansas): 411 W. Seventh Street, Fort Worth, Texas 76102. *Branch:* Scanlan Building, Suite 302, 405 Main Street, Houston, Texas 77002.

- **Zone 6** (Wyoming, Colorado, New Mexico, Nebraska, North Dakota, South Dakota, and Utah): 410 17th Street, Denver, Colorado 80202. *Branch:* Boston Building, Suite 810, 9 Exchange Place, Salt Lake City, Utah 84111.

- **Zone 7** (California, Nevada, Arizona, Hawaii, and Guam): 5757 Wilshire Boulevard, Suite 500 East, Los Angeles, California 90036-3648. *Branch:* 450 Golden Gate, Box 36042, San Francisco, California 94102.

- **Zone 8** (Washington, Oregon, Idaho, Montana, and Alaska): 13040 Federal Building, 915 Second Avenue, Seattle, Washington 98174.

- **Zone 9** (Virginia, West Virginia, Maryland, Delaware, District of Columbia, and Pennsylvania): Ballston Center Tower 3, 4015 Wilson Boulevard, Arlington, Virginia 22203. *Branch:* William J. Green, Jr., Federal Building, 600 Arch Street, Room 2204, Philadelphia, Pennsylvania 19106.

Small Business Administration

The Small Business Administration was created by Congress on July 30, 1953. The enabling legislation, known as the Small Business Act of 1953, provides formal governmental recognition of the importance of this country's ten million small businesses to the maintenance of a viable economy. Without a doubt, the most important activity of the SBA is the administration of a financial assistance program for small businesses. A staff of more than 4000 government employees, working through a network of 100 field offices, brings the benefits of SBA financial services to all qualified businesses. Current SBA loans outstanding total nearly $2 billion.

Although the SBA offers a number of forms of financial assistance, including disaster loans and lease guarantees, the discussion here will be restricted to four programs of primary practical interest to the average small business. A discussion of SBA-licensed Small Business Investment Companies will be presented in the next section.

Bank Participation Loans

Approximately two-thirds of the loans made by the SBA involve the participation of commercial banks or other private lending institutions. If a small business does not qualify for an ordinary bank loan because it fails to meet certain financial criteria, a bank may be willing to lend money to the enterprise, provided the Small Business Administration will guarantee the note. Such SBA-guaranteed loans may be used for:

1. Business construction, expansion, or conversion.

2. Purchase of machinery, equipment, facilities, supplies, or materials.

3. Working capital.

Provided the loan applicant is able to demonstrate an ability to repay a loan and any other debts out of company profits to the satisfaction of SBA examiners, the SBA may participate in a loan in either of two ways:

1. By guaranteeing up to ninety percent or $450,000 of a bank loan, whichever is less. (In this instance, the SBA merely *guarantees* ninety percent of the bank loan or $450,000, whichever is less; the SBA does not provide an immediate outlay of cash.)

2. By providing $150,000, as the SBA share of an immediate-participation loan with the bank.

The term of the loan may vary with a maximum maturity of twenty-five years. In the case of a working capital loan, the term may be as short as seven years or less.[113]

Direct Loans

If a bank or other private lending institution declines to participate in an SBA loan to a new or small enterprise, the SBA may choose to make a direct loan to the business subject to a $150,000 limit. Loan application evaluation criteria, interest rates, maturity dates, and repayment rates for such direct loans are normally the same as those that characterize bank-participation loans.[114]

In 1979 the SBA initiated a Certified Lenders Program to expedite the SBA loan guarantee process. Under this program, selected commercial banks are designated Certified Lenders. You can expect speedier processing of your loan application if you apply through one of these banks. Contact your local SBA office for a list of Certified Lenders in your area.

State Investment Development Corporations

Many states have business-development corporations formed in cooperation with the SBA for the purpose of supplying long-term loans and/or equity capital to small companies. The purpose of such programs is to induce new businesses to locate within a given state, thus enhancing industrial and commercial growth rates and providing employment for its citizens. These state development companies are usually in a position to obtain matching funds from the Small Business Administration to augment their capital. Loans to the development companies from the SBA may be for as long as twenty-five years. Assistance to state development companies from the SBA for such endeavors is made under the SBA 501 program, authorized under Section 501 of the Small Business Investment Act of 1958.[115]

Local Development Companies

Local development companies (LDCs) are sometimes established within a community to promote and partially fund industrial and commercial projects within the community. LDCs work with local lenders who finance projects in conjunction with SBA guarantees. This method of financing is provided under the SBA's 502 loan program.

An LDC is formed by a group of at least twenty-five community members (a broad range of backgrounds is preferable). These groups can operate either as for profit or nonprofit organizations. Businesses sponsored by LDCs may obtain SBA-guaranteed bank financing up to a maximum of $500,000 for a period of as much as twenty-five years. Use of funds is exclusively for real estate acquisition and/or construction. Interest rates are negotiated with the participating lender.[116] Your regional SBA office can supply you with details regarding both establishing an LDC or financing your business through the vehicle of LDC-sponsored loans.

Certified Development Companies

The SBA has created a new economic development tool for helping communities finance the real estate needs of local small businesses. It is called the 503 loan program and is administered by SBA-designated Certified Development Companies (CDCs). A listing of CDCs serving your community can be obtained from your regional SBA office. The 503 program provides funding for real estate acquisition and/or construction, and works as follows:[117]

- A private lending institution provides fifty percent of a project's costs, setting their own rates, terms, and loan conditions.

- The SBA provides forty percent of the project's costs by issuing a debenture which is sold through the Federal Finance Bank in Washington, D.C. The debenture is somewhat below market rates, and carries a fixed rate for the term of the loan (usually twenty-five years).

- The business seeking the project funding supplies the remaining ten percent of the cost.

The 503 program is the SBA's principal economic development tool, providing small businesses with low down-payment loans at favorable rates. More details on the program may be obtained from your regional SBA office.

Small Business Investment Companies

Although individual investors have been providing venture capital for new and small businesses in the United States since the birth of the nation, no federally sponsored source of such financing existed until 1958 when Congress passed the Small Business Investment Act. This Act authorized the founding of a special class of investment companies for the encouragement of small businesses.

Small business investment companies (SBICs) and minority enterprise small business investment companies (MESBICs) are financial institutions created to make equity capital and long-term credit (with maturities of at least five years) available to small, independent businesses. SBICs are licensed by the Federal Government's Small Business Administration, but they are privately-organized and privately-managed firms which set their own policies and make their own investment decisions.[118] Although all SBICs will consider applications for funds from socially and economically disadvantaged entrepreneurs, MESBICs normally make all their investments in this area.[119]

In return for pledging to finance only small businesses, SBICs may qualify for long-term loans from the Small Business Administration. By the end of 1983, the number of SBICs had grown to nearly 400. More than half are independent firms or units of nonfinancial companies; sixty-seven, or roughly twenty percent, are bank affiliates; thirty-one are subsidiaries of venture capital and other financial companies.[120]

While some SBICs provide only later-stage financing, others supply seed money for business start-ups. Perhaps surprisingly, bank-owned SBICs are leading a trend toward more start-up financing.[121]

To date, SBICs have disbursed over $4.5 billion by making over 66,000 loans and investments. The concerns they have financed have far out-performed all national averages as measured by increases in assets, sales, profits, and new employment.

Literally thousands of owners of profitable businesses can tell you how much they have benefited from the dollars and management counseling made available to them by SBICs for twenty-five years.[122]

The overwhelming majority of all business firms in this country qualify as "small." As a general rule, companies are eligible for SBIC financing if they have a net worth under $6 million and average after-tax earnings of less than $2 million during the past two years. A firm may also qualify as "small" under an employment standard or an amount-of-annual-sales standard. In most cases, a call to your local SBA office or the offices of one of your local SBICs will enable you, in short order, to resolve the question of eligibility.

All SBIC financing terms are tailored to meet the needs of the individual small business and the particular SBIC fund involved. Thus, the small business and the SBIC negotiate the terms for the financing arrangement—the SBIC might buy shares of stock in the company, might make a straight loan, or might agree upon some combination of the two.

Commonly, SBICs are interested in realizing capital gains from purchasing a stock at a low price and selling it at a later date at a much higher price. Thus, SBICs will purchase stock in a small company or advance funds through a debt instrument (a note or debenture) with conversion privileges or rights to buy stock at a predetermined later date.

According to a publication of the National Association of SBICs, "Industry averages show that for every SBIC dollar placed with a small business concern, two additional senior dollars become available from commercial banks or other sources."[123] Regarding the unique advantages of SBIC financing, this same publication states that

> Before it receives its license, an SBIC must prove that its management and directors are experienced individuals with a broad range of business and professional talents.
>
> This expertise will be applied to assist your business, supplementing the skills of your own management team. Here again, the actual pattern of management and financial counseling will be cut to fit each specific situation.
>
> SBICs can make only long-term loans or equity investments; therefore, their interests and yours will coincide—both of you will want your firm to grow and prosper.[124]

A fairly recent addition to the SBIC program is the Minority Enterprise SBIC (MESBIC). This special class of SBICs was created for the purpose of providing venture capital for socially and economically disadvantaged entrepreneurs. At the present time, more than 130 MESBICs are operational.

State and Local Industrial Development Commissions

Many cities, counties, and states across the nation have progressed in recent years in their willingness to provide financial encouragement for struggling new or small businesses. Although the amount of financial assistance offered may vary substantially from community to community and from state to state, the value of encouraging new business is recognized by all, and many localities have set up their own industrial development commissions.

In many instances, the financial assistance offered through state and local industrial development commissions is available in situations where banks or other conservative institutions are not willing to participate in the financing. This is particularly true if the new business does not meet AAA conventional credit requirements. The funds for industrial development commission financing are generally obtained through the issuance of municipal bonds. (Interest on these bonds is tax-free to the purchasers.)

Municipal legislative bodies may also appropriate public funds in their treasuries for the purpose of encouraging new businesses. Assistance rendered under these programs may include low-cost, long-term loans for the construction of manufacturing facilities or for the purchase of capital equipment, or it may provide for subsidized employee training programs. In some cases, working capital may be provided. Also, very favorable tax concessions may be offered to encourage new enterprises. Loan repayment periods may run anywhere from five to thirty-five years, depending on the community involved.

Advertisements are regularly run in the leading financial journals by many states and local communities that wish to encourage the growth of new industry within their borders. Information on the advantages of establishing a new enterprise in a given locality may be obtained by writing to the State Industrial Development Commissioner, Chamber of Commerce, or Economic Development Agency of any state in which the entrepreneur is interested in locating a facility. The State Commissioner or Chamber of Commerce representative will be more than happy to provide information on the special advantages that would accrue to the founders of a new business choosing to locate in his or her sovereign state. Information furnished ordinarily includes a discussion of municipal services and utilities, training programs, state and local tax-rate structures, housing, labor supply, availability of raw materials, transportation facilities, specifics on available buildings and building sites, and special financing that might be available through governmental or private sources. For a listing of economic development agencies across the country, you may purchase a directory, "Who's Who in Economic Development" by writing to the American Economic Development Council at 4849 North Scott Street, Suite 10, Schiller Park, Illinois 60176.

Tax-Exempt Foundations and Charitable Trusts

There are thousands upon thousands of foundations in this country that award grants for a wide variety of causes and to a broad array of businesses. The most comprehensive source of information about these organizations is *The Foundation Directory*.[125]

Ostensibly, the majority of the foundations in this country have been established for the purpose of serving and enhancing the general well-being of society, although many of these foundations are little more than tax-avoidance mechanisms for their creators.[126] However, there are a large number of foundations which *do* render a service to the community.

In some instances, entrepreneurs may wish to launch a business with a product or service that will benefit society. These entrepreneurs may be able to obtain significant financial assistance in the form of grants or loans from an interested foundation. If they do appropriate research on the subject (start by consulting *The Foundation Directory* mentioned above), they may be able to identify a foundation dedicated to serving a social need in consonance with the thrust of their planned enterprise. Thus, they may persuade the foundation to assist in the launching of their venture. Three examples illustrate this process:

1. An entrepreneur with a background in medical electronics may wish to launch an enterprise for the purpose of developing and manufacturing a badly needed new medical-electronic instrument. This entrepreneur may be able to persuade the foundation to provide a grant for the company for the purpose of developing such an instrument.

2. An entrepreneur may wish to start a profitable business for the purpose of providing management and technical assistance to minority enterprises. An interested foundation may be persuaded to make a low-interest-rate loan for launching the enterprise.

3. The entrepreneur with plans for the creation of a new business for the purpose of manufacturing products to reduce environmental pollution may afford a foundation a unique opportunity to simultaneously serve society and to realize gains for its portfolio through equity participation in the new enterprise.

These examples are intended merely to suggest only *some* of the avenues by which a tax-exempt foundation or charitable trust may be approached and subsequently induced to participate in financing a deserving venture. With a little imagination, I'm certain you can think of many others. *Remember:* The primary source in identifying a suitable foundation is the directory mentioned above.

Trade Suppliers

There are many characteristics in the trade supplier/new venture financial relationship that are similar to those of the customer/new venture financial relationship referred to above. Let's consider some of the more important elements that motivate trade supplier assistance.

Develop Customer Loyalty

A new company that receives substantial financial assistance from its trade suppliers will develop a sense of loyalty to those helpers. I have spoken with the presidents of many small firms who acknowledge that loyalty and appreciation remain for years after the new company becomes successful.

Expand Customer Base

By assisting in the creation of new customers, a trade supplier may enlarge its available market and increase the demand for its own output. The result may be greater profitability potential through economies of scale. (The unit cost for one hundred widgets should be significantly less than the unit cost of ten widgets.)

Create Markets for New Products

In some instances, a trade supplier may develop a product for which no market presently exists. For example, a textile manufacturer may produce a new synthetic yarn that existing customers may not be willing to accept. If this supplier encourages the launching of a new cloth or clothing manufacturer, a distribution channel (customer) will have been created.

The means available to a trade supplier for furnishing assistance to a new firm are many and include the following four.

Extended Credit Terms

The helpful trade supplier may ship goods to customers on extended credit terms. In some instances, the supplier may offer terms wherein no payment is due until the entrepreneurs are successful in securing payment from their own customers. Such terms can run anywhere from thirty days to periods in excess of six months. (Incidentally, should your company encounter a financial crisis down the line, trade suppliers could prove to be your major source of financing if you have proven yourself to be a good credit risk.) If trade suppliers wish to assist new customers without tying up their own working capital, they may guarantee bank loans for their customers' accounts, thereby permitting the customers to pay cash for their purchases. Of course, any interest which the bank or other financial institution may charge must be paid by the customers.

Direct Loans

In some instances, a major trade supplier may agree to provide the new firm with a direct loan.

Purchase of Stock in New Company

Through the expedient of providing equity capital to launch a new customer, a trade supplier may effectively set the stage for an eventual merger or acquisition.

Lend or Lease Equipment

Some trade suppliers are primarily engaged in furnishing customers with raw materials for processing. This processing may require the use of expensive equipment and machinery, which a new company may have difficulty financing. By lending or leasing the equipment to the customer, suppliers may very effectively expand the market for their output.

Trust Companies and Bank Trust Departments

Since trust companies and bank trust departments both function in the same manner, the following discussion will refer only to trust companies, including bank trust departments by inference. (It should be recognized, however, that bank trust departments far outnumber trust companies.)

A trust company is a financial institution organized primarily to administer funds assigned to its supervision for the advantage of the beneficiary. If the trust is discretionary, the trustee is permitted considerable latitude in the manner in which the funds are invested. Although trust company investment policies have always been extremely conservative, clients have recently begun to insist upon the type of portfolio appreciation that is possible only by investment in growth securities. In some instances, trust companies may even invest a part of a client's portfolio in the stock of a new company—particularly if authorized or directed to do so by the client.

Trust companies do not usually interact with the management of small new portfolio companies. Instead, they prefcr to invest portfolio assets on a limited partnership basis as members of large venture capital organizations staffed with management consultants, who monitor the progress of new enterprises. Citibank, Manufacturers Hanover Trust Company, and First National Bank of Chicago participate in venture capital via this avenue. As Raymond Held, director of venture capital investment for Manufacturers Hanover sees it, trust departments of commercial banks are well suited to get involved in this area since they "have the expertise and experience to tap the talents of the best venture capitalists in America, who in turn pick and capitalize promising emerging companies."[127] Although venture capital is quite unlikely to be forthcoming from a trust company, an entrepreneur may reasonably expect assistance from the trust officers in locating more suitable sources of such capital.

Footnotes

Notes

1. Peter F. Drucker, *The Age of Discontinuity* (New York: Harper and Row, 1969), p. 43.

2. This profile was written by Jeannine Marschner, based on a personal interview of Debbi Fields by Ms. Marschner and Don Dible.

3. The Pert-O-Graph kit is available from Halcomb Associates, Inc., 510 E. Maude Avenue, Sunnyvale, California 94086.

4. Hannah Campbell, *Why Did They Name it . . .?* (New York: Ace Books, 1964), p. 190.

5. Dr. Stanley F. Kaisel in a speech presented at the San Francisco Entrepreneurship Workshop Series on Managing a New Enterprise in Today's Economy. Sponsored by the Massachusetts Institute of Technology, Spring 1971, in Palo Alto, California.

6. Russell Freedman, *Thomas Alva Edison* (New York: American RDM Corporation, 1966), p. 43.

7. Arthur F. Snyder, Senior Vice President of the New England Merchants National Bank, Boston, Massachusetts, "Panel on Financing New Enterprises" (speech delivered at the MIT Seminar for Young Alumni, Palo Alto, California, May 1970).

8. *The Business Failure Record* (New York: The Dun & Bradstreet Corporation, 1983), p. 2.

9. Laurence J. Peter and Raymond Hull, *The Peter Principle* (New York: William Morrow and Co., 1969), p. 7.

10. L. Charles Burlage, *The Small Businessman and His Problems* (New York: Vantage Press, 1958), preface.

11. Zig Ziglar, President, Zig Ziglar Corporation, 13642 Omega at Alpha, Dallas, Texas 75234.

12. *Books in Print*, 14 vols. (New York: R. R. Bowker Co.), revised annually.

13. Introductory brochure from Dialog Information Services, Inc., 3460 Hillview Avenue, Palo Alto, California 94304, phone (800) 227-1927 if calling from outside California or (800) 982-5838 in state.

14. Informational brochure from Library of Congress, National Referral Center, Washington, D.C. 20540.

15. *Ibid.*

16. U. S. Department of Commerce, Patent Office, *Q and A About Patents* (Washington, D.C.: Government Printing Office, 1982), p. 3.

17. *Ibid.*

18. U. S. Department of Commerce, Patent Office, *The U. S. Patent Office's "Disclosure Document Program"* (Washington, D.C.: Government Printing Office, 1984).

19. U. S. Department of Commerce, Patent Office, *General Information Concerning Patents*, rev. (Washington, D.C.: Government Printing Office, 1983), p. 28.

20. C. Howard Mann, "Small Business Profits From Unpatentable Ideas," *Management Aids for Small Business,* annual no. 3, Small Business Administration (Washington D. C.: Government Printing Office, 1957), p. 48.

21. *Martindale-Hubbell Law Directory* (Summit, N.J.: Martindale-Hubbell, Inc.), 1985. (In seven volumes; 117th annual edition.)

22. "How to Start and Operate a Small Business" (speech delivered at the MIT Seminar for Young Alumni, Palo Alto, California, 19 May 1970).

23. Louis L. Allen, *Starting and Succeeding in Your Own Small Business* (New York: Grosset and Dunlap, 1968), p. 147.

24. E. F. Heizer, Jr., *Venture Capital and Management, Proceedings of the Second Annual Boston College Management Seminar,* 28-29 May 1970 (Chestnut Hill, Mass.: Boston College Press, 1970), p. 79.

25. Charles B. Smith, *Venture Capital and Management Proceedings* (see note 24), p. 88.

26. Mark Rollinson, "New Business: Innovative Technology, Management and Capital," *Proceedings of the Boston College Management Seminar*, 22-23 May 1969 (Chestnut Hill, Mass.: Boston College Press, 1969), p. 89.

27. G. Stanton Geary, "Venture Capital Financing for Small Business: A Symposium," *The Business Lawyer* 24, no. 3 (April 1969): 944. Reprint.

28. Benno C. Schmidt, "The Money Is There," *Forbes,* 1 December 1970, p. 45.

29. *Investment Companies* (New York: Wiesenberger Investment Companies Service, 1983), p. 19.

30. *ARD Annual Report, 1983* (Boston: American Research and Development Division, Textron, Inc.), p. 6.

31. *Investment Companies,* (New York: Wiesenberger Investment Companies Service, 1983), p. 19.

32. Stanley E. Pratt and Jane K. Morris, eds., *Guide to Venture Capital Sources,* 9th ed. (Wellesley Hills, Mass.: Venture Economics, 1985), p. 213.

33. Thomas P. Murphy, "Hatching Promises," *Forbes,* 4 June 1984, p. 232.

34. *Ibid.*

35. Reprinted with special permission of Venture Magazine, Inc., from June 1983, p. 26.

36. Jack Zwick, *A Handbook of Small Business Finance,* (Washington D. C.: Small Business Administration, 1965), Chapter 8.

37. *Ibid.*, p. 60.

38. Joel Kotkin, "The New Small Business Bankers," *Inc.* May 1984, p. 114.

39. *Commercial Financing: What It Is and What It Does,* (New York: Meinhard-Commercial Corporation, 1969), p. 8.

40. Reprinted by permission of Reston Publishing Company, a Prentice-Hall Company, from Olin S. Pugh and Jerry F. Ingram, *Credit Union Management* (Reston, Va.: Reston Publishing Co., 1984), p. 59.

41. *Ibid.*

42. "Financial Services in the 1980's," (Report of the American Council of Life Insurance, December 1982), p. 30.

43. Reprinted by permission of Reston Publishing Company, a Prentice-Hall Company, from Olin S. Pugh and Jerry F. In-

gram, *Credit Union Management* (Reston, Va.: Reston Publishing Co., 1984), p. 28.

44. *Ibid.*, p. 150.

45. *Ibid.*, p. 53.

46. "Financial Services in the 1980's" (Report of the American Council of Life Insurance), pp. 30-31.

47. Economic Development Administration, *Annual Report* (Washington, D.C.: U. S. Department of Commerce, 1983), p. 1.

48. *EDA Business Development Loans. Who Can Borrow. How to Apply* (Washington, D.C.: U. S. Department of Commerce, September 1970), p. 3.

49. *Federal Register,* Vol. 48, no. 241 (14 December 1983): p. 55597.

50. *Ibid.*, p. 55598.

51. "Essentials of Factoring," *Factoring: What It Is and What It Does* (New York: Meinhard-Commercial Corporation, 1969), p. 5.

52. Reprinted by special permission of Venture Magazine, Inc., from Kevin Farrell, "Franchising Hits a Snag," February 1982, p. 70.

53. Bart Fraust, "Fed Fears Regulatory Erosion From Industrial Bank Activity," *American Banker*, 9 February 1984, p. 31.

54. *Ibid.*, p. 30.

55. *Best's Insurance Reports: Life-Health* (Oldwick, N.J.: A.M. Best Company, 1983), p. vii.

56. *Best's Aggregates and Averages: Property-Casualty* (Oldwick, N.J.: A. M. Best Company, 1984), p. 23.

57. "Financial Services in the 1980's" (Report of the American Council of Life Insurance), p. 10.

58. "What Do You Do With $81 Million?," *Forbes,* 15 July 1970, pp. 42-44.

59. "The Most Active Investors of 1982," *Venture*, June 1983, p. 38.

60. Reprinted by special permission of Venture Magazine, Inc., from Lori Ioannou, "Venturesome . . . and Loaded," February 1983, p. 46.

61. Introductory brochure from ML Venture Partners I, L.P., Merrill Lynch Venture Capital Inc., 165 Broadway, New York, NY 10080.

62. "Financing Fast Growing Companies," pp. 17-18 (introductory

brochure from Bateman Eichler, Hill Richards, 700 So. Flower St., Los Angeles, Calif. 90017, (213) 625-3545).

63. Securities Act of 1933, Section 2 (11).

64. William G. Flanagan, ed., "Investment Clubs Are Hanging in There," *Forbes,* 4 June 1984, p. 190.

65. *The National Association of Investment Clubs: Its Organization and Its Operation* (Royal Oak, Mich.: National Assn. of Investment Clubs).

66. Introductory brochure from National Association of Investment Clubs, 1515 East Eleven Mile Road, Royal Oak, Mich. 48067, (313) 543-0612.

67. *Ibid.*

68. *Ibid.*

69. *1970 Mutual Fund Fact Book* (Washington, D.C.: Investment Company Institute, 1969), p. 5.

70. *Ibid.*

71. "Financial Services in the 1980's" (Report of the American Council of Life Insurance), p. 23.

72. Reprinted by permission of Reston Publishing Company, a Prentice-Hall Company, from Edward K. Gill, *Commercial Lending Basics* (Reston, Va.: Reston Publishing Co., 1983), p. 25.

73. *National Consumer Cooperative Bank, Annual Report 1983* (Washington, D.C.: National Consumer Cooperative Bank).

74. See "Orphan Products" in Chapter 2 of this text.

75. See "Corporate Venture Capital Departments or Subsidiaries" in Chapter 15 of this text.

76. Reprinted by special permission of Venture Magazine, Inc., from Richard Barbieri, "When a Former Employer Backs Your Startup," November 1983, p. 64.

77. *Ibid.,* pp. 64-65.

78. *Ibid.,* p. 65.

79. Clarence C. Elebash, "The Competition for Pension Capital," *Enterprise,* April 1983, p. 7.

80. *Ibid.*

81. Reprinted with permission of *Dun's Business Month,* copyright 1983, Dun & Bradstreet Publications Corporation from Thomas J. Murray, "Venturesome Pension Funds," January 1983, p. 64.

82. Reprinted by special permission of Venture Magazine, Inc., from Gail Gregg, "Investing in Entrepreneurs," June 1984, p. 46.

83. Reprinted with permission of *Dun's Business Month,* copyright 1983, Dun & Bradstreet Publications Corporation from Thomas J. Murray, "Venturesome Pension Funds," January 1983, p. 64.

84. Pavan Sahgal, "State Funds Venturing into New Investment," *Pensions & Investment Age,* 16 May 1983, p. 30.

85. Reprinted by special permission of Venture Magazine, Inc., from Ioannou, "Venturesome . . . and Loaded," p. 46.

86. Robert A. Mamis, "New Money," *Inc.* April 1984, p. 93.

87. Bruce G. Posner, "Venture Capital Discovers the Mass Market," *Inc.* July 1984, p. 50.

88. *Ibid.*

89. Based on an interview with Kenneth Guernsey, Administrative General Partner of Hambrecht and Quist, October 1984.

90. "The Money Is There," *Forbes* 1 December 1970, p. 45.

91. Pratt and Morris eds., *Guide to Venture Capital Sources,* 9th ed., p. 77.

92. Reprinted by special permission of Venture Magazine, Inc. from Lee Kravitz, "Venture Funds Stop to Catch Their Breath," June 1984, p. 55.

93. Pratt and Morris, eds., *Guides to Venture Capital Sources,* 9th ed., p. 77.

94. Introductory brochure from Heizer Corporation, 20 N. Wacker Drive, Chicago, Ill. 60606.

95. "What Do You Do with $81 Million?" *Forbes,* 15 July 1970, p. 42.

96. Introductory brochure from Heizer Corporation, 20 N. Wacker Drive, Chicago, Ill. 60606.

97. *1983 SEC Government-Business Forum on Small Business Capital Formation: Final Report* (Washington, D.C.: U.S. Securities and Exchange Commission, November 1983), p. 143.

98. Milton D. Stewart, "There's Gold in Them Thar Hills," *Inc.,* January 1984, p. 148.

99. *Ibid.*, p. 146

100. Michael Geczi, "The Equity Partnership as a Seed for Startups," *Inc.* December 1982, p. 127.

101. *Ibid.*

102. *The NBS/DOE Energy-Related Inventions Program: What It Is and How It Works* (Washington, D.C.: U. S. Department of Commerce, January 1980).

103. *Ibid.*

104. United States League of Savings Institutions, *'83 Savings and Loan Sourcebook* (Chicago: U.S. League of Savings Institutions, 1983), p. 5. (The U.S. League of Savings Institutions is at 111 E. Wacker Drive, Chicago, Ill. 60601.)

105. *Ibid.*, p. 9.

106. Bruce G. Posner, "How Savings and Loans Stalk the Business Market," *Inc.*, July 1983, p. 99.

107. Reprinted by special permission of Venture Magazine, Inc., from "You Should Know," March 1983, p. 30.

108. Securities Exchange Act of 1934, Section 3 (a) (5).

109. Securities Exchange Act of 1934, Section 3 (a) (4).

110. Data Recognition Corporation, Prospectus, Palo Alto, California, 9 March 1970, p. 1.

111. *Ibid.*

112. *Ibid.*

113. "Business Loans from the Small Business Administration," (Washington, D.C.: Office of Public Communications, 1983).

114. *Ibid.*, p. 5.

115. *Ibid.*, p. 7.

116. Based on interviews with Gary Welpley, Economic Development Specialist, U. S. Small Business Administration, September 1984.

117. *Ibid.*

118. National Association of Small Business Investment Companies, *1984 Membership Directory* (Washington, D.C.: National Association of Small Business Investment Companies, 1984), p. 2.

119. *Ibid.*

120. Reprinted with special permission of Venture Magazine, Inc., from Udayan Gupta, "SBICS" October 1983, p. 66.

121. *Ibid.*, p. 67.

122. National Association of Small Business Investment Companies, *1984 Membership Directory,* p. 2.

123. *Ibid.*, p. 4.

124. *Ibid.*

125. Marianna Lewis, ed., *The Foundation Directory,* 8th ed. (New York: The Foundation Center, 1981)

126. Joseph C. Goulden, *The Money Givers* (New York: Random House, 1971), pp. 19-50.

127. Reprinted with special permission of Venture Magazine, Inc., from Ioannou "Venturesome . . . and Loaded," p. 46.

Recommended Readings

The asterisk in the margin next to a reading indicates that title is out of print. You may find these books at your local library, or through the columns of A.B. Bookman's Weekly, Box AB, Clifton, New Jersey 07015. Some bookstores also offer book search services. In addition, facsimiles of out-of-print books may be obtained from University Microfilms International, 300 N. Zeeb Road, Ann Arbor, Michigan 48106.

Chapter 1

* Alberts, Robert C. *The Good Provider: H. J. Heinz and His 57 Varieties.* Boston: Houghton Mifflin Company, 1973.
* Allen, Frederick Lewis. *The Great Pierpont Morgan.* Perennial Library. New York: Harper & Row, Inc., 1965.
  Baty, Gordon B. *Entrepreneurs for the Eighties.* Reston, Va.: Reston Publishing Co., Inc., 1981.
  Boas, Max, and Chain, Steve. *Big Mac: The Unauthorized Story of McDonald's.* New York: New American Library, Mentor Books, 1977.
* Boesen, Victor. *William P. Lear: From High School Dropout to Space Age Inventor.* New York: Hawthorn Books, Inc., 1974.
* Brooks, John, ed. *The Autobiography of American Business.* New York: Doubleday & Company, 1974.

* Burlingame, Roger. *Henry Ford*. Chicago: Quadrangle Books, 1970.
* Cafarakis, Christian. *The Fabulous Onassis: His Life and Loves.* New York: Pocket Books, Inc., 1973.

Chamberlain, John. *The Enterprising Americans*. New York: Harper & Row Pubs., Inc., Perennial Library, 1967.

* Conn, Charles Paul. *The Possible Dream: A Candid Look at America*. Old Tappan, N.J.: Fleming H. Revell Company, 1977.

Cossman, E. Joseph. *How I Made $1,000,000 in Mail Order*. Englewood Cliffs, N.J.: Prentice-Hall, Inc., 1963.

Fortune Magazine Staff, eds. *Adventures in Small Business*. New York: McGraw-Hill Book Company, 1957.

Gardner, Ralph, Jr. *Young, Gifted and Rich*. New York: Simon & Schuster, Inc., 1984.

* Groner, Alex, et al., eds. *The History of American Business and Industry*. New York: McGraw-Hill Book Company, American Publishing Company, 1972.

* Gunther, Max. *Instant Millionaires*. Chicago: Playboy Press, 1973.

Hanson, Dirk. *The New Alchemists: Silicon Valley and the Microelectronics Revolution*. Boston: Little, Brown and Company, 1982.

* Lay, Beirne, Jr. *Someone Has to Make It Happen: The Inside Story of Tex Thornton, the Man Who Built Litton Industries*. Englewood Cliffs, N.J.: Prentice-Hall, Inc., 1969.

Miller, William, ed. *Men in Business*. Torchbook Edition. New York: Harper & Row Pubs., Inc., 1962.

* Rae, John B., ed. *Henry Ford*. Englewood Cliffs, N.J.: Prentice-Hall, Inc., Spectrum Books, 1969.

Shook, Robert L. *The Shaklee Story*. New York: Harper & Row Pubs., Inc., 1982.

* Wall Street Journal Staff. *The Innovators*. Princeton, N.J.: Dow Jones Books, 1968.

* Wright, Esmond, ed. *Benjamin Franklin, A Profile*. New York: Hill and Wang, Inc., 1970.

Chapter 2

Applegath, John. *Working Free: Practical Alternatives to the Nine to Five Job*. New York: American Management Associations, AMACOM, 1982.

Baty, Gordon B. *Entrepreneurs: Playing to Win*. Reston, Va.: Reston Publishing Co., Inc., 1974.

Bolles, Richard Nelson. *What Color Is Your Parachute?* Rev. ed. Berkeley, Calif.: Ten Speed Press, 1983.

* Brooks, John. *Business Adventures*. New York: Bantam Books, Inc., 1970.

* Collins, Orvis F., and Moore, David G. *The Organization Makers; a Behavioral Study of Independent Entrepreneurs.* New York: Appleton-Century-Crofts, 1970.

Davis, George, and Watson, Glegg. *Black Life in Corporate America: Swimming in the Mainstream.* New York: Doubleday & Company, 1982.

* Goodrich, David L. *Horatio Alger Is Alive and Well and Living in America.* New York: Cowles Book Company, 1971.

* Jay, Anthony. *Management and Machiavelli, An Inquiry into the Politics of Corporate Life.* New York: Bantam Books, Inc., 1969.

Komives, John L. *Some Characteristics of Selected Entrepreneurs.* Ph.D. dissertation, Michigan State University. Ann Arbor, Mich.: University Microfilms, 1965.

* Mancuso, Joseph R. *Fun and Guts: The Entrepreneur's Philosophy.* Reading, Mass.: Addison-Wesley Publishing Company, 1973.

———. *A Diagnostic Test for Entrepreneurs.* New York: The Center for Entrepreneurial Management, 1979.

McGregor, Douglas. *Human Side of Enterprise.* New York: McGraw-Hill Book Company, 1960.

Parkinson, C. Northcote. *Parkinson's Law & Other Studies in Administration.* New York: Ballantine Books, Inc., 1975.

Peter, Laurence J., and Hull, Raymond. *The Peter Principle.* New York: William Morrow and Co., Bantam Books, Inc., 1970.

Rand, Ayn. *Capitalism: The Unknown Ideal.* New York: The New American Library, Signet Books, 1967.

Schumacher, E. F. *Small Is Beautiful.* New York: Harper & Row Pubs., Inc., 1976.

* Seder, John, and Burrell, Berkeley G. *Getting it Together: Black Businessmen in America.* New York: Harcourt Brace Jovanovich, Inc., 1971.

Sher, Barbara. *Wishcraft: How to Get What You Really Want.* New York: Ballantine Books, Inc., 1983.

Townsend, Robert. *Further Up the Organization: How to Stop Management from Stifling People and Strangling Productivity.* New York: Alfred A. Knopf, 1984.

———. *Up the Organization: How to Stop the Corporation from Stifling People and Strangling Profits.* New York: Alfred A. Knopf, 1970.

Chapter 3

Allen, Louis L. *Starting and Succeeding In Your Own Small Business.* New York: Grosset & Dunlap, 1968.

Bank of America National Trust and Savings Association. "Steps to Starting a Business." *Small Business Reporter.* San Francisco:

Bank of America National Trust and Savings Association, 1984.

* Becker, Benjamin M., and Tillman, Fred. *The Family-Owned Business.* Chicago: Commerce Clearing House, 1975.

* Bush, Vannevar. *Pieces of the Action.* New York: William Morrow and Company, 1970.

Danco, Leon. *Beyond Survival: A Business Owner's Guide for Success.* Englewood Cliffs, N.J.: Prentice-Hall, Inc., 1982.

Dible, Donald M. *Small Business Success Secrets.* Reston, Va.: Reston Publishing Company, Inc., 1981.

Ferkauf, Eugene. *Going Into Business: How to Do It, by the Man Who Did It.* New York: Chelsea House, 1980.

Fixx, James. *Jackpot!* New York: Random House, Inc., 1982.

Goldsmith, Howard R. *How to Make a Fortune in Import/Export.* Reston, Va.: Reston Publishing Company, Inc., 1981.

* Greenburger, Francis, with Krieman, Thomas. *How to Ask for More and Get It.* New York: Doubleday & Company, 1978.

Jewkes, John; Sawers, David; and Stillerman, Richard. *The Sources of Invention.* 2nd ed. New York: W. W. Norton & Company, Inc., 1971.

Johnston, J., and Phillips, L. *Success in Small Business Is a Laughing Matter.* Durham, N.C.: Moore Publishing Company, 1978.

Maltz, Maxwell. *Psycho-Cybernetics.* Englewood Cliffs, N.J.: Prentice-Hall, Inc., 1969.

Maslow, Abraham H. *Eupsychian Management: A Journal.* Homewood, Ill.: Richard D. Irwin, Inc. and The Dorsey Press, 1965.

———. *Toward a Psychology of Being.* An Insight Book. Princeton, N.J.: Van Nostrand Reinhold Co., Inc., 1968.

McQuown, Judith H. *Inc. Yourself.* New York: The Macmillan Company, 1979.

Melton, James E. *Vital Enthusiasm.* Palm Springs, Calif.: Global Publications, 1983.

Metcalf, Wendell; Bunn, Verne; and Stugelman, C. Richard. *How to Make Money in Your Own Small Business.* Reston, Va.: Reston Publishing Company, Inc., 1981.

Miller, Donald B. *Personal Vitality.* Reading, Mass.: Addison-Wesley Publishing Company, 1974.

"Patterns for Success in Managing a Business." The Dun and Bradstreet Business Series Number 2. Business Edition. New York: Dun and Bradstreet, Inc., 1968.

Putt, William D., ed. *How to Start Your Own Business.* The Alumni Association of MIT. Cambridge, Mass.: Distributed by the MIT Press, 1974.

* Rockwell, Willard F., Jr. *The Twelve Hats of a Company President: What It Takes to Run a Company.* Englewood Cliffs, N.J.: Prentice-Hall, Inc., 1971.

Schwartz, David J. *The Magic of Thinking Big.* Cornerstone Library Publications. Englewood Cliffs, N.J.: Prentice-Hall, Inc., 1965.

Stern, Howard H. *Running Your Own Business.* Pasadena, Calif.: Crown Pubs., Inc., 1980.

Chapter 4

* Burlage, L. Charles. *The Small Businessman and His Problems.* New York: Vantage Press, 1958.

Carnegie, Dale. *How to Stop Worrying and Start Living.* Rev. ed. New York: Simon & Schuster, Inc., 1984.

Feinberg, Mortimer R., with Dempowolff, Richard F. *Corporate Bigamy: How to Rescue the Conflict Between Career and Family.* New York: William Morrow and Company, 1980.

Fish, George, ed. *The Frontiers of Management Psychology.* New York: Harper & Row Pubs., Inc., 1964.

Getty, J. Paul. *How to Be Rich.* Chicago: Playboy Press, 1965.

* Kirstein, George G. *The Rich: Are They Different?* Boston: Houghton Mifflin Co., Tower Books, 1970.

Mandino, Og. *The Greatest Salesman in the World.* New York: Frederick Fell, Inc., 1968.

Peale, Norman Vincent. *A Guide to Confident Living.* New York: Fawcett Book Group, Crest Books, 1977.

Piper, Watty. *The Little Engine That Could.* New York: Platt & Munk, Publishers, 1961.

* Scanzoni, John H. *Opportunity and the Family.* New York: The Free Press, 1970.

* Smith, Norman R. *The Entrepreneur and His Firm: The Relationship between Type of Man and Type of Company.* East Lansing, Mich.: Michigan State University Press, 1967.

Chapter 5

Bank of America National Trust and Savings Association. "Personnel Guidelines." *Small Business Reporter.* San Francisco: Bank of America National Trust and Savings Association, 1981.

DeFren, Burton J. *Partnership Desk Book.* Englewood Cliffs, N.J.: Institute for Business Planning, 1978.

Downs, Calvin W.; Smeyak, G. Paul; and Martin, Ernest. *Professional Interviewing.* New York: Harper & Row Pubs., Inc., 1980.

Fast, Julius. *Body Language.* New York: Pocket Books, Inc., 1971.

Fenlason, Anne F. *Essentials in Interviewing.* New York: Harper & Row Pubs., Inc., 1962.

* Freeman, G. L., and Taylor, E. K. *How to Pick Leaders.* New York: Funk and Wagnalls, 1950.

Chapter 6

Albert, Kenneth J. *How to Pick the Right Small Business Opportunity*. New York: McGraw-Hill Book Company, 1980.

Balliet, Gene. *Getting Started in Private Practice*. Oradell, N.J.: Litton Industries, Medical Economics Company, 1978.

Bauer, Robert O. *Small Business Goes to College*. Small Business Administration. Washington, D.C.: Government Printing Office, 1978.

Brandt, Steven C. *Entrepreneuring: The Ten Commandments for Building a Growth Company*. New York: New American Library, Mentor Executive Library, 1983.

* Burger, Ninki Hart. *The Executive's Wife*. New York: The Macmillan Company, Collier Books, 1970.

Burns, David, M.D. *Feeling Good: The New Mood Therapy*. New York: New American Library, Signet Books, 1980.

Cohn, Theodore, and Lindberg, Roy A. *Survival and Growth: Management Strategies for the Small Firm*. New York: American Management Associations, AMACOM, 1974.

Cooper, Kenneth H. *Aerobics*. New York: M. Evans and Company, Inc., 1968.

Dible, Donald M., ed. *What Everybody Should Know About Patents, Trademarks and Copyrights*. Reston, Va.: Reston Publishing Company, Inc., 1981.

Drucker, Peter F. *Managing for Results: Economic Tasks and Risk-taking Decisions*. New York: Harper & Row Pubs., Inc., 1964.

Fixx, James. *Jackpot!* New York: Random House, Inc., 1982.

Fowler, George T. *The Written Formula for Making Money*. Mobile, Ala.: Empress Press, 1974.

Gillis, Phyllis. *Entrepreneurial Mothers*. New York: Rawson Associates, 1984.

Grisham, Roy A., Jr., ed. *Encyclopedia of United States Government Benefits*. New York: Dodd, Mead and Co., 1981.

* Hammer, Marian Behan. *The Complete Handbook of How to Start and Run a Money-Making Business in Your Home*. West Nyack, N.Y.: Parker Publishing Company, 1975.

* Heller, Robert. *How to Make a Million*. New York: Dell Publishing Co., Inc., 1974.

Janezick, Elizabeth G., comp. *A Survey of Federal Government Publications of Interest to Small Business*. 3rd ed. Small Business Administration. Washington, D.C.: Government Printing Office, 1969.

Kepner, Charles H., and Tregoe, Benjamin G. *The Rational Manager; a Systematic Approach to Problem Solving and Decision Making*. New York: McGraw-Hill Book Company, 1965.

Klein, Bernard. *Guide to American Directories.* 10th ed. Coral Springs, Fla.: B. Klein Publications, 1978.

Kuppinger, Roger. *Everything You Always Wanted to Know About Mergers, Acquisitions and Divestitures, but Didn't Know Whom to Ask.* 2nd ed. Arcadia, Calif.: By the Author, 77 Woodland Lane, 1983.

Lane, Byron. *Free Yourself in a Business of Your Own.* An Astron Series Book. New York: The Guild of Tutors Press, 1979.

Lederman, Martin. *The Slim Gourmet.* New York: Simon & Schuster, Inc., 1955.

Machlup, Fritz. *The Production and Distribution of Knowledge in the United States.* Princeton, N.J.: Princeton University Press, 1972.

Mancuso, Joseph R. *The Small Business Survival Guide.* New York: The Center for Entrepreneurial Management, 1979.

——. *How to Start, Finance, and Manage Your Own Small Business.* Englewood Cliffs, N.J.: Prentice-Hall, Inc., 1978.

McGregor, Douglas. *The Human Side of Enterprise.* New York: McGraw-Hill Book Company, 1960.

Morehouse, Lawrence E., and Gross, Leonard. *Total Fitness in 30 Minutes a Week.* New York: Simon & Schuster, Inc., 1975.

Norback, Craig, and Norback, Peter. *Everything You Can Get From the Government for Free . . . or Almost for Free.* New York: Van Nostrand Reinhold Co., 1975.

Park, William R., and Chapin-Park, Sue. *How to Succeed in Your Own Business.* New York: John Wiley and Sons, 1978.

Peale, Norman Vincent. *The Power of Positive Thinking.* New York: Fawcett World Library, 1956.

Sher, Barbara. *Wishcraft: How to Get What You Really Want.* New York: Ballantine Books, Inc., 1983.

Sweetland, Ben. *I Can! The Key to Life's Golden Secrets.* New York: Cadillac Publishing Company, Inc., 1976.

Todd, Alden. *Finding Facts Fast.* Berkeley, Calif.: Ten Speed Press, 1979.

Vanek, Jaroslave, ed. *Self-Management: Economic Liberation of Man.* Baltimore: Penguin Books, Inc., 1975.

Vesper, Karl H. *Entrepreneurship and National Policy.* Chicago, Ill.: Heller Institute for Small Business Policy Papers, 1983.

Chapter 7

Carnegie, Dale. *How to Win Friends and Influence People.* Rev. ed. New York: Pocket Books, 1982.

* Fuchs, Jerome H. *Management Consultants in Action.* New York: Hawthorn Books, Inc., 1975.

Hill, Napoleon, and Keown, E. Harold. *Succeed and Grow Rich through Persuasion.* A Fawcett Crest Book. Greenwich, Conn.: Fawcett Book Group, 1970.

Lebell, Frank. *The Manufacturer's Representative.* Boston: Herman Publishing, Inc., 1981.

* Machlup, Fritz. *The Production and Distribution of Knowledge in the United States.* Princeton, N.J.: Princeton University Press, 1972.

National Trade and Professional Associations of the U.S. Washington, D.C.: Columbia Books, 1984.

Chapter 8

Albert, Kenneth J. *How to Pick the Right Small Business Opportunity.* New York: McGraw-Hill Book Company, 1980.

Amerongen, C. van, trans. *The Way Things Work; An Illustrated Encyclopedia of Technology.* New York: Simon & Schuster, Inc., 1967.

Bennett, Vivo, and Clapett, Cricket. *1001 Ways to Be Your Own Boss.* Englewood Cliffs, N.J.: Prentice-Hall, Inc., 1976.

* Bleum, A. William, and Squire, Jason C. *The Movie Business.* New York: Hastings House Publishers, Inc., 1973.

Botkin, James; Dimancescu, Dan; and Stat, Ray. *Global Stakes: The Future of High Technology in America.* New York: Harper & Row Pubs., Inc., 1982.

* Brabham, Vernon Jr. *How to Turn Your Ideas Into Big Money.* Marietta, Ga.: Craftmark Publishing Company, 1982.

* Bylinsky, Gene. *The Innovation Millionaires.* New York: Charles Scribner's Sons, 1976.

Campbell, Hannah. *Why Did They Name It . . . ?* Ace Books. New York: Fleet Publishing Corporation, 1964.

* Carlisle, Norman. *How to Make a Fortune From Your Invention.* New York: Warner Books, Inc., Paperback Library, 1972.

Cochrane, Diane. *This Business of Art.* New York: Watson-Guptill Pubs., Inc., 1978.

* De Bono, Edward, ed. *An Illustrated History of Inventions from the Wheel to the Computer.* New York: Holt Rinehart Winston, Inc., 1974.

* Dock, M. Russell, and Sanderson, William R. *A Fortune in Your Head.* New York: Clark Boardman Company, Ltd., 1963.

Dorland, Gilbert N., and Van der Wal, John. *The Business Idea: From Birth to Profitable Company.* New York: Van Nostrand Reinhold, 1978.

Fenner, Terrence W. *Inventor's Handbook.* New Orleans, La.: Associated Ideas International, 1968.

* Frantz, Forrest H., Sr. *Successful Moonlighting Techniques That Can Make You Rich.* West Nyack, N.Y.: Parker Publishing Co., 1970.

Genfan, Herb, and Taetzsch, Lyn. *How to Start Your Own Craft Business.* New York: Watson-Guptill Pubs., Inc., 1974.

Ghiselin, Brewster, ed. *The Creative Process.* New York: New American Library, Mentor Books, 1952.

* Hartman, Susan N., and Parrish, Norman C. *Inventors Source Book: How to Turn Ideas into Inventions.* Berkeley, Calif.: Inventors Resource Center, 1976.

* Henry, Leon, Jr. *The Home Office Guide.* Scarsdale, N.Y.: Home Office Press, 1968.

Horn, Yvonne Michie. *Dozens of Ways to Make Money.* New York: Harcourt Brace Jovanovich, Inc., 1977.

Hunt, Alfred. *The Management Consultant.* A Ronald Press Publication. New York: John Wiley and Sons, 1977.

Joffe, Gerardo. *How You Too Can Make at Least $1 Million in the Mail-Order Business.* San Francisco: Advance Books, 1979.

* Judge, Vira H. *Homework: The Stay-at-Home Money Book.* Salt Lake City, Utah: Deseret Book Company, 1977.

Kahm, H.S. *101 Businesses You Can Start With Less Than $1,000.* A Dolphin Book. Garden City, N.Y.: Doubleday & Company, 1973.

* Kaye, Marvin. *A Toy Is Born.* New York: Stein and Day, 1973.

Kracke, Don, with Honkanen, Roger. *How to Turn Your Idea Into a Million Dollars.* New York: Doubleday & Company, 1977.

* Lebell, Don. *The Professional Services Enterprise: Theory and Practice.* Sherman Oaks, Calif.: Los Angeles Publishing Company, 1973.

* LeBlanc, Jerry. *300 Ways to Moonlight.* New York: Paperback Library, 1969.

Lovinson, Jay Conrad. *Earning Money without a Job: The Economics of Freedom.* San Rafael, Calif.: Prosper Press, 1977.

Loye, David. *The Knowable Future: A Psychology of Forecasting and Prophecy.* New York: John Wiley and Sons, 1978.

McNair, Eric P., and Schwenck, James E. *How to Become a Successful Inventor.* New York: Hastings House Publishers, Inc., 1974.

Null, Gary, and Simonson, Richard. *How to Turn Ideas into Dollars.* Pilot Books. New York: Pilot Industries, Inc., 1969.

* Osborn, Alex F. *How to Become More Creative.* New York: Charles Scribner's Sons, 1952.

* Paige, Richard E. *Complete Guide to Making Money with Your Ideas and Inventions.* Englewood Cliffs, N.J.: Prentice-Hall, Inc., 1973.

* Philpot, F. A. *Three Months to Earn: A Guide to Summer Jobs for College Students*. New York: The Macmillan Company, Collier Books, 1970.
* Rines, Robert H. *Create or Perish; the Case for Inventions and Patents*. Washington, D.C.: Acropolis Books, 1969.
* Sanderson, William R. *Patent Your Invention and Make It Pay*. New York: Grosset & Dunlap (by arrangement with American Research Council, Larchmont, New York), 1966.
  Seltz, David D. *A Treasury of Business Opportunities for the Eighties*. 3rd ed. New York: Farnsworth Publishing Co., Inc., 1983.
  Shemel, Sidney, and Krasilousky, M. William. *More About This Business of Music*. Rev. ed. New York: Watson-Guptill Pubs., Inc., Billboard Books, 1982.
* Shulman, Morton. *Anyone Can Make a Million: How to Invest Your Money and Profit from Inflation*. New York: Bantam Books, Inc., 1968.
  United States Department of Commerce. *The Potential of Handicrafts as a Viable Economic Force: An Overview*. Washington, D.C.: U.S. Dept. of Commerce, May 1974.
  Von Oeck, Roger. *A Whack on the Side of the Head*. New York: Warner Books, 1983.
* Winter, Elmer L. *1015 Ways to Save Time, Trouble and Money in the Operation of Your Business*. Englewood Cliffs, N.J.: Prentice-Hall, Inc., 1970.
* Woods, Clinton, ed. *Ideas That Became Big Business*. Baltimore: Founders, Inc., 1959.
  Young, James Webb. *A Technique for Producing Ideas*. 3rd ed. Chicago: Crain Books, Crain Communications, 1975.
* Young, Jim, and Young, Jean. *The Kids' Money-Making Book*. New York: Doubleday & Company, 1976.

Chapter 9

Anthony, Michael. *Handbook of Small Business Advertising*. San Francisco: Auburn-Wolfe Publishing, 1981.

Baker, S. *The Systematic Approach to Advertising Creativity*. New York: McGraw-Hill Book Company, 1979.

Bank of America National Trust and Savings Association. "Advertising Small Business." *Small Business Reporter*. San Francisco: Bank of America National Trust and Savings Association, 1982.

Bellavance, Diane. *Advertising and Public Relations for a Small Business*. Boston: DBA Books, 1982.

Black, Sam. *Practical Public Relations*. 4th ed. Woodstock, N.Y.: Beckman Publishers, Inc., 1977.

Carlson, Linda. *The Publicity and Promotion Handbook: A Complete Guide for Small Business.* Boston: CBI Publishing Company, Inc. (Thompson Organization), 1982.

Cook, Harvey. *Profitable Advertising Techniques for Small Business.* Reston, Va.: Reston Publishing Company, Inc., 1981.

* D'Aprix, Roger M. *The Believable Corporation.* New York: American Management Associations, AMACOM, 1977.

Dudley, Jim. *Promoting the Organization: A Guide to Low Budget Publicity.* Philadelphia: International Ideas, Inc., 1975.

Mancuso, Joseph R. *How to Name a Business.* New York: The Center for Entrepreneurial Management, 1979.

Norins, Hanley. *The Compleat Copywriter; a Comprehensive Guide to All Phases of Advertising Communication.* New York: McGraw-Hill Book Company, 1966.

Ries, Al, and Trout, Jack. *Positioning: The Battle for Your Mind.* New York: McGraw-Hill Book Company, Inc., 1980.

Sackheim, Maxwell. *How to Advertise Yourself.* New York: Free Press, 1978.

Seiden, Hank. *Advertising Pure and Simple.* New York: American Management Associations, AMACOM, 1976.

Stanley, Richard E. *Promotion: Advertising, Publicity, Personal Selling, Sales Promotion.* 2nd Ed. Englewood Cliffs, N.J.: Prentice-Hall, Inc.

Winston, Martin Bradley. *Getting Publicity.* New York: John Wiley and Sons, 1982.

Chapter 10

Coffin, Royce A. *The Negotiator: A Manual for Winners.* New York: American Management Associations, AMACOM, 1973.

Fisher, Roger, and Ury, William. *Getting to Yes: Negotiating Agreement Without Giving In.* Reprint. New York: Penguin Books, 1983.

Ilich, John. *The Art and Skill of Successful Negotiation.* Englewood Cliffs, N.J.: Prentice-Hall, Inc., 1973.

Karrass, Chester L. *The Negotiating Game.* New York: World Publishing Company, 1972.

————. *Give & Take: The Complete Guide to Negotiating Strategies and Tactics.* New York: Thomas Y. Crowell Co., 1974.

Kennedy, Gavin. *Everything is Negotiable: How to Get a Better Deal.* Englewood Cliffs, N.J.: Prentice-Hall, Inc., 1983.

Nierenberg, Gerard I. *The Art of Negotiating: Psychological Strategies for Gaining Advantageous Bargains.* New York: Hawthorn Books, Inc., 1968.

————. *Creative Business Negotiating: Skills and Successful Strategies.* New York: Hawthorn Books, Inc., 1971.

———. *Fundamentals of Negotiating.* New York: Hawthorn Books, Inc., 1968.

Roth, Charles B., and Alexander, Roy. *Secrets of Closing Sales.* 4th ed. Englewood Cliffs, N.J.: Prentice-Hall, Inc., 1970.

Chapter 11

Bradford's Directory of Marketing Research Agencies and Management Consultants in the United States and the World, 1984. Fairfax, Va.: Bradford's Directory of Marketing Research Agencies and Management Consultants, 1983.

Lasser, J. K. *How to Run a Small Business.* 3d ed., rev. and enlarged. New York: McGraw-Hill Book Company, Inc., 1963.

* Luck, David J.; Wales, Hugh G.; and Taylor, Donald A. *Marketing Research.* 3d ed. Englewood Cliffs, N.J.: Prentice-Hall, Inc., 1970.

* Michman, Ronald. *Marketing Channels.* Columbus, Ohio: Grid Inc., 1974.

Chapter 12

American Marketing Association. *International Directory of Marketing Research Houses and Services.* New York: American Marketing Association, New York Chapter, 1984.

Bangs, David H., Jr., and Osgood, William R. *Business Planning Guide.* Rev. ed. New York: The Center for Entrepreneurial Management, 1978.

Baumback, Clifford M., and Mancuso, Joseph R. *Entrepreneurship and Venture Management.* Englewood Cliffs, N.J.: Prentice-Hall, Inc., 1975.

Baumback, Clifford, 7th ed. *How to Organize and Operate a Small Business.* Englewood Cliffs, N.J.: Prentice-Hall, Inc., 1985.

Brandt, Steven C. *Strategic Planning in Emerging Companies.* Reading, Mass.: Addison-Wesley, 1981.

Breen, George Edward. *Do-it-Yourself Marketing Research.* 2nd ed. New York: McGraw-Hill Book Company, 1982.

Brosterman, Robert. *The Complete Estate Planning Guide.* Rev. ed. New York: McGraw-Hill Book Company, 1981.

Brown, Deaver. *The Entrepreneur's Guide.* New York: Ballantine Books, Inc., 1981.

* Channing, Peter C. *The Career Alternative: A Guide to Business Venturing.* New York: Hawthorn Books, Inc., 1977.

Dible, Donald M., ed. *Business Startup Basics.* Reston, Va.: Reston Publishing Company, Inc., 1981.

————. *How to Plan and Finance a Growing Business.* Reston, Va.: Reston Publishing Company, Inc., 1981.

Elam, Houston G., and Paley, Norton. *Marketing for the Non-Marketing Executive.* New York: American Management Associations, AMACOM, 1978.

Halcomb, James. *Pert-O-Graph/PERT CPM Kit.* (Contains Project Manager's PERT/CPM Handbook and Pert-O-Graph II.) Sunnyvale, Calif.: Halcomb Associates, Inc.

* Jolson, Marian A. *Consumer Attitudes Toward Direct-to-Home Marketing Systems.* New York: Dunellen, 1970.

Kastins, Merritt. *Long-Range Planning for Your Business.* New York: American Management Associations, AMACON, 1976.

Kravitt, Gregory I; Grossman, Jeffrey E.; Keller, Karl P.; Mitra, Korak; Raha, Edward A; and Robins, Adam E. *How to Raise Capital: Preparing and Presenting the Business Plan.* Homewood, Ill.: Dow Jones-Irwin, 1984.

Krentzman, Harvey C.; White, L.T.; and Schabacker, Joseph C. *Techniques and Strategies for Effective Small Business Management.* Reston, Va.: Reston Publishing Company, Inc., 1981.

Management Information Systems for the Smaller Business. Management Services Technical Study No. 8. New York: Staff Study published by the American Institute of CPA's, Inc., 1969.

Mancuso, Joseph R. *How to Prepare and Present a Business Plan.* New York: The Center for Entrepreneurial Management, 1983.

* Markstein, David L. *Money Raising and Planning for the Small Business.* Chicago: Henry Regnery Company, 1974.

* McDonald, John. *Strategy in Poker, Business and War.* The Norton Library. New York: W. W. Norton & Company, Inc., 1963.

Michman, Ronald. *Marketing Channels.* Columbus, Ohio: Grid Inc., 1974.

* Mockler, Robert J. *Business Planning and Policy Formation.* New York: Meredith Corporation, 1972.

Morison, Robert S. *Handbook for Manufacturing Entrepreneurs.* Cleveland: Western Reserve Press, 1973.

Quagliaroli, John A. *How to Write a Marketing Plan.* New York: The Center for Entrepreneurial Management, 1979.

Rachlin, Robert. *Profit Strategies for Business.* New York: Marr Publications, 1980.

Randolph, Robert M. *Planagement—Moving Concept Into Reality.* New York: American Management Associations, AMACOM, 1975.

Shames, William H. *Venture Management.* New York: The Free Press, 1974.

Toffler, Alvin. *Future Shock.* New York: Bantam Books, Inc., 1971.

Vesper, Karl H. *New Venture Strategies.* Englewood Cliffs, N.J.: Prentice-Hall, Inc., 1980.

White, Richard M., Jr. *The Entrepreneur's Manual.* Radnor, Pa.: Chilton Book Company, 1977.

Young, Jerrald F. *Decision Making for Small Business Management.* New York: John Wiley and Sons, 1977.

Chapter 13

Bank of America National Trust and Savings Association. "Understanding Financial Statements." *Small Business Reporter.* San Francisco: Bank of America National Trust and Savings Association, 1980.

* Bean, Louis H. *The Art of Forecasting.* New York: Random House, Inc., 1969.

* Dudick, Thomas, ed. *How to Improve Profitability Through More Effective Planning.* New York: John Wiley and Sons, 1975.

Ellis, John. *A Financial Guide for the Self-Employed.* Chicago: Henry Contemporary Books Company, 1974.

* Harris, Clifford C. *The Break-Even Handbook: Techniques for Profit Planning and Control.* Englewood Cliffs, NJ: Prentice-Hall, Inc., 1978.

* Myer, John N. *Accounting for Non-Accountants.* 2nd ed. New York: Hawthorn Books, Inc., 1980.

———. *Understanding Financial Statements: A Handbook for Executives, Investors, and Students.* New York: The New American Library, Inc., Mentor Executive Library, 1968.

Ragan, Robert, and Zwick, Jack. *Fundamentals of Recordkeeping and Finance for the Small Business.* Reston, Va.: Reston Publishing Company, Inc., 1978.

Tracy, John A. *How to Read a Financial Report: Wringing Cash Flow and Other Vital Signs Out of the Numbers.* 2nd ed. New York: John Wiley and Sons, 1983.

Walker, Ernest W., and Petty, J. William. *Financial Management of the Small Firm.* Englewood Cliffs, N.J.: Prentice-Hall, Inc., 1978.

Chapter 14

* Berman, Daniel S. *Going Public: A Practical Handbook of Procedures and Forms.* Englewood Cliffs, N.J.: Prentice-Hall, Inc., 1974.

Brick, John R. *Financial Markets, Instruments and Concepts.* Reston, Va.: Reston Publishing Company, Inc., 1981.

Carey, Omer, and Olson, Dean. *Financial Tools for Small Businesses.* Reston, Va.: Reston Publishing Company, 1983.

Cook, John A., and Wool, Robert. *All You Need to Know About Banks.* New York: Bantam Books, Inc., 1983.

Craig, Gary H. *Unscrewing the Small Investor*. Menlo Park, Calif.: Van Nostrand Reinhold Company, 1976.

Dougall, Herbert E. *Capital Markets and Institutions*. Englewood Cliffs, N.J.: Prentice-Hall, Inc., 1970.

Hayes, Rick Stephan. *Business Loans: A Guide to Money Sources and How to Approach Them Successfully*. 2nd ed. Boston: CBI Publishers, 1980.

Kuppinger, Roger. *Everything You Always Wanted to Know About Mergers, Acquisitions and Divestitures, but Didn't Know Whom to Ask*. 2nd ed. Arcadia, Calif.: By the Author, 77 Woodland Lane, 1983.

Mackay, Charles. *Extraordinary Popular Delusions and the Madness of Crowds*. New York: Noonday Press. L. C. Page & Company, Inc., 1980.

McCarthy, George P., and Healy, Robert C. *Valuing a Company: Practices and Procedures*. New York: John Wiley and Sons, 1971.

* Meyer, Martin J., and McDaniel, Joseph M., Jr., *Don't Bank on It!* New York: Pocket Books, Inc.

* Noone, Charles M., and Rubel, Stanley M. *SBICs: Pioneers in Organized Venture Capital*. Chicago: Capital Publishing Company, 1970.

Pratt, Stanley E., and Morris, Jane K., eds. *Pratt's Guide to Venture Capital Sources*. 8th ed. Wellesley Hills, Mass. Venture Economics, Inc., 1984.

Silver, A. David. *Up Front Financing: The Entrepreneur's Guide*. A Ronald Press Publication. New York: John Wiley and Sons, 1982.

Stevens, Mark. *How to Pyramid Small Business Ventures*. West Nyack, N.Y.: Parker Publishing Company, 1977.

Thompson, Thomas W., and Edwards, Raoul. *The Changing World of Banking*. Richmond, Va.: Robert F. Dame, Inc., 1981.

Thompson, Thomas W.; Berry, Leonard L., and Davidson, Philip H. *Banking Tomorrow*. Reston, Va.: Reston Publishing Company, 1983.

Toffel, Egon W. *Financing Your Business*. A Hudson Group Book. New York: David McKay Company, Inc., 1977.

Wright, Don. *Banking: A Dynamic Business*. Richmond, Va.: Robert F. Dame, Inc., 1983.

Chapter 15

Bank of America National Trust and Savings Association. "Financing Small Business." *Small Business Reporter*. San Francisco: Bank of America National Trust and Savings Association, 1983.

* Belew, Richard C. *How to Negotiate a Business Loan.* New York: Van Nostrand Reinhold Company, 1973.

Fox, Jack, and Liberman, Paul S. *How to Obtain Your Own SBA Loan.* Kensington, Md.: Madison Financial Services, Inc., 1983.

Gill, Edward K. *Commercial Lending Basics.* Reston, Va.: Reston Publishing Company, Inc., 1983.

Gladstone, David J. *Venture Capital Handbook.* Reston, Va.: Reston Publishing Company, Inc., 1983.

Goodman, Steven C., ed. *Financial Market Place: A Directory of Major Corporations, Institutions, Services, and Publications.* New York: R. R. Bowker Company, 1972.

* Hanson, William C. *Capital Sources and Major Investing Institutions.* New York: Simmons-Boardman Publishing Corp., 1963.

Hayes, Rick S., and Howell, John O. *How to Finance Your Small Business with Government Money: Small Business Administration and Other Loans.* 2nd ed. New York: John Wiley and Sons, 1983.

McKiernan, John. *Planning and Financing Your New Business: A Guide to Venture Capital.* Warwick, R.I.: Technology Management, Inc., 1978.

* Nicholas, Ted. *Where the Money Is and How to Get It.* Wilmington, Del.: Enterprise Publishing Company, 1973.

Pratt, Stanley E., and Morris, Jane K., eds. *Pratt's Guide to Venture Capital Sources.* 8th edition. Wellesley Hills, Mass.: Venture Economics, Inc., 1984.

Pratt, Stanley E. *How to Raise Venture Capital.* New York: Charles Scribner's Sons, 1982.

* Sinclair, Leroy W., ed. *Venture Capital: The Source-Book of Small Business Financing.* New York: Technometrics, 1973.

Taylor, John Renford. *Consumer Lending.* Reston, Va.: Reston Publishing Company, Inc., 1983.

Thompson, Thomas W.; Berry, Leonard L.; and Davidson, Philip H. *Banking Tomorrow.* Reston, Va.: Reston Publishing Company, Inc. 1983.

Toffel, Egon W. *Financing Your Business.* New York: David McKay Company, Inc., Hudson Group Books, 1977.

Wright, Don. *Banking: A Dynamic Business.* Richmond, Va.: Robert F. Dame, Inc., 1983.

Annotated List of Information Sources Including Directories and Guides to Venture Capital Companies

This comprehensive list of business information sources, capital directories, and guides is designed to include a wide variety of publications that I have discovered in the course of doing research for this volume. As may be expected in a field of such universal interest as "how to make money," the quality and depth of the available material is subject to considerable variation. But since even a *poorly* presented statement of fact—not readily available elsewhere—is better than none at all, the compilation of this list is intentionally unselective. Accordingly, inclusion of a particular title in this list does not necessarily constitute my endorsement of it.

American Association of Minority Enterprise Small Business Investment Companies (AAMESBIC) Membership Directory. Washington, D.C.: AAMESBIC, annual.

Covers about 115 SBIC's serving minority-owned small businesses. Arranged geographically. Available from the AAMESBIC, 913 15th Street N.W., Washington, D.C. 20005.

American Banker, comp. "100 Largest Finance Companies in the U.S." *American Banker,* June 15, 1984.

This annual directory should prove quite helpful to the entrepreneur in lending perspective to this sector of the financial community. Available only through the American Banker, 1 State Street Plaza, New York, New York 10004.

American Institute of Certified Public Accountants. *Assisting Small Business Clients in Obtaining Funds.* (Small Business Consulting Practice Aid No. 1) New York: The Institute, undated.

This book is one of the Management Advisory Services series. Developed for use by professional accountants, it includes a review of procedures involved in locating external funding sources and assisting the small business in preparing data for lenders and investors. Available from the Institute at 1211 Avenue of the Americas, New York, New York 10036-8775.

Annual Register of Grant Support. Chicago: Marquis Who's Who, Inc., annual.

Covers more than 2400 current grant programs of government agencies, private foundations, and others. Available from the publisher at 200 E. Ohio Street, Chicago, Illinois 60611.

Bank of America. *Small Business Reporter.*

These helpful guidebooks are available at nominal cost by writing to the Small Business Reporter, Bank of America, Department 3120, P.O. Box 37000, San Francisco, California 94137. Titles include the following:

Business Operations:
- "How to Buy or Sell a Business" (1982)
- "Financing Small Business" (1983)
- "Management Succession" (1981)
- "Understanding Financial Statements" (1980)
- "Steps to Starting a Business" (1984)
- "Cash Flow/ Cash Management" (1984)
- "Advertising Small Business" (1982)
- "Personnel Guidelines" (1981)
- "Crime Prevention for Small Business" (1982)
- "Equipment Leasing" (1983)
- "Avoiding Management Pitfalls" (1982)

Business Profiles:
- "The Handcrafts Business" (1980)
- "Restaurants" (1983)
- "Gift Stores" (1980)
- "Bicycle Stores" (1981)
- "General Job Printing" (1979)

Professional Management:
- "Establishing an Accounting Practice" (1982)
- "Establishing a Veterinary Practice" (1974)
- "Establishing a Dental Practice" (1982)
- "Establishing a Medical Practice" (1982)

Baumback, Clifford M. *How to Organize and Operate a Small Business.* 7th ed. Englewood Cliffs, N.J.: Prentice-Hall, Inc., 1985.

Originally copyrighted in 1940 and now in its seventh edition, this updated classic is encyclopedic in its coverage of small business problems. New material includes a model business plan, presented in great detail. There are also sections on organizational structure and staffing, equipment leasing and product liability, and more. In addition, a separate *Study Guide* and Workbook has been prepared as a helpful student aid. Available through bookstores or directly from the publisher at Englewood Cliffs, New Jersey 07632.

Bernham, Mark, and Sickman, John. *How to Choose Your Small Business Computer.* Reading, Mass.: Addison-Wesley Company, 1982.

This is a handbook for very small businesses (professional practices or other businesses with a handful of employees). It contains good explanations of the functioning and application of computers, including how to select the computer and integrate it into your work flow. Simple, but valuable for those who are unfamiliar with computers. Available in bookstores or from the publisher at One Jacob Way, Reading, Massachusetts 01867.

Brownstone, David M., and Carruth, Gorton. *Where to Find Business Information.* 2nd ed. New York: John Wiley & Sons, 1982.

This book provides a ready reference to business information sources. It's easy to use and gives a good description of the sources of information, indicating how much each costs. More than 5000 publications are referenced. Available in libraries.

Bullock, Hugh. *The Story of Investment Companies.* New York: Columbia University Press, 1959.

Discusses the development of British, Canadian, and American investment companies and describes the adaptation of the American investment company to rapidly changing economic conditions. Available through your local bookstore or from the publisher at 440 West 110th Street, New York, New York 10025.

Business Books and Serials in Print. New York: R. R. Bowker Company, annual.

Gives bibliographic and ordering information for over 37,000 titles in 6000 categories, indexed by author, title, and subject. Serials listings cover 6000 titles in 170 categories. Available in libraries.

Business Capital Sources. Coral Springs. Fla.: B. Klein Publications, 1984.

This reference book lists hundreds of companies, banks, and

other lenders with funds available for business loans. Includes
many hints on running a business successfully. Available in libraries or from the publisher at P.O. Box 8503, Coral Springs,
Florida 33065.

Business Capital Sources. Merrick, N.Y.: International Wealth Success, Inc., 1983.
This guide to business capital sources lists over 2500 lenders
of various types—banks, insurance companies, commercial finance firms, factors, leasing firms, overseas lenders, venture capital firms, mortgage companies, and others. Names, addresses,
and phone numbers are included in this 150-page volume.

A Business Information Guidebook. New York: American Management Associations, AMACOM, 1980.
Excellent guide to locating business information you need
quickly. Tells you *what's* available and *where* to get it. Covers a
wide variety of subject areas and includes government information, directories, books, associations, etc., pertaining to your area
of interest. Available in libraries or from the publisher at 135
West 50th Street, New York, New York 10020.

Business Opportunities Journal. San Diego, Calif.: Business Services Corporation.
This semi-monthly journal covers real estate, investment
and business opportunities in the United States and Canada.
Over 2000 businesses, franchises, distributorships, and proper-
ties are listed in each issue. Available by ordering through Business Services Corporation, 5037 Newport Avenue, San Diego,
California 92107.

Carey, Omer, and Olson, Dean. *Financial Tools for Small Businesses.* Reston, Va.: Reston Publishing Company, Inc., 1983.
This book provides a step-by-step discussion of the financial
aspects of running a business, complete with problems and case
studies. Very readable and filled with valuable information. A
handy reference tool. Available in bookstores or from the publisher at 11480 Sunset Hills Road, Reston, Virginia 22090.

Carosso, Vincent P. *Investment Banking in America, a History.*
Cambridge, Mass.: Harvard University Press, 1970.
This excellent, comprehensive history of investment banking is a treasure house of background information for either the
novice or the professional who is interested in financial institutions. It is *must* reading for one who wishes to understand the
important role of investment banking in the growth of this bas-
tion of capitalism we call America. This work will take much of
the mystery out of the role investment banking institutions play

as fund raisers. Available from your local bookstore or from the publisher at 79 Garden Street, Cambridge, Massachusetts 02138.

Daniells, Lorna M. *Business Information Sources,* Berkeley, Calif.: University of California Press, 1976.

    This helpful guidebook is divided into two parts; the first part gives a description of the wide variety of business reference materials available to the researcher. The second focuses on a variety of business topics, and describes information sources and general literature relating to each subject area. Written by a highly qualified author, a Harvard University reference librarian.

Datapro Directory of Microcomputer Software. Delran, N.J.: Datapro Research Corporation.

    Lists over 1200 software vendors and 2500 software packages. Includes names, addresses, phone numbers of vendors, price, user availability, product descriptions, and more. Software is indexed by subject and application. Available at your local library.

Directory of Fee-Based Information Services. Woodstock, N.Y.: Information Alternative, annual.

    Covers more than 200 information brokers, freelance librarians, information specialists, public and institutional libraries, and others who provide information for a fee. Annual with bimonthly supplements in "Journal of Fee-Based Information Services." Available from the publisher at P.O. Box 657, Woodstock, New York 12498.

Directory of Members: United States League of Savings Associations. Chicago, Ill.: The League, annual.

    Alphabetical listings by state and city of thousands of members representing nearly all of the country's savings and loan associations. Includes Co-op Bank listings. Available from the League at 111 E. Wacker Drive, Chicago, Illinois 60601.

Directory of State Industrial and Economic Departments, Commerce Departments, and Purchasing Agencies. Coral Springs, Fla.: B. Klein Publications, 1983.

    Gives addresses and phone numbers of development agencies in the fifty states, as well as securities agencies. Includes contact names. Available in libraries or from the publisher at P.O. Box 8503, Coral Springs, Florida 33065.

Directory of Trust Institutions. Atlanta, Ga.: Communication Channels, Inc., annual.

    This directory provides a geographical list of active trust institutions, heads of trust and investment departments, and trust assets. Available from the publisher at 6255 Barfield Road, Atlanta, Georgia 30328. (Included in subscription to *Trusts and Estates*.)

Dougall, Herbert E. *Capital Markets and Institutions*. Englewood Cliffs, N.J.: Prentice-Hall, Inc., 1980.

This book by the C.O.G. Miller Professor of Finance, Emeritus of Stanford University, provides a clear study of a complex subject: The institutions through which long-term financing is made available to industry. An excellent bibliography is included. Available through your local bookstore or from the publisher at Englewood Cliffs, New Jersey 07632.

Encyclopedia of Associations. 19th ed. Detroit, Mich.: The Gale Research Company, 1985.

Lists and describes national and international associations in the United States in a wide variety of subject areas, including business. Detailed information on over 18,000 active organizations in seventeen subject categories. Published annually in three volumes. Available at your local library.

An Entrepreneur's Guide to Starting a Business. Chicago: Arthur Andersen and Company, 1983.

This twenty-nine-page booklet covers the fundamentals of a business plan, discusses forms of doing business (corporation, proprietorship, etc.), tax aspects, financing sources, and accounting methods. Includes helpful charts on federal forms and information reporting requirements for each form of business. Available from Arthur Andersen and Company, Distribution Clerk, 33 W. Monroe, Chicago, Illinois 60603.

Ethridge, James M., ed. *The Directory of Directories*. 2nd ed. Detroit, Mich.: Gale Research Company, 1983.

This directory describes approximately 6800 directories covering a wide variety of subject areas, including business and government. Indexed by title and subject. An excellent reference. Available at your local library.

Financing Small and Growing Businesses. New York: Deloitte, Haskins and Sells, 1981.

This booklet provides a good discussion of external sources of financing, indicating which types of financing are appropriate for various stages of corporate development and where you're most likely to secure funding at each stage. Available from any local office of Deloitte, Haskins and Sells.

Finding Co-ops: A Resource Guide and Directory. Washington, D.C.: Cooperative Information Consortium, undated.

This guide lists 20,000 cooperatives and includes information on resources available to co-ops, how co-ops can market to each other, how to entice prospective members to join your co-op, and much more. For ordering information, write to the National Consumer Cooperative Bank, 1630 Connecticut Avenue, Washington, D.C. 20009.

Franchise Annual. Coral Springs, Fla.: B. Klein Publications, 1984.

A comprehensive directory of 2500 franchisors, distributors, licensors, and franchise consultants in the United States and Canada. Includes government regulations and tips on how to get into each field. Available in libraries or from the publisher at P.O. Box 8503, Coral Springs, Florida 33065.

Ganly, John; Sciattara, Diane; and Pedolsky, Andrea; eds. *Small Business Sourcebook.* Detroit, Mich.: The Gale Research Co., 1983.

This reference book is a *must* for anyone thinking of starting a small business. It's written in two parts. Part 1 profiles 100 popular small businesses and includes information sources for each business. Part 2 is a compilation of small business resources; nearly 1000 books and periodicals are annotated, and government services, trade associations, educational institutions, consultants, and venture capitalists are referenced. Available in libraries.

Gill, Edward K. *Commercial Lending Basics.* Reston, Va.: Reston Publishing Company, Inc., 1983.

This book discusses the commercial lending process from the point of view of the banker making the loan. A valuable book for understanding how your loan application will be evaluated. Available in bookstores or from the publisher at 11480 Sunset Hills Road, Reston, Virginia 22090.

Gladstone, David J. *Venture Capital Handbook.* Reston, Va.: Reston Publishing Company, 1983.

This is not a directory of venture capitalists. Rather, it's an excellent overview of the venture capital process, including frank discussions of what it takes to make it as an entrepreneur and how to deal with venture capitalists. Available in bookstores or from the publisher at 11480 Sunset Hills Road, Reston, Virginia 22090.

Guide to Venture Capital Sources. Coral Springs, Fla.: B. Klein Publications, 1983.

Lists over 500 active venture capital firms and small issue

underwriters in the United States and Canada, giving investor preferences and contact names. Includes articles on venture capital by industry members. Available in libraries or from B. Klein Publications at P.O. Box 8503, Coral Springs, Florida 33065.

Handbook of Business Finance and Capital Sources. New York: American Management Associations, AMACOM.

Lists several hundred private sources of venture capital, including investment companies, development companies, leasing companies, investment bankers, mortgage bankers, etc., and approximately 150 federal and state financing sources. Published irregularly. Available from the American Management Associations, 135 W. 50th Street, New York, New York 10020.

Helping High Technology Companies Grow. New York: Arthur Young and Company, 1983.

This fifteen-page brochure identifies six phases of growth that high-tech firms pass through, providing a good discussion of the problems and opportunities inherent in each stage. Available from any local office of Arthur Young or by calling 800-344-8324.

Hicks, Tyler G. *How to Borrow Your Way to a Great Fortune.* Englewood Cliffs, N.J.: Prentice-Hall, Inc., 1970.

This book purports to provide information on more than 10,-000 sources of capital. The style is of the "getting-rich-quick-is-as-easy-as-falling-off-a-log" school. The author has a knack for making sometimes complex financial topics easier to understand. Available from your local bookstore or from the publisher at Box 500, Englewood Cliffs, New Jersey 07632.

Hicks, Tyler G. *Smart Money Shortcuts to Becoming Rich.* Englewood Cliffs, N.J.: Prentice-Hall, Inc., 1966.

This get-rich-quick book contains many chapters devoted to the raising of other people's money ("OPM" as the author calls it). A large amount of complex source material has been broken down into terms readily understood by the financial novice. Available from your local bookstore or from the publisher at Box 500, Englewood Cliffs, New Jersey 07632.

IBP Research and Editorial Staff. *How to Raise Money to Make Money.* Englewood Cliffs, N.J.: Institute for Business Planning, Inc., 1980.

This loose-leaf publication is an authoritatively prepared compendium on the subject of raising money for business ventures. Many examples of business agreements, forms, and other contracts are provided. Many aspects of business finance not treated elsewhere are covered in this volume. Available only from the publisher at 210 Sylvan Avenue, Englewood Cliffs, New Jersey 07632.

The Index of Active Registered Investment Companies. Washington, D.C.: Securities and Exchange Commission, 1983.

This list includes all companies which are engaged primarily in the business of investing, reinvesting, and trading in securities and which have issued their own securities that are offered to, sold to, and held by the investing public. Available to individuals and firms having a demonstrable, bona fide need for this information from the Securities and Exchange Commission Public Reference Room, 450 5th Street N.W., Washington, D.C. 20549.

Industry and Trade Administration, U.S. Department of Commerce. *Franchise Opportunities Handbook.* Washington, D.C.: Government Printing Office, 1983.

Part of the Commerce Department's program to assist minority businesses. Provides complete information on nondiscriminatory franchisors. Indexed by product/service category and alphabetically by franchisor. Includes government information on franchising, checklists, suggestions, and leads to other information sources. Available in business or government libraries or from the Government Printing Office, Washington, D.C. 20402.

The Investment Adviser Directory. Washington, D.C.: Securities and Exchange Commission, 1983.

This 358-page directory includes all investment advisers registered with the Securities and Exchange Commission. Available from the Securities and Exchange Commission Public Reference Room, 450 5th Street N.W., Washington, D.C. 20549.

Investment Companies. New York: Wiesenberger Investment Companies Service (Warren, Gorham and Lamont, Inc.), 1983.

Contains information on mutual funds, closed-end investment companies, tax-exempt bond funds, money market funds, and separate accounts. Provides good discussions of the various funds and includes a directory of funds. Available in libraries or from the publisher at 1633 Broadway, New York, New York 10019.

Kibel, H. Ronald. *How to Turn Around a Financially Troubled Company.* New York: McGraw Hill Book Company, 1982.

This is a good book to read *before* your business falls on hard times. The author gives valuable advice on dealing with suppliers, bankers, or others who might pressure you when financial times are tough. It includes a "health check questionnaire" so you can pinpoint trouble spots before they become disaster areas. Available in bookstores or from the publisher at 1221 Avenue of the Americas, New York, New York 10020.

Klein, B., ed. *Guide to American Directories*. 11th ed. Coral Springs, Fla.: B. Klein Publishers, 1983.

    Lists more than 6500 directories covering a wide variety of subject areas. Describes contents of directories, cost, frequency of publication, and other relevant information. Available from the publisher at P.O. Box 8503, Coral Springs, Florida 33065.

Kryszak, Wayne D. *The Small Business Index*. Metuchen, N.J.: The Scarecrow Press, 1978.

    Covers a wide variety of small businesses. The index is arranged by subject. For each subject, it lists books, pamphlets, periodicals, associations, and directories pertaining to the business. Includes a bibliography of small business periodicals. Available in libraries or from the Scarecrow Press at 52 Liberty Street, Box 656, Metuchen, New Jersey 08840.

Levy, Robert S., and Granik, T. *Directory of State and Federal Funds for Business Development*. New York: Pilot Books.

    This is a single source for basic data on the financial assistance programs of the fifty states and a few federal agencies. This concise directory is the starting point for any business, large or small, which seeks to relocate or expand. The book helps management to "shop," compare, select, and discard from a wide range of aid programs without collecting and sorting through mountains of promotional literature. Published irregularly. Available from the publisher at 103 Cooper Street, Babylon, New York 11702.

Lewis, Marianna, ed. *The Foundation Directory*. 8th ed. New York: The Russell Sage Foundation Center, 1981.

    This directory lists over 3500 of the largest foundations in the United States, many of which invest portions of their portfolios in new ventures. Each entry includes a description of the assets and primary areas of interest for the foundations listed. The directory is available in libraries or can be purchased from The Foundation Center, 888 Seventh Avenue, New York, New York 10106.

Mancuso, Joseph R. *Checklist for Starting a Successful Business*. New York: Center for Entrepreneurial Management, 1983.

    This booklet contains questionnaires and worksheets to help you assess whether or not you have what it takes to make it as an entrepreneur, and to guide you along the way if you do. Very practical. Available only through the Center for Entrepreneurial Management, 83 Spring Street, New York, New York 10012.

Mangold, Maxwell J. *How Public Financing Can Help Your Company Grow: A Guide to the Advantages and Ways of Securing*

Equity Capital through Sales of Stock to the Public. 4th rev. ed. New York: Pilot Books, Inc., 1975.

This is a compact, factual guide to the advantages and ways of securing equity capital through sales of stock to the public. It includes twenty-five brief case histories of actual public offerings. Available from Pilot Books, 103 Cooper Street, Babylon, New York 11702.

McNierney, Mary A., ed. *Directory of Business and Financial Services.* 8th ed. New York: Special Libraries Association, 1984.

A selected listing by the Special Libraries Association of more than 1000 business, economic, and financial publications printed periodically, with a regular supplement. Available by ordering from Special Libraries Association, 235 Park Avenue South, New York, New York 10003.

Meinhard-Commercial Corporation. *Factoring: The Financial Alternative to Bank Loans with Built-in Credit Protection.* New York: Meinhard-Commercial Corporation, undated.

This informative brochure provides a good overview of the factoring business, including a discussion of company profiles that are suitable candidates for factoring. Available from Meinhard-Commercial at 135 W. 50th Street, New York, New York 10020.

Money Market Directory. Charlottesville, Va.: Money Market Directory, Inc., annual.

This directory covers approximately 18,000 tax-exempt funds and some 1300 investment management services, bank trust departments, and insurance companies. Names, addresses, and telephone numbers of contacts are included. Classified by fund types and services as well as geographically. Available by ordering from the publisher at Box 1608, Charlottesville, Virginia 22902.

Moody's Bank and Finance Manual. New York: Moody's Investors Service, Inc., annual.

This manual contains financial statements and earnings reports for American and Canadian investment companies and includes several tables classifying investment companies by net assets and management performance. Semi-weekly supplements and weekly indexes keep the manual up to date. Available at your local library.

Mutual Funds Almanac. Holliston, Mass.: Donoghue's Money Fund Report, annual.

This publication covers about 600 open- and closed-end mutual funds, individual money market, and municipal bond funds.

Company names, assets, rank, history, management policies and objectives, financial, and statistical information are included. Available in bookstores or by ordering from Donoghue's Money Fund Report, Box 540, Holliston, Massachusetts 01746.

Myers, Darlene, ed. *Computer Science Resources*. White Plains, N.Y.: Knowledge Industry Publications, 1981.

Lists roughly 850 publishers of books and periodicals in the computer science field. Also lists computer industry associations, software resources, etc. A good source for anyone starting a computer-related business. Available from the publisher at 701 Westchester Avenue, White Plains, New York 10604.

National Association of Small Business Investment Companies. *Membership Directory*. Washington, D.C.: National Association of Small Business Investment Companies, 1984.

This little directory (reproduced in Appendix 3) is a *must* for anyone interested in raising venture capital. The introduction includes a brief but highly informative discussion of SBICs and how they operate. All entries are coded to indicate preferred limit for loans or investment, financing preferences (i.e., equity, loans, or both), and industry preferences. Available free of charge from the National Association of Small Business Investment Companies, 618 Washington Building, Washington, D.C. 20005.

National Commercial Finance Companies of New York, Inc. *Roster of Membership of National Commercial Finance Association. Including Membership of Affiliate-Association of Commercial Finance Companies of New York, Inc.* New York: National Commercial Finance Association, July, 1984.

This directory, although free, is available only to authorized individuals and agencies. Should you request a copy of it, you must indicate for what purpose you require it. One of the restrictions the conference has regarding this listing is that it not be used for solicitation purposes. Available from the National Commercial Finance Association, One Penn Plaza, New York, New York, 10001.

National Science Foundation. *Federal Funds for Research and Development, Fiscal Years 1981, 1982 and 1983*. NSF 82-326, Vol. 28 of Surveys of Science Resources Series. Washington, D.C.: Government Printing Office, 1982.

This report provides a comprehensive body of statistical information on the size and scope of federal obligations for scientific activities, the purposes to which funds are directed, and the important trends in major funding areas. This information can be of considerable assistance in helping scientifically oriented entrepreneurs to identify federal funds to which they may gain access for use in starting their enterprises. Available by ordering from the Superintendent of Documents, U.S. Government Printing Office, Washington, D.C. 20402.

National Venture Capital Association. *Membership Directory.* Arlington, Va.: National Venture Capital Assn., 1985.

    This directory (reproduced in Appendix 2) lists more than 100 venture capital firms, including subsidiaries of banks and insurance companies, as well as individual investors. Complimentary copies of this directory are available from the Association at 1655 North Fort Myer Drive, Suite 700, Arlington, Virginia 22209.

No Load Mutual Fund Association. *Your Guide to Mutual Funds.* New York: The Association, 1984–1985.

    This directory lists approximately 300 no load (no sales charge) mutual funds, indicating the investment policies and objectives of each fund. There is also a general discussion of these types of mutual funds. Available from the No Load Mutual Fund Association, Inc., 11 Penn Plaza, New York, New York 10001.

Outline for a New High Technology Business Plan. New York: Arthur Young and Company, 1983.

    While this brochure was written with high technology firms in mind, its discussion of the components of a business plan should prove useful to any startup seeking venture capital financing. Available from any local office of Arthur Young, or by calling 800-344-8324.

Payne, Jack. *The Complete New Encyclopedia of Little-Known, Highy Profitable Business Opportunities.* Rev. ed. New York: Frederick Fell, Inc., 1980.

    This book is a real potpourri of business ideas, providing the names and addresses of hundreds of contacts in business fields as varied, for example, as mines and oil wells, real estate, merger and acquisition brokerage, and franchising. It should make interesting and entertaining reading for the entrepreneur looking for the unusual in business opportunities. Available from the publisher at 386 Park Avenue South, New York, New York 10016.

R. L. Polk & Co. *Polk's World Bank Directory.* Nashville, Tenn.: R. L. Polk & Co., semi-annual with supplements.

    This directory lists all banks in the U.S. by state and city. Financial statements and names of officers and directors are included for each. Also included are lists of discontinued banks and foreign banks. Available by ordering from the publisher at 2001 Elm Hill Pike, Nashville, Tennessee 37202.

Pratt, Stanley E., and Morris, Jane K., eds. *Guide to Venture Capital Sources*. 8th ed. Wellesley Hills, Mass.: Venture Economics, Inc., 1984.

This 500-page volume includes a wealth of information about the venture capital industry. Several articles, written by industry experts, provide insight into all aspects of venture financing. There is also a comprehensive directory of venture capital firms, which includes information about the size and types of deals preferred by each. An indispensable resource for anyone seeking venture capital financing. Available in libraries or from Venture Economics, Inc., 16 Laurel Avenue, Box 348, Wellesley Hills, Massachusetts 02181.

Raising Venture Capital: An Entrepreneur's Guidebook. New York: Deloitte, Haskins and Sells, 1982.

This excellent 104-page booklet covers all the basics of starting a business, from organization through venture capital negotiations. The appendices contain good examples of pro forma financial statements. Available from any local office of Deloitte, Haskins and Sells.

Ricotta, Anthony V., ed. *Corporate Financing Directory*. New York: Investment Dealers' Digest, Inc., semi-annual.

This unique directory, published by one of the leading news magazines of the financial industry, serves as an extremely important source of hard-to-find information for the entrepreneur seeking insight into the operating details of the investment community. Detailed semi-annual summaries are provided on subjects such as rights, exchange and purchase offers, secondary offerings, and listings of underwriting managers and participations. Published by Investment Dealers' Digest, Inc., 150 Broadway, New York, New York 10038.

Rohrlich, Chester. *Organizing Corporate and Other Business Enterprises*. 4th ed. New York: Matthew Bender, undated.

This legal reference work provides a lawyer's-eye view of the new business formation process. One chapter is devoted to stock subscriptions and promoter's compensation; another offers an extensive discussion of initial capitalization and financing; while still another discusses legal issues in the marketing of securities, including an analysis of blue-sky laws. Available from the publisher at 235 East 45th Street, New York, New York 10017.

T. K. Sanderson Organization. *Directory of American Savings and Loan Associations*. Baltimore, Md.: T. K. Sanderson Organization, annual.

This directory is arranged geographically by state. It includes mention of officers, assets, and, in some cases, current interest rates. Available through your local bookstore or from T. K. Sanderson Organization, 25th and Calvert Streets, Baltimore, Maryland 21218.

SBIC Directory and Handbook of Small Business Finance. Merrick, N.Y.: International Wealth Success, Inc., undated.

Part of the title reads: *SBIC Directory.* The one included in this publication is substantially derived from the free Small Business Administration directory included elsewhere in this bibliography. The last part of the title reads: *Handbook of Small Business Finance.* Approximately half of the pages in this publication have been photographically reproduced directly from the excellent SBA publication, *A Handbook of Small Business Finance,* which costs less than $1. One might conclude that this IWS publication at $15 is overpriced. Available from the publisher at 24 Canterbury Road, Rockville Center, New York 11570.

Schmittroth, John, Jr. *Encyclopedia of Information Systems and Services.* 5th ed. Detroit, Mich.: Gale Research Company, 1982.

This directory lists more than 2500 "storage and retrieval services, database producers and publishers, online vendors, computer service companies, computerized retrieval systems" and a variety of other information services too numerous to mention. If you need current information quickly on a specific topic, these services, while somewhat expensive, can be invaluable. Published irregularly. Available at your local library.

Securities Industry Association. *Profile of Investment Banking.* New York: The Association, undated.

Readers learn how the investment banker fills a dual function by helping businesses to grow and by aiding investors to put their savings to work. Available free of charge by ordering from the Securities Industry Association, 120 Broadway, New York, New York 10271.

Small Business Administration. *Free Management Assistance Publications.*

These helpful brochures can be obtained by writing to the Small Business Administration at P.O. Box 15434, Ft. Worth, Texas 76119. The following titles are available.

Small Business Bibliographies (SBBs):
• Handcrafts
• Home Businesses
• Selling By Mail Order
• Marketing Research Procedures
• Retailing

- Statistics and Maps for National Market Analysis
- National Directories for Use in Marketing
- Recordkeeping Systems—Small Store and Service Trade
- Basic Business Reference Sources
- Advertising—Retail Store
- Retail Credit and Collection
- Buying for Retail Stores
- Personnel Management
- Inventory Management
- Purchasing for Owners of Small Plants
- Training for Small Business
- Financial Management
- Manufacturing Management
- Marketing for Small Business
- New Product Development
- Ideas into Dollars (Inventors' Guide)
- Effective Business Communication
- Productivity Management in Small Business
- Decision Making in Small Business

Starting Out Series (SOSs):
- Building Service Contracting
- Radio-Television Repair Shop
- Retail Florists
- Franchised Businesses
- Hardware Store or Home Centers
- Sporting Goods Store
- Drycleaning
- Cosmetology
- Pest Control
- Marine Retailers
- Retail Grocery Stores
- Apparel Store
- Pharmacies
- Office Products
- Interior Design Services
- Fish Farming
- Bicycles
- Roofing Contractors
- Printing
- The Bookstore
- Home Furnishings
- Ice Cream
- Sewing Centers
- Personnel Referral Service
- Selling By Mail Order

- Solar Energy
- Breakeven Point for Independent Truckers
- Starting a Retail Travel Agency
- Starting a Retail Decorating Products Business
- Starting an Independent Consulting Practice
- Starting an Electronics Industry Consulting Practice

Small Business Administration. *For Sale Management Assistance Publications.*

The following publications can be purchased from the Government Printing Office. For a current listing of books for sale and an order form, write to the Small Business Administration at P.O. Box 15434, Ft. Worth, Texas 76119.

Small Business Management Series: The books in this series discuss specific management techniques or problems.

- *An Employee Suggestion System for Small Companies*
- *Cost Accounting for Small Manufacturers* (assists managers of small manufacturing firms in establishing accounting procedures that help control production and business costs)
- *Handbook of Small Business Finance*
- *Ratio Analysis for Small Business*
- *Practical Business Use of Government Statistics* (available only from SBA.)
- *Guide for Profit Planning* (guides for computing and using the breakeven point, the level of gross profit, and the rate of return on investment)
- *Small Business and Government Research and Development* (includes a discussion of the procedures necessary to locate and sell to Government agencies)
- *Management Audit for Small Manufacturers* (a questionnaire for manufacturers)
- *Insurance and Risk Management for Small Business*
- *Management Audit for Small Retailers* (gives 149 questions for reviewing business operations)
- *Financial Recordkeeping for Small Stores* (covers merchandising, advertising and display, and provides checklists to increase sales)
- *Franchise Index/Profile* (presents an evaluation process that may be used to investigate franchise opportunities)
- *Training Salesmen to Serve Industrial Markets*
- *Financial Control by Time-Absorption Analysis*
- *Management Audit for Small Service Firms* (a questionnaire for service firms)
- *Decision Points in Developing New Products*
- *Management Audit for Small Construction Firms* (available only from SBA)

- *Purchasing Management and Inventory Control for Small Business*
- *Managing the Small Service Firm for Growth and Profit*
- *Credit and Collections for Small Stores*

  Starting and Managing Series: This series is designed to help the small entrepreneur "to look before leaping" into a business.

- *Starting and Managing a Small Business of Your Own*
- *Starting and Managing a Small Service Business*

  Business Basics: Each of the twenty-three self-study booklets in this series contains text, questions, and exercises that teach a specific aspect of small business management.

- *The Profit Plan*
- *Capital Planning*
- *Understanding Money Sources*
- *Evaluating Money Sources*
- *Asset Management*
- *Managing Fixed Assets*
- *Understanding Costs*
- *Cost Control*
- *Marketing Strategy*
- *Retail Buying Function*
- *Inventory Management—Wholesale/Retail*
- *Retail Merchandise Management*
- *Consumer Credit*
- *Credit and Collections: Policy and Procedures*
- *Purchasing for Manufacturing Firms*
- *Inventory Management—Manufacturing/Service*
- *Inventory and Scheduling Techniques*
- *Risk Management and Insurance*
- *Managing Retail Salespeople*
- *Job Analysis, Job Specifications, and Job Descriptions*
- *Recruiting and Selecting Employees*
- *Training and Developing Employees*
- *Employee Relations and Personnel Policies*

Small Business Administration. *List of Small Business Investment Companies*. Washington, D.C.: Government Printing Office, rev. semi-annually.

 This is a list of all functioning small business investment companies, including their branch offices, whose licenses, issued by the SBA, remain outstanding. This list does not purport to characterize the relative merits, as investment companies or otherwise, of the licensees. Inclusion on this list may in no way be construed as an endorsement of a company's operations or as a recommendation by the Small Business Administration. All entries are coded relative to the size of capital investment preferred. Available free of charge from the Small Business Administration, Investment Division, Washington, D.C. 20416.

Spohr, Anthony P., and Wat, Leslie. *Forming R & D Partnerships: An Entrepreneur's Guidebook*. New York: Deloitte, Haskins and Sells, 1983.

    The third publication in Deloitte, Haskins and Sells' Entrepreneur's Guidebook series, this book discusses the structure of R & D partnerships, advantages and disadvantages of this financing method, and includes case studies of firms which have chosen this route. Along with the other two books in the series, an excellent resource. Available at any local office of Deloitte, Haskins and Sells.

Standard & Poor's Corporation. *Security Dealers of North America*. New York: Standard & Poor's Corporation, semi-annual.

    This work is a geographical listing of all investment firms in the U.S. and Canada, giving the nature of the business of each, branch locations, and officers' names. North American securities administrators, foreign offices and representation, discontinued listings, and an alphabetical list of firms are other useful features. Available by ordering from Standard and Poor's Corporation, 25 Broadway, New York, New York 10014. Cumulative revision service available.

Start-Up Manuals. Santa Maria, Calif.: International Entrepreneur's Association.

    These "do-it-yourself kits" provide detailed information on starting a variety of businesses. Discussions of markets, profits, costs, financing, and a number of other aspects of business start-ups are included. Available from the publisher at 631 Wilshire Blvd, Santa Maria, California 90401.

United States Securities and Exchange Commission. *1983 SEC Government—Business Forum on Small Business Capital Formation*. Washington D.C.: Securities and Exchange Commission, November 1983.

    This is a summary of findings of a forum mandated by the Small Business Incentive Act of 1980, for the purpose of exploring the status of problems and programs related to small business capital formation. Tedious to read, but it contains a vast amount of information on the workings of small business and is a good reference document. Available from the Securities and Exchange Commission, Washington, D.C. 20549.

Vancil, Richard F., ed. *Financial Executive's Handbook*. Homewood, Ill.: Dow Jones-Irwin, Inc., 1970.

This is a compendium of information on financial matters, consisting of ten sections and sixty-six chapters and covering the wide range of responsibilities of business executives in the area of finance and financial management. In its 1264 pages, this comprehensive book brings together the practical experience of leading corporate executives. Available through your local bookstore or from Dow Jones-Irwin, Inc., at 1818 Ridge Road, Homewood, Illinois 60430.

Venture Capital Journal. Wellesley Hills, Mass.: Capital Publishing Corporation.

This monthly magazine gives a comprehensive picture of current trends, news and views of the world of venture capital. Each issue is compiled by industry analysts and researchers. Available in business libraries or from the publisher at P.O. Box 348, Wellesley Hills, Massachusetts 02181.

Wasserman, Paul, ed. *Encyclopedia of Business Information Sources*. 5th ed. Detroit, Mich.: Gale Research Company, 1983.

Covers publishers of thousands of books on business-oriented topics, as well as other sources of business information, including trade associations, professional societies, and others. Classified by highly specific subjects (e.g. helicopters, industrial diamonds, and so forth). Published biennially. Available in libraries or from the publisher at Book Tower, Detroit, Michigan 48226.

Wat, Leslie. *Strategies for Going Public: An Entrepreneur's Guidebook*. New York: Deloitte, Haskins and Sells, 1983.

Another of the entrepreneurship series published by Deloitte, Haskins and Sells, this publication discusses the pros and cons of going public, regulations and timing, as well as the added responsibilities you will face after going public. An appendix suggests alternatives to a public offering. An excellent reference book. Available at any local office of Deloitte, Haskins and Sells.

World Wide Chamber of Commerce Directory. Boulder, Colo.: Johnson Publishing Co., Inc., annual.

This directory includes (1) a complete list of Chambers of Commerce in the U.S., including the name of the manager or president of each; (2) a list of foreign embassies and governmental agencies located in the U.S.; (3) a list of foreign Chambers of Commerce with offices in the U.S.; (4) a list of Chambers of Commerce outside of the U.S., arranged alphabetically by country. Since Chambers of Commerce regularly function as clearinghouses for information regarding community assistance to new and relocating businesses, this directory could be of significant help to the entrepreneur. Available from the publisher at 8th and Van Buren Streets, Loveland, Colorado 80537.

Directory of the Membership of the National Venture Capital Association

Following is a comprehensive listing of the membership of the National Venture Capital Association (NVCA), headquartered at 1655 North Fort Myer Drive, Suite 700, Arlington, Virginia 22209. The NVCA was organized "to foster a broader understanding of the importance of venture capital to the vitality of the United States economy. The Association is also interested in stimulating the free flow of capital to young companies." The directory includes company names, addresses and telephone numbers as well as the names of key contacts within the organizations.

Members

ABS Ventures Limited Partnership
135 E. Baltimore St.
Baltimore, MD 21202
301/727-1700
301/727-2154 (night line)

Bruns Grayson
Arthur Reidel

ACCEL Partners
One Palmer Square
Princeton, NJ 08540
609/683-4500

Also:
ACCEL Partners
One Embarcadero Center
31st Floor
San Francisco, CA 94111
415/989-5656

Arthur C. Patterson
James R. Swartz

Adler & Company
375 Park Ave.
Suite 3303
New York, NY 10152
212/319-7373

Also:
Adler & Company
1245 Oakmead Parkway
Suite 103
Sunnyvale, CA 94086
408/720-8700

Frederick R. Adler (NY)
Yuval Binur (NY)
John Harlow (NY)
James J. Harrison (CA)
Joy London (NY)
James E. Long (CA)
Daniel C. O'Neill (CA)

Advanced Technology Ventures
50 Broad St.
New York, NY 10004
212/344-0622

Also:
Advanced Technology Ventures
1000 El Camino Real
Suite 210
Menlo Park, CA 94025-4327
415/321-8601

Also:
Advanced Technology Ventures
Ten Post Office Square
Suite 1230
Boston, MA 02109
617/423-4050

Robert C. Ammerman (NY/Boston)
Jos C. Henkens (CA)
Robert G. Loewy (NY/Boston)
Ralph J. Nunziato (CA)
Albert E. Paladino (NY/Boston)
Robert F. Sproull (NY/Boston)
Ivan E. Sutherland (NY/Boston)
William R. Sutherland (CA)

R.W. Allsop & Associates
2750 First Ave., NE
Suite 210
Cedar Rapids, IA 52402
319/363-8971 (Iowa)
913/642-4719 (Kansas)
314/434-1688 (Missouri)
414/271-6510 (Wisconsin)

Robert W. Allsop (IA)
Gregory B. Bultman (WI)

Robert L. Kuk (MO)
Larry C. Maddox (KS)
Paul D. Rhines (IA)

Allstate Insurance Co.
Venture Capital Division
Allstate Plaza
Building E-2
Northbrook, IL 60062
312/291-5681

Leonard A. Batterson
Donald R. Johnson
Robert L. Lestina
Sharri E. Marcin
Marcy H. Shockey

American Research and Development
45 Milk St., 7th Floor
Boston, MA 02109
617/423-7500

Luc Beaubien
Wade Blackman
Charles Coulter
Frank Hughes
Gary Katz
George McKinney
Courtney Whitin, Jr.

Ameritech Development Corp.
233 South Wacker Dr.
Suite 6960
Chicago, IL 60606
312/993-1900

Louis A. Sands
John E. Wray

Ampersand Management Co.
100 Federal St.
31st Floor
Boston, MA 02110
617/423-8264
617/423-8500
(see also Paine Webber Ventures
   Management Company)

Daniel Alexander
Richard A. Charpie
William C. Mills, III
Merlin D. Schulze
Donald W. Stacey

Anatar Investments, Inc.
#2218 Gas Light Tower
235 Peachtree St., N.E.
Atlanta, GA 30303
404/588-0770

Douglas A.P. Hamilton

Anderson Investment Co.
39 Locust Ave.
P.O. Box 426
New Canaan, CT 06840
203/966-5684

Harlan E. Anderson

Androck Capital Corp.
803 N. Church St.
Rockford, IL 61103
815/987-9070

John R. Anderson
R. Steven Holdeman

Arscott, Norton & Associates
369 Pine St., Suite 506
San Francisco, CA 94104
415/956-3386

David G. Arscott
Dean C. Campbell
Leal F. Norton

Asset Management Co.
1417 Edgewood Dr.
Palo Alto, CA 94301
415/321-3131

Daniel Flamen
Pitch Johnson
Craig C. Taylor

Atlantic Venture Co., Inc.
801 North Fairfax St.
Alexandria, VA 22314
703/548-6026

Also:
Atlantic Venture Co., Inc.
815 Seventh and Franklin Bldg.
P.O. Box 1493
Richmond, VA 23212
804/644-5496

Wallace L. Bennett (Alexandria)
Edward C. McCarthy (Alexandria)
Robert H. Pratt (Richmond)

BankAmerica Capital Corp.
42nd Floor
555 California St.
San Francisco, CA 94104
415/622-6164

Robert W. Gibson
Philip J. Gioia
Patrick J. Topolski

Basic Search Co.
Park Place—10 West Streetsboro St.
Hudson, OH 44236
216/650-2045
216/650-4321

Burton D. Morgan
Louis J. Weisz

Bay Partners II/III
1927 Landings Dr.
Suite B
Mountain View, CA 94043
415/961-5800

John E. Bosch
John Freidenrich
W. Charles Hazel
Terrence M. Morris

Bernhard Associates
1211 Avenue of the Americas
New York, NY 10036
212/921-7755

Robert A. Bernhard
David N. Nutt

Bessemer Venture Partners
630 Fifth Ave.
New York, NY 10111
212/708-9300

Also:
Bessemer Venture Partners
3000 Sand Hill Rd., #3-225
Menlo Park, CA 94025
415/854-2200

Also:
Bessemer Venture Partners
83 Walnut St.
Wellesley Hills, MA 02181
617/237-6050

Robert H. Buescher (NY)
Robert B. Field (CA)
G. Felda Hardymon (MA)

William Blair Venture Partners
135 South LaSalle St.
Chicago, IL 60603
312/236-1600

James E. Crawford, III
Samuel B. Guren
Scott F. Meadow

Boston Capital Ventures
One Devonshire Place
Suite 2913
Boston, MA 02109
617/227-6550

A. Dana Callow, Jr.
Donald J. Steiner
H.J. von der Goltz

Bow Lane Capital Corp.
2401 Fountainview, Suite 950
Houston, TX 77057
713/977-7421

Also:
Bow Lane Capital Corp.
3305 Graybuck Road
Austin, Texas 78748
512/282-9330

Hugh Batey (Austin)
Stuart Schube (Houston)

Brentwood Associates
11661 San Vicente Blvd.
Suite 707
Los Angeles, CA 90049
213/826-6581

Also:
Brentwood Associates
601 California St.
Suite 450
San Francisco, CA 94108
415/788-2416

William M. Barnum, Jr. (LA)
George M. Crandell (LA)
Roger C. Davisson (LA)
Michael J. Fourticq (LA)
B. Kipling Hagopian (LA)
G. Bradford Jones (LA)
Brian P. McDermott (LA)
Timothy M. Pennington (LA)
Toby Schreiber (SF)
Frederick J. Warren (LA)

Broventure Capital Management
16 West Madison St.
Baltimore, MD 21201
301/727-4520

Harvey C. Branch
Philip D. English
William M. Gust

Bryan & Edwards
3000 Sand Hill Rd.
Building Two
Suite 260
Menlo Park, CA 94025
415/854-1555

Also:
Bryan & Edwards
600 Montgomery St.
35th Floor
San Francisco, CA 94111
415/421-9990

Alan R. Brudos (SF and MP)
John M. Bryan (SF)
Guy H. Conger (MP)
William C. Edwards (MP)
Robert W. Ledoux (SF)

Burr, Egan, Deleage & Co., Inc.
One Post Office Square
Suite 3800
Boston, MA 02109
617/482-8020

Also:
Burr, Egan, Deleage & Co., Inc.
Three Embarcadero Center
25th Floor
San Francisco, CA 94111
415/362-4022

Brion B. Applegate (CA)
Craig L. Burr (MA)
Shirley Cerrudo (CA)
Jean Deleage (CA)
William P. Egan (MA)
Jean-Bernard Schmidt (CA)
Thomas E. Winter (CA)

Butcher & Singer/Keystone Venture
211 South Broad St.
Philadelphia, PA 19107
215/985-3616
215/985-5519

Timothy W. Cunningham
G. Kenneth Macrae

CW Ventures
1041 Third Ave.
New York, NY 10021
212/308-5266

Walter Channing
Charles M. Hartman
Jesse Trev
Barry Weinberg

Cable, Howse, & Cozadd, Inc.
999 Third Ave., Suite 4300
Seattle, WA 98104
206/583-2700

Also:
Cable, Howse, & Cozadd, Inc.
1800 One Main Place
101 S.W. Main
Portland, OR 97204
503/248-9646

Also:
Cable, Howse, & Cozadd, Inc.
3000 Sand Hill Rd.
Building 1, Suite 190
Menlo Park, CA 94025
415/854-3340

L. Barton Alexander (OR)
Thomas J. Cable (WA)
Bennett A. Cozadd (WA)
Michael E. Ellison (WA)
Elwood D. Howse, Jr. (WA)
Greg Turnbull (CA)
Wayne C. Wager (WA)

Capital Southwest Corp.
12900 Preston Rd.
Suite 700
Dallas, TX 75230
214/233-8242

J. Bruce Duty
Patrick F. Hamner
William R. Thomas

Cardinal Development Capital Fund
155 East Broad St.
Columbus, OH 43215
614/464-5552

Richard F. Bannon

The Centennial Fund
600 South Cherry
Suite 1400
Denver, CO 80222
303/329-9474

Steven C. Halstedt
G. Jackson Tankersley, Jr.
Larry H. Welch

Century IV Partners
1760 Market St.
Philadelphia, PA 19103
215/751-9444

Walter M. Aikman
Charles A. Burton
Thomas R. Morse
Michael Radow

Charles River Partnership
133 Federal St.
Suite 602
Boston, MA 02110
617/482-9370

Richard M. Burnes, Jr.
Donald W. Feddersen
Robert F. Higgins
John T. Neises

Cherry Tree Ventures
640 Northland Executive Ctr.
3600 West 80th St.
Minneapolis, MN 55431
612/893-9012

Buzz Benson
Michael K. Butler
Tony J. Christianson
Thomas W. Jackson
Gordon F. Stofer

Churchill International
444 Market St.
25th Floor
San Francisco, CA 94111
415/398-7677

Also:
Churchill International
545 Middlefield Rd.
Suite 160
Menlo Park, CA 94025
415/328-4401

Also:
Churchill International
9 Riverside Rd.
Weston, MA 02193
617/893-6555

Julie Dunbar (SF)
Janet G. Effland (MA)
Anthony J. Manlove (MP)
David M. Smith (MA)
Robert C. Weeks (MP)

Citicorp Venture Capital, Ltd.
399 Park Ave.
20th Floor
New York, NY 10043
212/559-1127

Also:
Citicorp Venture Capital, Ltd.
2200 Geng Rd.
Suite 203
Palo Alto, CA 94303
415/424-8000

Also:
Citicorp Venture Capital, Ltd.
717 N. Harwood
Suite 2920-LB87
Dallas, TX 75221
214/880-9670

William T. Comfort (NY)
Guy de Chazal (NY)
Peter G. Gerry (NY)
J. Matthew Mackowski (CA)
George M. Middlemas (NY)
Thomas F. McWilliams (TX)
Stanley Nitzburg (NY)
Allan G. Rosenburg (CA)
Stephen C. Sherrill (NY)
Newell Starks (TX)
Kilin To (NY)
David A. Wegmann (CA)
Larry J. Wells (CA)
John R. Whitman (NY)

City Ventures
404 N. Roxbury Dr.
Suite 800
Beverly Hills, CA 90210
213/550-0416

Neill B. Lawton
Mimi Shepard

Columbine Venture Fund, Ltd.
5613 DTC Parkway, Suite 510
Englewood, CO 80111
303/694-3222

Mark Kimmel
David Miller
Sherman Muller
Duane Pearsall
Terry Winters

Concord Partners
535 Madison Ave.
New York, NY 10022
212/906-7000

Also:
Concord Partners
600 Montgomery St.
San Francisco, CA 94111
415/362-2400

John B. Clinton (NY)
Charles L. Lea, Jr. (NY)
Edgar A. Miller (NY)
E. Payson Smith, Jr. (SF)

Continental Capital Ventures
555 California St.
Bank of America Center
Suite 5070
San Francisco, CA 94104
415/989-2020

Also:
Continental Capital Ventures
3000 Sand Hill Rd.
Building 1, Suite 135
Menlo Park, CA 94025
415/854-6633

William A. Boeger (MP)
Lawrence A. Brown (MP)
Frank G. Chambers (SF)
Donald R. Scheuch (MP)
Robert G. Spencer (MP)

Continental Illinois Venture Corp.
231 South LaSalle St.
Chicago, IL 60697
312/828-8021

John L. Hines
Judith Bultman Meyer
Seth L. Pierrepont
William Putze

Criterion Venture Partners
333 Clay, Suite 4300
Houston, TX 77002
713/751-2400

M. Scott Albert
Crichton W. Brown
Harvard H. Hill, Jr.
Gregory A. Rider
David O. Wicks, Jr.

Crosspoint Venture Partners
1015 Corporation Way
Palo Alto, CA 94303
415/964-3545

Also:
Crosspoint Venture Partners
4600 Campus Dr., Suite 3
Newport Beach, CA 92660
714/852-1611

Also:
Crosspoint Venture Partners
6 New England Exec. Park
Suite 400
Burlington, MA 01803
617/229-8920

Roger J. Barry (Palo Alto)
William P. Cargile (Palo Alto)
Frederick J. Dotzler (Boston)
Robert A. Hoff (Newport Beach)
John B. Mumford (Palo Alto)
James F. Willenborg (Palo Alto)

Curtin & Co., Inc.
2050 Houston Natural Gas Bldg.
Houston, TX 77002
713/658-9806

Charles A. Armbrust
Stewart Cureton, Jr.
John D. Curtin, Jr.

DSV Partners III
221 Nassau St.
Princeton, NJ 08542
609/924-6420

James R. Bergman
John K. Clarke
Morton Collins
Robert S. Hillas

Davis Skaggs Capital
160 Sansome St.
San Francisco, CA 94104
415/392-0274

Charles P. Stetson, Jr.

DeMuth, Folger and Terhune
1 Exchange Plaza at 55 Broadway
New York, NY 10006
212/509-5580

Donald F. DeMuth
Thomas W. Folger
J. Michael Terhune

Doan Associates
333 East Main St.
P.O. Box 1431
Midland, MI 48640
517/631-6852

Ian R. N. Bund
Herbert D. Doan

Dougery, Jones & Wilder
Three Embarcadero Center
Suite 1980
San Francisco, CA 94111
415/434-1722

Also:
Dougery, Jones & Wilder
Two Lincoln Centre
5420 LBJ Freeway, Suite 1100
Dallas, Texas 75240
214/960-0077

John R. Dougery (CA)
David A. Jones (CA)
Henry L.B. Wilder (CA)
A. Lawson Howard (TX)

Drexel Burnham Lambert Inc.
Lambda Funds
55 Broad St.
New York, NY 10004
212/480-6018

Richard J. Dumler
Anthony M. Lamport

Eastech Management Co., Inc.
One Liberty Square, 9th Floor
Boston, MA 02109
617/338-0200

Fontaine K. Richardson
Michael H. Shanahan
G. Bickley Stevens, II

Electro-Science Management Corp.
600 Courtland St., Suite 490
Orlando, FL 32804
305/645-1188

Paul F. Curry
G. Arthur Herbert

Elron Technologies, Inc.
1211 Avenue of the Americas
New York, NY 10036
212/819-1644

Gideon Tolkowsky

Euclid Partners Corp.
50 Rockefeller Plaza
New York, NY 10020
212/489-1770

Jeffrey T. Hamilton
Vivian Lee
A. Bliss McCrum, Jr.
Milton J. Pappas

Fairfield Venture Management Co., Inc.
999 Summer St.
Stamford, CT 06905
203/358-0255

Pedro A. Castillo
John C. Garbarino
Randall R. Lunn
Eugene E. Pettinelli

Faneuil Hall Associates
One Boston Place
Boston, MA 02108
617/723-1955

David T. Riddiford

Fidelity Venture Associates, Inc.
82 Devonshire St.
Boston, MA 02109
617/726-0450

William R. Elfers
Donald R. Young

The First Boston Corp.
Park Avenue Plaza
New York, NY 10055
212/909-2000

Harold W. Bogle
John F. Kenny, Jr.
William E. Mayer
W. Barry McCarthy, Jr.
Denis Newman

First Capital Corp. of Boston
100 Federal St.
Boston, MA 02110
617/434-2442

Diana F. Frazier
Paul F. Hogan
Edwin M. Kania
Charles R. Klotz
Jeffrey W. Wilson

First Chicago Investment Advisors
Institutional Venture Capital Fund
Three First National Plaza
Suite 1040
Chicago, Illinois 60670
312/732-6743

Gary P. Brinson
T. Bondurant French
Marshall L. Greenwald
Patrick A. McGivney
Daniel J. Mitchell

First Chicago Investment Corp.
One First National Plaza
Suite 2628
Chicago, IL 60670
312/732-5400

Also:
First Chicago Investment Corp.
133 Federal Street
Boston, Massachusetts 02110
617/542-9185

John A. Canning, Jr. (IL)
Kent P. Dauten (IL)
Kevin M. McCafferty (MA)
Paul R. Wood (IL)

First Interstate Capital, Inc.
515 South Figueroa St.
Suite 1900
Los Angeles, CA 90071
213/622-1922

Also:
First Interstate Capital, Inc.
1300 S.W. Fifth Ave.
Suite 2323
Portland, OR 97201
503/223-4334

Kenneth M. Deemer (CA)
Jonathan E. Funk (CA)
David B. Jones (CA)
Wayne B. Kingsley (OR)

First Midwest Capital Corp.
1010 Plymouth Bldg.
12 South Sixth St.
Minneapolis, MN 55402
612/339-9391

William R. Franta
Walter L. Tiffin

Fleet Venture Resources, Inc.
111 Westminster St.
Providence, RI 02903
401/278-5597

Margaret A. DePodwin
Carlton B. Klein
Robert M. Van Degna

Foster Management Co.
437 Madison Ave.
New York, NY 10022
212/753-4810

Michael J. Connelly
Timothy E. Foster

Fostin Capital Corp.
415 Holiday Dr.
P.O. Box 67
Pittsburgh, PA 15230
412/928-8900

Andrew S. Harris
Thomas M. Levine
William F. Woods

Frontenac Venture Co.
208 South LaSalle St.
Suite 1900
Chicago, IL 60604
312/368-0044

David A.R. Dullum
Rodney L. Goldstein
Martin J. Koldyke

**General Electric Venture
  Capital Corp.**
3135 Easton Turnpike
Fairfield, CT 06431
203/373-2154

Also:
General Electric Venture
  Capital Corp.
3000 Sand Hill Rd.
Building 1, Suite 230
Menlo Park, CA 94025
415/854-8092

Also:
General Electric Venture
  Capital Corp.
33 Riverside Ave.
Westport, CT 06880
203/373-3238

Also:
General Electric Venture
  Capital Corp.
7100 Regency Square Blvd.
Suite 108
Houston, TX 77036

Also:
General Electric Venture
  Capital Corp.
53 State St.
Boston, MA 01209
617/227-7922

Preston H. Abbott (Fairfield)
Andrew C. Bangser (Boston)
Robert L. Burr (Menlo Park)
James J. Fitzpatrick (Westport)
David C. Fries (Westport)
Stephen L. Green (Fairfield)
Harry T. Rein (Fairfield)
Eric A. Young (Menlo Park)

Golder, Thoma & Cressey
120 South LaSalle St.
Suite 630
Chicago, IL 60603
312/853-3322

Also:
Golder, Thoma & Cressey
17330 Preston Rd.
Dallas, TX 75252
214/248-7848

Bryan C. Cressey (IL)
Stanley C. Golder (IL)
Bruce V. Rauner (IL)
Carl D. Thoma (IL)
F. Dan Blanchard (TX)

Grace Ventures Corp.
630 Hansen Way
Suite 260
Palo Alto, CA 94304
415/424-1171

Charles A. Bauer
Christian F. Horn
William B. Wittmeyer
Susan A. Woods

**Greater Washington Investors,
Inc.**
5454 Wisconsin Ave.
Chevy Chase, MD 20815
301/656-0626

Don A. Christensen
Cyril W. Draffin, Jr.
Martin S. Pinson

Greylock Management Corp.
One Federal St.
Boston, Mass. 02110
617/423-5525

Howard E. Cox, Jr.
Daniel S. Gregory

Robert P. Henderson
Henry F. McCance
David N. Strohm
Charles P. Waite

Hambrecht & Quist
235 Montgomery St.
San Francisco, CA 94104
415/576-3300

David Best
D. Kirkwood Bowman
Dan Case
William R. Hambrecht
Grant Inman
Robert J. Kunze
Robert Morrill
W. Denman Van Ness

**Hambro International Venture
Fund**
17 East 71st St.
New York, NY 10021
212/288-7778

Also:
Hambro International Venture
Fund
1 Boston Place
Suite 923
Boston, MA 02108
617/722-7055

Anders Brag (NY)
Richard D'Amore (MA)
Edwin A. Goodman (NY)
Frances Janis (NY)
Robert Sherman (MA)
Arthur Spinner (NY)

**John Hancock Venture Capital
Fund**
John Hancock Pl., 57th Fl.
P.O. Box 111
Boston, MA 02117
617/421-6350
617/421-6760

William A. Johnston
Edward W. Kane
Robert J. Lepkowski
D. Brooks Zug

Harvest Ventures, Inc.
767 Third Ave.
New York, NY 10017
212/838-7776

Also:
Harvest Ventures, Inc.
3000 Sand Hill Rd.
Building 3, Suite 125
Menlo Park, CA 94025
415/854-8400

Harvey Mallement (NY)
Cloyd Marvin (CA)
Cydney Meltzer (NY)
Harvey Wertheim (NY)

Hawley & Associates
999 Summer St.
Stamford, CT 06905
203/348-6669

Alexander H. Dunbar
Frank J. Hawley, Jr.
Norman W. Johnson

Hewlett-Packard Co.
P.O. Box 10301 Bldg. #20BL
Palo Alto, CA 94303-0890
415/857-2314

Robert E. Greeley
Elizabeth Obershaw

The Hill Partnership
885 Arapahoe Ave.
Boulder, CO 80302
303/442-5151

John G. Hill
Robert H. Keeley
Paul J. Kirby

Hillman Ventures, Inc.
2000 Grant Building
Pittsburgh, PA 15219
412/281-2620

Also:
Hillman Ventures, Inc.
40 Orville Dr., Suite 104
Bohemia, NY 11716
516/563-1790

Stephen J. Banks (PA)
Catharine C. Burkett (NY)
Kent L. Engelmeier (PA)
Howard W. Geiger (PA)
Jay D. Glass (PA)
Kenneth H. Levin (PA)
March Yagjian (PA)

The Holland Financial Group, Ltd.
370 Campbell Centre
8350 North Central Expressway
Dallas, TX 75206
214/987-6481

Alvin E. Holland, Jr.

Horsley Keogh & Associates, Inc.
11 Tobey Village Office Park
Pittsford, NY 14534
716/385-9830

G.C. Belden, Jr.
Phillip Horsley
Kevin Keogh
John P. Ragard
Thomas G. Washing

Idanta Partners
201 Main St.
Suite 3200
Fort Worth, TX 76102
817/338-2020

Also:
Idanta Partners
3344 North Torry Pines Court
Suite 200
La Jolla, CA 92037
619/455-5280

David J. Dunn (TX)
Michael J. Kucha (CA)
Harry W. Lange (CA & TX)
Dev Purkayastha (TX)

InnoVen Group
Park 80 Plaza West—One
Saddle Brook, NJ 07662
201/845-4900

Bart Holaday
John H. Martinson

Institutional Venture Partners
3000 Sand Hill Rd.
Building 2, Suite 190
Menlo Park, CA 94025
415/854-0132

Reid W. Dennis
Mary Jane Elmore
John K. Poitras

Interscope Investments
10900 Wilshire Blvd.
#1400
Los Angeles, CA 90024
213/208-8636

J. Murray Hill, II
Peter Samuelson

Interwest Partners
2620 Augustine Dr.
Suite 201
Santa Clara, CA 95051
408/727-7200

Eugene F. Barth
Philip T. Gianos
Wallace R. Hawley
W. Scott Hedrick
Robert R. Momsen

Investors in Industry Corp.
99 High St.
Suite 1200
Boston, MA 02110
617/542/8560

Also:
Investors in Industry Corp.
450 Newport Center Dr.
Suite 250
Newport Beach, CA 92660
714/720-1421

David R. Shaw (MA)
Geoff N. Taylor (CA)
Frederick M. Haney (CA)
Anna Henry (CA)
William N. Holm, Jr. (MA)
Russ J. Salisbury (MA)
Peter J. Bollier (MA)
David Warnock (MA)

Johnston Associates, Inc.
Research Park
300 Wall St.
Princeton, NJ 08540
609/924-3131

Robert F. Johnston
James R. Mrazek
Harold V. Smith
Robert B. Stockman

**Kleiner, Perkins, Caufield, &
  Byers**
Four Embarcadero Center
Suite 3520
San Francisco, CA 94111
415/421-3110

Also:
Kleiner, Perkins, Caufield & Byers
Two Embarcadero Place
2200 Geng Road, Suite 205
Palo Alto, CA 94303
415/424-1660

Brook H. Byers (SF)
Frank J. Caufield (SF)
L. John Doerr (SF)
Eugene Kleiner (Palo Alto)
Floyd Kvamme (Palo Alto)
James P. Lally (Palo Alto)
Thomas J. Perkins (SF)

Lawrence WPG Partners
One New York Plaza
30th Floor
New York, NY 10004
212/908-9553

Also:
Lawrence WPG Partners
555 California St.
Suite 4720
San Francisco, CA 94104
415/622-6864

Philip Greer (CA)
Larry J. Lawrence (NY)
Robert J. Loarie (CA)
John C. Savage (CA)
Richard W. Smith (NY)
Eugene M. Weber (CA)

Lubar & Co., Inc.
777 East Wisconsin Ave.
Milwaukee, WI 53202
414/291-9000

William T. Donovan
David J. Lubar
Sheldon B. Lubar
James C. Rowe
James S. Vaughan

Lubrizol Enterprises, Inc.
29400 Lakeland Blvd.
Wickliffe, OH 44092
216/943-4200

David R. Anderson
James R. Glynn
Bruce H. Grasser
Donald L. Murfin

MIP Equity Fund
47 Lafayette Place
Suite 6F
Greenwich, CT 06830
203/661-6342

Also:
MIP Equity Fund
The Hague
Bezuidenhoutseweg 27
P.O. Box 11592
2502 An The Hague
70/814891

Daniel J. Piliero

ML Venture Partners 1
165 Broadway
New York, NY 10080
212/766-6215

George Kokkinakis
R. Stephen McCormack
George L. Sing
Stephen J. Warner

MSI Capital Corp.
650 Peoples Bank Bldg.
6510 Abrams Rd.
Dallas, TX 75231
214/341-1553

Nick Stanfield
Rich Wierzbicki

Carl Marks & Co., Inc.
CM Capital Corp.
77 Water St.
New York, NY 10005
212/437-7080

Robert Davidoff
Jeffrey L. Kenner

Matrix Partners, LP
224 West Brokaw Rd.
Suite 395
San Jose, CA 95110
408/298-0270

Also:
Matrix Partners, LP
One Post Office Square
Boston, MA 02109
617/482-7735

Paul J. Ferri (MA)
Frederick K. Fluegel (CA)
F. Warren Hellmman (CA)
W. Michael Humphreys (MA)
Glen McLaughlin (CA)

Mayfield Fund
2200 Sand Hill Rd.
Suite 200
Menlo Park, CA 94025
415/854-5560

Thomas J. Davis, Jr.
Norman A. Fogelsong
A. Grant Heidrich
Michael J. Levinthal
Glenn M. Mueller
F. Gibson Myers, Jr.

Memorial Drive Trust
20 Acorn Park
Cambridge, MA 02140
617/864-5770, ext. 2611

Jean E. de Valpine
Paul D. Shuwall

Menlo Ventures
3000 Sand Hill Rd.
Menlo Park, CA 94025
415/854-8540

Also:
Menlo Ventures
230 Park Ave.
New York, NY 10169
212/697-7667

Douglas C. Carlisle (CA)
Robert Finzi (NY)
Ken E. Joy (CA)
Kirk L. Knight (CA)
Richard P. Magnuson (CA)
H. DuBose Montgomery (CA)
Denise M. O'Leary (CA)
Yung Wong (NY)

Merrill, Pickard, Anderson & Eyre
Two Palo Alto Square, Suite 425
Palo Alto, CA 94304
415/856-8880

James C. Anderson
Stephen E. Coit
Chris A. Eyre
Steven L. Merrill
W. Jeffers Pickard

Michigan Capital & Service, Inc.
500 First National Bldg.
Ann Arbor, MI 48104
313/663-0702

Anthony F. Buffa
Gerard L. Buhrman
Joseph F. Conway
James A. Parsons

Montgomery Securities
600 Montgomery St.
Suite 2200
San Francisco, CA 94111
415/627-2000

R. Stephen Doyle
Thomas E. Mancino
Alan L. Stein
James I. Valentine
Thomas W. Weisel

Morgan, Holland Ventures Corp.
One Liberty Square
Boston, MA 02109
617/423-1765

Jay Delahanty
Dan Holland
Jim Morgan
Bob Rosbe

Morgenthaler Management Corp.
700 National City Bank Bldg.
Cleveland, OH 44114
216/621-3070

Robert C. (Robin) Bellas, Jr.
Paul S. Brentlinger
David T. Morgenthaler
Robert D. Pavey

NBR II
P.O. Box 796
Addison, TX 75001
214/233-6631

J.R. Hanschen
Richard J. Hanschen
Stephen R. Hanschen (Austin)

Narragansett Capital Corp.
40 Westminster St.
Providence, RI 02903
401/751-1000

Gregory P. Barber
Arthur D. Little
Robert D. Manchester
Roger A. Vandenberg

New England Capital Corp.
One Washington Mall
7th Floor
Boston, MA 02108
617/722-6400

Thomas A. Ballantyne
Melvin W. Ellis
Z. David Patterson
Thomas C. Tremblay

New Enterprise Associates, L.P.
1119 St. Paul St.
Baltimore, MD 21201
301/244-0115

Also:
New Enterprise Associates, L.P.
235 Montgomery St.
Suite 1025
San Francisco, CA 94104
415/956-1579

R. John Armor (CA)
Cornelius C. Bond, Jr. (CA)
Frank A. Bonsal, Jr. (MD)
Curran W. Harvey (MD)
C. Richard Kramlich (CA)
Arthur J. Marks (MD)
Charles W. Newhall, III (MD)
C. Woodrow Rea, Jr. (CA)

North American Co.
111 East Las Olas Blvd.
Fort Lauderdale, FL 33302
305/463-0681

Charles L. Palmer

North Star Ventures, Inc.
1501 First Bank Place West
Minneapolis, MN 55402
612/333-1133

Keith M. Eastman
Terrence W. Glarner
David W. Stassen

Northwood Ventures
420 Madison Ave.
13th Floor
New York, NY 10017
212/935-4679

Peter G. Schiff

Norwest Venture Capital Management, Inc.
1730 Midwest Plaza Bldg.
801 Nicollet Mall
Minneapolis, MN 55402
612/372-8770, Minnesota
503/223-6622, Oregon
303/297-0537, Colorado

Leonard J. Brandt (MN)
Mark Dubovoy (CO)
Daniel J. Haggerty (MN)
Douglas E. Johnson (MN)
John E. Lindahl (MN)
Anthony J. Miadich (OR)

Timothy A. Stepanek (MN)
Dale J. Vogel (OR)
John P. Whaley (MN)
Larry R. Wonnacott (CO)
Robert F. Zicarelli (MN)

Oak Management Corp.
257 Riverside Ave.
Westport, CT 06880
203/226-8346

Edward F. Glassmeyer
Stewart H. Greenfield
Carla Haugen
Michael D. Kaufman
Annie Lamont
Ginger M. More
Catherine A. Pierson
Dennis G. Sisco
Karen Vinjamuri
Jeffrey D. West

Orange Nassau Companies, Inc.
1 Post Office Square
Suite 1760
Boston, MA 02109
617/451-6220

Also:
Orange Nassau Companies, Inc.
13355 Noel Rd.
Suite 635
Dallas, TX 75240
214/385-9685

Also:
Orange Nassau Companies, Inc.
Westerly Place
Suite 520
1500 Quail St.
Newport Beach, CA 92660

Also:
Orange Nassau Companies, Inc.
P.O. B. 85578
2508 cg, The Hague
The Netherlands
Phone # 011-31-70-469-670

Also:
Orange Nassau Companies, Inc.
10 Rue de Clichy
75009 Paris
FRANCE
Phone # 011-33-1878-6629

John W. Blackburn (Newport
    Beach)
Paul A. Deiters (The Netherlands)
Guy R. Eugene (Paris)
Linda S. Linsalata (Boston)
Gregory B. Peters (Boston)
Frederick L. Russell (Newport
    Beach)
Martin J. Silver (Dallas)
Rene Smits (The Netherlands)
Richard D. Tadler (Dallas)
Joost E. Tjaden (Boston)

Oxford Partners
Soundview Plaza
1266 Main St.
Stamford, CT 06902
203/964-0592

Also:
Oxford Partners
233 Wilshire Blvd.
Suite 730
Santa Monica, CA 90401
213/458-3135

Stevan A. Birnbaum (CA)
William R. Lonergan (CT)
Kenneth W. Rind (CT)
Cornelius T. Ryan (CT)

PNC Venture Corp.
Pittsburgh National Bank Bldg.
Fifth Avenue & Wood—19th Floor
Pittsburgh, PA 15222
412/355-2245

David McL. Hillman
Jeffrey H. Schutz

**Paine Webber Ventures
    Management Co.**
100 Federal Street, 31st Floor
Boston, MA 02110
617/423-8264
617/423-8500

Daniel Alexander
Richard A. Charpie
William C. Mills, III
Merlin D. Schulze
Donald W. Stacey

The Palmer Organization
300 Unicorn Park Dr.
Woburn, MA 01801
617/933-5445

Karen S. Camp
William H. Congleton
Michael T. Fitzgerald
Stephen J. Ricci
Alison J. Seavey
John A. Shane

Palo Alto Ventures
3000 Sand Hill Rd.
Building 1, Suite 140
Menlo Park, CA 94025
415/854-8770

Daniel L. Larson
Peter von Raits

Paragon Partners
3000 Sand Hill Rd.
Building 4, Suite 130
Menlo Park, CA 94025
415/854-8000

Robert F. Kibble
John S. Lewis
Jess R. Marzak
Palyn Partners

**Pathfinder Venture Capital
    Fund**
7300 Metro Boulevard, Suite 585
Minneapolis, MN 55435
612/835-1121

Jack Ahrens
Marv Bookin
Norm Dann
Andy Greenshields
Gary Stoltz

Alan Patricof Associates, Inc.
545 Madison Ave.
New York, NY 10022
212/753-6300

Also:
Alan Patricof Associates, Inc.
1245 Oakmead Parkway
Suite 105
Sunnyvale, CA 94086-4041
408/737-8788

Also:
Alan Patricof Associates, Ltd.
24 Upper Brook St.
London, W1Y 1PD ENGLAND
493-3633

Also:
Alan Patricof Associés, S.A.R.L.
67 rue de Monceau
Paris 75008 FRANCE
563-4025

John C. Baker (NY)
Jonathan Ben-Cnaan (NY)
Charles Cheskiewicz (NY)
Ronald M. Cohen (UK)
Robert G. Faris (NY)
Camilla Jackson (NY)
Barbara Lundberg (CA)
James W. Newton (NY)
Alan J. Patricof (NY)
Lewis Solomon (NY)
Maurice Tchenio (FRANCE)

Pioneer Ventures Co.
113 East 55th St.
New York, NY 10022
212/980-9090

R. Scott Asen
Neil A. McConnell
James G. Niven

T. Rowe Price Threshold Fund
100 East Pratt St.
Baltimore, MD 21202
301/547-2000

Jonathan M. Greene
Anita M. Iannone
Edward J. Mathias
Philip J. Rauch
Eugene M. Waldron

**Prime Capital Management Co.,
  Inc.**
1 Landmark Square, Suite 800
Stamford, CT 06901
203/964-0642

Theodore H. Elliott, Jr.
Dean E. Fenton
H. Thomas Gnuse

Prince Venture Partners
One First National Plaza
Suite 4950
Chicago, IL 60603
312/726-2232

Also:
Prince Venture Partners
767 Third Ave.
New York, NY 10017
212/319-6620

Angus M. Duthie (IL)
James W. Fordyce (NY)

Quantum Venture Partners, L.P.
650 Fifth Ave.
New York, NY 10019
212/975-1285

John R. Cullinane
Roger P. Williams

Rain Hill Group, Inc.
90 Broad St.
New York, NY 10004
212/483-9162

Diane Lupi

Regional Financial Enterprises
51 Pine St.
New Canaan, CT 06840
203/356-1730

Also:
Regional Financial Enterprises
Burlington Executive Center
325 East Eisenhower Pkwy.
Suite 108
Ann Arbor, MI 48104
313/769-0941

Howard C. Landis (CT)
Robert R. Sparacino (CT)
George E. Thomassy (CT)
John V. Titsworth (CT)
Barry P. Walsh (MI)
Robert M. Williams (CT)

Republic Venture Group, Inc.
Republic Venture Capital Corpora-
  tion
P.O. Box 225961
Dallas, TX 75265
214/653-5078

Bart A. McLean
Christian A. Melhado
William W. Richey
Robert H. Wellborn
Wayne C. Willcox

Robertson, Colman & Stephens
One Embarcadero Center
San Francisco, CA 94111
415/781-9700

Robert L. Cummings
Sanford R. Robertson
Paul H. Stephens
Nywood Wu

Robinson Venture Partners
6507 Wilkins Ave.
Pittsburgh, PA 15217
412/661-1200

Stephen G. Robinson

Rothschild Ventures Inc.
One Rockefeller Plaza
New York, NY 10020
212/757-6000

Robert A. Bettigole
James C. Blair
Douglas S. Luke, Jr.
Archie J. McGill
Kathryn A. Minckler
Thomas L. Phillips, Jr.
Ivan L. Wolff

Ruddick Investment Co.
2000 First Union Plaza
Charlotte, NC 23282
704/333-7144
704/334-2867

William R. Starnes

The Rust Group
—Rust Capital, Ltd.
—Rust Ventures, L.P.
114 West 7th St.
Austin, TX 78701
512/479-0055

Joseph C. Aragona
Kenneth P. DeAngelis
Jeffrey C. Garvey
Jack L. Locy

SAS Associates
515 South Figueroa St.
6th Floor
Los Angeles, CA 90071
213/624-4232

Robert W. Campbell
Bruce P. Emmeluth
Joseph E. Giansante
James E. Moore

Santa Fe Private Equity Fund
524 Camino del Monte Sol
Santa Fe, NM 87501
503/983-1769

A. David Silver
Kay Tsunemori

Schroder Venture Managers
One State St.
New York, NY 10004
212/269-6500

Also:
Schroder Venture Managers
755 Page Mill Rd.
Bldg. A-Suite 280
Palo Alto, CA 94304
415/424-1144

Jeffrey J. Collinson (NY)
Michael A. Hentschel (CA)
Judith E. Schneider (NY)
David Walters (CA)

Scientific Advances, Inc.
601 West Fifth Ave.
Columbus, OH
614/294-5541

Thomas W. Harvey
Charles G. James
Paul F. Purcell
Daniel J. Shea

Security Pacific Capital Corp.
9th Floor
4000 MacArthur Blvd.
Newport Beach, CA 92660
714/754-4780

Also:
Security Pacific Capital Corp.
333 South Hope St., H25-4
Los Angeles, CA 90071
213/613-5215

Also:
Security Pacific Capital Corp.
P.O. Box 512
Washington, PA 15301
412/223-0707

Dmitry Bosky (NB)
Al Brizzard (NB)
Everett Cox (NB)
Michael Cronin (NB)
Daniel Dye (PA)
Gregory Forrest (NB)
John Geer (NB)
Tim Hay (NB)
Brian Jones (NB)
James McElwee (NB)
James McGoodwin (NB)
John Padgett (LA)
Tony Stevens (LA)

Seidman Jackson Fisher & Co.
233 North Michigan Ave.
Suite 1812
Chicago, IL 60601
312/856-1812

Margaret G. Fisher
Douglas L. Jackson
David C. Seidman

Sequoia Capital
3000 Sand Hill Rd.
Building 4, Suite 280
Menlo Park, CA 94025
418/854-3927

Walter F. Baumgartner
Jonathan M. Hamren
Pierre R. Lamond
Gordon Russell
Robert G. Spencer
Donald T. Valentine

Sevin Rosen Management Co.
5050 Quorum Dr.
Dallas, TX 75240
714/960-1744

Also:
Sevin Rosen Management Co.
200 Park Ave.
#4503
New York, NY 10166
212/687-5115

Also:
Sevin Rosen Management Co.
1245 Oakmead Pkwy.
Sunnyvale, CA 94086
408/720-8590

L.J. Sevin
Benjamin M. Rosen
Jon W. Bayless
Roger S. Borovoy

Sierra Ventures
3000 Sand Hill Rd.
Menlo Park, CA 94025
415/854-9096

Also:
Sierra Ventures
645 Madison Ave.
New York, NY 10022
212/758-8500

Peter C. Wendell (CA)
Gilbert H. Lamphere (NY)
Thomas A. Barron (NY)
Jeffrey M. Drazan (CA)

Slater Carley Group, Inc.
4221 Malsbary Rd.
Cincinnati, OH 45242
513/793-1130

John G. Slater

Smith Barney Venture Corp.
1345 Avenue of the Americas
New York, NY 10105
212/399-6382

Also:
Smith Barney Venture Corp.
350 California St.
San Francisco, CA 94014
415/955-1672

Byron K. Adams (SF)
Steven P. Bird (NY)
Roberto Buaron (NY)
C. Sage Givens (SF)

Walter C. Johnsen (SF)
David S. Lobel (NY)
Michael J. Myers (NY)
David Gliba (SF)

South Atlantic Capital Corp.
220 East Madison
Suite 530
Tampa, Florida 33602
813-229-7400

Sandra P. Barber
Donald W. Burton
P. Thomas Vogel

**The Southwest Venture
    Partnerships**
300 Convent St., Suite 1400
San Antonio, TX 78205
512/227-1010

Also:
The Southwest Venture
    Partnerships
5080 Spectrum Drive
Suite 610 East
Dallas, TX 78248
214/960-0404

Michael Bell (San Antonio)
J. Edward McAteer (Dallas)
C.D. Grojean (San Antonio)
Thomas R. Crawford (Dallas)
John L. Long, Jr. (San Antonio)

Spectrum Capital Ltd.
208 South LaSalle St.
Suite 1230
Chicago, IL 60604
312/236-5231

William C. Douglas
Michael V. Fox

The Sprout Group
140 Broadway
New York, NY 10005
212/902-2492

Also:
The Sprout Group
5300 Stevens Creek Blvd.
Suite 320
San Jose, CA 95129
408/554-1515

Peter T. Grauer (NY)
Gary W. Kalbach (CA)
Richard E. Kroon (NY)
David L. Mordy (NY)
Larry E. Reeder (NY)
Lloyd D. Ruth (NY)

Stephenson Merchant Banking
899 Logan St.
Denver, CO 80203
303/837-1700

Einar Nagell-Erichsen
A. Emmet Stephenson, Jr.

The Sterling Group, Inc.
Eight Greenway Plaza
Suite 702
Houston, TX 77046
713/877-8257

Gordon A. Cain
Frank J. Hevrdejs
Gregory S. Buck
Cameron Adair

Sunwestern Management, Inc.
6750 LBJ Freeway
One Oaks Plaza—Suite 1160
Dallas, TX 75240
214/239-5650

Floyd W. Collins
Thomas W. Wright

Sutter Hill Ventures
Two Palo Alto Square
Suite 700
Palo Alto, CA 94306
415/493-5600

David L. Anderson
G. Leonard Baker, Jr.
Paul M. Wythes
William H. Younger, Jr.

**Swedish Industrial
    Development Corp.**
600 Steamboat Rd.
Greenwich, CT 06830
203/661-2500

Tord Carmel

TA Associates
45 Milk St.
Boston, MA 02109
617/338-0800

Also:
TA Associates
525 University Ave.
Suite 420
Palo Alto, CA 94301
415/328-1210

John L. Bunce, Jr. (MA)
Jeffrey T. Chambers (CA)
Michael C. Child (CA)
Brian J. Conway (MA)
Robert Daly (MA)
Arthur G. Epker III (MA)
Donald J. Kramer (MA)
C. Kevin Landry (MA)
P. Andrews McLane (MA)
Jacqueline C. Morby (MA)
Edwina B. Shealy (MA)
Paul A. White (MA)
Linda C. Wisnewski (MA)

Taylor & Turner
220 Montgomery St.
Penthouse 10
San Francisco, CA 94104
415/398-6821

Also:
Taylor & Turner
c/o Rotan Mosle Technology Inc.
3800 Republic Bank Center
Houston, TX 77253
713/236-3180

Also:
Taylor & Turner
c/o VenWest Inc.
Westinghouse Electric Bldg.
Gateway Center
Pittsburgh, PA 15222
412/642-5858

William Taylor (CA)
Marshall Turner (CA)
John Jaggers (TX)
Jack Brock (PA)

Technology Venture Investors
3000 Sand Hill Rd.
Building 4, Suite 210
Menlo Park, CA 94025
415/854-7472

James J. Bochnowski
Robert C. Kagle
James A. Katzman
David F. Marquardt
Burton J. McMurtry
Pete Thomas

Tenneco Ventures Inc.
1010 Milam
POB2511-Suite T2919
Houston, TX 77001
713/757-5599

Carl S. Stutts
Richard L. Wambold

Torchmark Venture Capital, Inc.
Federal Reserve Plaza
Boston, MA 02210
617/722-6030

Julius Jensen III
David J. Ryan

Union Venture Corp.
445 South Figueroa St.
Los Angeles, CA 90071
213/236-6292

Lee R. McCracken
Christopher L. Rafferty
John W. Ulrich
Jeffrey A. Watts

United Venture Capital, Inc.
P.O. Box 109
Genoa, NV 89411
702/782-5114
702/883-6395

Seth L. Atwood
Fraser d'Avignon

U.S. Venture Partners
2180 Sand Hill Rd.
Suite 300
Menlo Park, CA 94025
415/854-9080

William K. Bowes, Jr.
Robert Sackman
Stuart G. Moldaw
H. Joseph Horowitz
Bruce J. Boehm
Jane H. Martin

Vanguard Capital Corp.
101 Lions Dr.
Barrington, IL 60010
312/381-2330

Kenneth M. Arenberg

Venrock Associates
30 Rockefeller Plaza
Suite 5508
New York, NY 10112
212/247-3700

Peter O. Crisp
Anthony B. Evnin
David R. Hathaway
Ted H. McCourtney
Henry S. Smith
Anthony Sun

**The Venture Capital Fund of
    New England**
100 Franklin St.
Boston, MA 02110
617/451-2575

Richard A. Farrell
Harry J. Healer, Jr.
E. Janice Leeming

Venture Founders Corp.
100 Fifth Ave.
Waltham, MA 02154
617/890-1000

Also:
Venture Founders Corp.
39 The Green, South Bar Street
Banbury, Oxon OX16 9AE
ENGLAND

Also:
Venture Founders Corp.
Old Bank House
Haddington, E. Lothian E H41 3JS
SCOTLAND

Charles F.M. Cox (UK)
Alexander L.M. Dingee (MA)
Joseph M. Fyre, Jr. (Europe)
Edward H. Getchell (MA)
David T. Riddiford (MA)
Leonard E. Smollen (MA)
Ross Yeiter (MA)

VIMAC Corp.
12 Arlington St.
Boston, MA 02116
617/267-2785

Max J. Steinmann

Vista Ventures
36 Grove St.
New Canaan, CT 06840
203/972-3400

Gerald B. Bay
Edwin Snape
John Tomlin

Wallner & Company
P.O. Box 8329
La Jolla, CA 92038
619/454-3805

J. Terrence Greve
Willard C. McNitt
Peter S. Redfield
Nicholas Wallner, Ph.D.

Warburg, Pincus Ventures, Inc.
466 Lexington Ave.
New York, NY 10017
212/878-0600

Nissan Boury
Christopher W. Brody
Stephen W. Fillo
John H. Friedman
Fred Fruitman
Andrew Gaspar
Jeffrey A. Harris
Henry Kressel
Sidney Lapidus
Barbara L. Manfrey
W. Edward Massey
Edward McKinley
Cornelia Mitchell
Rodman W. Moorhead III
Howard Newman

Lionel I. Pincus
Ernest H. Pomerantz
Adam Solomon
John L. Vogelstein

Welsh, Carson, Anderson & Stowe
45 Wall St.
New York, NY 10005
212/422-3232

Bruce K. Anderson
Russell L. Carson
Charles G. Moore
Andrew M. Paul
Richard H. Stowe
Patrick J. Welsh

Whitehead Associates
15 Valley Dr.
Greenwich, CT 06830
203/629-4633

William E. Engbers
Joseph A. Orlando
Edwin C. Whitehead
Andrew M. Ziolkowski

J.H. Whitney & Co.
630 Fifth Ave., Room 3200
New York, NY 10111
212/757-0500

Also:
J.H. Whitney & Co.
3000 Sand Hill Rd.
Suite 2-215
Menlo Park, CA 94025
415/854-0500

Don E. Ackerman
Levi W. Goodrich
John W. Larsen
Harry A. Marshall
David T. Morgenthaler II
Russell E. Planitzer
Robert E. Pursley
Edward V. Ryan
Benno C. Schmidt

Wood River Capital Corp.
645 Madison Ave.
New York, NY 10022
212/750-9420

Also:
Wood River Capital Corp.
3000 Sand Hill Rd.
Menlo Park, CA 94025
415/854-4150

W. Wallace McDowell, Jr. (NY)
Elizabeth W. Smith (NY)
Peter C. Wendell (CA)

Xerox Corp.—Venture Capital
2029 Century Park East
Suite 740
Los Angeles, CA 90067
213/278-7940

Also:
Xerox Corp.—Venture Capital
800 Long Ridge Rd.
Stamford, CT 06904
203/329-8700

Richard J. Hayes
Worth Z. Ludwick
Lawrence R. Robinson III
Al Talbot

APPENDIX 3
Directory of the Membership of the National Association of Small Business Investment Companies

The following comprehensive directory constitutes the membership roster of the National Association of Small Business Investment Companies (NASBIC), with headquarters at 618 Washington Building, Washington, D.C. 20005. The resources of these companies represent approximately 90 percent of the SBIC industry assets. The NASBIC code of ethics states that

> the constant goal of each SBIC shall be to improve the welfare of the small business concerns which it serves. Each SBIC shall promote and maintain ethical standards of conduct and deal fairly and honestly with all small business concerns seeking its assistance.

This directory of the NASBIC membership includes the corporate name, the name of the chief executive, and the address and telephone number of the company. The investment preferences of each company are also provided and are keyed to the codes on the following page.

This directory also lists several companies which invest in small businesses, but which are not SBICs. These non-SBIC venture capitalists are Associate Members of NASBIC.

Codes

Preferred Limit for Loans or Investments
A Up to $100,000
B Up to $250,000
C Up to $500,000
D Up to $1 million
E Above $1 million

Investment Policy
   *   Will consider either loans or investments
  **   Prefers to make long-term loans
 ***   Prefers financings with right to acquire stock interest

Industry Preferences
   1. Communications
   2. Construction and development
   3. Natural resource
   4. Hotels, motels, and restaurants
   5. Manufacturing and processing
   6. Medical and other health services
   7. Recreation and amusements
   8. Research and technology
   9. Retailing, wholesaling, and distribution
  10. Service trades
  11. Transportation
  12. Diversified

SBIC Members

ALABAMA
Firrst SBIC of Alabama
Mr. David C. DeLaney, Pres.
16 Midtown Park E.
Mobile, AL 36606
(205) 476-0700
C ** 12

Tuskegee Capital Corp.
Mr. E. Taylor Harmon, Pres.
P.O. Drawer GG
Tuskegee Institute, AL 36088
(205) 727-2850
MESBIC A * 2,5,12

ALASKA
Alaska Business Investment Corp.
Mr. James L. Cloud, VP
301 W. Northern Lights Blvd.
P.O. Box 600
Anchorage, AK 99510
(907) 265-2816
C * 1,5,6,8,12

Alaska Pacific Inv. Corp.
Mr. Robert R. Richards, Pres.
P.O. Box 420
Anchorage, AK 99510
(907) 276-0002
A * 12**

Calista Business Investment Corp.
Mr. Alex Raider, Pres.
516 Denali St.
Anchorage, AK 99501
(907) 279-5516
MESBIC B * 12

ARIZONA _____
Rocky Mountain Equity Corp.
Mr. Anthony J. Nicoli, Pres.
4530 N. Central Ave., Ste. 3
Phoenix, AZ 85012
(602) 274-7558
A * 4,7,8,10

Sun Belt Capital Corporation
Mr. Brian Burch, VP
14255 N. 76th Pl., Ste. A-1
Scottsdale, AZ 85260
(602) 998-4444
A * 2,9,10

ARKANSAS _____
Capital Management Services, Inc.
Mr. David L. Hale, Pres.
1910 N. Grant, Ste. 200
Little Rock, AR 72207
(501) 664-8613
MESBIC A * 12**

First SBIC of Arkansas, Inc.
Mr. Fred C. Burns, Pres.
1400 Worthen Bank Bldg.
Little Rock, AR 72201
(501) 378-1876
A * 12**

Independence Financial Services,
    Inc.
Mr. Preston Grace, Jr., Pres.
P.O. Box 3878
Batesville, AR 72503
(501) 793-4533
D * 12

Kar-Mal Venture Capital, Inc.
Mr. Thomas Karam, Pres.
610 Plaza West Bldg.
Little Rock, AR 72205
(501) 661-0010
MESBIC B * 12**

Power Ventures, Inc.
Mr. Dorsey D. Glover, Pres.
829 Highway 270 N.
P.O. Box 518
Malvern, AR 72104
(501) 332-3695
MESBIC A * 12**

CALIFORNIA _____
AMF Financial, Inc.
Mr. William A. Temple, Pres.
9910-D Mira Mesa Blvd.
San Diego, CA 92131
(619) 695-0233
A * 12**

Branch Office
Atalanta Investment Co., Inc.
Mr. Alan W. Livingston, Pres.
141 El Camino Dr.
Los Angeles, CA 90212
(213) 273-1730
D * 1,2,5,6,7,8**
(Main office in NY)

Bay Venture Group
Mr. William Chandler, Gen. Ptnr.
One Embarcadero Ctr., Ste. 3303
San Francisco, CA 94111
(415) 989-7680
B * 1,6,8**

Beverly Glen Venture Capital
Mr. Herman Jacobs, Pres.
1964 Westwood Blvd., Ste. 450
Los Angeles, CA 90025
(213) 550-0431
B * 5,12

Brantman Capital Corp.
Mr. W. T. Brantman, Pres.
P.O. Box 877
Tiburon, CA 94920
(415) 435-4747
A * 1,4,5,6,8,9,10,11,12**

Brentwood Associates
Mr. Timothy Pennington, Gen.
    Ptnr.
11661 San Vicente Blvd., Ste. 707
Los Angeles, CA 90049
(213) 826-6581
E * 1,8**

Business Equity and Development
   Corp.
Mr. Ricardo J. Olivarez, Pres.
1411 W. Olympic Blvd.
Ste. 200
Los Angeles CA 90015
(213) 385-0351
MESBIC B *** 1,5,6,12

Cal Fed Venture Capital Corp.
Ms. Anna Henry, Pres.
5670 Wilshire Blvd., Ste. 2135
Los Angeles, CA 90036
(213) 932-4077
C *** 1,5,6,7,8,9,10,12

California Capital Investors, Ltd
Mr. Arthur Bernstein, Gen. Ptnr.
11812 San Vicente Blvd.
Los Angeles, CA 90049
(213) 820-7222
B *** 1,5,6,11,12

California Partners
Mr. Alan R. Brudos, Sec.
3000 Sand Hill Rd.
Bldg. 2, Ste. 260
Menlo Park, CA 94025
(415) 854-1555
A *** 1,8

CFB Venture Capital Corp.
Mr. Piet Westerbeek III, CFO
530 B St., 2nd Fl.
San Diego, CA 92101
(619) 230-3304
C * 1,6,8

Charterway Investment Corp.
Mr. Harold Chuang, Pres.
222 S. Hill St., Ste. 800
Los Angeles, CA 90012
(213) 687-8534
B *** 2,4,5,7,9

Churchill International Oceanic
   Capital Corp.
Mr. Robert C. Weeks, Pres.
545 Middlefield Rd.
Ste. 160
Menlo Park, CA 94025
(415) 328-4401
C * 1,5,8

Churchill International Pan American Investment Co.
Mr. Robert C. Weeks, Mng. Dir.
545 Middlefield Rd., Ste. 160
Menlo Park, CA 94025
(415) 328-4401
D * 1,5,8,

Branch Office
Citicorp Venture Capital, Ltd.
Mr. Peter G. Gerry, Pres.
44 Montgomery St.
San Francisco, CA 94104
(415) 954-1154
E *** 1,3,5,6,8,10,11
(Main office in NY)

City Ventures, Inc.
Mr. Neill B. Lawton, Pres.
404 N. Roxbury Dr., Ste. 800
Beverly Hills, CA 90210
(213) 550-0416
D *** 1,5,6,8,12

Continental Investors, Inc.
Mr. Lac Thantrong, Pres.
8781 Seaspray Dr.
Huntington Beach, CA 92646
(714) 964-5207
MESBIC B * 4,6,9,10,12

Branch Office
Cornell Capital Corp.
Mr. Alan B. Newman
2049 Century Park E., 12th Fl.
Century City, CA 90067
(213) 277-7993
D *** 4,9,12
(Main office in NY)

Crocker Ventures, Inc.
Mr. Jordan Burkart, VP
One Montgomery St.
San Francisco, CA 94104
(415) 983-3636
A * 12

Crosspoint Investment Corp.
Mr. Max S. Simpson, Pres.
1015 Corporation Way
PO Box 10101
Palo Alto, CA 94303
(415) 964-3545
B *** 1,5,6,

Developers Equity Capital Corp.
Mr. Larry Sade, Pres.
9201 Wilshire Blvd., Ste. 204
Beverly Hills, CA 90210
(213) 278-3611
C * 2,4,6

Enterprise Venture Capital Corp.
Mr. Ernest de la Ossa, Pres.
1922 The Alameda, Ste. 306
San Jose, CA 95126
(408) 249-3507
B * 1,4,5,6,8,10,12

Equitable Capital Corp.
Mr. John C. Lee, Pres.
855 Sansome St., Ste. 200
San Francisco, CA 94111
(415) 434-4114
MESBIC B * 1,2,11,12

First Interstate Capital
Mr. David B. Jones, Pres.
515 S. Figueroa, Ste. 1900
Los Angeles, CA 90071
(213) 622-1922
E *** 12

First SBIC of California
Mr. Timothy Hay, Pres.
Mr. Gregory Forrest, Sr. VP
Mr. Michael Cronin, VP
Mr. Brian Jones, VP
Mr. James McElwee, VP
4000 MacArthur Blvd., Ste. 950
Newport Beach, CA 92660
(714) 754-4780
E *** 12

Branch Office
First SBIC of California
Mr. John D. Padgett, VP
Mr. Tony Stevens, VP
25th Fl., H25-4
333 S. Hope St.
Los Angeles, CA 90071
(213) 613-5215
E *** 12

Glover Capital Corp.
Mr. J. David Ray, Pres.
1000 E. Dominquez St.
Carson, CA 90746
(213) 532-6187
A * 1,3,6,7,8,12

Hamco Capital
Mr. William R. Hambrecht, Pres.
235 Montgomery St.
San Francisco, CA 94104
(415) 986-5500
B *** 1,6,8

HUB Enterprises, Ltd.
Mr. Jack M. Atkin, Gen. Mgr.
5878 Doyle St.
Emeryville, CA 94608
(415) 428-2181
MESBIC A * 2,5,9,12

Imperial Ventures, Inc.
Mr. Donald B. Prell, Pres.
9920 S. LaCienega Blvd.
14th Floor
Inglewood, CA 90301
(213) 417-5888
A * 12

Ivanhoe Venture Cap., Ltd.
Brigadier Gen. Alan R. Toffler,
   Managing Partner
737 Pearl St., Ste. 201
La Jolla, CA 92037
(619) 454-8882
C *** 1,5,6,12

Lasung Investment & Finance Co.
Mr. Jung Su Lee, Pres.
3600 Wilshire Blvd., Ste. 1410
Los Angeles, CA 90010
(213) 384-7548
MESBIC B * 9,12

Latigo Capital Partners
Mr. Donald Peterson, Gen. Ptnr.
23410 Civic Ctr. Way, Ste. E-2
Malibu, CA 90265
(213) 456-5054
C * 1,6,8

Marwit Capital Corp.
Mr. Martin Witte, Pres.
180 Newport Ctr. Dr., Ste. 200
Newport Beach, CA 92660
(714) 640-6234
D * 1,2,4,6,8,12**

MCA New Ventures, Inc.
Mr. W. Roderick Hamilton, Pres.
100 Universal City Pl.
Universal City, CA 91608
(213) 508-2933
MESBIC C * 1,12

Merrill, Pickard, Anderson & Eyre
Mr. Steven L. Merrill, Mng. Ptnr.
Two Palo Alto Sq., Ste. 425
Palo Alto, CA 94306
(415) 856-8880
E * 1,6,8**

Metropolitan Venture Co.
Mr. Rudolph J. Lowy, Chmn.
8383 Wilshire Blvd., Ste. 360
Beverly Hills, CA 90211
(213) 651-2175
B * 1,2,6,8**

Myriad Capital, Inc.
Mr. Kuo-Hung Chen, Sec.
8820 S. Sepulveda Blvd., Ste. 204
Los Angeles, CA 90045
(213) 641-7936
MESBIC E * 12

Branch Office
Nelson Capital Corp.
Mr. Norman Tulchin, Chmn.
1901 Ave. of the Stars, Ste. 584
Los Angeles, CA 90067
(213) 556-1944
E * 12
(Main Office in NY)

New West Ventures
Mr. Tim Haidinger, Pres.
180 Newport Ctr. Dr., Ste. 200
Newport Beach, CA 92660
(714) 759-0884
E * 1,5,6,9,11,12**

Opportunity Capital Corp.
Mr. J. Peter Thompson, Pres.
50 California St., Ste. 2505
San Francisco, CA 94111
(415) 421-5935
MESBIC B * 1,5,11**

PCF Venture Capital Corporation
Mr. Miguel L. Guerrero, Pres.
3420 E. Third Ave., Ste. 200
Foster City, CA 94404
(415) 571-5411
B * 1,6

San Joaquin Capital Corp.
Mr. Chester W. Troudy, Pres.
PO Box 2538
1675 Chester Ave., Ste. 330
Bakersfield, CA 93303
(805) 323-7581
B * 5,8,9,12**

San Jose SBIC, Inc.
Mr. Robert T. Murphy, Pres.
100 Park Ctr. Pl., Ste. 427
San Jose, CA 95113
(408) 293-8052/7708
B * 1,5,6,8,12

Seaport Ventures, Inc.
Mr. Michael Stolper, Pres.
770 B St., Ste. 420
San Diego, CA 92101
(619) 232-4069
B * 12**

Space Ventures, Inc.
Mr. Leslie R. Brewer, Pres.
3931 MacArthur Blvd., Ste. 212
Newport Beach, CA 92660
(714) 851-0855
MESBIC C * 12**

Union Venture Corp.
Mr. Brent T. Rider, Pres.
445 S. Figueroa St.
Los Angeles, CA 90071
(213) 236-6292
E * 1,5,6,8,12**

Unity Capital Corp.
Mr. Frank W. Owen, Pres.
4343 Morena Blvd., Ste. 3A
San Diego, CA 92117
(619) 275-6030
MESBIC B * 1,2,8,12**

Vista Capital Corp.
Mr. Fred J. Howden, Jr., Chmn.
701 "B" St., Ste. 760
San Diego, CA 92101
(619) 236-1900
D * 1,3,5,6,8,12**

Wells Fargo Equity Corp.
Mr. Michael F. Park, Sr. VP
Mr. Louis Gerken, VP
One Embarcadero Ctr., Ste. 1814
San Francisco, CA 94111
(415) 396-3291
D * 12**

Wesco Capital, Ltd.
Mr. Peter J. Madigan, Gen. Ptnr.
3471 Via Lido, Ste. 204
Newport Beach, CA 92663
(714) 673-4733
B * 12**

Westamco Investment Co.
Mr. Leonard G. Muskin, Pres.
8929 Wilshire Blvd., Ste. 400
Beverly Hills, CA 90211
(213) 652-8288
B * 2,4,6,7,9,12

Branch Office
Wood River Capital Corp.
3000 Sand Hill Rd., Ste. 280
Menlo Park, CA 94025
(415) 854-7145
C * 1,5,6,**
(Main Office in NY)

Yosemite Capital Investment
Mr. J. Horace Hampton, Pres.
448 Fresno St.
Fresno, CA 93706
(209) 485-2431
MESBIC A * 12**

COLORADO
Colorado Growth Capital, Inc.
Mr. Nicholas Davis, Chmn./Pres.
1600 Broadway, Ste. 2125
Denver, CO 80202
(303) 629-0205
B * 5,12**

Enervest, Inc.
Mr. Mark Kimmel, Pres.
7000 E. Bellevue Ave., Ste. 310
Englewood, CO 80111
(303) 771-9650
D * 1,5,6,8**

Mile Hi SBIC
Mr. Joseph Chavez, Inv. Adv.
1355 S. Colorado Blvd., Ste. 400
Denver, CO 80222
(303) 830-0087
MESBIC B * 1,5,6,8,12**

Branch Office
Norwest Venture Cap. Mgmt., Inc.
Mr. Larry R. Wonnacott, V.P.
Mr. Mark Dubovy, V.P.
1801 California St., Ste. 585
City Center Four
Denver, CO 80202
(303) 297-0537
E * 1,5,8**
(Main Office in MN)

CONNECTICUT
Asset Capital & Management Corp.
Mr. Robert N. Nolting, VP
608 Ferry Blvd.
Stratford, CT 06497
(203) 375-0299
C ** 1,6

Capital Resource Co. of Connecticut
Mr. I. Martin Fierberg, Ptnr.
699 Bloomfield Ave.
Bloomfield, CT 06002
(203) 243-1114
B * 12

The First Connecticut SBIC
Mr. James Breiner, Chmn.
Mr. David Engelson, Pres.
177 State St.
Bridgeport, CT 06604
(203) 366-4726
D * 1,2,4,5,6,9,12

Marcon Capital Corp.
Mr. Martin Cohen, Pres.
49 Riverside Ave.
Westport, CT 06880
(203) 226-7751
A ** 1,9,10

Northeastern Capital Corp.
Mr. Louis W. Mingione, VP
310 Main St.
East Haven, CT 06512
(203) 469-7901
A * 12

Regional Financial Enterprises
Mr. Robert M. Williams, Chmn.
51 Pine St.
New Canaan, CT 06840
(203) 966-2800
E * 1,5,6,8,9,12**

SBIC of Connecticut
Mr. Kenneth F. Zarrilli, Pres.
1115 Main St., Rm. 610
Bridgeport, CT 06604
(203) 367-3282
A ** 12

DISTRICT OF COLUMBIA _____
Allied Capital Corp.
Mr. George C. Williams, Pres.
Mr. David Gladstone, Exec. VP
1625 I St., NW. Ste. 603
Washington, DC 20006
(202) 331-1112
C * 12**

Broadcast Capital, Inc.
Mr. John E. Oxendine, Pres.
1771 N St., NW, Ste. 420
Washington, DC 20036
(202) 293-3575
MESBIC C * 1**

Capital Investment Co. of Wash.
Mr. John Katkish, Pres.
1208—30th St., NW
Washington, DC 20007
(202) 333-2281
A * 2,6

Branch Office
Continental Investors, Inc.
Mr. Lac Thantrong, Pres.
2020 K Street, NW, Ste. 350
Washington, DC 20006
(202) 466-3709
MESBIC B * 4,6,9,10,12
(Main Office in CA)

Fulcrum Venture Cap. Corp.
Mr. Divakar Kamath, VP
2021 K St., NW, Ste. 301
Washington, DC 20006
(202) 833-9590
MESBIC B * 1,5,6,9,11,12**

Snycom Capital Corp.
Mr. Herbert P. Wilkins, Pres.
1625 I St., NW, Ste. 412
Washington, DC 20006
(202) 293-9428
MESBIC C ***1

FLORIDA _____
Branch Office
Allied Capital Corp.
Mr. G. Cabell Williams, Asst. VP
One Financial Pl., Ste. 1614
Ft. Lauderdale, FL 33394
(305) 763-8484
C * 12**
(Main Office in DC)

Caribank Capital Corp.
Mr. Michael E. Chaney, Pres.
255 E. Dania Beach Blvd.
Dania, FL 33004
(305) 925-2211/ext. 400
C * 1,3,5,6,8**

CUBICO, Ltd.
Mr. Anthony G. Marina, Pres.
7425 NW 79th St.
Miami, FL 33166
(305) 885-8881
MESBIC B * 12

First American Investment Corp.
Mr. Joseph N. Hardin, Jr., Pres.
3250 Mary St., Ste. 308
Coconut Grove, FL 33133
(305) 441-0881
C * 2,8,12**

First Tampa Capital Corp.
Mr. Thomas L. du Pont, Pres.
4600 N. Dale Mabry Hwy.
Tampa, FL 33614
(813) 879-4058
B * 12**

Ideal Financial Corp.
Mr. Mario Pineda, Gen. Mgr.
85 Grand Canal Dr., Ste. 105
Miami, FL 33144
(305) 264-1468
MESBIC B * 12

J & D Capital Corp.
Mr. Jack Carmel, Pres.
12747 Biscayne Blvd.
North Miami, FL 33181
(305) 893-0303
B * 5,9,12

Mansfield Capital Corp.
Mr. Stephen H. Farrington, Pres.
2900 14th St., N
Naples, FL 33940
(813) 263-3660
A * 12

Market Capital Corp.
Mr. E. E. Eads, Pres.
PO Box 22667
Tampa, FL 33622
(813) 248-5781
A * 2,9

Massachusetts Capital Corp.
Ms. Mary Helen Blakeslee, Pres.
3250 Mary St., Ste. 308
Coconut Grove, FL 33133
(305) 441-0924
C * 1,5,6,8

Safeco Capital, Inc.
Dr. Rene J. Leonard, Pres.
835 SW 37th Ave.
Miami, FL 33135
(305) 443-7953
MESBIC B * 12**

Servico Capital Corp.
Mr. Gary O. Marino, Pres.
1601 Belvedere Rd., Ste. 201
West Palm Beach, FL 33406
(305) 689-4906
A * 1,4,5,11

Small Business Assistance Corp. of
    Panama City, FL
Mr. Charles S. Smith, Pres.
2612 W. 15th St., PO Box 1627
Panama City, FL 32401
(904) 785-9577
C * 12

Southeast Venture Capital, Inc.
Mr. C. L. Hofmann, Pres.
100 S. Biscayne Blvd.
Miami, FL 33131
(305) 577-4680
D * 1,5,6,8,11,12**

Branch Office
Threshold Ventures, Inc.
Mr. T. Denny Sanford, Chmn.
2566D McMullen Booth Rd.
Clearwater, FL 33519
(813) 797-7697
B * 1,5,6,9,12**
(Main Office in MN)

Trans Florida Capital Corp.
Mr. Alex Echevarria, VP
1450 Avenida Madruga, #402
Coral Gables, FL 33146
(305) 665-5489
MESBIC B * 12

Universal Financial Services, Inc.
Mr. Norman Zipkin, Pres.
225 NE 35th St., Ste. B
Miami, FL 33137
(305) 573-6326
MESBIC B * 12

Venture Group, Inc.
Mr. Ellis W. Hitzing, Pres.
5433 Buffalo Ave.
Jacksonville, FL 32208
(904) 355-6265
MESBIC A * 9

Venture Opportunities Corp.
Mr. A. Fred March, Pres.
444 Brickell Ave., Ste. 930
Miami, FL 33131
(305) 358-0359
MESBIC B * 1,2,5,12**

Verde Capital Corp.
Mr. Jose Dearing, Pres.
6701 Sunset Dr., Ste. 104
South Miami, FL 33143
(305) 666-8789
MESBIC B * 2,5,9,12

Western Financial Cap. Corp.
Dr. Fredric M. Rosemore, Pres.
12550 Biscayne Blvd., Ste. 406
N. Miami, FL 33181
(305) 891-0823
C ** 6,12

GEORGIA _____
Affiliated Investment Fund, Ltd.
Mr. Samuel Weissman, Pres.
2225 Shurfine Dr.
College Park, GA 30337
(404) 766-0221
A ** 9

Central Georgia Capital Funding
    Corp.
Mr. H. Edward Downey, Pres.
P.O. Box 218
Ellenwood, GA 30349
(404) 474-2892
MESBIC B * 12

Mighty Capital Corp.
Mr. Gary Korynoski, VP/Gen. Mgr.
50 Technology Park
Atlanta—Ste. 100
Norcross, GA 30092
(404) 448-2232
A * 9,10

Sunbelt Funding Corp.
Mr. Charles H. Jones, Pres.
PO Box 7006
Macon, GA 31298
(912) 474-5137
MESBIC A * 12

HAWAII _____
Pacific Venture Capital, Ltd.
Mr. Dexter J. Taniguchi, Pres.
1405 N. King St., Ste. 302
Honolulu, HI 96817
(808) 847-6502
MESBIC A * 12**

IDAHO _____
First Idaho Venture Capital Corp.
Mr. Ron Twilegar, Pres.
900 W. Washington
Boise, ID 83701
(208) 345-3460
B * 12**

ILLINOIS _____
Abbott Capital Corp.
Mr. Richard E. Lassar, Pres.
9933 Lawler Ave., Ste. 125
Skokie, IL 60077
(312) 982-0404
A * 1,6,10**

Alpha Capital Corp.
Mr. Andrew H. Kalnow, Pres.
3 First National Pl. Ste. 1400
Chicago, IL 60602
(312) 372-1556
B * 12**

Business Ventures, Inc.
Mr. Milton Lefton, Pres.
20 N. Wacker Dr., Ste. 550
Chicago, IL 60606
(312) 346-1580
A * 12

CEDCO Capital Corp.
Mr. J. C. Taylor, VP/Gen. Mgr.
180 N. Michigan Ave., Ste. 333
Chicago, IL 60601
(312) 984-5971
MESBIC A * 12

Chicago Community Ventures Inc.
Ms. Phyllis George, Pres.
108 N. State St., Ste. 902
Chicago, IL 60602
(312) 726-6084
MESBIC B * 4,5,12**

Combined Opportunities, Inc.
Mr. E. Patric Jones, Pres.
1525 E. 53rd St.
Chicago, IL 60615
(312) 752-5355
MESBIC B * 12

Continental Illinois Venture Corp.
Mr. John L. Hines, Pres.
231 S. LaSalle St.
Chicago, IL 60697
(312) 828-8021
E * 1,5,6,7,8,9,10**

First Capital Corp. of Chicago
Mr. John A. Canning, Jr., Pres.
One First National Pl., Ste. 2628
Chicago, IL 60670
(312) 732-5400
E * 12**

Frontenac Capital Corp.
Mr. David A. R. Dullum, Pres.
208 S. LaSalle St., Rm. 1900
Chicago, IL 60604
(312) 368-0044
C * 1,5,6,8,12**

FUND'S Inc.
Mr. William R. Breihan, Gen. Mgr.
1930 George St.
Melrose Park, IL 60068
(312) 921-5100
A * 6,9

Golder, Thoma & Cressey
Mr. Stanley C. Golder, Gen. Ptnr.
120 S. LaSalle St., Ste. 630
Chicago, IL 60603
(312) 853-3322
D * 1,5,6,11,12**

Heizer Corp.
Mr. E. F. Heizer, Jr., Chmn./Pres.
20 N. Wacker Dr., Ste. 4100
Chicago, IL 60606
(312) 641-2200
E * 1,4,5,6,7,8,9,12**

Mesirow Capital Corp.
Mr. James C. Tyree, Exec. VP
135 S. LaSalle St., Ste. 3713
Chicago, IL 60603
(312) 443-5757
E * 1,4,5,6,7,9,10,11,12**

Branch Office
Nelson Capital Corp.
Mr. Irwin B. Nelson, Pres.
8550 W. Bryn Mawr Ave., Ste. 515
Chicago, IL 60631
(312) 693-5990
E * 12
(Main Office in NY)

Tower Ventures, Inc.
Mr. James M. Troka, Pres.
Sears Tower, BSC 43-50
Chicago, IL 60684
(312) 875-0583
MESBIC B * 12

The Urban Fund of Illinois, Inc.
Mr. E. Patric Jones, Pres.
1525 E. 53rd St.
Chicago, IL 60615
(312) 752-5355
MESBIC B * 12

Walnut Capital Corp.
Mr. Burton W. Kanter, Chmn.
Three First Nat'l. Pl., 22nd Fl.
Chicago, IL 60602
(312) 269-1732
C * 12**
(Branch Office in NY)

INDIANA _____
First Indiana Equity Group
Mr. Samuel Sutphin
20 N. Meridian St., 3rd Fl.
Indianapolis, IN 46240
(317) 635-4551
B * **12**

Heritage Venture Group, Inc.
Mr. Arthur A. Angotti, Pres.
One Indiana Sq., Ste. 2400
Indianapolis, IN 46204
(317) 635-5696
D *** **1,5,6,**

Mt. Vernon Venture Capital Co.
Mr. Thomas Grande, Gen. Mgr.
9102 N Meridian St.
P.O. Box 40177
Indianapolis, IN 46240
(317) 846-5106
B * **12**

White River Capital Corp.
Mr. John H. Cragoe, Pres.
Mr. David J. Blair, VP
500 Washington St.
Columbus, IN 47201
(812) 376-1759
B *** **1,5,6,8,9,10,11,12**

IOWA _____
R. W. Allsop Capital Corp.
Mr. Robert W. Allsop, Pres.
Mr. Paul D. Rhines, Exec. VP
2750 First Ave., NE
Ste. 210
Cedar Rapids, IA 52402
(319) 363-8971
C * **1,5,6,12**

MorAmerica Capital Corp.
Mr. Jerry M. Burrows, Pres.
300 American Bldg.
Cedar Rapids, IA 52401
(319) 363-8249
D *** **1,5,6,9,12**

KANSAS _____
Branch Office
R. W. Allsop Capital Corp.
Mr. Larry C. Maddox, VP
35 Corporate Woods
Ste. 244
9101 W. 110th St.
Overland Park, KS 66210
(913) 642-4719
C ** **1,5,6,12**
(Main office in Iowa)

Kansas Venture Capital, Inc.
Mr. George L. Doak, Pres.
First Nat'l Bank Tower
Ste. 1030
One Townsite Pl.
Topeka, KS 66603
(913) 233-1368
B *** **5**

KENTUCKY _____
Blackburn-Sanford Venture Capital
    Corp.
Mr. Charles Arensberg, Gen. Mgr.
3120 First National Tower
Louisville, KY 40202
(502) 585-9612
C *** **1,4,5,9,11,12**

Equal Opportunity Finance, Inc.
Mr. Frank P. Justice, Pres.
420 Hurstbourne Ln., Ste. 201
Louisville, KY 40222
(502) 423-1943
MESBIC B * **12**

Financial Opportunities, Inc.
Mr. Gary F. Duerr, Gen. Mgr.
981 S. Third St.
Louisville, KY 40203
(502) 584-1281
A * **12**

Mountain Ventures, Inc.
Mr. Frederick Beste III, Pres.
Box 628, 911 N. Main St.
London, KY 40741
(606) 878-6635
D *** **1,3,5,6,7,8,11,12**

LOUISIANA _____
Business Capital Corp.
Mr. David R. Burrus, Pres.
PO Drawer 57329
New Orleans, LA 70157
(504) 581-4002
MESBIC E * 2,4,12

Caddo Capital Corp.
Mr. Thomas L. Young, Jr., Pres.
3010 Knight St., Ste. 240
Shreveport, LA 71105
(318) 869-1689
A * 6,8**

Capital Equity Corp.
Mr. Arthur Mitchell, Sr. VP
1885 Wooddale Blvd.
Baton Rouge, LA 70806
(504) 924-9205
B * 6,12**

Commercial Capital, Inc.
Mr. A. R. Blossman, Sr., Treas.
200 Belle Terre Blvd.
Covington, LA 70433
(504) 892-4921
A * 12

Dixie Business Investment Co.
Mr. L. Wayne Baker, Pres.
PO Box 588
Lake Providence, LA 71254
(318) 559-1558
A * 12

EDICT Investment Corp.
Mr. Gregory G. Johnson, Exec. VP
2908 S. Carrollton Ave.
New Orleans, LA 70118
(504) 861-2364
MESBIC A ** 12

First Southern Capital Corp.
Mr. John H. Crabtree, Pres.
6161 Perkins Rd., Ste. 2-C
Baton Rouge, LA 70808
(504) 769-3004
D * 1,3,5,6,8,11,12

Louisiana Equity Capital Corp.
Mr. Melvin L. Rambin, Pres.
451 Florida St.
Baton Rouge, LA 70801
(504) 389-4421
C ** 5,9,10

Savings Venture Capital Corp.
Mr. David R. Dixon, Exec. VP
6001 Financial Pl.
Shreveport, LA 71130
(318) 687-8996
B ** 12

Walnut Street Capital Co.
Mr. William D. Humphries,
    Managing General Partner
702 Cotton Exchange Bldg.
New Orleans, LA 70130
(504) 525-2112
D * 12**

MAINE _____
Maine Capital Corp.
Mr. David M. Coit, Exec. VP
70 Center St.
Portland, ME 04101
(207) 772-1001
B * 12**

MARYLAND _____
Albright Venture Capital, Inc.
Mr. William A. Albright, Pres.
8005 Rappahannock Ave.
Jessup, MD 20794
(301) 799-7935
MESBIC B ** 2,4,5,6,9,10,12

Greater Washington Investors, Inc.
Mr. Don A. Christensen, Pres.
5454 Wisconsin Ave., Ste. 1565
Chevy Chase, MD 20815
(301) 656-0626
D * 1,5,6,8,12**

Suburban Capital Corp.
Mr. Henry P. Linsert, Jr., Pres.
6610 Rockledge Dr.
Bethesda, MD 20817
(301) 493-7025
D * 1,6,8,12**

MASSACHUSETTS _____
Advent III Capital Company
Mr. David D. Croll, Mng. Ptnr.
45 Milk St.
Boston, MA 02109
(617) 338-0800
E *1,3,5,6,8,12

Advent IV Capital Company
Mr. David D. Croll, Mng. Ptnr.
45 Milk St.
Boston, MA 02109
(617) 338-0800
E * 1,3,5,6,8,12

Alta Capital Corp.
Mr. William P. Egan, Pres.
One Post Office Sq. Ste. 3800
Boston, MA 02109
(617) 482-8020
B *** 1,6,8,12

Atlas Capital Corp.
Mr. Herbert Carver, Treas.
55 Court St., Ste. 200
Boston, MA 02108
(617) 482-1218
B ** 12

Branch Office
Boston Hambro Capital Co.
Mr. Robert Sherman, VP
One Boston Pl., Ste. 723
Boston, MA 02106
(617) 722-7055
D *** 1,5,6,9,12
(Main Office in NY)

Chestnut Capital Corp.
Mr. David D. Croll, Chmn/CEO
45 Milk St.
Boston, MA 02109
(617) 338-0800
E * 1,3,5,6,8,12

Branch Office
Churchill International
    Pan American Investment Co.
Dr. Terry K. Dorsey, Inv. Dir.
Nine Riverside Rd.
Weston, MA 02193
(617) 893-6555
D * 1,5,8
(Main Office in CA)

Devonshire Capital Company
Mr. David D. Croll, Mng. Ptnr.
45 Milk St.
Boston, MA 02109
(617) 338-0800
E * 1,3,5,6,8,12

First Capital Corp. of Boston
Mr. Bruce G. Rossiter, Pres.
100 Federal St.
Boston, MA 02110
(617) 434-2442
D *** 5,6,8,12

Branch Office
First Capital Corp. of Chicago
Mr. Kevin M. McCafferty, VP
200 Claredon St.
Boston, MA 02116
(617) 247-4856
E *** 1,6,8,9
(Main Office in IL)

Massachusetts Venture Capital
    Corp.
Ms. Irene E. Sax
59 Temple Pl.
Boston, MA 02111
(617) 426-0208
MESBIC B * 12

New England Capital Corp.
Mr. Z. David Patterson, Exec. VP
One Washington Mall
Boston, MA 02108
(617) 722-6400
C *** 1,5,6

New England MESBIC, Inc.
Dr. Jeff Yeh, Gen. Mgr.
50 Kearney Rd., Ste. 3
Needham, MA 02194
(617) 449-2066
MESBIC A * 2,4,5,6,8,9,12

Orange Nassau Capital Corp.
Mr. Joost E. Tjaden, Pres.
One Post Office Sq., Ste. 1760
Boston, MA 02109
(617) 451-6220
C * 1,3,5,6,8,9,12**

Transatlantic Capital Corp.
Mr. Bayard Henry, Pres.
Mr. John O. Flender, VP/Treas.
24 Federal St.
Boston, MA 02110
(617) 482-0015
C * 1,5,6,8,10,11,12**

UST Capital Corp.
Mr. Richard Kohn, VP
30 Court St.
Boston, MA 02108
(617) 726-7137
B * 1,6,8,12**

Worcester Capital Corp.
Mr. W. Kenneth Kidd, VP
446 Main St.
Worcester, MA 01608
(617) 793-4508
A * 1,6,8**

MICHIGAN _____
Comerica Capital Corp.
Mr. John D. Berkaw, Pres.
243 W. Congress, PO Box 59
Detroit, MI 48231
(313) 222-3907
C * 1,5,6,8,12**

Detroit Metropolitan SBIC
Ms. Charlotte Doud
150 Michigan Ave.
Detroit, MI 48226
(313) 964-4000
B * 12

Doan Resources Corp.
Mr. Ian R. N. Bund, Pres.
333 E. Main St., PO Box 1431
Midland, MI 48640
(517) 631-2471
D * 1,5,6,8**

Federated Capital Corp.
Mr. Jack Takala, VP Fin.
20000 W. Twelve Mile Rd.
Southfield, MI 48076
(313) 557-9100
B * 12

Metro-Detroit Investment Co.
Mr. William J. Fowler, Pres.
30777 Northwestern, Ste. 300
Farmington Hills, MI 48018
(313) 851-6300
MESBIC A ** 9

Michigan Cap. & Service, Inc.
Mr. Joseph F. Conway, Pres.
440 City Ctr. Bldg.
Ann Arbor, MI 48104
(313) 663-0702
D * 1,5,6,8,12

Michigan Tech Capital Corp.
Mr. Edward J. Koepel, Pres.
PO Box 20
Hubbell, MI 49934
(906) 487-2643
A * 3,5,8

Motor Enterprises, Inc.
Mr. James Kobus, Mgr.
3044 W. Grand Blvd., Rm 13-152
Detroit, MI 48202
(313) 556-4273
MESBIC B ** 5,12

Mutual Investment Co., Inc.
Mr. Timothy J. Taylor, Treas.
18501 W. Ten Mile Rd.
Southfield, MI 48075
(313) 559-5210
MESBIC B * 9

Tyler Refrigeration Cap. Corp.
Mr. Gary J. Slock, Pres.
1329 Lake St.
Niles, MI 49120
(616) 683-1610
A * 10

MINNESOTA

Control Data Capital Corp.
Mr. W. D. Anderson, Sec./Treas.
3600 W. 78th., 7th Fl.
Minneapolis, MN 55435
(612) 921-4391
C * 1,5,6,12

Eagle Ventures, Inc.
Mr. Lawrence L. Horsch, Pres.
700 Soo Line Bldg.
Minneapolis, MN 55402
(612) 339-9693
B *** 1,6,8

FBS Venture Capital Co.
Mr. Donald Soukup, Mng. Agent
7515 Wayzata Blvd.
Minneapolis, MN 55426
(612) 544-2754
D *** 1,5,6,8

First Midwest Capital Corp.
Mr. Alan K. Ruvelson, Chmn.
Mr. Thomas M. Neitge, Pres.
1010 Plymouth Bldg.
12 S. 6th St.
Minneapolis, MN 55402
(612) 339-9391
C *** 1,5,6,7,8,9,10,12

Northland Capital Corp.
Mr. George G. Barnum, Jr., Pres.
613 Missabe Bldg.
277 W. 1st St.
Duluth, MN 55802
(218) 722-0545
B *** 12

North Star Ventures, Inc.
Mr. Terrence W. Glarner, Pres.
1501 First Bank Place W.
Minneapolis, MN 55402
(612) 333-1133
D *** 1,5,6,7,8,12

Norwest Growth Fund, Inc.
Mr. Robert F. Zicarelli, Chmn.
1730 Midwest Plaza Bldg.
801 Nicollet Mall
Minneapolis, MN 55402
(612) 372-8770
E *** 1,6,8,12

P. R. Peterson Venture Capital
  Corp.
Mr. P. R. Peterson, Pres.
7301 Washington Ave. S.
Edina, MN 55435
(612) 941-8282
A * 5,6,8

Retailers Growth Fund, Inc.
Mr. Cornell L. Moore, Pres.
5100 Gamble Dr., Ste. 380
Minneapolis, MN 55416
(612) 546-8989
A ** 9,11,12

Shared Ventures, Inc.
Mr. Howard Weiner, Pres.
6550 York Ave. S., Ste. 419
Edina, MN 55435
(612) 925-3411
B *** 12

Threshold Ventures, Inc.
Mr. Michael J. Meyer, Pres.
430 Oak Grove St., Ste. 303
Minneapolis, MN 55403
(612) 874-7199
B *** 1,5,6,9,12

MISSISSIPPI

Invesat Capital Corp.
Mr. J. Thomas Noojin, Pres.
162 E. Amite St., Ste. 204
PO Box 3288
Jackson, MS 39207
(601) 969-3242
D *** 12

Vicksburg SBIC
Mr. David L. May, Pres.
PO Box 1240
302 First National Bank Bldg.
Vicksburg, MS 39180
(601) 636-4762
A * 12

MISSOURI _____

Branch Office
R. W. Allsop Capital Corp.
Mr. Robert L. Kuk, VP
111 Westport Plaza, Ste. 600
St. Louis, MO 63146
(314) 434-1688
C * 1,5,6,12**
(Main Office in Iowa)

Bankers Capital Corp.
Mr. Raymond E. Glasnapp, Pres.
4049 Pennsylvania Ave., Ste. 304
Kansas City, MO 64111
(816) 531-1600
A * 12

Capital For Business, Inc.
Mr. James Hebenstreit, Pres.
720 Main St.
Executive Plaza Bldg.
Kansas City, MO 64105
(816) 234-2381
D * 5,12**

Branch Office
Capital For Business, Inc.
Mr. James Hebenstreit, Pres.
7931 Forsyth Blvd.
St. Louis, MO 63105
(314) 725-0900
D * 5,12**

Intercapco West, Inc.
Mr. Thomas E. Phelps, Pres.
7800 Bonhomme Ave.
St. Louis, MO 63105
(314) 863-0600
A * 12**

Branch Office:
MorAmerica Capital Corp.
Mr. Kevin F. Mullane, VP
Ste. 2724—Commerce Tower
911 Main St.
Kansas City, MO 64105
(816) 842-0114
D * 1,5,6,9,12**
(Main Office in Iowa)

MONTANA _____
Rocky Mountain Ventures, Ltd.
Mr. James H. Koessler, Pres.
315 Securities Bldg.
Billings, MT 59101
(406) 256-1984
D * 12

NEBRASKA _____
Community Equity Corp, of NE
Mr. Herbert M. Patten, Sec.
6421 Ames Ave.
Omaha, NE 68104
(402) 455-7722
MESBIC A ** 12

NEVADA _____
United Capital Corp. of Illinois
Mr. Seth L. Atwood, Pres.
P.O. Box 109, 2001 Foothill Rd.
Genoa, NV 89411
(702) 782-5114
C * 1,4,5,12

NEW HAMPSHIRE _____
Granite State Capital, Inc.
Mr. Stuart D. Pompian, Mng. Dir.
10 Fort Eddy Rd.
Concord, NH 03301
(603) 228-9090
B * 12**

Hampshire Capital Corp.
Mr. Philip G. Baker, Pres.
One Middle St., PO Box 468
Portsmouth, NH 03801
(602) 431-1415
A * 12**

NEW JERSEY _____
Engle Investment Co.
Mr. Murray Hendel, Pres.
35 Essex St.
Hackensack, NJ 07601
(201) 489-3583
B * 12

ESLO Capital Corp.
Mr. Ronald Lokos, CEO
485 Morris Ave.
Springfield, NJ 07081
(201) 467-2545
A * 12

First Princeton Capital Corp.
Mr. S. Lawrence Goldstein, Pres.
227 Hamburg Tpke.
Pompton Lakes, NJ 07442
(201) 831-0330
D * 1,2,5,9,10,11,12**

Loyd Capital Corp.
Mr. Solomon T. Scharf, Pres.
77 State Hghwy. 5
P.O. Box 180
Edgewater, NJ 07020
(201) 947-6000
C ** 2,4,5,9,10,12

Monmouth Capital Corp.
Mr. Eugene W. Landy, Pres.
Mr. Charles P. Kaempffer, Exec
P.O. Box 335
125 Wyckoff Rd.
Eatontown, NJ 07724
(201) 542-4927
C * 12

Raybar SBIC
Mr. Patrick McCort, VP
255 W. Spring Valley Ave.
Maywood, NJ 07607
(201) 368-2280
B * 12**

Rutgers Minority Investment Co.
Mr. Oscar Figueroa, Pres.
180 University Ave., 3rd Fl.
Newark, NJ 07102
(201) 648-5627
MESBIC B * 1,5,6,9,12**

Unicorn Ventures, Ltd.
Mr. Frank P. Diassi, Gen. Ptnr.
Mr. Arthur B. Baer, Gen. Ptnr.
14 Commerce Dr.
Cranford, NJ 07016
(201) 276-7880
C * 12**

Venray Capital Corp.
Mr. Raymond Skiptunis, Pres.
981 Rt. #22
P.O. Box 6817
Bridgewater, NJ 08807
(201) 725-1020
B * 2**

NEW MEXICO _____
Albuquerque SBIC
Mr. Albert T. Ussery, Pres.
501 Tijeras Ave., NW
Ste. 202
P.O. Box 487
Albuquerque, NM 87103
(505) 247-0145
A * 12**

Associated SW Investors, Inc.
Mr. John R. Rice, Pres.
2425 Alamo, SE
Albuquerque, NM 87106
(505) 842-5955
MESBIC C * 1,5,6,12

Equity Capital Corp.
Mr. Jerry A. Henson, Pres.
231 Washington Ave., Ste. 2
Santa Fe, NM 87501
(505) 988-4273
B * 12**

Fluid Capital Corp.
Mr. George T. Slaughter, Pres.
8421 B Montgomery Blvd., NE
Albuquerque, NM 87111
(505) 292-4747
A * 1,2,4,5,12**

Fluid Financial Corp.
Mr. George T. Slaughter, Pres.
8421 B Montgomery Blvd, NE
Albuquerque, NM 87111
(505) 292-4747
MESBIC A * 1,2,4,5,12**

New Mexico Capital Corp.
Mr. Phillip G. Larson, Chmn.
2900 Louisiana Blvd., NE, #201
Albuquerque, NM 87110
(505) 884-3600
C * 12**

Southwest Capital Investments
Mr. Martin J. Roe, Pres./Tres.
3500 Commanche Rd., NE, Bldg. E
Albuquerque, NM 87107
(505) 884-7161
C * 12

Venture Capital Corp. of NM
Mr. Gary L. McPherson, Chmn.
5301 Central Ave., NE, Ste. 1600
Albuquerque, NM 87108
(505) 266-0066
A * 4,12**

NEW YORK _____
American Commercial Capital
  Corp.
Mr. Gerald J. Grossman, Pres.
310 Madison Ave., Ste. 1304
New York, NY 10017
(212) 986-3305
B ** 1,2,4,5,7,11,12

AMEV Capital Corp.
Mr. Martin S. Orland, Pres.
Two World Trade Ctr., Ste. 9766
New York, NY 10048
(212) 775-1912
D * 1,4,5,6,7,8,9,11,12**

Amistad DOT Venture Capital Inc.
Mr. Percy E. Sutton, Pres.
801 Second Ave., Ste. 303
New York, NY 10017
(212) 697-9210
MESBIC C * 1,5,8,11

Atalanta Investment Co., Inc.
Mr. L. Mark Newman, Chmn.
450 Park Ave., Ste. 1802
New York, NY 10022
(212) 832-1104
D * 1,2,5,6,7,8,**

BanCap Corp.
Mr. William L. Whitely, Pres.
155 E. 42nd St., Ste. 305
New York, NY 10017
(212) 687-6470
MESBIC B * 1,5,6,12**

Beneficial Capital Corp.
Mr. John J. Hoey, Pres.
645 Fifth Ave.
New York, NY 10022
(212) 752-1291
B * 12**

Bohlen Capital Corp.
Mr. Harvey J. Wertheim, Pres.
767 Third Ave.
New York, NY 10017
(212) 838-7776
D * 1,5,6,8**

Boston Hambro Capital Co.
Mr. Edwin A. Goodman, Pres.
17 E. 71st St.
New York NY 10021
(212) 288-7778
D * 1,5,6,9,12**

BT Capital Corp.
Mr. James G. Hellmuth, Pres.
280 Park Ave.
New York, NY 10017
(212) 850-1916
E * 5, 12**

The Central New York SBIC, Inc.
Mr. Albert Wertheimer, Pres.
351 S. Warren St., Ste. 204
Syracuse, NY 13202
(315) 478-5026
A ** 1,4,7

Citicorp Venture Capital
Mr. Peter G. Gerry, Pres.
399 Park Ave., 20th Fl.
New York, NY 10043
(212) 559-1117
E * 1,3,5,6,8,10,11**

Clinton Capital Corp.
Mr. Mark Scharfman, Pres.
35 Middagh St.
Brooklyn, NY 11201
(212) 858-0920
D * 12

CMNY Capital Co., Inc.
Mr. Robert Davidoff, VP
77 Water St.
New York, NY 10005
(212) 437-7078
C *** 1,5,6,7,12

College Venture Equity Corp.
Mr. Francis M. Williams, Pres.
256 3rd St.
P.O. Box 135
Niagara Falls, NY 14305
(716) 285-8455
A *** 2,6,7,11

Cornell Capital Corp.
Mr. Barry M. Bloom, Pres.
Mr. Alan B. Newman
230 Park Ave., Ste. 3440
New York, NY 10169
(212) 490-9198
D *** 4,9,12

County Capital Corp.
Mr. Myron Joffe, Pres.
25 Main St.
Southampton, NY 11968
(516) 283-2943
A * 2,4,6,11,12

EAB Venture Corp.
Mr. Richard C. Burcaw, Pres.
90 Park Ave.
New York, NY 10016
(212) 687-6010
C * 1,3,5,6,9,10,11,12

Edwards Capital Co.
Mr. Edward Teitlebaum, Mng.
  Ptnr.
215 Lexington Ave., Rm. 805
New York, NY 10016
(212) 686-2568
C ** 11

Elk Associates Funding Corp.
Mr. Gary C. Granoff, Pres.
31 East Mall
Plainview, NY 11803
(516) 249-3387
MESBIC A ** 11

Branch Office
Engle Investment Co.
Mr. Murray Hendel, Pres.
135 W. 50th St.
New York, NY 10020
(212) 757-9580
B * 12
(Main Office in NJ)

Equico Capital Corp.
Mr. Duane E. Hill, Pres./CEO
1290 Ave. of the Americas
Ste. 3400
New York, NY 10019
(212) 554-8413
MESBIC C *** 12

Equities Capital Co., Inc.
Mr. Leon Scharf, Pres.
890 West End Ave.
New York, NY 10025
(212) 866-6008
A ** 12

European Development Cap. Corp.
Mr. Harvey J. Wertheim, Pres.
767 Third Ave.
New York, NY 10017
(212) 838-7776
D *** 1,5,6,8,

Fairfield Equity Corp.
Mr. Matthew A. Berdon, Pres.
200 E. 42nd St.
New York, NY 10017
(212) 867-0150
B *** 1,5,6,9,10

Ferranti High Technology, Inc.
Mr. Sanford R. Simon, Pres.
505 Park Ave.
New York, NY 10022
(212) 688-9828
E *** 1,8,12

Fifty-Third Street Ventures
Mr. Alan J. Patricof, Chmn.
545 Madison Ave., 15th Fl.
New York, NY 10022
(212) 753-6300
E *** 1,6,9

Branch Office
The First Connecticut SBIC
Mr. James Breiner, Chmn.
Mr. David Engelson, Pres.
680 Fifth Ave.
New York, NY 10153
(212) 355-6540
D * **1,2,4,5,6,9,12**
(Main office in CT)

J. H. Foster & Co., Inc.
Mr. John H. Foster, Ptnr.
437 Madison Ave.
New York, NY 10022
(212) 753-4810
C *** **1,3,5,6,8,11**

The Franklin Corp.
Mr. Herman E. Goodman, Pres.
1185 Ave. of Americas
27th Floor
New York, NY 10036
(212) 719-4844
D * **1,2,4,5,6,7,8,11,12**

Fundex Capital Corp.
Mr. Howard F. Sommer, Pres.
525 Northern Blvd.
Great Neck, NY 11746
(516) 466-8550
B * **12**

Genesee Funding, Inc.
Mr. A. Keene Bolton, Pres.
Ste. 1450—183 E. Main St.
Rochester, NY 14604
(716) 262-4716
A * **12**

Hanover Capital Corp.
Mr. John A Selzer, VP
150 E. 58th St., Ste. 3520
New York, NY 10155
(212) 486-2411
A *** **5,12**

Heller Capital Services
Mr. Jack A. Prizzi, Exec. VP
101 Park Ave.
New York, NY 10178
(212) 880-7047
D *** **1,5,6,8,9,11,12**

Holding Capital Mgmt. Corp.
Mr. James W. Donaghy, VP
685 Fifth Ave., 14th Fl.
New York, NY 10022
(212) 486-6670
A *** **1,2,3,5,6,9,10,12**

Ibero-American Investors Corp.
Mr. Emilio L. Serrano, Pres./CEO
Chamber of Commerce Bldg.
55 St. Paul St.
Rochester, NY 14604
(716) 262-3440
MESBIC A * **5**

Intercoastal Capital Corp.
Mr. Herbert Krasnow, Pres.
380 Madison Ave., 18th Fl.
New York, NY 10017
(212) 986-0482
D * **1,2,4,5,6,7,10,11,12**

Intergroup Venture Cap. Corp.
Mr. Ben Hauben, Pres.
230 Park Ave., Ste. 210
New York, NY 10169
(212) 661-5428
A * **12**

International Paper Cap. Formation, Inc.
Mr. Bernard Riley, Chmn.
77 W. 45th St.
New York, NY 10036
(212) 536-6606
MESBIC B * **12**

Irving Capital Corp.
Mr. J. Andrew McWethy, Exec. VP
1290 Ave. of Americas, 3rd Fl.
New York, NY 10019
(212) 922-8790
E *** **12**

Japanese American Capital Corp.
Mr. Benjamin Lin, Pres.
120 Broadway, Rm. 1755
New York, NY 10271
(212) 964-4077
MESBIC A * **2,4,6,12**

Key Venture Capital Corp.
Mr. John M. Lang, Pres.
Mr. Mark R. Hursty
60 State St.
Albany, NY 12207
(518) 447-3180
B * 8,12**

Korean Capital Corp.
Ms. Min ja OH, Pres.
144-43 25th Rd.
Flushing, NY 11354
(212) 762-8866
MESBIC C * 12

Kwiat Capital Corp.
Mr. Jeffrey M. Greene, Pres.
576 Fifth Ave.
New York, NY 10036
(212) 391-2461
C * 1,5,6,7,8,12**

Lincoln Capital Corp.
Mr. Martin Lifton, Pres.
41 E. 42nd St., Ste. 1510
New York, NY 10017
(212) 697-0610
B ** 12

M & T Capital Corp.
Mr. Joseph V. Parlato, Pres.
One M & T Pl.
Buffalo, NY 14240
(716) 842-5881
D * 1,5,6,8,9,10,11,12**

Medallion Funding Corp.
Mr. Alvin Murstein, Pres.
205 E. 42nd St., Ste. 2020
New York, NY 10017
(212) 682-3300
MESBIC A ** 11

Midland Venture Capital, Ltd.
Mr. Edwin B. Hathaway, Asst. VP
950 Third Ave.
New York, NY 10022
(212) 753-7799
E * 3,5**

Minority Equity Capital Co., Inc.
Mr. Patrick Owen Burns, Pres.
275 Madison Ave., Ste. 1901
New York, NY 10016
(212) 686-9710
MESBIC C * 1,5,6,9,12**

Multi-Purpose Capital Corp.
Mr. Eli B. Fine, Pres.
31 S. Broadway
Yonkers, NY 10701
(914) 963-2733
A * 12**

Nelson Capital Corp.
Mr. Irwin B. Nelson, Pres.
591 Stewart Ave.
Garden City, NY 11530
(516) 222-2555
E * 12

New Oasis Capital Corp.
Mr. James Huang, Pres.
114 Liberty St., Ste. 304
New York, NY 10006
(212) 394-2804
MESBIC B * 12

New Publications Fund, Inc.
Mr. Richard Ekstract, Pres.
350 E. 81st St.
New York, NY 10028
(212) 734-4440
B * 1

Noro Capital Ltd.
Mr. Harvey J. Wertheim, Gen. Ptnr.
767 Third Ave.
New York, NY 10017
(212) 838-7776
D * 1,5,6,8**

North American Funding Corp.
Mr. Franklin Wong, VP
177 Canal St.
New York, NY 10013
(212) 226-0080
MESBIC A * 12

North Street Capital Corp.
Mr. Ralph L. McNeal, Sr., Pres.
250 North St., RA-6S
White Plains, NY 10625
(914) 335-6306
MESBIC B * 12**

NPD Capital, Inc.
Mr. David A. Rapaport, VP
375 Park Ave., Ste. 2201
New York, NY 10152
(212) 826-8500
B * 6,8,12**

NYBDC Capital Corp.
Mr. Marshall R. Lustig, Pres.
41 State St.
Albany, NY 12207
(518) 463-2268
A * 3,5,6,8,9,10,12**

Pan Pac Capital Corp.
Dr. In-Ping J. Lee, Pres.
120 Broadway
New York, NY 10271
(212) 966-2296
MESBIC A * 12

Pioneer Investors Corp.
Mr. James G. Niven, Pres.
113 E. 55th St.
New York, NY 10022
(212) 980-9090
C * 1,3,5,6,8,9**

Questech Capital Corp.
Dr. Earl W. Brian, Pres.
600 Madison Ave.
New York, NY 10022
(212) 758-8522
D * 1,5,6,8**

R & R Financial Corp.
Mr. Herbert Glick
1451 Broadway
New York, NY 10036
(212) 790-1400
A * 12

Rand Capital Corp.
Mr. George F. Rand III, Chmn.
Mr. Donald A. Ross, Pres.
Mr. Keith B. Wiley, VP
1300 Rand Bldg.
Buffalo, NY 14203
(716) 853-0802
C * 1,5,8,9**

Realty Growth Capital Corp.
Mr. Lawrence A. Benenson, Pres.
575 Lexington Ave.
New York, NY 10022
(212) 755-9044
A ** 2,11

Retzloff Capital Corp.
Mr. James K. Hines, Pres.
PO Box 41250
Houston, TX 77240
(713) 466-4633
C * 12**

Peter J. Schmitt Co., Inc.
Mr. Denis G. Riley, Mgr.
355 Harlem Road
P.O. Box 2
Buffalo, NY 14240
(716) 821-1400
A ** 9

Securities First Corp.
Mr. Norman M. Kanterman, Treas.
c/o Jericho Management Associates
41-11 39th St.
Long Island City, NY 14240
(212) 392-7000
D ** 11,12

Sherwood Business Capital Corp.
Mr. Anthony R. Russo, Pres.
175 Main St.
White Plains, NY 10601
(914) 761-1946
D * 12**

Small Business Electronics
    Investment Corp.
Mr. Stanley Meisels, Pres.
60 Cutter Mill Rd.
Great Neck, NY 11021
(516) 466-6451
A ** 12

Southern Tier Capital Corp.
Mr. Milton Brizel, Pres.
55 S. Main St.
Liberty, NY 12754
(914) 292-3030
A * 12

Sprout Capital Corp.
Mr. Richard E. Kroon, Pres.
140 Broadway, 48th Fl.
New York, NY 10005
(212) 902-2482
D * 1,5,6,8,9**

Tappan Zee Capital Corp.
Mr. Jack Birnberg, Exec. VP
120 N. Main St.
New City, NY 10956
(914) 634-8890
A ** 12

Taroco Capital Corp.
Mr. David R. C. Chang, Pres.
19 Rector St., 35th Fl.
New York, NY 10006
(212) 344-6690
MESBIC A * 12

TLC Funding Corp.
Mr. Philip G. Kass, Pres.
141 S. Central Ave.
Hartsdale, NY 10530
(914) 683-1144
B * 5,6,9,10,12**

Transportation SBIC, Inc.
Mr. Melvin L. Hirsch, Pres.
122 E. 42nd St., 46th Fl.
New York, NY 10168
(212) 986-6050
MESBIC B ** 11

Transworld Ventures, Ltd.
Mr. Jack H. Berger, Pres.
331 W. End Ave., Ste. 1A
New York, NY 10023
(212) 496-1010
A * 5,10,12**

Van Rietschoten Capital Corp.
Mr. Harvey J. Wertheim, Pres.
767 Third Ave.
New York, NY 10017
(212) 838-7776
D * 1,5,6,8**

Vega Capital Corp.
Mr. Victor Harz, Pres.
720 White Plains Rd.
Scarsdale, NY 10583
(914) 472-8550
D * 12

Venture SBIC, Inc.
Mr. Arnold Feldman, Pres.
249-12 Jericho Tpke.
Bellerose, NY 11426
(516) 352-0068
B * 12

Branch Office
Walnut Capital Corp.
Mr. Burton W. Kanter, Chmn.
110 E. 59th St., 37th Fl.
New York, NY 10022
(212) 980-4665
C * 12**
(Main Office in IL)

Watchung Capital Corp.
Mr. Thomas S. T. Jeng, Pres.
431 Fifth Ave., 5th Fl.
New York, NY 10016
(212) 889-3466
MESBIC A * 12

Winfield Capital Corp.
Mr. Stanley Pechman, Pres.
237 Mamaroneck Ave.
White Plains, NY 10605
(914) 949-2600
D * 12**

Wood River Capital Corp.
Ms. Elizabeth W. Smith, Exec. VP
645 Madison Ave.
New York, NY 10022
(212) 750-9420
C * 1,5,6**

Yang Capital Corp.
Mr. Maysing Yang, Pres.
41-40 Kissena Blvd.
Flushing, NY 11355
(516) 482-1578
(212) 445-4585
MESBIC B * 2,6**

NORTH CAROLINA
Delta Capital, Inc.
Mr. Alex B. Wilkins, Jr., Pres.
227 N. Tryon St., Ste 201
Charlotte, NC 28202
(704) 372-1410
C * 12**

Heritage Capital Corp.
Mr. J. Randolph Gregory, Pres.
2290 First Union Pl.
Charlotte, NC 28282
(704) 334-2867
C * 12**

Kitty Hawk Capital, Ltd.
Mr. Walter Wilkinson Jr.,
   General Partner
2030 One Tryon Ctr.
Charlotte, NC 28284
(704) 333-3777
C * 1,5,6,9,12**

Vanguard Investment Co., Inc.
Mr. Marion Rex Harris, Pres.
4517 Bragg Blvd., Ste. 3
Fayetteville, NC 28303
(919) 864-4447
MESBIC B * 1,5,8,11,12**

NORTH DAKOTA
Dakota First Capital Corp.
Mr. Alexander P. McDonald, Pres.
51 Broadway, Ste. 601
Fargo, ND 58102
(701) 237-0450
A * 1,5,8,12**

OHIO
Center City Minority Enterprises
   Investment Co.
Mr. Claude Patmon, Pres.
40 S. Main St., Ste. 762
Dayton, OH 45402
(513) 229-2416
MESBIC A * 12

Clarion Capital Corp.
Mr. Morton A. Cohen, Pres.
1801 E. 12th St., Ste. 201
Cleveland, OH 44114
(216) 687-1096
C * 5,6,8,12**

First Ohio Capital Corp.
Mr. Michael Aust, Gen. Mgr.
606 Madison Ave.
Toledo, OH 43604
(419) 259-7146
B * 12**

Glenco Enterprises, Inc.
Dr. Lewis F. Wright, Jr., VP
1464 E. 105th St., Ste. 101
Cleveland, OH 44106
(216) 721-1200
MESBIC A * 12**

Gries Investment Co.
Mr. Robert D. Gries, Pres.
720 Statler Office Tower
Cleveland, OH 44115
(216) 861-1146
B * 12**

Intercapco, Inc.
Mr. Robert B. Haas, Pres.
One Erieview Pl.
Cleveland, OH 44114
(216) 241-7170
D * 1,3,5,6,8,9,12**

Miami Talley Capital, Inc.
Mr. Everett F. Telljohann, Pres.
131 N. Ludlow, Ste. 315
Dayton, OH 45402
(513) 222-7222
B * 5**

National City Capital Corp.
Mr. Michael Sherwin, Pres.
623 Euclid Ave.
Cleveland, OH 44114
(216) 575-2491
C * 1,5,12**

Branch Office:
RIHT Capital Corp.
Mr. Peter Van Oosterhout, Pres.
796 Huntington Bldg.
Cleveland, OH 44115
(216) 781-3655
D * 12**
(Main Office in RI)

Tamco Investors SBIC, Inc.
Mr. Nathan H. Monus, Pres.
375 Victoria Rd., PO Box 1588
Youngstown, OH 44501
(216) 792-3811
A ** 9

Tomlinson Capital Corp.
Mr. Donald R. Calkins, VP
3055 E. 63rd St.
Cleveland, OH 44127
(216) 271-2103
B * 12**

OKLAHOMA
Alliance Business Investment Co.
Mr. Barry M. Davis, Pres.
One Williams Ctr., Ste. 2000
Tulsa, OK 74172
(918) 584-3581
D * 1,3,5,6,8,11,12**

Bartlesville Investment Corp.
Mr. J. L. Diamond, Pres.
P.O. Box 548
Bartlesville, OK 74003
(918) 333-3022
A * 2,3

First OK Investment Cap. Corp.
Mr. O. Stuart Brown, Pres.
PO Box 25189
Oklahoma City, OK 73125
(405) 272-4660
D * 1,3,4,5,6,7,9**

Investment Capital, Inc.
Mr. James J. Wasson, Pres.
300 N. Harrison
Cushing, OK 74023
(918) 225-5850
B * 12

Southwest Venture Capital, Inc.
Mr. Donald J. Rubottom, Pres.
4120 E. 51st St., Ste. E
Tulsa, OK 74135
(918) 742-3177
A * 12**

Utica Investment Corp.
Mr. David S. Nunneley, Pres.
1924 South Utica
Tulsa, OK 74104
(918) 743-3376
A * 2,3,5,10,12**

OREGON
Branch Office
First Interstate Capital, Inc.
Mr. Wayne B. Kingsley, Exec. VP
1300 S.W. Fifth Ave., Ste. 2323
Portland, OR 97201
(503) 223-4334
E * 1,5,6,8**
(Main office in CA)

Northern Pacific Cap. Corp.
Mr. John Tennant, Jr., Pres.
1201 S.W. 12th Ave.
Portland, OR 97202
(503) 241-1255
B * 5,9,11**

Branch Office:
Norwest Growth Fund, Inc.
Mr. Anthony Miadich, VP
1300 S.W. Fifth Ave., Ste. 3018
Portland, OR 97201
(503) 223-6622
E * 1,6,8,12**
(Main Office in MN)

PENNSYLVANIA _____

Alliance Enterprise Corp.
Mr. Duane C. McKnight, VP
1801 Market St., 3rd Fl.
Philadelphia, PA 19103
(215) 972-4230
MESBIC C * 2,5,6,9,10,12

American Venture Capital Co.
Mr. Knute Albrecht, Pres./CEO
Ste. 122, Blue Bell W.
Blue Bell, PA 19422
(215) 278-8907
B * 12**

Branch Office
First SBIC of California
Mr. Daniel A. Dye, VP
PO Box 512
Washington, PA 15301
(412) 223-0707
E * 12**
(Main Office in CA)

First Valley Capital Corp.
Mr. Carl B. Bear, Pres.
One Bethlehem Pl.
Bethlehem, PA 18018
(215) 865-8675
C * 5,6,7,9,10,11**

Greater Philadelphia Venture
  Capital Corp., Inc.
Mr. Martin Newman, Pres.
225 S. 15th St., Ste. 920
Philadelphia, PA 19102
(215) 732-1666
(215) 732-3415
MESBIC B * 1,4,6,7,12**

PNC Capital Corp.
Mr. David McL. Hillman, Exec. VP
Fifth Ave. & Wood St.—PNB Bldg.
Pittsburgh, PA 15222
(412) 355-2245
C * 1,5,6,8,9

PUERTO RICO _____

First Puerto Rico Capital, Inc.
Mr. Eliseo E. Font, Pres.
PO Box 1300
Mayaguez, PR 00709
(809) 832-9171
MESBIC A * 12

North America Investment Corp.
Sr. Santiago Ruiz-Betancourt, Pres.
Banco Popular Ctr., Ste. 1710
Hato Rey, PR 00928
(809) 754-6177
MESBIC B * 5,6,9,10,12**

Venture Capital P.R., Inc.
Mr. Manuel L. Prats, Inv. Adv.
Banco Cooperativo Plz
Ste. 604-B
Hato Rey, PR 00917
(809) 751-8040
MESBIC A * 2,5,12

RHODE ISLAND _____

Fleet Venture Resources, Inc.
Mr. Robert M. Van Degna, Pres.
111 Westminster St.
Providence, RI 02903
(401) 278-6770
C * 1,6,8**

Narragansett Capital Corp.
Mr. Arthur D. Little, Chmn.
40 Westminster St.
Providence, RI 02903
(401) 751-1000
E * 1,5,6,9**

Old Stone Capital Corp.
Mr. Bruce D. Moger, Pres.
150 S. Main St.
Providence, RI 02901
(401) 278-2544
E * 12**

RIHT Capital Corp.
Mr. Peter Van Oosterhout, Pres.
Mr. Robert A. Comey, VP
One Hospital Trust Plaza
Providence, RI 02903
(401) 278-8819
D * 12**

SOUTH CAROLINA ____ ____
Carolina Venture Capital Corp.
Mr. Thomas Harvey III, Pres.
14 Archer Rd., PO Box 3110
Hilton Head Island, SC 29928
(803) 842-3101
B *** 1,2,4,7,11,12

Reedy River Ventures
Mr. Jack Sterling, Pres.
PO Box 17526
Greenville, SC 29606
(803) 297-9198
B *** 12

TENNESSEE _____
Chickasaw Capital Corp.
Mr. Wayne J. Haskins, Pres.
PO Box 387, 67 Madison
Memphis, TN 38147
(901) 523-6404
MESBIC A *** 5,6,12

DeSoto Capital Corp.
Mr. William B. Rudner, Pres.
5050 Poplar Ave., Ste. 2429
Memphis, TN 38157
(901) 682-9072
A *** 12

Financial Resources, Inc.
Mr. Milton C. Picard, Chmn.
2800 Sterick Bldg.
Memphis, TN 38103
(901) 527-9411
B *** 1,5,6,8,10,12

Inverness Capital Corp.
Mr. Floyd W. Kephart, Jr., Pres.
127 Woodmont Blvd.
Nashville, TN 37205
(615) 297-1970
C *** 5,6,8

Suwannee Capital Corp.
Mr. Peter R. Pettit, Pres.
1991 Corporate Ave.
Memphis, TN 38132
(901) 345-4235
B ** 9

Tennessee Equity Capital Corp.
Mr. Walter S. Cohen, Pres.
1102 Stonewall Jackson Ct.
Nashville, TN 37220
(615) 373-4502
MESBIC C *** 12

Valley Capital Corp.
Ste. 806, Krystal Bldg.
Chattanooga, TN 37402
(615) 265-1557
MESBIC A *** 1,5,8,9,10,11

West Tennessee Venture Capital
    Corp.
Mr. Bennie L. Marshall, Mgr.
Ste. 1701, Sterick Bldg.
8 N. Third St.
Memphis, TN 38103
(901) 527-6091
MESBIC B * 1,6,12

TEXAS _____
Branch Office
Alliance Business Investment Co.
2660 S. Tower, Pennzoil Pl.
Houston, TX 77002
(713) 224-8224
D *** 1,3,5,6,11,12

Allied Bancshares Capital Corp.
Mr. D. Kent Anderson, Chmn.
Mr. Philip A. Tuttle, Pres.
PO Box 3326
Houston, TX 77001
(713) 224-6611
C * 3,5,10,12

American Energy Investment Corp.
Mr. Robert J. Moses, Pres.
1010 Lamar, Ste. 1680
Houston, TX 77002
(713) 651-0220
C * 3

Americap Corp.
Mr. James L. Hurn, Pres.
6363 Woodway, Ste. 200
Houston, TX 77057
(713) 780-8084
B *** 3,12

BancTexas Capital Inc.
Mr. Byron G. Berger, Exec. VP
1601 Elm St., PO Box 2249
Dallas, TX 75221
(214) 969-6382
B * 1,3,5,6,8,12**

Bow Lane Capital Corp.
Mr. Stuart Schube, Pres.
2401 Fountainview, Ste. 950
Houston, TX 77057
(713) 977-7421
E * 1,6,8,12**

Branch Office
Bow Lane Capital Corp.
Mr. Hugh Batey
3305 Graybuck Rd.
Austin, TX 78748
(512) 456-8698
E * 1,6,8,12**

Brittany Capital Corp.
Mr. Robert E. Clements, Pres.
2424 LTV Tower, 1525 Elm St.
Dallas TX 75201
(214) 742-5810
B * 12**

Business Capital Corp. of Arlington
Mr. Keith Martin, Pres.
1112 Copeland Rd., Ste. 420
Arlington, TX 76011
(817) 261-4936
B * 1,5,9**

Capital Marketing Corp.
Mr. John King Myrick, Pres.
P.O. Box 1000
Keller, TX 76248
(214) 281-4417
E ** 2,12

Central Texas SBIC
Mr. David G. Horner, Pres.
514 Austin Ave.
Waco, TX 76710
(817) 753-6461
A * 12

Charter Venture Group, Inc.
Mr. Kent E. Smith, Pres.
5150 N. Shepherd, Ste. 218
PO Box 10816
Houston, TX 77018
(713) 699-3588
B * 12**

CSC Capital Corp.
Mr. William R. Thomas, Pres.
Mr. J. Bruce Duty, VP
12900 Preston Rd., Ste. 700
Dallas, TX 75230
(214) 233-8242
D * 1,3,5,6,8,9,11,12**

Energy Assets, Inc.
Mr. L. E. Simmons, VP
1800 S. Tower, Pennzoil Pl.
Houston, TX 77002
(713) 236-9999
A * 3

Energy Capital Corp.
Mr. Herbert Poyner, Jr., Pres.
953 Esperson Bldg.
Houston, TX 77002
(713) 236-0006
D * 3

Enterprise Capital Corp.
Mr. Fred S. Zeidman, Pres.
3401 Allen Pkwy., Ste. 108
Houston, TX 77019
(713) 524-5170
E * 1,2,5,6,12**

Equity Capital Corp. of Texas
Mr. John M. Fooshee, Pres.
5333 Spring Valley Rd.
Dallas, TX 75240
(214) 991-2961
B * 4,9,12**

Evergreen Capital Co., Inc.
Mr. Richard Shen-Lim Lin, Pres.
8502 Tybor, Ste. 201
Houston, TX 77074
(713) 778-9889
MESBIC B * 12**

First City Capital Corp.
Mr. William E. Ladin, Pres.
One West Loop S., Ste. 809
Houston, TX 77027
(713) 623-6151
D * 12**

FSA Capital, Ltd.
Mr. G. Felder Thornhill, Pres.
PO Box 1987
Austin, TX 78767
(512) 472-6720
C * 1,3,6,8,12

Grocers SBIC
Mr. Milton Levit, Pres.
3131 E. Holcombe Blvd.
Houston, TX 77021
(713) 747-7913
B ** 9

InterFirst Venture Corp.
Mr. J. A. O'Donnell, Pres.
PO Box 83644
Dallas, TX 75283
(214) 744-8050
E * 1,2,3,6,12**

Livingston Capital Ltd.
Mr. J. Livingston Kosberg, Pres.
5701 Woodway, Ste. 332
Houston, TX 77057
(713) 977-4040
D * 12**

Mapleleaf Capital Corp.
Mr. Michael P. Zuk, Pres.
One West Loop S., Ste. 603
Houston, TX 77027
(713) 627-0752
C * 3,8,10,12**

Mercantile Dallas Corp.
Mr. J. Wayne Gaylord, Exec. VP
P.O. Box 222090
Dallas, TX 75222
(214) 741-1469
D * 5,6,12

MESBIC Financial Corp. of Dallas
Mr. Walter W. Durham, Pres.
7701 N. Stemmons Freeway
Ste. 836
Dallas, TX 75247
(214) 637-0445
MESBIC C * 12**

MESBIC Financial Corp. of
    Houston
Mr. Richard Rothfeld, Pres.
1801 Main St., Ste. 320
Houston, TX 77002
(713) 228-8321
MESBIC B * 5,8,9,10,11,12

MESBIC of San Antonio, Inc.
Mr. Ruben M. Saenz, VP
2300 W. Commerce
San Antonio, TX 78207
(512) 224-0909
MESBIC A * 2,3,4,5,6,9,12**

Omega Capital Corp.
Mr. Ted E. Moor, Jr., Pres.
755 S. 11th St., Ste. 250
Beaumont, TX 77701
(409) 835-5928
A * 12

Red River Ventures, Inc.
Mr. Thomas Schnitzius, Pres.
2050 Houston Natural Gas Bldg.
Houston, TX 77002
(713) 658-9806
C * 3,8**

Republic Venture Group, Inc.
Mr. Robert H. Wellborn, Pres.
PO Box 225961
Dallas, TX 75265
(214) 653-5078
E * 1,2,3,5,6,11,12

Retail Capital Corp.
Mr. William J. Boschma, Pres.
7915 FM 1960 W., Ste. 300
Houston, TX 77070
(713) 890-4242
A * 9

Retzloff Capital Corp.
Mr. James K. Hines, Pres.
PO Box 41250
Houston, TX 77240
(713) 466-4633
C * 12**

Rice County Capital, Inc.
Mr. W. H. Harrison, Jr., Pres.
PO Box 215
Eagle Lake, TX 77434
(409) 234-2504
A * 12

Rust Capital Ltd.
Mr. Jeffrey C. Garvey, Pres.
114 W. 7th St., Ste. 1300
Austin, TX 78701
(512) 479-0055
D * 1,4,5,6,12**

San Antonio Venture Group, Inc.
Mr. Domingo Bueno, Pres.
2300 W. Commerce
San Antonio, TX 78207
(512) 224-0909
B * 12**

SBI Capital Corp.
Mr. William E. Wright, Pres.
6305 Beverly Hill Ln.
Houston, TX 77057
(713) 975-1188
D * 1,3,4,5,6,8,12**

Southern Orient Capital Corp.
Mr. Min-Hsiung Liang, Pres.
2419 Fannin, Ste. 200
Houston, TX 77002
(713) 225-3369
MESBIC A * 4,9,10,12

Southwestern Venture Capital of
    Texas, Inc.
Mr. J. A. Bettersworth, Pres.
PO Box 1169
Seguin, TX 78155
(512) 379-0380
B * 12

Branch Office
Southwestern Venture Capital of
    Texas, Inc.
Mr. James A. Bettersworth, Pres.
North Frost Center
1250 N.E. Loop 410, Ste. 300
San Antonio, TX 78209
B * 12

Sunwestern Capital Corp.
Mr. Floyd W. Collins, VP
Ste. 816, South Tower
2720 Stemmons Freeway
Dallas, TX 75207
(214) 638-2100
C * 1,3,5,6,8,12**

Texas Capital Corp.
Mr. W. Grogan Lord, Chmn.
333 Clay St., Ste. 2100
Houston, TX 77002
(713) 658-9961
D * 1,6**

Texas Commerce Investment Co.
Mr. Fred Lummis, VP
707 Travis St., 7th Fl.
PO Box 2558
Houston, TX 77002
(713) 236-5332
D * 1,2,6,8**

Trammell Crow Investment Corp.
Mr. Henry Billingsley, Pres.
2001 Bryan, Ste. 3900
Dallas, TX 75201
(214) 747-0643
A ** 2

TSM Corp.
Mr. L. Joe Justice, Inv. Adv.
444 Executive Ctr. Blvd.
Ste. 222
El Paso, TX 79902
(915) 533-6375
A * 5,9

United Oriental Cap. Co.
Mr. Don J. Wang, Pres.
13432 Hempstead Hwy.
Houston, TX 77040
(713) 462-6264
MESBIC B * 12

VERMONT _____
Vermont Investment Capital, Inc.
Mr. Harold Jacobs, Pres.
Box 590
South Royalton, VT 05068
(802) 763-7716
A * 12

VIRGINIA _____
Basic Investment Corp.
Mr. Frank Luwis, Pres.
6723 Whittier Ave.
McLean, VA 22101
(703) 356-4300
MESBIC A * 12

East West United Investment Co.
Mr. Doug Bui, Pres.
6723 Whittier Ave.
Ste. 206
McLean, VA 22101
(703) 821-6616
MESBIC A * 4,9,12

James River Capital Associates
Mr. A. Hugh Ewing, III, Pres.
9 S. 12th St.
Richmond, VA 23219
(804) 643-7358
B * 1,5,6,8,9,12**

Metropolitan Capital Corp.
Ms. M. A. Riebe, Pres.
2550 Huntington Ave.
Alexandria, VA 22303
(703) 960-4698
B * 12**

Norfolk Investment Co., Inc.
Mr. Kirk W. Saunders, Pres.
100 W. Plume St., Ste. 208
Norfolk, VA 23502
(804) 623-1042
MESBIC A * 1,5,6,8,11,12**

Tidewater SBIC
Mr. Robert H. Schmidt, Pres.
1106 Maritime Tower
Norfolk, VA 23510
(804) 627-2315
A * 12

WASHINGTON _____
Capital Resource Corp.
Mr. Theodore M. Wight, Pres.
1001 Logan Bldg.
Seattle, WA 98101
(206) 623-6550
B * 1,5,6,8,9,12**

Clifton Capital Corp.
Mr. John S. Wiborg, VP
1408 Washington Bldg.
Tacoma, WA 98406
(206) 272-1875
A * 1,5,9,12**

Peoples Capital Corp.
Mr. Robert E. Karns, Pres.
2411 Fourth Ave., Ste. 990
Seattle, WA 98121
(206) 344-8105
A * 1,5,12**

Seafirst Capital Corp.
Mr. Steven G. Blanchard, Pres.
Fourth & Blanchard Bldg.
Seattle, WA 98121
(206) 583-3278
C * 2,5,6,

Seattle Trust Capital Corp.
Mr. Willard E. Skeel, Jr., VP
804 Second Ave.
Seattle, WA 98104
(206) 223-2237
B * 12**

Washington Trust Equity Corp.
Mr. Jack Snead, Pres.
PO Box 2127
Spokane, WA 99210
(509) 455-4106
B * 1,5,6,9,10,11,12**

WISCONSIN _____
Branch Office
R. W. Allsop Capital Corp.
Mr. Gregory B. Bultman, VP
Ste. 1501, 815 E. Mason St.
P.O. Box 1368
Milwaukee, WI 53201
(414) 271-6510
C * 1,5,6,12**
(Main Office in Iowa)

Bando-McGlocklin Investment Co., Inc.
Mr. Sal Bando, Pres.
13555 Bishops Ct., Ste. 205
Brookfield, WI 53005
(414) 784-9010
D ** 5,6,9,10

CERTCO Capital Corp.
Mr. Donald E. Watzke, Pres.
P.O. Box 7368
Madison, WI 53707
(608) 271-4500
A ** 9

Madison Capital Corp.
Mr. Roger H. Ganser, Exec. VP
102 State St.
Madison, WI 53703
(608) 256-2799
B * 1,5,6,8,10,11**

Branch Office:
MorAmerica Capital Corp.
Mr. Steven H. Massey
    Investment Analyst
600 East Mason St.
Milwaukee, WI 53202
(414) 276-3839
D * 1,5,6,9,12**
(Main Office in Iowa)

SC Opportunities, Inc.
Mr. Robert Ableman, VP/Sec.
1112 7th Ave.
Monroe, WI 53566
(608) 325-3134
MESBIC A * 9**

Super Market Investors, Inc.
Mr. John W. Andorfer, Pres.
c/o ROUNDY's, Inc.
PO Box 473, 11300 W. Burleigh St.
Milwaukee, WI 53201
(414) 783-4956
A ** 9

WYOMING _____
Capital Corp. of Wyoming, Inc.
Mr. Larry J. McDonald, Exec. VP
PO Box 612
Casper, WY 82602
(307) 234-5438
A * 12

Non-SBIC Members

Allstate Insurance Co.
Venture Capital Division
Mr. Charles L. Rees, Dir.
Allstate Plaza E-2
Northbrook, IL 60062
(312) 291-5681
E * 1,5,6**

Arthur Andersen & Co.
Mr. Richard J. Strotman, Ptnr.
33 W. Monroe St.
Chicago, IL 60603
(312) 580-0033

Atlantic Venture Partners
Mr. Robert H. Pratt, Gen. Ptnr.
PO Box 1493
Richmond, VA 23212
(804) 644-5496
D * 12**

Bacon Stifel Nicolaus
Mr. George Hendrick, 1st VP
208 S. LaSalle St., Ste. 400
Chicago, IL 60604
(312) 368-0050

Beacon Partners
Mr. Leonard Vignola, Mng. Ptnr.
111 Hubbard Ave.
Stamford, CT 06905
(203) 348-8858
D * 1,4,5,6,7,8,9,10,11,12

William Blair Venture Partners
Mr. Samuel B. Guren, Gen. Ptnr.
135 S. LaSalle St.
Chicago, IL 60603
(312) 236-1600
D *** 12

Bridge Capital Advisors, Inc.
Mr. Donald P. Remey, Mng. Dir.
Mr. Hoyt J. Goodrich, Mng. Dir.
50 Broadway
New York, NY 10004
(212) 514-6700
E *** 1,5,6,8,10,12

Broventure Capital Management
Mr. William M. Gust, Ptnr.
16 W. Madison St.
Baltimore, MD 21201
(301) 727-4520
D *** 1,5,6,8

Brownstein, Zeidman & Schomer
Mr. Thomas C. Evans, Ptnr.
1025 Conn. Ave., NW
Ste. 900
Washington, DC 20036
(202) 457-6560

Canadian Enterprise Dev. Corp.
   Ltd.
Mr. Gerald D. Sutton, Pres.
199 Bay St., Ste. 1103
Toronto, Ontario M5J 1L4
(416) 366-7607
C *** 1,6,8

Capital Publishing Corp.
Mr. Stanley E. Pratt, Pres.
16 Laurel Avenue, PO Box 348
Wellesley Hills, MA 02181
(617) 431-8100

Capital Services & Resources, Inc.
Mr. Charles Y. Bancroft, Treas.
5159 Wheelis Dr., Ste. 104
Memphis, TN 38117
(901) 761-2156
D * 1,5,6,12

Cardinal Development Cap. Fund I
Mr. Richard Bannon, Ptnr.
155 E Broad St.
Columbus, OH 43215
(614) 464-5552
D * 1,4,5,6,8,9

The Charles River Partnerships
Mr. John T. Neises, Gen. Ptnr.
Mr. Richard Burnes Jr, Gen. Ptnr.
Mr. Robert F. Higgins, Gen. Ptnr.
133 Federal St., Ste. 602
Boston, MA 02110
(617) 482-9370
E *** 1,6,8

Commonwealth Development
   Finance Company Limited (CFC)
Mr. Peter Duce, Pres.
One London Bridge Walk
London, England SE1 2SS
(01) 407-9711
E *** 12

Corp. for Innovation Development
Mr. Marion C. Dietrich, Pres.
One North Capitol Ave., Ste. 520
Indianapolis, IN 46204
(317) 635-7325
C *** 1,5,6,8

Criterion Venture Partners
Mr. Gregory A. Rider, Gen. Ptnr.
4300 Capital Bank Plaza
Houston, TX 77002
(713) 751-2400
D *** 1,3,5,6,8,9,11

Deloitte, Haskins & Sells
Mr. Daniel A. Bailey, Ptnr.
One World Trade Ctr.
New York, NY 10048
(212) 669-5140

Development Credit Corp. of MD
Mr. W. G. Brooks Thomas, Pres.
40 W. Chesapeake Ave., Ste. 211
PO Box 10629
Towson, MD 20204
(301) 828-4711
D ** 12

The Early Stages Partnership
Mr. W. P. Lanphear IV, Ptnr.
244 California St., Ste. 300
San Francisco, CA 94111
(415) 986-5700
C * 1,9**

EastWest Capital Corp.
Mr. Charles H. Bruce, Pres.
390 Union Blvd., Ste. 390
Denver, CO 80228
(303) 986-1113
C * 1,5,6,8,9,12

Enterprise Finance Capital
   Development Corp.
Mr. Robert N. Hampton, Pres.
P.O. Box 5840
Snowmass Village, CO 81615
(303) 923-4144
B ** 12

Enventure Capital Group, Inc.
Mr. Ronald E. Allen, CEO
1000 Guaranty Bldg.
Church & Pearl Streets
Buffalo, NY 14202
(714) 849-9329
C * 1,2,3,5,6,8**

EntreSource
Mr. S. Albert Hanser, Gen. Ptnr.
1300 First Bank Pl. W.
Minneapolis, MN 55402
(612) 375-9655
C * 1,3,5,6,7,8

Equity Resource Company, Inc.
Mr. Michael J. Hammes, VP
202 S. Michigan St.
South Bend, IN 46624
(219) 237-5344
B * 12**

Ernst & Whinney
Mr. Oscar Jimenez, Ptnr.
515 S. Flower St., Ste. 2700
Los Angeles, CA 90071
(213) 621-1666

Exchange Nat'l. Bank of Chicago
Mr. Joseph Chevalier, VP
120 LaSalle St.
Chicago, IL 60603
(312) 781-7046

Executive Capital Corp.
Mr. John A. Hall, Jr., Pres.
4144 N. Central Expy., Ste. 1222
Dallas, TX 75204
(214) 823-6990
C * 1,2,5,9,12**

Fine & Ambrogne
Mr. Arnold M. Zaff, Ptnr.
133 Federal St.
Boston, MA 02110
(617) 482-0100

Fine Art Funds Inc.
Mr. Stephen Maitland-Lewis, Pres.
25 E. 77th St.
New York, NY 10021
(212) 737-2330
B ** 12

The First National Bank of Atlanta
Mr. Richard S. Downey, VP
Two Peachtree St., Ste. 212
Atlanta, GA 30383
(404) 588-6504

The First Worcester SBIC
Mr. Carl Cervini, Pres.
420 Boston Tpke.
Shrewsbury, MA 01545
(617) 842-4000
C * 4,5,8,9**

G. E. Venture Capital Corporation
Mr. Harry T. Rein, Pres.
Mr. Robert L. Burr, Sen. VP
3000 Sand Hill Road
Bldg. 1, Ste. 230
Menlo Park, CA 94025
(415) 854-8092

Harrison Capital, Inc.
Mr. W. T. Corl, Pres.
2000 Westchester Ave.
White Plains, NY 10650
(914) 253-7845
D * 12**

Hawley & Associates
Mr. Frank J. Hawley, Jr., Pres.
999 Summer St.
Stamford, CT 06905
(203) 348-6669
D * 1,2,3,5,6,11,12**

Haynes and Boone
Mr. Marc H. Folladori, Corp. Div.
4300 InterFirst Two
Dallas, TX 75270
(214) 744-0550

Helms, Mulliss & Johnston
Mr. B. Bernard Burns, Jr., Ptnr.
227 N. Tryon St., PO Box 31247
Charlotte, NC 28231
(704) 372-9510

IEG Venture Partners
Mr. F. I. Blair, Man. Ptnr.
Three First National Pl.
Ste. 1400
Chicago, IL 60602
(312) 899-0185
D * 1,3,6,8**

Investment Management Group of
   the First National Bank of
   Chicago
Mr. Daniel O'Connell, VP
Three First Nat'l. Pl. Ste. 0140
Chicago, IL 60607
(312) 732-7974
D * 12**

Investors in Industry
Mr. David R. Shaw, Pres.
99 High St., Ste. 1200
Boston, MA 02110
(617) 542-8560
E * 12**

JVIG U.S. Management, Inc.
Mr. John Ross, CEO
1008 N. Bowen Rd.
Arlington, TX 76012
(817) 860-5222
E ** 12

Knight & Irish Associates, Inc.
Dr. Joan S. Irish, Pres.
420 Lexington Ave., Ste. 2358
New York, NY 10170
(212) 490-0135

Leighton, Lemov, Jacobs & Buckley
Mr. James L. Watts
2033 M St., NW
Washington, D.C. 20036
(202) 785-4800

Lewis, D'Amato, Brisbois &
   Bisgaard
William F. Greenhalgh, Esq.
261 S. Figueroa St., Ste. 300
Los Angeles, CA 90012
(213) 628-7777

Lord, Bissell & Brook
Mr. John K. O'Connor, Ptnr.
115 S. LaSalle St.
Chicago, IL 60603
(312) 443-0265

M&I Capital Corporation
Mr. Daniel P. Howell, Asst. VP
770 N. Water St.
Milwaukee, WI 53201
(414) 765-7800
C * 6,12**

Marine Venture Capital, Inc.
Mr. H. Wayne Foreman, Pres.
111 E. Wisconsin Ave.
Milwaukee, WI 53202
(414) 765-2151
C * 1,5,6,12**

Herbert B. Max, Esq.
77 Water St.
New York, NY 10005
(212) 437-7132

Med-Wick Associates, Inc.
Mr. A. A. T. Wickesham,
   Chmn/Pres
1902 Fleet National Bank Bldg.
Providence, RI 02903
(401) 751-5270

Menlo Ventures
Mr. Kirk L. Knight, Gen. Ptnr.
3000 Sand Hill Rd.
Menlo Park, CA 94025
(415) 854-8540
E *** 1,5,6,8

New Enterprise Associates
Mr. Charles Newhall III,
   General Partner
300 Cathedral St., Ste 110
Baltimore, MD 21201
(301) 244-0115
E * 1,6

Nippon Inv. & Fin. Co. Ltd.
Mr. Yasutoshi Sasada, Pres.
1-25-1 Nishi-Shinjuku, Shinjuku-ku
Tokyo 160 Japan
(03) 349-0961
B * 12

NMB Participatie B.V.
Mr. Michiel A. de Haan, Drs.
Eekholt 26, DIEMEN-Zuid
PO Box 1800
1000 BV AMSTERDAM
The Netherlands
(020) 903311
D * 12

North American Capital Corp.
Mr. Stanley P. Roth, Chmn.
510 Broad Hollow Rd., Ste. 205
Melville, NY 11747
(516) 752-9696
E * 12

North American Capital Group
Mr. Gregory I. Kravitt, Pres.
449 N. Wells St., Ste. 1E
Chicago, IL 60610
(312) 645-0831
E *** 1,2,4,5,6,9,10,12

I. Gordon Odell & Company
Mr. I. Gordon Odell, Pres.
77 N. Oak Knoll Ave., Ste. 108
Pasadena, CA 91101
(213) 793-6858

Opportunity Capital, Inc.
Mr. Chip Glaser, Pres.
8300 Norman Ctr. Dr., #838
Bloomington, MN 55437
(612) 893-9270
B *** 4,6,8,12

Oxford Partners
Mr. Kenneth Rind, Gen. Ptnr.
Mr. Cornelius T. Ryan, Gen. Ptnr.
Mr. Williams Lonergah, Gen. Ptnr.
72 Cummings Point Rd.
Stamford, CT 06902
(203) 964-0592
E *** 1,6,8

Parker Hyde Corp.
Mr. Anthony W. Parker, Pres.
2000 L St., N.W., Ste. 200
Washington, D.C. 20036
(202) 466-3810
C * 12

Pathfinder Venture Cap. Fund
Mr. A. J. Greenshields, Gen. Ptnr.
7300 Metro Blvd., Ste. 585
Minneapolis, MN 55435
(612) 835-1121
E *** 1,5,6,8,12

Peat, Marwick, Mitchell & Co.
Mr. Donald T. Briggs, Jr., Ptnr.
Three Embarcadero Ctr.
San Francisco, CA 94111
(415) 335-5300

Peat, Marwick, Mitchell & Co.
Mr. Paul H. Phillips, Ptnr.
1700 IDS Center
Minneapolis, MN 55402
(612) 341-2222

Peat, Marwick, Mitchell & Co.
Mr. Edgar R. Wood, Jr., Ptnr.
1800 First Union Pl.
Charlotte, NC 28282
(704) 335-5300

Pennsylvania Dev. Credit Corp.
Mr. C. Drew Moyer, Exec. VP
2595 Interstate Dr., Ste. 103
Harrisburg, PA 17110
(717) 652-9434
B ** 5,9

Pepper, Hamilton & Scheetz
Mr. Michael B. Staebler, Ptnr.
36th Fl., 100 Renaissance Ctr.
Detroit, MI 48226
(313) 259-7110

Peregrine Associates
Mr. Gene I. Miller, Gen. Ptnr.
606 Wilshire Blvd., Ste. 602
Santa Monica, CA 90401
(213) 458-1441
E * 1,5,6,8,9,10,12**

Pernovo, Inc.
Mr. Robert P. Whipple, Exec. VP
15233 Ventura Blvd., Ste. 716
Sherman Oaks, CA 91403
(213) 789-0666

Plante and Moran
Mr. Robert C. Law, Dir.
220 E. Huron St., Ste. 600
Ann Arbor, MI 48104
(313) 665-9494

Price Waterhouse
Mr. L. Michael Larrenaga
5950 Canoga Ave., Ste. 100
Woodland Hills, CA 91367
(213) 704-1117

Quidnet Capital Corp.
Mr. Reid White, Pres.
909 State Rd.
Princeton, NJ 08540
(609) 924-7665
B * 1,3,5,6,9,12**

Richards, O'Neil & Allegaeret
Mr. Craigh Leonard, Ptnr.
660 Madison Ave.
New York, NY 10021
(212) 207-1200

Rodi, Pollock, Pettker, Galbraith &
  Phillips
Michael P. Ridley, Esq.
611 W. 6th St., Ste. 1600
Los Angeles, CA 90017
(213) 680-0823

L. F. Rothschild, Unterberg,
  Towbin
Mr. T. I. Unterberg, Mng. Dir.
55 Water St.
New York, NY 10041
(212) 425-3300
C * 1,6,8,9,11**

Scientific Advances, Inc.
Mr. Charles G. James, Pres.
601 W. Fifth Ave.
Columbus, OH 43201
(614) 294-5541
D * 1,5,6,8**

Security Pacific Bus. Credit, Inc.
Mr. Robert Spitalnic, VP
228 E. 45th St.
New York, NY 10017
(212) 309-9302

The Small Business Advocacy, Inc.
Mr. Marc E. Brown, Pres.
526 Nilles Rd., Ste. 5
Fairfield, OH 45014
(513) 829-0800
C * 1,3,5,6,7,8,9**

Standard Ventures, Ltd.
Mr. Michael R. Thomas, Mng. Ptnr.
225 Peachtree St., N.E.
Atlanta, GA 30303
(404) 577-8773
D ** 12

Stephenson Merchant Banking
Mr. A. Emmet Stephenson,
  Sr. Ptnr.
899 Logan St.
Denver, CO 80203
(303) 837-1700
C * 1,3,5,6,9,10**

Steuben Partners
Mr. Amory Houghton, Jr., Chmn.
717 Fifth Ave.
New York, NY 10022
(212) 752-1100
E * 1,3,5,6,8,10,11,12

TDH Capital Corp.
Mr. J. Mahlon Buck, Jr., Pres.
Box 234, Two Radnor Corp. Ctr.
Radnor, PA 19089
(215) 293-9787
D * 12**

Technology Transfer Institute
Mr. Shingo Tanaka, Exec. Mng. Dir.
Kokusai Shin Akasaka West Bldg.
12F 1-20, Akasaka 6-chome
Minato-ku, Tokyo 107
(03) 585-6451

Tulsa Industrial Authority
Mr. Rick L. Weddle, Gen. Mgr.
616 S. Boston
Tulsa, OK 74119
(918) 585-1201
E ** 5,6

The Venture Capital Fund of
  New England
Mr. Richard Farrell, Gen. Ptnr.
100 Franklin St.
Boston, MA 02110
(617) 451-2575
C * 1,8,12**

Venture Capital International
Mr. Robert S. Froug, Pres.
720 S. Colorado Blvd., Ste. 940
Denver, CO 80222
(303) 759-4860
C * 5,6,7,8,10,11,12

Venture Founders Corp.
Mr. Alexander Dingee, Jr., Pres.
100 Fifth Ave.
Waltham, MA 02154
(617) 890-1000
D * 1,5,6,8**

Vista Ventures
Mr. Gerald Bay, Mng. Gen. Ptnr.
1600 Summer St.
Stamford, CT 06905
(203) 359-3500
D * 1,5,6,8**

Whitehead Associates
Mr. Joseph A. Orlando, Pres.
15 Valley Dr.
Greenwich, CT 06830
(203) 629-4633
D * 12**

Arthur Young & Co.
Mr. Jerome S. Engel, Ptnr.
One Post St.
San Francisco, CA 94104
(415) 393-2733

Arthur Young & Co.
Mr. Robert J. Brennan, Ptnr.
1111 Summer St.
Stamford, CT 06905
(203) 356-1800

Arthur Young & Co.
Mr. John Spencer, Jr., Ptnr.
235 Peachtree St., NE
2100 Gas Light Tower
Atlanta, GA 30043
(404) 581-1300

Arthur Young & Co.
Mr. Al Boos, Ptnr.
200 Lomas Blvd., N.W.
Ste. 300
Albuquerque, NM 87102
(505) 842-9273

Arthur Young & Co.
Mr. Dennis Serlen, Ptnr.
277 Park Ave.
New York, NY 10172
(212) 407-1611

Arthur Young & Co.
Mr. Robert M. Feerick, Ptnr.
777 E. Wisconsin Ave.
Milwaukee, WI 53202
(414) 273-3340

Six Business Start-up Checklists

Information Required from Applicant for Financing

The following checklist has been provided through the courtesy of Goodman & Mautner, Inc., a private venture capital firm. It outlines the information that a company seeking financing should supply and suggests a format for the presentation of this information.

A. Corporate Structure

1. Give the name of the company, the state in which it was incorporated, and the date of its incorporation.

2. Predecessor companies: if any, give their particulars and their history up to the incorporation of the subject company.

3. Subsidiaries of subject: show the degree of ownership by the subject company and identify any minority interests. Also give the dates and state of the incorporation of any subsidiaries.

4. Outstanding securities, including bank loans involving the subject company and any subsidiaries that are not 100 percent in the ownership of the subject company: state the principal terms of such securities. Wherever bank loans or institutional obligations exist, identify lender, and name, if possible, the individual at the lending institution who is most familiar with the account.

5. Name and state the other holdings of the principal holders of the subject company's common stock and/or other types of equity securities (convertible debt or preferred stock). If any such principal holders are not members of executive management, identify them and describe briefly the history and reasons for their stock purchases; also state if such holders have been in the past or are currently suppliers, vendees, or lessees or if they have any other business relationships with the subject company. If they do have such relationships, describe them in full, including the financial details of any transactions with the subject company.

6. Give a chronological record of the subject company's sales of its equity securities, stating prices, number of buyers, identity of principal buyers, and any other pertinent facts.

B. Executive Management and Work Force

1. Provide an abbreviated schematic diagram of the organization.

2. Provide personal resumes, including academic and business backgrounds, of all executive officers and any other supervisory personnel who may be considered of special value to the organization (for example, director of research, production manager, etc.). Business backgrounds should be as specific as possible regarding the positions held and the functions of such positions. Name three business references for each executive officer. State the present salaries and/or other remunerations.

3. If a restricted stock option plan is in effect or is contemplated, deliver a copy of such a plan or an outline of the proposed plan, along with a schedule of options granted or to be granted, exercise prices, and grantees.

4. Include a statistical table showing, for the last five years, if applicable, the number of employees at year-end and the total payroll expense. If profit-sharing or bonus plans were in effect for this period or any portion thereof, show such payments or appropriations in separate columns.

5. Include a statistical table that shows the departmental breakdown of the work force at the most recent date available. Show a further breakdown for the research department, if any, between engineers and nonengineers.

C. Business

1. Prepare a narrative description of historical development of the business, including the dates of any significant changes, such as acquisitions, introduction of new products, etc.

2. Describe the present product lines, providing as full a quantitative analysis as possible of the relative importance of each. If possible, provide a sales analysis for the past several years. Provide an evaluation of each product with respect to quality, performance, etc., in comparison with competitors' products. Identify competitors in each line of products and compare percent of market possessed by subject company's product(s) with percentage possessed by the products of competitors in each product line. Describe in what ways the subject company believes its products have special competitive advantages over those of other producers.

3. Where products are of a technical nature, describe briefly the uses to which each principal product is put.

4. Describe marketing methods, including any significant changes in methods introduced in the last five years and the reasons for them. Provide a list of principal distributors, dealers, manufacturers' representatives, foreign agents, etc.

5. Identify and describe any patents believed to be of value to the subject; give expiration dates.

6. Provide an analysis of twenty principal customers in each of the last five years, giving annual dollar sales made to each. Describe any special agreements with any such customers. Briefly give the background facts explaining any relatively sharp gain or decline in sales to each of such customers in the last five years.

7. With respect to proprietary items, describe pricing policies on each important product line, including the current prices to distributors and the distributors' prices to ultimate consumers or users. Compare subject company's prices with those of the principal competitors.

8. Describe as concretely as possible management planning in regard to product and market development over the next five years.

D. Industry

1. Where possible, give a statistical record of the industry or sub-industry in which the subject operates; indicate the sources of such statistical data.

2. Evaluate future prospects for the industry or sub-industry of the subject company. Any judgments should be supported by logical reasoning that leads to the conclusion.

3. Describe any technological trends or potentialities in or out of

the subject company's industry that might materially and/or adversely affect the subject company's business.

E. Financial Statements and Operating Statistics

1. Furnish annual audited statements for the last five years. If audits are short forms only (i.e., no supporting schedules for major balance sheet items, cost of sales, and expense categories), also furnish internal fiscal year-end reports.

2. Furnish the most recent interim financial statements (need not be audited) in comparative form.

3. If the financial statements contain items or involve methods of treatment peculiar to the industry or to the subject company, describe them.

4. Where applicable, furnish historical operating statistics as to unit sales, average realized prices, costs per unit, etc.

F. Financing Sought

1. Describe as specifically as possible the financing sought, including the amount, suggested form, and other concurrent financing if this is part of a larger plan.

2. As concretely as possible, describe the application of financing. If funds are to be used in whole or in part for construction or capital additions, provide detailed estimates of the cost of the program.

3. Furnish independent engineering reports, if any, which have been prepared in connection with the contemplated financing or business program.

4. If financing is in whole or in part for the purpose of buying out in whole or in part the subject company's stockholders, give details as to the individuals desiring to divest themselves of their holdings.

5. Estimate as concretely as possible the incremental earning power to be generated by the application of financing proceeds.

6. If further financing requirements are anticipated for the purpose of carrying out the subject company's future program, state the amount, timing, and management's thinking as to the form of the financial arrangements.

7. Furnish a balance sheet showing the projected effects of the financing that is presently sought.

8. Furnish cash flow and/or profit and loss forecasts covering the twenty-four months succeeding this financing. Describe all pertinent reasoning that supports such forecasts.

A Twenty-Four-Point Checklist for Preparing a Business Plan

The following checklist has been provided through the courtesy of Robert R. Kley Associates, Inc. The items listed below represent the salient points to be considered in planning and financing a new venture that is centered around the development of a new product. They are presented in the order in which a business plan is normally arranged.

1. Provide a one-page summary of the idea, the market need, and the amount of money required.

2. Describe the key goals and objectives. Specify what you are setting out to achieve, particularly in the sense of sales and profitability.

3. Provide an in-depth market analysis, and cite external sources of market research data.

4. List the names of six close competitors.

5. List for each product the anticipated selling price to an ultimate consumer, and present a brief summary that compares these prices with those of major competitors.

6. Provide a list of potential customers who have expressed an interest in the proposed products.

7. Provide a one-page summary of the functional specifications for the new product.

8. Illustrate the physical forms of the products with drawings and/or photographs.

9. Provide a profile of the most important patents.

10. Categorize and list the key technologies and skills required to develop and manufacture the proposed products, and indicate which technologies and skills the company plans to emphasize.

11. Describe the alternative channels of sales distribution; e.g., direct sales, sales through manufacturers' representatives, sales through original equipment manufacturers (OEMs), etc.

12. Describe the basis for determining, from the purchaser's point of view, if the new products are typically "lease" or "buy" items.

13. Describe the type and geographical distribution of the anticipated field service organization.

14. Describe the building block modularity of the new products (a module is something that can be independently manufactured, is testable, and can be inventoried).

15. Portray the cost vs. volume curves for each module, and illustrate the cost breakdown for material, labor, and factory burden.

16. Describe the manufacturing process involved; illustrate it by means of a block diagram.

17. Describe the types and quantities of capital equipment needed, and determine when this equipment will be required.

18. Portray a Flow-Event-Logic-Feedback chart that illustrates achievement milestones and portrays stepped levels of when and how additional funds should go into the venture.

19. Project staff and plant space requirements over a five-year period.

20. List the rationale for choosing a particular manufacturing plant location.

21. Provide cash flow projections by month for twenty-four months and then every quarter for the following three years.

22. Provide pro-forma balance sheets for five years.

23. Provide pro-forma profit and loss statements for five years.

24. State the degree of ownership control being sought and the limits to which these can be varied in regard to time and profitability.

Several examples of growth industries to which this checklist has been applied are:

- Health Sciences
- Education
- Computers and Peripherals
- Solid State Electronics
- Electronic Communications
- Power and Energy
- Metals and Alloys
- Chemicals and Plastics
- Pollution Control
- Infrared, Optics, and Holography

Development of a Marketing Program

This marketing checklist was provided by special arrangement with the international management consulting firm of William E. Hill and Co., Inc., now a part of Hayes/Hill Inc., Chicago, Illinois.

A. Planning Stage

1. Identify and Measure Market Segments
   a. Identify total market, including size and growth.
   b. Break market down into meaningful "business" segments, again including size and growth.
   c. Identify (typical) customers in each segment.
   d. Identify (typical) competitors in each segment, including profit and growth records of competitor.

2. Identify Market Characteristics for Each Segment (through Field Research)
   a. Identify end-user functional requirements (e.g., prestige, appeal).
   b. Identify end-user product requirements (types, extent of line, prices, quality, packaging service, product service, warranties, etc.).
   c. Determine end-user buying practices.
   d. Determine competitor marketing practices.

3. Determine Major Requirements for Success in Each Segment
   a. Determine concept of the business or basic business policies.
   b. Determine product line.
   c. Plan marketing.
   d. Plan operations or production.
   e. Plan engineering, research, and new product development.

4. Project the Business and Our Company Profit Potential
   a. Project growth forces in the market (or lack of same).
   b. Project technical trends (including product/process obsolescence).
   c. Project competitive trends (including capacity and vertical/horizontal integration).
   d. Project market trends (including approaching saturation, population shifts, changes in merchandising, and changes in buying habits).
   e. Make market and industry projections (physical units and dollar volume).
   f. Make projection of pricing climate (factors causing improvement or decline).

g. Make projection of "our share" of market attainable.

h. Project costs, investment, return on investment (five-year pro forma financial statements).

5. Develop Marketing Objective and Strategies

   a. Evaluate company objectives versus profit opportunities, company skills and resources, and company needs.

   b. Develop marketing objectives and strategies for each market segment.

B. Execution Stage

1. Determine Sales Force Requirements

   a. Established customers: determine requirements in regard to frequency and types of calls, persuasive selling, engineering selling, pesonal selling, executive selling, technical service, etc.

   b. Potential customers: identify prime and secondary potential customers and their needs; determine requirements in regard to frequency and type of primary sales contacts; bird dogging (i.e., persistently following a potential customer until you make contact with him).

2. Determine Sales Administration to Facilitate Above Functions

   a. Decide upon a policy of determining sales "territories" and for distributing salesmen's accounts.

   b. Develop sales organization and management.

   c. Plan method for sales compensation and for review of salesmen's performance, quotas, or other standards; customer contact.

   d. Plan methods of stimulating salesmen.

3. Determine Requirements for Service to Fill Customer Needs

   a. Plan for price and delivery quotations, order processing, scheduling and expediting of deliveries, and order follow-up.

   b. Plan for technical service of product, if necessary.

   c. Plan for shipping and physical distribution.

   d. Plan for distributing sales correspondence, product information, and advertising literature.

4. Determine Advertising and Sales Promotion Requirements

   a. Advertising must reach both present and potential customers.

5. Determine Marketing Administration to Facilitate Above Functions

   a. Market research determines market trends and forecasting, makes sales analyses, identifies prime prospects, analyzes competitors, and obtains trade intelligence.

b. The marketing administration must work in conjunction with the developers of new products so that the new products can be marketed effectively.

c. Plan for advertising and sales promotion.

d. Adopt a positive pricing administration.

e. Select distributors and/or dealers carefully.

f. Recruit adequate personnel, then train them well, compensate them adequately, and frequently review their performance.

g. Plan marketing budgets, cost controls, and inventory control.

h. Plan to take care of both credits and collections.

i. Evaluate trade association affiliations.

j. Determine whether or not product or market managers can act as specialized assistants in marketing administration.

k. Plan for the handling of national or multi-salesmen accounts.

l. Plan the total organization structure of marketing activities.

Marketing Functions Checklist

This checklist, also provided by special arrangement with William E. Hill and Co., Inc., indicates the many functions that must be considered in establishing a well-rounded marketing organization.

A. Sales Operations

1. Customer maintenance
   - Periodic follow-up
   - Engineering selling
   - Personal selling
   - Executive selling
   - Service selling

2. New customer development

3. Bird dogging

4. Customer service

5. Intelligence feedback

B. Marketing Research and Planning

1. Sales analysis by product

2. Market share analysis

3. Territory analysis

4. Distribution analysis

 5. Account profitability analysis

 6. Market measurement

 7. Market forecasts

 8. Market characteristics

 9. Identification and classification of potential accounts

10. New products research

11. Test marketing

12. Product planning

13. Package planning

14. "Long-range" planning

15. Competitive, technical, and market trends

16. Market intelligence center

C. Sales Management

1. Sales organization

2. Territories

3. Use of account or other specialists

4. Quotas and other performance standards

5. Performance review

6. Salesman stimulation

7. Time and expense controls

8. Call reports

9. Compensation review

D. Advertising and Sales Promotion

1. Advertising
   * Creative development
   * Media selection
   * Sales coordination
2. Sales promotion
   * Salesman aids
   * Merchandise displays
   * Trade promotion literature
   * Public relations

E. Customer Service

1. Quotation and estimating
2. Order processing
3. Scheduling
4. Expediting and delivery
5. Specials
6. Technical service
7. Sales correspondence
8. Warranties
9. Adjustments

F. Physical Distribution

1. Warehousing
2. Shipping
3. Repackaging
4. Inventory control

G. Marketing Management

1. Marketing objectives
2. Market segments to pursue
3. Volume and profit goals
4. Overall marketing concept
5. Marketing strategy selection
6. Sales policies
7. Pricing policies
8. Policies in other areas
9. Credit, allowances
10. Budget and cost controls
11. Inventory control
12. Trade association membership
13. New product marketing-customer liaison
14. Use of product and/or market specialists
15. Key account aid
16. Overall marketing organization

H. Marketing Personnel

1. Selction

2. Recruitment

3. Training

4. Personnel records

5. Manpower planning

Information Needed from Prospective Portfolio Companies Making Application for Investment by the SBIC of New York

The following checklist was provided for the original printing of this book through the courtesy of the Small Business Investment Company of New York, a publicly held SBIC affiliated with the International Bank (no longer active).

1. Short introductory statement giving facts as to incorporation of company (date, state), location of executive offices, and *brief* description of business (what is made, how it is used, who uses it).

2. Statement regarding amount of funds needed from SBIC-NY and use to which said funds are to be put.

3. Statement regarding amount of capital already supplied by applicant. How much in cash? How much in the form of patents, processes, or property? How much as compensation for past services rendered?

4. Statement regarding capitalization of company, listing short-term debt, long-term debt, preferred stock, common stock, and surplus (or deficit). Specify interest rates and term on debt (options?).

5. Summary of earnings and a projection of earnings for coming years; also a cash flow statement if it seems appropriate.

6. More detailed outline of business, indicating products, method of manufacture, markets, method of sales, research and development, patents, competition, plant, property, equipment, and backlog.

7. Description of management, including previous experience, education, and age.

8. Accounting of remuneration of management if over $20,000 per year.

9. List of principal shareholders, with amounts held.

10. Audited financial statements for past five years or whatever is available.

Checklist for Organizing and Operating
a Small Business

This checklist is reproduced from the book *How to Organize and Operate a Small Business,* Seventh Edition, 1985 by Clifford M. Baumback, through the courtesy of the publisher, Prentice-Hall, Inc.

I. The Role of Small Business in the Economy

1. Can you correctly define what your proposed product or service business is?

2. Can you identify this business by its Standard Industrial Classification (SIC) number?

3. Can you state in detail how your product or service business is related to other businesses, large and small, in your community or trading area?

II. The Problems and Risks of Business Ownership

1. What are the most serious problems for the small businessperson in your chosen line of business? What are the common risks faced in this business?

2. How would these problems and risks affect *you* as a business owner?

III. The Decision for Self-Employment

1. Have you rated yourself and had some acquaintances rate you on the personal qualities necessary for success as your own boss, such as leadership, organizing ability, perseverance, and physical energy?

2. Have you taken steps to improve yourself in those qualities in which you are weak but which are needed for success?

3. Have you saved money, made business contacts, taken special courses, or read particular books for the purpose of preparing yourself for business ownership?

4. Have you had training or experience in your proposed line of business or in one similar to it?

5. Are you (*a*) good at managing your own time and energy? (*b*) not easily discouraged? (*c*) willing to work harder in your own business than as an employee?

6. Have you estimated the net income from sales or services you can reasonably expect in the crucial "first two years"?

7. Have you compared this income with what you could earn work-ing for someone else?

8. Are you willing to risk the uncertainty or irregularity of your self-employment income during the early years of the enter-prise?

9. Have you carefully considered and enumerated the reasons why you want to enter business on your own?

IV. Acquiring a Franchised Business

1. Have you viewed the franchise offer in terms of its economic justification or business potential?

2. Have you contacted personally several of the company's fran-chise holders to see how they like the deal?

3. Have you asked for a business responsibility report on the fran-chise promoter from your local Better Business Bureau or Chamber of Commerce?

4. Have you engaged the services of a lawyer to go over provisions of the franchise contract concerning territory, competition from other franchisees, renewal, termination, transfer, franchise fees, sales quotas, and other matters?

V. Buying a Going Concern

1. Have you analyzed conditions in the line of business you are planning to enter? How well are this firm and similar business ventures in your community and in the rest of the country doing?

2. Have you asked for a business responsibility report on this firm from your local Better Business Bureau or Chamber of Com-merce?

3. Are the firm's physical facilities in satisfactory condition?

4. Are its accounts receivable, inventory, and goodwill fairly val-ued?

5. Have you determined why the present owner wants to sell?

6. Have you compared what it would take to start a similar busi-ness of your own with the price asked for the business you are considering buying?

7. Has your lawyer checked to see that the title is good, that there are no liens against the business, and no past due taxes or public utility bills?

8. Have you compared several independent appraisals of the business, arrived at by different methods?

9. If it is a bulk sale, have the bulk sale provisions of the Uniform Commercial Code been complied with?

10. Have you investigated possible developments, such as new shopping centers, new traffic patterns, or changes in zoning or parking regulations that might affect the business adversely?

11. Have you talked with the company's suppliers, customers, competitors, banker, and other businesspersons in the area to see what they think of the business?

12. Have you prepared a business plan covering the first three to five years of operation?

VI. Justifying a New Business

1. Have you analyzed conditions in the line of business you are planning to enter? How well are similar business ventures in your community and in the rest of the country doing?

2. Have you prepared a customer "profile"? Do you know what kinds of people will want to buy what you plan to sell?

3. Are there enough potential customers in your trading area to support another business of this type?

4. If your business will be based on an entirely new idea, have you attempted to secure actual contracts or commitments from potential customers instead of merely getting their polite approval of your idea?

5. Have you discussed your proposition with competent advisers who are in different occupations or who have different viewpoints?

6. Have you prepared a business plan covering the first three to five years of operation?

VII. Market Analysis and Business Location

1. Did you compare several different locations before making your final choice?

2. Have you determined the number, buying habits, income level, and other characteristics of the people in the trading area?

3. Have you determined the growth potential of this area?

4. With regard to the business site, have you investigated possible developments such as new shopping centers, new traffic patterns, or changes in zoning or parking regulations?

5. Have you checked the zoning of your proposed business?

6. Have you arranged for legal counsel before signing the lease and any similar contracts?

7. Are you, and the members of your family affected, satisfied that the community in which you plan to locate will be a desirable place in which to live and rear your children?

8. If your proposed location is not wholly suitable, are there sound reasons (not merely your impatience to get started) why you should not wait and try to secure a more nearly ideal location?

VIII. Advertising and Sales Promotion

1. Have you analyzed your probable competition in connection with the direct and indirect sales promotional methods you plan to use?

2. Have you planned definite ways to build and maintain superior customer relations?

3. Have you defined your potential customers so precisely that you could describe them in writing?

4. Have you decided how you can measure and record the degree of success achieved with each sales promotion so that you can repeat the "hits" and avoid the "duds"?

5. Have you considered different features of your business that would be appropriate for special promotions timed to your customers' needs and interests?

6. Have you made a list of all the media suitable for advertising *your* business, with some evaluation of each?

7. Have you selected the most promising reasons why people should patronize your business, and have you incorporated them in plans for your opening advertising?

8. Have you made use of all appropriate sources in the preparation of a good initial mailing list?

9. Have you prepared an advertising budget?

10. Have you made plans for some unusual gesture of welcome and appreciation for all customers during the opening days of your business?

11. Have you planned how you can measure the effectiveness of your advertising?

IX. Credit Policies and Practices

1. Have you carefully investigated the need for credit extension in your business?

2. Have you decided on your credit terms?

3. Have you weighed the advantages and disadvantages of joining a credit-card plan?

4. Have you planned specifically the various ways you will secure and use information obtainable from your charge account customers?

5. Have you made a personal investigation of the services and costs of affiliating with the local credit bureau?

6. Have you planned the basic procedures you will *always* follow before extending credit to any applicant?

7. Have you formulated plans to *control* all credit accounts?

8. Have you prepared a procedure for follow-up of delinquent accounts?

X. Pricing Policies and Strategies

1. Have you thought through the advantages and disadvantages of acquiring the price reputation you plan for your business?

2. Have you considered the probable reaction of competitors to your pricing practices?

3. Have you decided how and to what extent you will meet probable price competition?

4. Have you investigated possible legal limitations on your pricing plans?

5. Have you considered possible applications of price-lining to your business?

6. Have you decided on the formula or method you will use in pricing each class of goods and services?

XI. Reaching Foreign Markets

1. Have you carefully considered the marketability of your product or service to foreign customers?

2. Have you decided on the channels of distribution for the products you wish to export?

3. Have you considered all the factors for and against establishing your business or a branch of it in a foreign country?

XII. Physical Plant and Layout

1. Have you studied your proposed building with function, construction, and modernization in mind? If it is an existing building, is it adaptable to your type of business?

2. Will the building in its present or converted state meet local health, building, and other regulations applying to your business?

3. If the proposed building does not meet all of your major needs, are there any *good* reasons for deciding to use it?

4. Have you determined your equipment needs, and the cost of this equipment?

5. Have you considered the possibility, and the advantages and disadvantages, of leasing rather than buying fixtures and equipment?

6. Have you made a personal inspection of the physical plant of successful businesses that are similar to the one you plan to start?

7. Have you made a scaled layout drawing of your store or shop?

XIII. Inventory Procurement

1. Have you devised a plan or procedure for determining what your customers want?

2. Have you made a careful analysis to determine what major lines should be carried?

3. Have you contacted suppliers to determine their range of merchandise, prices, terms of sale, and special services, such as merchandising assistance, inventory planning aid, bookkeeping assistance, and store layout service?

4. Have you carefully analyzed the points for and against concentrating your purchases with one or a few vendors, taking into account your personal skill and ability as well as conditions in your line of business?

5. Have you given adequate attention to each of the fundamentals of buying in making your plans for this function?

6. Have you investigated your field of business with reference to the existence of cooperative buying groups, and the advantages of affiliating with one of these groups?

XIV. Inventory Control

1. Have you determined carefully what constitutes a *balanced* inventory for your business?

2. Have you recorded on paper the exact information you will need for effective inventory control?

3. Have you planned the best methods for securing this information?

4. Have you selected the most appropriate inventory control *system* to use?

5. Have you planned the best procedures to use for stock or stores keeping?

6. Have you listed the purposes and uses of the information you plan to secure from your inventory control system?

XV. Personnel and Employee Relations

1. Have you prepared your wage structure, and are your wage rates in line with prevailing wage rates in your area?

2. Have you considered what fringe benefits, if any, you will offer your employees?

3. Have you determined your employee needs, and your wage and salary costs?

4. Will you be able to hire employees, locally, who possess the requisite skills?

5. If you plan to employ friends and relatives, are you sure you have determined their qualifications objectively?

6. Have you planned working conditions to be as desirable and practical as possible?

7. Are you certain the employee incentives you plan to use represent the workers' viewpoint rather than what *you* think they want?

8. Have you planned your employment, induction, and training procedures?

XVI. Organization and Management

1. Have you considered the way you will organize duties and responsibilities? Have you prepared an organization chart?

2. Have you prepared job descriptions and specifications?

3. Have you made up a tentative plan or schedule to guide the distribution of your own time and effort?

4. Have you thought about how you would go about preparing standards, budgets, schedules, and other management aids as discussed in the text?

5. Have you provided some check on your own actions to ensure that you do adequate management planning before making commitments or important decisions covering future activities of the business?

6. Have you arranged to use periodically some checklist covering detailed activities regarding customer relations, maintenance, safety, or whatever type of activity will require close attention to details in your particular business?

7. Have you written down the main provisions of your general and major policies?

8. Have you discussed your proposed policies with competent advisers to counteract the beginners' tendency to offer what *they* like and want instead of what their potential *customers* like and want?

9. Have you written down an adequate statement of the reputation you want your business to acquire with customers, suppliers, and competitiors?

10. Have you made adequate provisions to ensure that your policies will be understood and enforced and that you will receive ample warning of the need for policy adjustments?

11. Have you prepared plans for succession on your retirement or in the event of your untimely death or disability?

XVII. Manufacturing and Contract Construction

1. Have you prepared a production planning and control procedure to suit your manufacturing or construction processes?

2. Have you anticipated future production requirements, and have you made plans for increasing the capacity of the plant as needed?

3. Have you made provision for assessing the *quality* of your production?

XVIII. Capital Requirements and Sources

1. Have you written down a complete, itemized list of all capital needs for starting your kind of business, including a fair allowance for operating expenses and your own living expenses until the business is able to support itself *and* provide a substantial

reserve for the "one serious error" most business owners make during their first year of operation?

2. Have you prepared *pro forma* financial statements, including cash flow statements, for at least three years?

3. Have you discussed this financial prospectus with a banker and a successful business owner in the line of business you propose to enter?

4. Have you used as a guide the standard operating ratios for your business in calculating your capital requirements?

5. If you plan to secure much of your initial capital from friends or relatives, are you *certain* that your business will remain free of "friendly" domination?

XIX. Insurance and Risk Management

1. Have you evaluated all the hazards to which your business will be exposed?

2. Have you determined the hazards for which you should provide insurance coverage?

3. Have you determined how much of each kind of insurance you should purchase, and the costs of this insurance?

4. Have you made allowances in your budget of estimated expenses for losses resulting from predictable, uninsured risks (such as shoplifting and bad debts)?

5. Have you considered the nature of the protective devices and precautionary control measures you will need to reduce the business risks you will face?

XX. Accounting Records and Financial Statements

1. Have you decided what records will be adequate for each division and need of your business?

2. Have you secured the necessary forms to enable you to start keeping adequate records from the first day of operation of the business?

3. Have you planned your record system so that appropriate use will be made of standard operating ratios?

4. Have you figured out how to keep your payroll records and take care of tax reports and payments?

5. Have you investigated the record-keeping system recommended by the trade association in your type of business?

6. Have you decided by whom each record needed will be kept?

XXI. Depreciation and Inventory Valuation

1. Have you considered the advantages and disadvantages of writing off the cost of your plant and equipment as rapidly as the law allows?

2. Have you considered the tax consequences of the various methods of valuing your inventories?

XXII. Profit Planning and Cost Control

1. Do you know what your "break-even" volume is?

2. Have you made an estimate of what your volume is likely to be during the early years of your business?

2. Have you carefully considered your financial goals by preparing *pro forma* financial statements?

4. Have you investigated the standard systems of expense classifications used in your type of business and selected the most appropriate one for your use?

5. Have you determined what are usually the largest items of expense for your type of business and made definite plans for controlling these expenses from the very beginning of the business?

6. Have you determined which, if any, expense items, though normally small for your type business, very easily become excessively large unless carefully controlled *at all times?*

7. Have you prepared on paper a *flexible* expense budget for two or three different probable amounts of volume of business, including provisions for frequent operating expense reports to be compared with planned figures in your budget?

8. Have you determined the standard operating ratios for your field that you plan to use as guides?

9. Have you compared the expense of "farming out," or having certain activities of the business done by outside agencies, with what it would cost you to do the work yourself?

XXIII. Cash Flows and Capital Expenditures

1. Have you set up a budget that estimates your working capital needs in different months of the year?

2. Have you set up a budget that estimates your long-term needs to replace existing plant and equipment or to purchase additional plant and equipment?

XXIV. Legal Forms of Business Organization

1. Have you considered all the factors for and against each legal form of organization?

2. If you plan to form a partnership, have you prepared a formal partnership agreement? If you will be incorporating, have you prepared the articles of incorporation and by-laws?

3. In either case, have you sought the counsel of an attorney?

XXV. Regulation of Business Operations

1. Have you checked the licensing requirements and fees for your type of business?

2. Have you complied with regulations governing the use of a firm or trade name, brand names, or trademarks?

3. Have you ascertained from reliable sources all other regulations that must be complied with in the operation of your business?

XXVI. Taxes and Economic Security Legislation

1. Have you listed all your firm's tax-paying and tax-collecting obligations?

2. Have you provided for securing all information from employees required by law?

3. Have you provided for an adequate system of record keeping that will furnish essential information for all taxation purposes?

4. Have you obtained a social security number and IRS employer identification number?

_____ **Applause** _____

_____ **Act I (First Edition)** _____

The author would like to take this opportunity to thank the many people who provided information and assistance in the preparation of this manuscript. Although a comprehensive listing is not practical and no slight is intended toward those whose names are not included, I would like to acknowledge the particularly helpful assistance of the following individuals and organizations (listed alphabetically):

- Alameda County Library, Hayward Business Branch
- American Bankers Association
- American Bar Association
- American Institute of Certified Public Accountants
- Center for Venture Management
- Library of Congress, National Referral Center for Science and Technology Division
- Massachusetts Institute of Technology, Alumni Association
- National Consumer Finance Association
- Newark Public Library, Business Branch

- San Francisco Public Library, Business Branch
- San Jose Public Library
- San Jose State College Library
- University of Toronto, School of Business

The technical advice and assistance of Dr. Herbert E. Dougall, C.O.G. Miller Professor of Finance, Stanford University Graduate School of Business, proved invaluable in the preparation of Chapter 15. (Any errors in the text, however, are *entirely* my own responsibility.) The comments of Mr. Karl S. Kropf, Manager, Special Industries Group and Vice President, Wells Fargo Bank were most helpful in the formulation of my discussion of commercial banking. The editorial assistance of Joan Rogers, Director of Grammatical Sciences and an entrepreneur in her own right, who coddled my commas, smoothed my syntax, and mended my split infinitives, saved me months in the preparation of this book. The secretarial services provided by Elsie L. Kuntz and Iris M. Tralle, two cheerful ladies who typed this manuscript, were invaluable in helping me keep production on schedule. The index was prepared by Janette Leppe.

Act II (Second Edition)

I'd like to thank my seminar attendees and many others who have written to me recommending ways in which this book could be improved. I'd also like to thank my wife, Alice, for assisting me with these revisions.

Act III (Third Edition)

First of all I'd like to thank my publisher, Fred Easter, for proposing that I revise this book. I sincerely appreciate his patience and that of Howard Schneider, editor at Reston Publishing Company, for giving me the opportunity to undertake these revisions while I simultaneously ran my own seminar company with a faculty and staff of well over one hundred people.

This project could not have been accomplished without the very capable research assistance of Jeannine Marschner who has labored for months. The fine staff of reference librarians at the University of California at Berkeley's Kelson Library provided invaluable assistance in the research effort. I'd like to thank Peter Turla, our time management expert, for inspiring me to do most of my revision work during the many hours I spent aboard the airlines of America. Pearl Henry certainly deserves a vote of thanks for her computer skills in manuscript production. I would like to acknowledge the very helpful comments of Paul Foote, a New York University researcher doing grant-supported research in the field of venture capital. I'd like also to thank my assistant, Ursula Anderson, for helping to keep me organized. And finally, I'd like to thank my wife, Alice, for her support while I seek fortune and fulfillment in the service of America's information needs through my books and the more than 2000 management seminars presented annually by my company, Dible Management Development Systems, Inc.

Index

A

Accountant
  Certified Public, 133, 151
  tax, 48
Accounting, 29
Accounting firm, selecting, 154–155
Advertising, 7
  classified, 75
  direct mail, 17, 34, 168–169
  display, 34
  space, 17
Age of Discontinuity, 3
Allen, Louis L., 203
Allstate Insurance Company, 237
American Express, 27
American Financial Services Association, 237
American Industrial Bankers' Association, 237
American Management Association, 82
American Research and Development (ARD) Corporation, 213
American Telephone and Telegraph, 249

Ampex Corporation, 12
Apprenticeship, 59
ARCO, 27
Armstrong, Neil, 34
Assistance in preparation of business plan (See Business plan)
Attorney, 133, 135, 256
  and the Board of Directors, 151
  and the business plan, 133, 135
  company, 123
  and the company name search, 123
  patent, 115–116, 117
Audacity, 25, 26, 97
Auditing, 155
Avon, 27

B

Balance sheet, 183
Bank participation loan, 266–267
Bank publications, 89–90
Bank trust departments, 274–275
Bankers, 100–101
  and the Board of Directors, 151
Bankruptcy, 58, 199

Bateman Eichler, Hill Richards,
      Inc., 240
Bauer, Richard, 12
Bell, Alexander Graham, 122
Bell Laboratories, 36–37
Bendix Corporation, 37
"Blue sky" laws, 265
Board of Directors
   compensation of, 151–152
   composition of, 150–151
   duties, 148–150
   size of, 150
Book clubs, 87–88
Books, resource, 85–86
   bank publications, 89–90
   book clubs, 87–88
   bookstores, 87
   business magazines, 90
   financial papers, 90
   libraries, 86–87
   newsletters, 90–91
   newspapers, 91
   periodicals, 88–89
   trade journals, 89
Bookstores, 87
Breakeven analysis, 167
"Bridge" financing, 141
Broker, securities, 262
Bureau of Census, U.S. Depart-
      ment of Commerce, 111
Burlage, L. Charles, 71
Business consultants, 74
Business magazines, see Trade
      magazines
Business plan, 13, 114
   another company's, 133
   Appendix to, 161, 179–191
   assistance in preparing, 132–134
   authority of, 130–131
   credibility of, 130
   formal (See Formal business
      plan)
   importance of, 129–131
   ingenuity of, 130, 131
   Introduction to, 145–146
   packaging of, 134–135
   preparation of, 132–134
   responsibilities of, 131–132
   as a sales document, 129–131

supporting documentation for,
      190–191
   table of contents, 146
Business proposal, 129
Business stationery, 123–124
Business Week, 24, 47, 90
Buyer's agent, 112

C

Capital
   equity, 14, 198–199
   gains, 220
   initial, 140
   venture, 24, 33–34
Cash flow statement, 181–182
"Cashing out", 208–209
Center for Venture Management,
      73
Certified development company
      (CDC), 268
Certified Lender Program, 267
Certified Public Accountant, 133,
      151
   and the Board of Directors, 151
Classified advertising, 75
Closed-end investment companies,
      212, 213 (See also Invest-
      ment companies, closed-end)
Clubs,
   investment, 241–242
   Toastmasters, 94–95
College seminars, 82–83
Commerce, U.S. Department of
      (See U.S. Department of
      Commerce)
Commercial bank, 215–217
   selecting, 155–157
Commercial bankers, 65
Commercial finance company,
      218
Commissioner of Corporations, 34,
      132
Company
   legal structure of, 184–186
   name selection, 123
Competence, 58
Computerized information services,
      91–92
Conference command center, 29

Consultants, 74
  and the Board of Directors, 151
  business, 74
  management, 232
Consumer finance company, 219
Control Data Institute, 27, 83
Convertible debt, 199
Co-op Bank, 246
Corporate
  communications, 45, 49
  contributions and financial re-
    ward, 45, 49–50
  nepotism, 45, 52
  orphan products, 45, 53–54
  politics, 45, 52
  red tape, 45, 52–53
  venture capital department,
    219–221
Corporations, 34, 185 (See also
    Commissioner of Corpora-
    tions)
Cost control, 18
Credit Unions, 221–222
Customers, 99
  as a money source, 223–224
  potential, 38, 160–170
  proximity of, 175

D

Dale Carnegie Institute, 83
Datrix, 109
Datura/DTI Security, 16–19
Debt, capital, 198
Dedication of founders, 58–59
Department of Commerce, U.S.
    (See U.S. Department of
    Commerce)
Department of Economic Develop-
    ment, 111
Department of Energy, 259
Department of Housing and Urban
    Development (See U.S. De-
    partment of Housing and
    Urban Development)
Design, product, 13
Desire of founders, 58–59
Determination of founders, 58–59
Dialog Information Services, 91

Dible, Donald M., Seminars, 13, 83
Digital Equipment Corporation, 28,
    147
Direct loan, 267
Direct mail advertising, 17, 34,
    168–169
Directory of Continuing and Pro-
    fessional Education Pro-
    grams, 84
Display advertising, 34
Distributors, 100
Divorce, 69
Doctoral Dissertations, 108–109
Drucker, Peter F., 3
DTI Security, 11–16
Dyer, Wayne, 59

E

Earned equity, 207–208
Eastman, George, 46
Economic Development Administra-
    tion (EDA), 224–226
  loan eligibility, 225–226
  loan terms, 225
  regional offices, 226
Edison, Thomas Alva, 32, 49
Education, in-house, 23
Educational requirements of cor-
    porations, 45, 54–55
Electronic voice mail system, 8
Employee Retirement and Income
    Security Act (ERISA), 249
Employee stock purchase program,
    228
Employees, as money sources,
    226–228
Employment security, 45, 51
Endowed institutions, 213–215
Endowment, 213
Energy-Related Inventions Pro-
    gram, 259
Envelopes, business, 123–124
Equipment manufacturers, as in-
    vestors, 228–229
Equity
  capital, 14, 198–199
  financing, 217
  formula, 188–190

Export broker, 15
Export sales, 15, 17
"Extramarital affair," 68–69

F
Factoring
    advantages of, 229–230
    company, as an investor, 229–231
    nonrecourse, 230
Fame, 45, 46–47
Federal Credit Union Act of 1934,
        221
Federal Home Loan Bank, 245
Federal Research in Progress
        (FEDRIP), 114
Fields, Debbi, 6
Financial
    consultants, as investors, 231–233
    papers, 90
    resources, 64–65
    statements, 180–183, 187
Finders, 217, 231–233
Fixed expenses, 63
Forbes Magazine, 89, 90
Formal business plan
    and the Board of Directors,
        148–152
    founders' resumes, 146, 186
    Introduction to, 145–146
    marketing strategy, 167–172
    organization chart, 147
    plant location, 174–177
    references, 146–147
    research and development,
        172–174
    review of the product/service,
        162–167
    supporting professional service
        agencies, 152–159
    table of contents, 146
Former business associates, 73–74
Formula, equity, 188–190
Fortune (personal), 45, 47–48
Fortune Magazine, 89
Founders
    "backyard of", 175
    investment of, 233–235
    responsibility of, 131–132
    resumes of, 146, 186

Franchising, 9, 235–236
Friends, 74

G
*Gale Research Company Encyclo-
        pedia of American Associa-
        tions,* 81
Garn-St. Germain Depository Insti-
        tutions Act of 1984, 261
Geary, G. Stanton, 207
General Electric, 36, 37, 249
General Telephone, 37
"Getting out", 208–209
Gillette, King C., 172
Glass-Steagall Banking Act of 1933,
        238
Good Humor Man, 59
"Goodwill", 121

H
Halcomb, James, 22, 178
Halcomb Associates, 21–30
Hambrecht, William R., 252
Hambrecht and Quist, 252
Harvard Business Review, 89
Heizer, E.F., Jr., 206, 237
Hewlett-Packard, 37, 169, 249
Honeywell, Inc., 37, 249
"Horizontal" promotion, 61
Housing and Urban Development,
        U.S. Department of (See
        U.S. Department of Housing
        and Urban Development)

I
IBM, 24, 37
Idea
    books, 109–110
    file, 25
Image, importance of, 122–123
Inc. Magazine, 90
Income statement, 182
Individual investors, 247–248
Industrial
    banks, 236–237
    distributors, 169
    Research "100" Award, 36, 39
Info World Magazine, 22

Insurance, 157–159
    key man, 157–158
    partnership, 158
    shareholder, 158
    sole proprietorship, 158
    underwriter, 136
Insurance agency, selecting, 157,
    159
Insurance companies, 237–238
Intermediate term loan, 216
Internal Revenue Code, 250–251,
    252
Internal Revenue Service, 227, 250,
    252
International Business Machines,
    24, 37
International Platform Association,
    95
International Security Conference,
    15
Inventors, 120
    warning to, 120
Inventory control, 29
Investment
    adviser, 9
    banking, 238–241
    clubs, 241–242
Investment companies
    closed-end, 212–213
    open-end (See Mutual funds)
Investor
    objectives of, 141
    preferences of, 139–141, 177

J

Jobbers, 169

K

Kaisel, Stanley F., Dr., 48
Key man insurance, 157–158
"Kickers", 141, 199, 216
Kodak, 46
Komives, John L., 73

L

Lapidary work, 30
Laser, 31, 33
Laser Technology, Inc., 31–39
Law Directory, The, 153

Law firm, selecting, 152–154
Leasing companies, as investors,
    242–244
Legal counsel, 106 (See also Law-
    yer and Attorney)
Legal structures, business, 184–186
License for a flat fee or royalty, 120
Limited partnership agreement, 251
Local development company
    (LCD), 268
Location, plant, 174–177
    customer proximity, 175
    educational facilities, 176–177
    investor preferences, 177
    personnel availability, 176
    supplier proximity, 175–176
    tax climate, 177
    transportation services, 176
Logotype, 124
Long-term loan, 216–217
Lotus 1-2-3®, 181

M

Maltz, Maxwell, 59
Management consultant (See Con-
    sultant, management)
Managerial ability, 61
Manufacturers' representatives,
    99–100, 170
Market analysis, 159–162
Market survey, 130
Marketing strategy, 167–172
    advertising, 168
    delivery/performance timing,
        171–172
    distribution, 168–170
    promotional methods, 167–168
    terms of sale, 170
Masonite Corporation, 29
Merrill Lynch Venture Capital,
    Inc., 239
Mini-proposal
    contents of, 141–143
    length of, 143
Minority Enterprises Small Busi-
    ness Investment Company
    (MESBIC), 270
Mrs. Fields Cookies, 5–10
Montgomery Ward, 169

Morris Plan Bank, 236
Motivation, 58–59
Mutual fund, 212, 244–245
Mutual Savings Bank, 245

N

Name, company, 123
NASA, 27, 37
National Association of Investment
    Clubs, 241–242
National Association of State De-
    velopment Agencies
    (NASDA), 111–112
National Bureau of Economic Re-
    search, 219
National Consumer Co-operative
    Bank, 246
National Consumer Finance Asso-
    ciation, 237
National Credit Union Administra-
    tion (NCUA), 221
National Directory of Newsletters
    and Repository Services, 91
National Referral Center, 113–114
National Speakers Association
    (NSA), 95
National Technical Information
    Service (NTIS), 92–93, 113,
    114
*National Trade and Professional
    Associations,* 82
Nation's Business, 89
Nepotism, 45, 52
Net thirty days, 171
New York Stock Exchange, 24, 212,
    213
*New York Times Book Review,
    The,* 88
New York Times Magazine, The,
    89
Newsletters, 90–91
Newspapers, 91
Newsweek, 89

O

Offering, public, 132–133
Open-end investment company
    (See Investment company,
    open-end)

Operation Breakthrough, 23
Organization chart, 147
Organizational structure, 184–186
Orphan products, 45, 53

P

Papers, financial, 90
Parent company, 247–248
Partners, 73–74
Partnership, 73–77, 107, 151,
    184–185
  agreement, 251
  candidates for, 73
  insurance, 158
  limited, 251
  private investment, 251–252
  venture capital, 200–204
Patent, 106, 115–117, 120, 142,
    165
  broker, 112–113
  rights, 106–107
  Patent and Trademark Office,
    108, 115, 116
Payroll, 63
Peale, Norman Vincent, 59
Pension funds, 248–249
Periodicals, new product, 107–108
Persistence, 25, 97
Personal autonomy, 45, 46
Personal fortune, 47–48
Personal motivation, 80
Pert-O-Graph Computer, 22, 24,
    107
Pert-O-Graph Kit, 22, 28
Physical conditioning, 79
Physical well-being, 63–64
Plan, business (See Business plan)
Plant
    location of, 174–177
    requirements for, 183–184
Point-of-sale manufacturing, 168
Premiums, 170
Private individual investors,
    247–248
Private investment partnerships
    (See Partnership, private in-
    vestment)
Private label manufacturing, 15, 17,
    169–170

Privately-owned venture capital corporations, 253–254
Pro forma financial statements, 180–181
Product
  convenience of, 163–164
  cost of, 166–167
  customer service of, 164–165
  durability of, 163
  leasing, 171
  manufacturing, 166
  price of, 164
  proprietory content, 165–166
  quality of, 164
  research, 7, 18
  selection, 105
  size of, 162
  specifications of, 162–167
  standardization-compatibility, 165
  timing of, 161–162
  weight of, 162
Professors, 101–102
Profit and loss statement, 182
Program Evaluation and Review Technique/Critical Path Method (PERT/CPM), 22, 23, 24, 25, 26, 27, 177–178
Promotions, 45, 50–51
Proposal, mini (See Mini-proposal)
Prospectus, public-offering, 132–133
Protection, product, 114–119
Prototype, 34–35, 140
Public offering (See Offering, public)
Public speaking, 94
Publications
  bank, 89–90
  trade, 12, 26, 89, 90
Publicity, 25, 26
  releases, 34, 35

Q

Qualified stock option plan, 227
Quality control, 6
Quist, George, 252

R

Raborn, William F. (Red), Admiral, 22

Raiding competitors' staff, 74–75
Ratio
  price-to-earnings, 121
  risk-rewards, 205–206
RCA, 36
RCA Astro Electronics, 28
Red tape, 45, 52
References, founders', 186–187
Referrals, 75, 98
Rensselaer Polytechnic Institute, 214
Rent, 63
Representatives, manufacturers', 99–100, 170
Research and development, 18, 36, 38, 172–174
  development of new products, 173
  payment for, 173–174
  process improvement, 173
  product improvement, 172–173
Research and Development (R & D) Partnership, 258
Resources, 85–86
  bank publications, 89–90
  book clubs, 87–88
  bookstores, 87
  business magazines, 90
  financial papers, 90
  libraries, 86–87
  newsletters, 90–91
  newspapers, 91
  periodicals, 88–89
  trade journals, 89
Return on Investment (ROI), 206–207, 208
Reward-risk ratio, 205–206
Risk, 50, 52, 205–206
  capital, 253–254
Rockefeller family, 48
Rollinson, Mark, 207
Royalty, 107, 113, 120

S

Salary, 45, 50–51, 188
Sales finance company, 259–260
Savings banks, 245
Savings and Loans Associations, 260–261

Schmidt, Benno C., 207
Schuldt, David, 12
Schuller, Robert, 59
Sears Roebuck and Company, 169, 237
Securities Act of 1933, 240, 265
Securities and Exchange Commission (SEC), 132, 262, 264, 265
  regional and branch offices, 256–266
Securities dealers, 261–263
Securities Exchange Act, 261
Self-underwriting, 263–266
Seminars, 8, 80, 83–85, 137
Service Corps of Retired Executives (SCORE), 93
Shareholder insurance, 158
Sharp, William, 247–248
Short-term loan, 215–216
Small Business Act of 1953, 266
Small Business Administration (SBA), 81, 92, 93–94, 157, 266–268
Small Business Innovation Research (SBIR), 257–258
Small Business Institutions, 94
Small Business Investment Act of 1958, 269
Small Business Investment Company (SBIC), 157, 266, 269–270
  subsidiaries and affiliates, 271
Small Business Reporter, 89, 90
Small Businessman and His Problems, The, 71
Smith, Charles B., 207
Sole proprietorship, 184
  insurance, 158
Space advertising, 17
Staff, projected requirements for, 183
Stamina, 63–64
Stanford University Endowment Fund, 214
State Invention Expositions, 111–112

State Investment Development Corporations, 267
Stationery, business, 123–124
Stock brokers, 101, 148, 149, 150
Subcontracting, 14
Subsidiary plants, 67
Supplier, 99
  captive, 224
  proximity of, 175
Supply and demand, 196–197
"Sweeteners", 141, 199, 216
Symphony®, 181
Syndication, 232

T
Table of contents, business plan, 146
Taxes, 63
  planning for, 188
Tax-exempt foundations, 271–272
Teledyne, 48
Term loan, 216
Testing, product, 13
Time Magazine, 89
Toastmasters Clubs, See Clubs, Toastmasters
Toastmasters International, 94
Trade
  associations, 81–82
  journals, 12, 26, 89
  magazines, 90
  secrets, 106
  shows, 15, 16, 111
  supplier, 273–274
Trademark, 46
Truman, Harry, 132
Trust, charitable, 271–272
Trust companies, 274–275

U
Underwriter, 130, 262
Underwriting, self, 263–266
Union Carbide, 36
Unpatentable ideas, 117–119
U.S. Department of Commerce, 81, 92–93, 111, 160
U.S. Department of Housing and Urban Development, 23

U.S. Department of Labor, 249
U.S. Patent Office, 108, 115, 116
Utilities, 63

V

Varian Associates, 23
Venture, 90
Venture capital, 24, 33–34
Venture capitalist, 73, 130, 136, 137,
    200–204, 205, 207
VisiCalc®, 181

W

Wall Street Journal, The, 47, 107
Westinghouse, 36
Wharton Innovation Center, 214
Wholesalers, 169
Wiesenberger Investment Services,
    213
Winning, importance of, 45, 48–49

/